White Collar Crime

*Current Perspectives
from InfoTrac®*

Danielle Lively Neal

University of Nebraska, Kearney

WADSWORTH
CENGAGE Learning™

Australia • Brazil • Japan • Korea • Mexico • Singapore • Spain • United Kingdom • United States

ISBN-13: 978-1-111-82817-2
ISBN-10: 1-111-82817-2

Wadsworth
20 Davis Drive
Belmont, CA 94002-3098
USA

Cengage Learning is a leading provider of customized learning solutions with office locations around the globe, including Singapore, the United Kingdom, Australia, Mexico, Brazil, and Japan. Locate your local office at: **www.cengage.com/global**

Cengage Learning products are represented in Canada by Nelson Education, Ltd.

To learn more about Wadsworth, visit
www.cengage.com/wadsworth

Purchase any of our products at your local college store or at our preferred online store
www.cengagebrain.com

Printed in the United States of America
1 2 3 4 5 6 7 15 14 13 12 11

TABLE OF CONTENTS

Preface

White-collar crime has become an area of increasing research and attention in the last several years due to the increasing public attention on the United States' economic situation, as well as the increase in publicly maligned corporate scandals and exorbitant executive salaries, to name a few. Scams such as Enron and WorldCom have brought the public's attention to white-collar criminals. Cullen, Hartman, and Johnson (2009) note that due to these scandals, "High-profile offenders are now seen not as respected community citizens, but as 'bad guys' whose crimes reflect inordinate greed and a disturbing lack of concern for victims" (31). This has led to increasing research in the area of white-collar crime, as is evidenced by the articles included in this InfoTrac Edition, however, there are still many areas left to be investigated by researchers. Several issues tend to manifest themselves in the research on white-collar crime. There is the obvious lack of research due to definitional issues, the large span of disciplines research on white-collar crime covers, and the lack of data available for extensive quantitative analysis.

The definitional issues associated with white-collar crime are some of the most significant issues confronted by researchers in this area of research. These issues were brought to light by Edwin H. Sutherland and were elaborated upon in his seminal work on white-collar crime in 1983. Sutherland explained the necessity of conducting research on this oft ignored area of crime, fraught with difficulty as crime was often considered to be a "poor man's" issue. In contrast, Sutherland (1983) defined white-collar crimes as those "crimes committed by a person of respectability and high social status in the course of his occupation" (7). Oftentimes there is also a lack of definition by governmental bodies whose legislation is heavily influenced by those of "high social status" that Sutherland describes. Dodge and Geis note (2009), "The idea of morality comes into play when actions that clearly are injurious fail to be included in penal codes because those who benefit from them have imposed their will on legislative bodies, typically through financial contributions to politicians" (1). Thus, how and by whom the term of "white-collar criminal" is defined is paramount in the examination of the issues surrounding this area of research and most especially how these criminals and their victims are examined, the punishments available, and the impact these crimes have on society.

The lack of data and research on white-collar crime is a pervasive issue. Some of this is a result of white-collar crime being viewed as simply a subfield rather than a significant area of research or criminality in the academic field of criminal justice (Schichor, 2009). The majority of research focuses more on case studies instead of in depth quantitative analysis. Dodge and Geis (2009) explain "None of these manifestations of white-collar crime readily lend themselves to the fashionable, highly-sophisticated statistical models and experimental designs now in vogue in criminological circles" (1). This detracts from scholars wanting to study and work in this field, and combined with the lack of data and definitional issues, it is a very tough topic area in criminal justice for researchers to tackle.

As white-collar criminal activity covers more areas than just criminal behavior, the span of disciplinary fields that must be examined to understand the nature of white-collar crime is quite large. In order to adequately cover the pervasive issue of white-collar crime, researchers of this topic must be able to branch out into various other fields, such as law, economics, business, technology, and medicine, to name a few (Dodge and Geis, 2009, 2). Combined with the definitional issues and the lack of data and focus of the criminal justice discipline on the area of white-collar crime, researchers are not often reaching out to these other disciplines in the way that they should. This problem is becoming less of an issue more recently, however, because there is the realization that research on white-collar crime, in order to be comprehensive, must span a variety of disciplines and must be give more focus as an important area of academic research in criminal justice (Schichor, 2009).

These readings were selected from Wadsworth InfoTrac College Edition. This compilation is designed to be as diverse as the perspectives that surround the field of research in white-collar crime. Definitional issues and an explanation of white-collar crime is provided, as well as an examination of the various different types and trends in white-collar crime. Not to be forgotten are the victims of white-collar crimes, the cost of white-collar crime to society, as well as the prosecution, defense and punishment of these criminals. The InfoTrac College Edition readings help the student gain a more in depth insight into the field of research in white-collar crime, as well as the realities of this criminal activity, as a supplement to a text.

Danielle Lively Neal, University of Nebraska at Kearney

References

Cullen, F., J. Hartman, and C. Lero Johnson. (2009). "Bad guys: Why the public supports punishing white-collar criminals." *Crime, Law, and Social Change*, 51: 31-44.

Dodge, M. and G. Geis. (2009). "Social and political transformations in white-collar crime scholarship: introductory notes." *Crime, Law, and Social Change*, 51: 1-3.

Schichor, D. (2009). "'Scholarly influence' and white-collar crime scholarship." *Crime, Law, and Social Change*, 51: 175-187..

Sutherland, E. H. (1983). *White collar crime: The uncut version.* New Haven, CT: Yale University Press.

Part I

STUDYING TRENDS IN WHITE COLLAR CRIME AND ASSESSING ITS COSTS

1

Remarks by Lanny A. Breuer, Assistant Attorney General for the Criminal Division at the American Bar Association National Institute on White Collar Crime

MIAMI, Feb. 25 /PRNewswire-USNewswire/ -- The following are remarks by Lanny A. Breuer, Assistant Attorney General for the Criminal Division at the American Bar Association National Institute on White Collar Crime:

Thank you for that very kind introduction.

It is a pleasure to be with you and to see so many friends and former colleagues in the audience today. As always, the ABA has put together a terrific program for this 24th National Institute on White Collar Crime, and I am honored to be here.

In April 2009, I was confirmed by the Senate to what truly is my dream job. As the Assistant Attorney General for the Criminal Division, I have the honor and privilege of representing the Department of Justice and leading a Division of more than 400 dedicated and exceptional attorneys. Each day, the Criminal Division's lawyers come to work with the singular purpose of

Remarks by Lanny A. Breuer, Assistant Attorney General for the Criminal Division at the American Bar Association National Institute on White Collar Crime. PR Newswire Feb 25, 2010

combating our nation's most serious criminal threats. They do so not for glory or riches, but because they believe to their core in the cause of justice and in serving the American people. Across a broad range of areas - from international organized crime and drug trafficking conspiracies to complex computer crime, financial fraud, and corruption - our prosecutors routinely disrupt and dismantle the most sophisticated criminal conduct. And they do so with limited resources, making their efforts and accomplishments all the more worthy of our thanks and admiration.

Many of you were former prosecutors yourselves, and so you, like me, know what it means to work alongside these public servants. You, like me, know what it means to walk into the RFK Main Justice Building or a United States Attorney's Office knowing that your duty, above all else, is to seek firm and fair justice. It is a remarkable and humbling responsibility.

What do I mean by "firm and fair" justice?

Well, I mean that tough and certain penalties are necessary to punish criminal conduct, deter future criminal conduct, and make society safer and more prosperous, all of which serve the interests of justice. I also mean that our prosecutors are committed to a fair process in which the defendant's rights are protected throughout criminal proceedings. Not only is this necessary to ensure actual fairness, but it is critical so that the public perceives our laws and our system of justice as fundamentally fair.

These notions of "firm and fair justice" inform all that we do in the area of white collar crime.

FINANCIAL FRAUD

As you know, in the wake of the economic crisis, pursuing financial fraud is one of the Department's top priorities. That means stepped up resources and focus on financial fraud in all its forms - corporate, securities, and commodities fraud; mortgage fraud; health care fraud; foreign bribery; and fraud in connection with the massive amounts of taxpayer funds that have been devoted to the rescue and recovery of our economy from the brink of economic collapse.

In tackling financial fraud, we are not on a witch hunt. We are - as I said a moment ago - seeking fairly but firmly to go after criminal conduct where it exists. We also are striving to innovate in how we do business. That could mean utilizing data and intelligence more strategically, or it could mean - as we've seen in a couple of prominent cases recently - going undercover. However we do it, we will be more targeted, more creative, and more strategic in where and how we look for criminal conduct.

By now, many of you are aware of the new, inter-agency Financial Fraud Enforcement Task Force, which was established by Executive Order of the President in November 2009. The Task Force really is the spearhead of the Obama Administration's financial fraud enforcement strategy. It is chaired by the Attorney General and includes among its senior leadership the Secretary of the Treasury, the Chairwoman of the SEC, and the Secretary of Housing and Urban Development.

The mission of the Task Force is simple: to strengthen our collective efforts to combat financial crime and to prevent fraudulent practices from contributing to a future financial meltdown. Through education and training, information sharing, and coordinated enforcement strategies, the Task Force is well positioned to achieve this mission. Indeed, in the enforcement realm, the various working groups focused on securities and commodities, mortgage, rescue, and Recovery Act fraud are already hard at work and already are improving coordination and cooperation across the law enforcement community.

Luckily, even though it is relatively new, the Task Force is building on a very solid foundation - indeed, one could say that it began with a head start.

The U.S. Attorney community has successfully prosecuted numerous billion-dollar-plus frauds, including the Rothstein case here in the Southern District of Florida, the well-known Madoff and Dreier cases in the Southern District of New York, and the Petters case in the District of Minnesota.

We also have been very busy in the Criminal Division. For example, working closely with the Manhattan DA's office, we recently resolved a long-running investigation of Credit Suisse AG for its efforts to help sanctioned countries avoid U.S. banking regulations. The bank ultimately forfeited $536 million, representing the largest forfeiture ever entered against an entity for violations of what's known as the International Emergency Economic Powers Act, or IEEPA. We also have indicted defendants involved in a massive, $8 billion Ponzi scheme allegedly perpetrated by Allan Stanford.

As I alluded a few moments ago, in pursuing financial fraud, we are aggressively using all of the tools at our disposal, including tools not often seen in white collar cases.

There has been much discussion, for example, of the Galleon case brought by the U.S. Attorney's Office in the Southern District of New York, the FBI, and the SEC. Through the use of court-authorized wiretaps, the Department uncovered an alleged insider trading scheme netting more than $20 million - believed to be the largest hedge fund insider trading case ever charged by the Department.

And, as I'm sure many of you are aware, in a recent FCPA investigation, the Criminal Division's Fraud Section used undercover law enforcement techniques to uncover what we allege to be widespread fraud and corruption. As a result, 22 executives and employees of companies in the military and law enforcement products industry were indicted for their involvement in schemes to bribe foreign government officials. This investigation involved the most expansive use ever of undercover techniques to uncover FCPA violations.

Taken together, these two cases reflect a new chapter in white collar criminal enforcement - one that I'm confident has not gone unnoticed by many of you, or by your clients. Out are the days of resting easy in the belief that only self-reporting or tipsters will bring criminality to light. In are the days of proactive and innovative white collar enforcement.

FCPA

Let me say a few more words about our very robust FCPA program, because it, in many ways, typifies how we are approaching crime in corporate America.

The FCPA investigation I just referenced is the largest single prosecution of individuals in the history of DOJ' s enforcement of the FCPA. It thus vividly illustrates one cornerstone of our FCPA enforcement policy: the aggressive prosecution of individuals. Put simply, the prospect of significant prison sentences for individuals should make clear to every corporate executive, every board member, and every sales agent that we will seek to hold you personally accountable for FCPA violations. As we focus on the prosecution of individuals, we will not shy away from tough prosecutions, and we will not shy away from trials. We are ready, willing, and able to try FCPA cases in any district in the country-as we demonstrated with our three FCPA trial victories just last year.

To be sure, we are not focusing on individuals to the exclusion of corporations. We will continue to insist on corporate guilty pleas or to bring criminal charges against corporations in appropriate cases - when the criminal conduct is egregious, pervasive and systemic, or when the corporation fails to implement compliance reforms, changes to its corporate culture, and undertake other measures designed to prevent a recurrence of the criminal conduct. We will continue to insist on appropriately stiff corporate fines, applying a consistent, principled approach that considers the facts and circumstances within the Department's established framework and that is guided by the Sentencing Guidelines in arriving at an appropriate sanction.

I also want to assure you that the Department's commitment to meaningfully reward voluntary disclosures and full and complete corporate cooperation will continue to be honored in both letter and spirit. I know that many of you often grapple with the difficult question of whether to advise your client to make a voluntary disclosure. I strongly urge any corporation that discovers an FCPA violation - or any other criminal violation, for that matter - to seriously consider making a voluntary disclosure and to cooperate with the Department. The Sentencing Guidelines and the Principles of Federal Prosecution of Business Organizations obviously encourage such conduct, and your clients will receive meaningful credit for that disclosure and cooperation.

HEALTH CARE FRAUD

Our efforts at fraud prevention are not limited to corporate America or protecting the financial markets. By now, the expression is well worn, but the focus really is on combating fraud from Wall Street to Main Street.

Health care fraud is a perfect example. Our Medicare Strike Force prosecutors and agents are using billing data to target Medicare abuses and a range of fraudulent health care schemes in hot spots around the country. Since it began operating here in 2007, the Strike Force in Miami has charged more than 300 defendants in 200 cases totaling approximately $860 million in fraud. All told to date, more than 230 defendants have been convicted, and nearly 200 have been sentenced to prison. The success of the Strike Force is not limited to prosecution, however. It also contributes to deterring health care fraud before it happens. Here in Miami-Dade County, for example, after the Strike Force began operation, we saw an estimated reduction of $1.75 billion in fraudulent claims for durable medical equipment alone.

Because this is a model that works, we are devoting resources to expanding our Strike Force operations. The Strike Force, which started operations in Miami and Los Angeles, is now operating in Detroit, Houston, Brooklyn, Tampa, and Baton Rouge as part of the DOJ and HHS-led Healthcare Fraud Prevention & Enforcement Action Team, or "HEAT" as it is known. Nationwide, more than 500 defendants have been charged by the Strike Force in cases involving approximately $1.1 billion in fraudulent claims submitted to Medicare.

MORTGAGE FRAUD

Of course, no effort at tackling fraud on Main Street can overlook the very serious problem of mortgage fraud. Mortgage fraud has swept through housing and credit markets across the country in a variety of forms. Everyone from borrowers, to appraisers, to real estate professionals, to lawyers, have been implicated.

The United States Attorneys' Offices, the Criminal Division, the FBI, and our state and local partners have been hard at work in this area. Right here in Miami, representatives of the Financial Fraud Enforcement Task Force met yesterday with members of the community and local industry representatives to discuss the impact of mortgage fraud locally, as part of our efforts to be even more proactive and targeted in combating mortgage fraud.

In addition, the Department has deployed an array of bold and innovative enforcement strategies to combat mortgage fraud. For example, as in the health care fraud arena, we are pursuing mortgage fraud enforcement strategies that are threat-based and intelligence-driven. The FBI has established a Financial Intelligence Center in order to provide tactical data-driven analysis that can be used to effectively target the most egregious mortgage fraudsters.

The Criminal Division intends to utilize the FBI's analytical products as part of its own new Mortgage Fraud Enforcement Initiative. Working closely with the FBI's National Mortgage Fraud Team and other federal, state, and local law enforcement agencies, the Initiative will focus Criminal Division resources on the prosecution of high-impact mortgage fraud cases where mortgage fraud is most acute. This focused effort by the Criminal Division should effectively complement the already outstanding work going on in United States Attorneys' Offices around the country.

So, as you can see, there is much going on in financial fraud enforcement, and our efforts are only going to increase, as new resources are brought to bear. Music to your ears, I'm sure!

This stepped-up resource commitment is only one part of the equation, however. We realize that, to achieve "firm and fair" justice in the area of white collar crime, we must do more than simply bring successful prosecutions. We must tend to our own house - ensuring that we are constantly evaluating the Department's organization, policies, and practices.

Let me say a few words about this process of self-evaluation.

CHANGES WITHIN THE CRIMINAL DIVISION

In the ten months since I took over at the helm of the Criminal Division, we have taken a hard look at the Criminal Division to make sure that we have the necessary focus, resources, talent, leadership, and structure to accomplish our ambitious goals. Whether that means changing policies to ensure, for example, that asset forfeiture is sought in every case in which it can be pursued, or re-organizing sections in the Division to better rationalize our approach in key programmatic areas, we are making those changes.

Right now, for example, we are looking closely at our white collar crime program. A new Chief of the Public Integrity Section will soon be selected, and we have begun searching for a new Chief of the Asset Forfeiture & Money Laundering Section, the Section that prosecuted the Credit Suisse case I mentioned earlier.

We also have seen some changes in our Fraud Section. After an extensive national search, Denis McInerney, a former deputy criminal chief in the Southern District of New York and partner at Davis Polk & Wardwell, recently began as the Chief of the Section. And Greg Andres, the criminal chief in the Eastern District of New York, now serves as the Acting Deputy Assistant Attorney General supervising the Fraud Section, among others. Denis and Greg are already hard at work at the forefront of financial fraud enforcement, along with our colleagues at the United States Attorneys' Offices, the SEC, the FBI, and our many other law enforcement partners around the country, and, indeed, around the world. And, while we're on the topic, we expect in the near term to be advertising for other senior leadership positions in the Fraud Section, so stay tuned.

SENTENCING AND CORRECTIONS POLICY

In addition to all that is going on in the Criminal Division, the Department is also hard at work on key issues of policy and practice.

One prominent example is the current effort to review sentencing and corrections policy and to identify areas for reform. As you may know, the Attorney General established a Sentencing and Corrections Working Group last year to take a fresh look at federal sentencing and charging practices, prisoner re-entry issues, alternatives to incarceration, and unwarranted disparities in federal sentencing. He cares deeply about such issues, as do I.

Our goal in this effort is a sentencing and corrections system that protects the public, is fair to both victims and defendants, eliminates unwarranted sentencing disparities, reduces recidivism, and controls the federal prison population. Low-hanging fruit, right? Well, the goals may be lofty, but I think we're up to the challenge. Indeed, in my experience, this Working Group has been remarkably effective, both in terms of its organization and its very thoughtful approach toward what are very complicated issues of law and policy.

Let me say a few more words in that regard.

As you know, the sentencing guidelines continue to provide us with a sentencing baseline in all federal criminal cases. However, Sentencing Commission data shows that the percentage of defendants sentenced within the guidelines has decreased in the wake of the Booker line of cases. Although the full impact of recent trends in sentencing jurisprudence is still unclear, these developments must be monitored carefully.

We are especially concerned about increased disparity in white-collar sentencing. It is not uncommon for a health care fraud defendant to be sentenced to 15 or more years in one district court, while, in the same week, another defendant in another court involved in a larger fraud is sentenced to a very short prison term. A few weeks ago, the Ninth Circuit affirmed a 25-year sentence for a fraudster involved in a $40 million fraud just a few days after another defendant on the East Coast who had been involved in a $1 billion fraud was sentenced to just five years.

We must determine the reasons for these disparities. Public trust and confidence are essential elements of an effective criminal justice system. Our laws and their enforcement must not only be fair, they also must be perceived as fair. Accordingly, we must create a system where the factual basis for sentencing in a particular case is clear to all parties and to the public, and where the sentences themselves are truly commensurate with the crime committed.

The work of the Sentencing and Corrections Working Group is an important step in that direction.

CRIMINAL DISCOVERY POLICY

Criminal discovery is, of course, another area that is absolutely essential to the fairness of the criminal justice system and to how the system is perceived.

To that end, last spring, the Attorney General convened a Discovery and Case Management Working Group, which I co-chaired along with Karen Immergut, the then-Chair of the Attorney General's Advisory Committee. The working group examined our discovery and case management practices from top to bottom, as well as our discovery resources and training. Based on our work and the input of groups across the Department, then-Deputy Attorney General David Ogden issued new guidance on discovery to all federal prosecutors.

The new guidance recognizes that our duty is to seek justice, and encourages broad discovery - above and beyond what is required under the Constitution and the Federal Rules. At the same time, the guidance recognizes that, because of longstanding differences in local practice, a one-size-fits-all approach is not appropriate; thus, it requires each U.S. Attorney's Office and Department litigating component to establish its own discovery policy that meets the standards established by the new guidance, but also takes into account controlling precedent, existing local practices, and judicial expectations. In addition, the new policy establishes a methodical approach to handling discovery, including providing guidance on where to look, what to review, how to conduct the review, and how best to make disclosures.

The new guidance is only one piece of our overall effort to further enhance our discovery practices. Beginning in 2009, every federal criminal prosecutor, new and old, was required to undergo several hours of discovery training. Going forward, every federal prosecutor is required to undertake annual refresher training on discovery obligations.

The Department also has appointed a national coordinator for discovery issues - Andrew Goldsmith - as well as a discovery expert in each U.S. Attorney's Office and Main Justice litigating component. I know from working with Andrew on the Discovery and Case Management Working Group that he is deeply committed to ensuring the success of the Department's initiatives in this crucial area.

Along those lines, just to give you a preview, we are creating a discovery handbook similar to the Grand Jury Manual, so that prosecutors will have a one-stop resource relating to discovery obligations. We also are implementing a mandatory, comprehensive discovery curriculum for all federal prosecutors. Moreover, we already have implemented, among other things, specialized training for paralegals and law enforcement agents, as well as enhanced computer forensics, and we are exploring and testing available case management software.

We are confident that, through this comprehensive approach, we are equipped to meet our discovery obligations and minimize prosecutorial error.

OUR SHARED RESPONSIBILITY TO DO JUSTICE

Now, I know there are skeptics among you, and that's fine. I'm realistic. But I also know what I have seen since joining the Department.

From my vantage point, I can tell you that, across the country, our line prosecutors are doing an outstanding job ensuring that the administration of justice is both firm and fair. Over the past ten months, I've worked with the Department's career lawyers around the country. And whether dealing with a seasoned trial lawyer or a rookie prosecutor, I have found our lawyers overwhelmingly to be bright in their understanding of the law, wise in their judgment, and unswerving in their desire to do their jobs faithfully and responsibly. In a word, they are faithful to our Nation's highest traditions of public service.

We all should think about what it means to be a federal prosecutor. The Department's career lawyers are on the front lines every day, conscientiously investigating and prosecuting all kinds of criminal wrongdoing on behalf of the American people. Each of our line prosecutors sacrifices a great deal in service to our country. Multi-defendant complex criminal cases can take years to build, and weeks or even months to try. Cases frequently take Department lawyers away from their families for extended periods of time. Violent crime and other cases can lead to death threats against our prosecutors - sadly, a chilling reality that is confronted more often than people realize. And all the while, these career lawyers earn a fraction of what they could in the private sector. They do a terrific job, and I commend their efforts and their sacrifices for the cause of justice.

CONCLUSION

None of this is to suggest that we don' t occasionally make mistakes. We do, because just like defense attorneys, our prosecutors are human. But there is, of course, a big difference between honest mistakes and intentional misconduct.

Let me say a few words about this issue. Our continuing dialogue about criminal discovery is, to be sure, an incredibly valuable one. The Department benefits immeasurably from the thoughtful comments and perspectives of those in the defense bar, in academia, and on the bench.

My concern, though, is that there are a few in the defense bar who see blood in the water and are determined to attack the Department's prosecutors indiscriminately - and without any factual basis. Some think it is acceptable to use motions for sanctions, or threats of OPR referrals, as a way to gain some sort of strategic litigation advantage.

Now, I realize that such attacks are coming from only a very small number of you. But to those so inclined, I say that such tactics are not acceptable. They're just not. And as officers of the court, we must all come together to cry foul when we see such overreaching.

Remember, it was not so long ago that I was one of you. I was a defense lawyer, and an aggressive one at that. I know the meaning of zealous advocacy. And I know the stakes and stresses that come about when someone's liberty is on the line. But I also know the meaning of fair play. And I know the meaning of proportionality. And I know that no one benefits - not the defense bar, not the defendant, not the government, and certainly not the American people - when discovery violations by the government are pitched in legal briefs, in oral arguments, or in commentary as endemic. Nothing could be further from the truth - and those who engage in such tactics know it.

So, as we move forward in our dialogue, let's deliver on our shared responsibility not to distort the truth. Let's deliver on our shared responsibility not to suggest the sky is falling when it isn't.

But above all else, let's deliver on our shared responsibility to serve the interests of justice.

Thank you for the privilege of being with you. It really is wonderful to see so many dear friends and colleagues here today. Enjoy the South Florida sunshine and the remainder of the conference. My best wishes to you all.

2

The Changing Nature of U.S. Card Payment Fraud

Industry and Public Policy Options

Richard J. Sullivan

AUTHOR'S ABSTRACT

As credit and debit card payments have become the primary payment instrument in retail transactions, awareness of identity theft and concerns over the safety of payments has increased. Traditional forms of card payment fraud are still an important threat, but fraud resulting from unauthorized access to payment data appears to be rising, and we are only beginning to get a sense of the dimensions of the problem.

Thus far, the role of public policy has been to encourage the card payment industry to limit fraud by developing its own standards and procedures. Whether this policy stance is sufficient depends on the effectiveness of industry efforts to limit fraud in light of the dramatic shift toward card payments.

Sullivan provides an overview of card payment fraud in the United States. He develops a preliminary estimate of the rate of U.S. card payment fraud and suggests that such fraud is higher than in several other countries for which data are available. The U.S. payment industry is taking steps to combat payment fraud, but progress has been slowed by conflicts of interest, inadequate incentives, and lack of coordination. Thus, policymakers should monitor the card payment industry to see if it better coordinates

The changing nature of U.S. card payment fraud: industry and public policy options. Richard J. Sullivan. Economic Review (Kansas City) Spring 2010 v95 i2 p101(34).

security efforts, and if not, consider actions to help overcome
barriers to effective development of security.

Debit and credit card payments are convenient for consumers, widely accepted by merchants, and more efficient than paper forms of payments. But as cards have become the primary payment instrument in retail transactions, awareness of identity theft and concerns over the safety of payments has increased. For example, a recent data breach at Heartland Payment Systems compromised 130 million records of payment cards--the largest in a succession of security failures that have compromised growing numbers of payment records.

Like all forms of payment, cards have security vulnerabilities. Traditional forms of card payment fraud are still an important threat, but fraud resulting from unauthorized access to payment data appears to be rising. Payment providers are exploring options to protect sensitive data, such as the recently implemented payment card industry data security standard. But the damage from card payments fraud is a rising concern, and we are only beginning to get a sense of the dimensions of the problem.

As the central bank of the United States, the Federal Reserve has responsibility to ensure that payments are safe, efficient, and accessible. Confidence in the safety of payments is particularly important. Thus far, the role of public policy has been to encourage the card payment industry to develop its own standards and procedures that limit fraud. Whether this policy stance is sufficient depends on the effectiveness of industry efforts to limit fraud in light of the dramatic shift towards card payments.

This article provides an overview of card payment fraud in the United States. The process for approving card payments depends to a large extent on information. Thus, criminals have a strong incentive to steal that information, leading to attacks on computer systems, data breaches, and ultimately payment fraud. Such criminal efforts are increasing in organization and scale. To assess the resulting damage, this article presents a preliminary estimate of the rate of card payment fraud in the United States. According to the estimate, card fraud is higher in the United States than in several other countries for which data are already available. While the U.S. payment industry is taking steps to combat payment fraud, progress has been slowed by conflicts of interest, inadequate incentives, and lack of coordination. The principal conclusion is that policymakers should monitor the card payment industry to see if it better coordinates security efforts, and if not, consider actions to help the industry overcome barriers to effective development of security.

The first section examines the information-intensive card payment approval process and the security vulnerabilities that emerge as a result of shifting to electronic forms of payments. The second section explores what we know about how criminals gather and use payments information to commit fraud. The section also addresses the monetary harm that fraud inflicts on participants in the payment system. The third section reviews several important initiatives, in the United States and elsewhere, designed to combat card payment fraud. It goes on to discuss the limited effectiveness of industry efforts to establish payment security standards on its own and the resulting policy concerns.

1. EMERGING VULNERABILITIES OF CARD PAYMENTS

The primary aim of card payment security is to ensure that only payments authorized by the account holder are allowed. Vulnerabilities exist in the card payment approval process, however, that enable criminals to make fraudulent card payments. These vulnerabilities are related to an information-intensive payment approval process. Criminals have begun concerted efforts to collect and exploit this information, especially targeting electronic records.

While traditional forms of card payment fraud (such as from lost or stolen cards) remain important, this section will focus on newer forms of payment fraud, which are often a result of breaches of personal information. (1) Large data breaches are especially damaging, and many of these breaches expose payment-related data. Criminals are specializing in activities to gather sensitive information (such as writing malevolent software or establishing fake Internet sites), to commit fraud, and to launder associated funds. These groups are international in scope and organize themselves in underground online markets where they can buy and sell services that aid in stealing data or perpetrating payment fraud.

Card payment approval and fraud

Payment fraud occurs when someone gains financial or material advantage by using a payment instrument, or information from a payment instrument, to complete a transaction that is not authorized by the legitimate account holder. (2) In this definition, the lack of an account holder's authorization is the crucial distinguishing characteristic of payment fraud. (3) A card payment approval system screens transactions to limit fraud. The system authenticates the card, identifies the cardholder, and determines whether the transaction satisfies certain limits set by the card issuer or merchant.

Card issuers and merchants face numerous challenges in making a correct approval decision. The payment cards that issuers provide are not sufficiently difficult to counterfeit. (4) To accommodate merchants and consumers, card issuers continue to allow payments via mail order, the telephone, and now the Internet, with only the information from a payment card. Some merchants do not properly check payment cards for counterfeits or review signatures of cardholders. Some consumers write their personal identification numbers (PINs) on their payment cards or do not sufficiently protect their personal computers. Criminals take advantage of these and other vulnerabilities either to gather or to exploit information that lets them commit fraud.

The common underlying cause of these vulnerabilities is an information-intensive payment approval process. (5) Criminals have incentives to gather and use the information to commit fraud. Because more information will generally lead to a more accurate approval decision, card issuers (and merchants) have an incentive to continuously expand the data on which they rely (Roberds and Schreft 2008). The result appears to be an escalating cycle of card issuers adding information to their databases and criminals devising ways to gather the information.

The recent transition to electronic payments processing has opened new avenues for gathering payment card data. Small handheld card readers are used in locations such as restaurants to read and save card information. (6) A disguised card reader can be fit over a legitimate slot on ATMs or other payment terminals to electronically capture card information (skimming). Video cameras placed in hard-to-detect locations can capture PIN numbers. (7) Criminals also exploit the Internet by, for example, sending out millions of e-mail messages that trick a small number of recipients into revealing sensitive account or card information (phishing). On a larger scale, hackers can penetrate computer systems and steal information where it is stored and transmitted.

Stolen data circulate among criminals in underground Internet markets. Evidence shows that stolen credit card information is most commonly available at a cost of $.85 to $30 per card number (Symantec). Bank account information is the second most common type of data available, at a cost of $15 to $850 per account number.

Other information, such as full identities, online auction accounts, email accounts, and passwords are also for sale.

More broadly, a specialized electronic payment fraud industry appears to be growing. Security experts argue that since 2004 "criminals who were carrying out card fraud and attacks on electronic banking got organized, thanks to a small number of criminal organizations and a number of chat-rooms and other electronic fora, where criminals can trade stolen card and bank account data, hacking tools and other services" (Anderson and others). Elements of this industry specialize in activities such as writing malware, hacking databases, organizing underground electronic marketplaces, and laundering money.

Data breaches

Criminals exploit card information from any source to commit card payment fraud. But data breaches deserve special attention because electronic processing of payments provides new means of accessing data and can substantially increase the amount of data that is compromised. Organizations do not always report data breach incidents but recently the public record has become more complete as states have implemented laws that require disclosure. (8)

Data breaches occur when individuals gain unauthorized access to digitized information. Until recently, insiders of an organization were mostly responsible for data breaches, but with the arrival of the Internet, outsiders gained access to this information. The majority of publicly disclosed data breaches are committed by outsiders, although insiders account for a significant share (Table 1). Most incidents are a result of stolen laptops or desktop computers, followed by exposure of information on the Internet or e-mail and by hacking.

Since 2005, at least 2,221 data breaches have been made public. The number of breaches rose until the middle of 2006, which can be partly attributed to data breach notification laws (Chart 1). The number of publicly announced breaches fell, then rose, and fell again from mid-2006 to mid-2009. For about a year it has been fairly steady at a relatively low level of about 30 per month. The recent decline in breaches may have multiple causes, such as increased difficulty in tracking the data breaches due to waning news organization interest or better security of data. (9)

A recent example shows the damage that can result from a data breach. In November 2008, computer hackers broke into RBS Worldpay, a U.S. payment processing subsidiary of the Royal Bank of Scotland, and gained access to data on 1.5 million cardholders (Gorman and Perez). They distributed the information to a worldwide network of confederates. While these "cashiers" counterfeited payment cards, the hackers modified computer systems at RBS Worldpay to raise the available funds on the cards and the limits on the cash that could be withdrawn at ATMs. Then, over the course of just 12 hours, the cashiers went on a cash withdrawal spree, obtaining $9 million from 2,100 ATMs in some 280 cities.

While this is a large-scale example, lesser attacks occur on a regular basis. According to one law enforcement official, more money is stolen from banks by data breaches than by robbery (Gorman and Perez).

[GRAPHIC 1 OMITTED]

[GRAPHIC 2 OMITTED]

The damage resulting from a breach may relate more to the records compromised than to the number of breaches. Since early 2005, at least 494 million records of sensitive information have been compromised in publicly announced data breaches. Just eight large data breaches have accounted for 79 percent of the compromised records (Chart 2). Because large incidents occur infrequently, it will take time to know if their occurrence has slowed.

A closer look at the origin of data breaches shows that the distribution of incidents and records compromised varies considerably across sectors of the economy. Among the sectors shown in Chart 3, nonbank payment processors account for a small share of breach incidents but are responsible for the largest share of records compromised. Retail and commerce account for the largest share of incidents and the third-largest share of records compromised. The education sector stands out with a significant share of incidents but few compromised records. Government entities have a significant share of both. Banks and credit unions have a good record by comparison.

[GRAPHIC 3 OMITTED]

Some tentative conclusions can be made from the record of publicly announced data breaches. First, much exposure results from a relatively few large breaches. Second, sectors that process or store payment data, such as nonbank payment processors and retailers, are major targets. Third, nonbank payment processors have avoided a large number of potential attacks, but when their security systems are successfully penetrated, exposure can be extensive. (10) Fourth, the relatively good record of banks and credit unions, despite their storage of data useful for payments fraud, suggest they have done a good job protecting sensitive data.

Links from stolen data to fraud

It is challenging to track stolen data to its misuse. After a data breach, determining what information has been compromised is difficult. In the case of large breaches involving millions of payment records, criminals may not be able to take advantage of the data quickly and may exploit it over a period of time. As a result, consumers may not be aware that a data breach has led to fraudulent use of their payment card. (11)

Two common ways to use stolen data for card payment fraud are to purchase goods from Internet, mail order, or telephone merchants or to counterfeit a payment card and use it in an ATM cash withdrawal or in a face-to-face transaction at a point-of-sale (POS). Internet, mail order, or telephone transactions, referred to as card-not-present (CNP) transactions, are vulnerable to stolen data because payment cards cannot be inspected.

A recent study of banks found that, between 2006 and 2008, fraud losses from counterfeit cards rose on each of signature debit, PIN debit and ATM transactions (American Bankers Association 2009). Costs related to online payments fraud (lost sales, direct payment fraud losses, and fraud management) rose steadily from 2000 to 2008 (Cybersource 2010). The 2009 costs declined somewhat, to $3.3 billion (1.2 percent of sales revenue), in part due to the economic slowdown. Unfortunately, we do not have good statistics on sources of credit card fraud, which is twice as likely as debit card fraud (Javelin).

These statistics are only suggestive because the information used for the fraudulent transactions do not necessarily come from data breaches. More direct information is available from a 2008 survey of banks. The survey reports that 43 percent of respondents suffered payment fraud losses due to data breaches, up from 22 percent in 2006 (American Bankers Association 2009). The increase is significant because, as shown below, banks bear the largest share of card payment fraud loss.

There is also some evidence on what characteristics of data breaches are more likely to lead to payment fraud. Misuse of data was more likely if it was identity-level information, such as Social Security numbers, and obtained through deliberate hacks or stolen computer hardware (ID Analytics). The potential for fraudulent use of stolen data was less related to the size of a data breach than to the resources available to hackers.

An indirect consequence of stolen data and associated fraud is public concern over the safety of payments. News reports of data breaches and identity theft have become routine. To protect themselves, consumers and businesses must use security software (firewall and antivirus software, etc.) on their personal computers to prevent criminals from stealing personal information directly or from installing malware that allows secret control of the computer. (12) These attacks on personal computers contribute to consumer anxiety and suspicion about the safety of some forms of payment. (13)

In short, attention has turned to new threats to card payment security, such as stolen payment data obtained in data breaches and other sources. Stolen data is linked to card payment fraud by a complex and developing chain. Preventing hackers from breaching computer security and committing fraud is widely viewed as a major challenge. The bottom line, however, is that payment participants bear a significant loss. The next section reviews the evidence on losses caused by card payment fraud.

II. HOW LARGE ARE PAYMENT CARD FRAUD LOSSES?

To gauge the extent of debit and credit card fraud, this section examines the direct monetary losses. It first reviews two alternatives for measuring card fraud losses and the comparability of the measurement. It then presents a new estimate of the fraud loss rate (total fraud losses divided by the value of total card payments) in the United States for 2006. The estimate suggests that the loss rate was higher in the United States than in Australia, France, Spain, and the UK. Finally, the section discusses factors that explain the international differences. For the United States, significant factors include continued reliance on older payment card technology, the use of signatures to identify the cardholders, and a highly developed Internet economy.

Alternatives for measuring fraud

One measure of the damage caused by card payment fraud is the value of associated losses for all participants in various card payment networks. (14) In recent years, several countries around the world have begun to regularly publish such statistics (Sullivan 2009). The data that feed these statistics originate in financial institutions when account holders report fraudulent transactions. The financial institution puts a marker in the computer record of the transaction, indicating that it was reported fraudulent. Periodic summary statistics on the number and value of fraudulent payments can then be easily generated from computer records. Typically, an industry organization gathers data from card issuers and networks to calculate aggregate statistics. Often, information on the sources of payments fraud is also reported.

These statistics are unavailable for payment card fraud in the United States, but an alternative method can provide comparable statistics. The estimate of U.S. fraud presented here is based on the sum of direct losses borne by card issuers, POS merchants, and merchants in Internet, mail order, and telephone transactions. (15) This estimate should be comparable to those from other countries because the value of a fraudulent payment when first reported should approximate the sum of the losses of payment participants who ultimately bear the loss.

The person or merchant who first reports a fraudulent payment will not necessarily bear all or even part of the loss. For example, a merchant typically receives a payment guarantee by the card issuer for a properly approved payment where the card is present at the time of purchase. In this case, the loss is borne by the financial institution that issued the payment card. While the merchant may first report the fraudulent transaction, it does not bear the loss. (16)

Some merchants, however, do bear losses due to card payment fraud. Merchants who accept CNP payments cannot inspect cards for authenticity or confirm that a customer has possession of the card. As a result, CNP transactions are not generally guaranteed. Relative to their sales, card payment fraud losses fall most heavily on Internet, mail order, and telephone merchants because nearly all of their payments are CNP transactions.

Another important example concerns consumer payments. A consumer might find a $200 fraudulent debit card payment on his monthly account statement. U.S. regulations say that if the consumer reports the transaction to his financial institution in a timely manner, the consumer would be responsible for no more than $50 of the value of the transaction, and the financial institution would lose the remaining $150. (17) In practice, however, consumers often avoid any of the cost of a fraudulent card payment. All of the major credit card networks provide zero liability to cardholders in cases of fraudulent payments. (18) As a result, consumer losses are excluded from the estimates in this section.

Finally, the estimated fraud losses for the United States reported here relies on the best sources available and informed assumptions. By comparison, other countries have developed and refined their methods for collecting data and reporting fraud statistics over several years. As a result, the U.S. statistics should be viewed as preliminary and may be subject to change as more information becomes available.

Fraud losses in the United States and other countries

In 2006, total U.S. fraud losses are estimated at $5.718 billion (Table 2). Card issuers paid the largest dollar cost, followed by POS merchants and Internet, mail order, and telephone merchants. Internet, mail order, and telephone merchants had the lowest cost of card payment fraud, but the annual sales volume of POS merchants was approximately 30 times that of Internet, mail order, and telephone merchants. Fraud as a share of sales volume was much higher for Internet, mail order, and telephone merchants than for POS merchants. (19)

The shares of fraud losses in the United States in 2006 were divided between card issuers (59 percent) and merchants (41 percent). For comparison, losses in France are shared more equally. In 2007, 51 percent of French losses were attributed to issuers and acquirers and 46 percent to merchants (Observatory for Payments Card Security 2007). This comparison is tentative, however, because of the preliminary nature of the estimate of U.S. losses. Additional research will be needed to further refine the distribution of fraud losses.

Table 3 compares loss rates on payment card transactions in the United States to losses in Australia, France, Spain, and the UK. (20) The United States had the highest rate of fraud losses in 2006; Australia and Spain had the lowest; and France and the UK were in the middle. The extent of the difference is significant: The highest rate of fraud is almost four times that of the lowest.

While there is some uncertainty in the calculations, the difference between U.S. fraud rates and those in other countries, shown in Table 3, is sufficiently large that added accuracy would not close the gap--but probably increase it. First, the U.S. statistics are based on net losses for those who bore the loss, while other countries use the gross losses when the fraudulent transaction is reported. The difference between net and gross is the amount of funds recovered or prevented from being fraudulently transferred. If the estimate for the United States were based on gross losses, the difference would be greater. Second, conservative assumptions are generally used to calculate the losses of U.S. merchants. More realistic assumptions would likely widen the gap as well.

Why fraud loss rates differ

The cross-country differences in fraud rates are due to a number of factors, including the mix of payment cards in use, transaction authorization systems, the types of payments made using cards, evolving security standards, and the use of older card technology that has relatively weak security features.

The rate of fraud is lower on PIN debit cards than on signature debit cards (Pulse). As a consequence, countries that rely more heavily on PIN codes to authenticate payment cards will have less payment fraud. In Australia, for example, approximately 90 percent of debit transactions in 2006 used PIN codes, compared to only about 40 percent in the United States.

The quality of transaction authorization systems is also important. Both the Spanish and Australian payment networks have strong reputations for the use of transaction history analysis to help identify and avoid fraudulent transactions.

Another factor contributing to the difference in fraud rates is the extent of Internet, mail order, and telephone shopping, where relatively risky CNP transactions are necessary. A recent European Commission study showed that only 20 percent of individuals ordered goods over the Internet in Spain, compared to 57 percent in the UK (EC Staff Working Document). A 2008 survey of U.S. consumers found that 83 percent of them made purchases on the Internet (Hitachi). Thus, the relatively high rate of card fraud in the United States and in the UK is likely due, in part, to more fully developed online commerce.

Yet another factor contributing to cross-country differences in fraud rates is evolving security standards that help to prevent debit and credit card fraud. For example, "chip-and-PIN" payment cards have an embedded computer chip and require use of a PIN to initiate a transaction. These cards are more secure because they better protect data used to authorize a payment, and they make it difficult to counterfeit a payment card. These cards are being adopted in many countries around the world. Chip-and-PIN cards have been successful at reducing fraud in face-to-face transactions, ATM withdrawals, and from lost or stolen cards (UK Cards Administration).

In countries that adopt chip-and-PIN cards, experience shows that fraud will migrate to payment types with relatively weak security. This occurs because issuers of chip-and-PIN cards also add magnetic stripes to their cards to allow backward compatibility with older transaction equipment. The magnetic stripe allows fraudsters to use information from a chip-and-PIN card to counterfeit cards for use in locations that continue to accept such cards. Prior to the adoption of chip-and-PIN cards, about 18 percent of fraud on counterfeit cards of UK issuers occurred on transactions outside of the UK, but today it is over 80 percent (APACS). Much of this growth has been on transactions in the United States, where magnetic stripes are still used on payment cards.

To sum up, the United States has a higher card fraud loss rate than Australia, France, Spain, and the UK. International differences are due to a number of factors, including underlying card payment technology and security standards. For the United States, important factors that lead to a relatively high fraud loss rate include a comparatively weak approval process for debit and credit card transactions and a highly developed Internet economy.

III. THE WAY FORWARD

Led by various segments of the industry in the United States and elsewhere, several initiatives to further protect card payments are under way. Outside the United States, card issuers and networks are implementing new card technology and publishing payment fraud statistics. Projects in the United States include enhancing data security standards, supplementing approval systems of contactless payment cards, developing methods to encrypt payment data, and disguising card numbers. While these are positive steps, barriers remain, such as conflicts of interest, inadequate incentives, poor governance, and potential redundancy. U.S. policymakers face mixed signals on how well the card payment industry controls payment fraud. On one hand, considerable efforts are aimed at reducing fraud. On the other, some initiatives appear redundant, new security standards are adopted slowly, and the rate of card fraud losses is relatively high.

Industry initiatives

A major initiative occurring in other countries is the implementation of the EMV standard for payment cards. EMV is an acronym for the card schemes Europay, MasterCard and Visa, but the standard has also been accepted by American Express, Discover, and JCB.

The EMV standard defines technical rules and protocols for payment cards that use computer chips. The standard has some flexibility, allowing card issuers to adopt various configurations for their cards that best fit their business needs. The chip-and-PIN card mentioned above is an example and is currently the most common implementation of the EMV standard. Chip-and-PIN cards are fully implemented in a few countries, but many other countries, including Canada and Mexico, are either in transition to chip-and-PIN or plan to adopt it in the near future. Chip-and-PIN payment cards have proven to be very good at preventing certain types of fraud, such as on lost or stolen cards. In countries where merchants will only accept these cards, counterfeit fraud has fallen as well.

Another initiative that other countries are pursuing is the collection and publication of payment fraud statistics. These statistics provide guidance for the card industry in its efforts to combat fraud. After implementation of chip-and-PIN, for example, statistics revealed to UK issuers that fraud on their cards was migrating to areas of relative security weakness. Specifically, CNP fraud in the UK and counterfeit card fraud outside of the UK grew rapidly. The information helped the industry take steps to counter these sources of fraud, and it appears the efforts have had some success. Total fraud losses on UK-issued payment cards fell 28 percent in 2009 over the previous year, a decline partly attributed to sophisticated fraud detection screening and to fraud prevention tools applied to online shopping (UK Cards Association).

In the United States, the major credit card companies are leading the most significant recent initiative to improve security and control fraud in card payments. While the card companies have long maintained their own security standards, a cooperative effort in 2004 between Visa and MasterCard led to a common standard. Other card companies joined the effort, and in 2006 the group formed the Payment Card Industry (PCI) Security Standards Council to oversee the standard. Card companies themselves manage compliance validation and enforcement.

The PCI Council oversees several industry-wide standards. The most important is the PCI Data Security Standard (PCI DSS), which helps merchants and payment processors protect sensitive data. This goal is accomplished by creating secure networks, strong access controls, data encryption, computers protected with firewalls and antivirus programs, and security policies designed to establish an effective internal control environment. (21)

Data breaches and their consequences have led elements of the U.S. payment industry to explore ways to improve card payment security. Card issuers have been deploying contactless payment cards, which have a small radio to transmit card information to a payment terminal. Because it is difficult to counterfeit these cards, they are considered more secure than magnetic stripe cards. Issuers are considering an upgrade to EMV-compliant contactless cards, which will use a cryptogram (an encrypted identifying number for the transaction) to allow the card issuer to check the authenticity of the payment card and the uniqueness of the transaction.

Two initiatives are being developed in the merchant community in cooperation with payment service providers. One initiative targets a weakness in the PCI DSS, which requires encryption of sensitive card data when it is transmitted over public networks, but not when transmitted over private networks. Merchants are investigating "end-to-end encryption," which would encrypt payment data over the entire communications channel from the point-of-sale terminal to the card issuer (Hernandez). Another initiative disguises a card account number by replacing it with a token number. This "tokenization" would occur after a card payment has been authorized so that a merchant can store the transaction information without having to store the card account number (Taylor). Merchants can retrieve the card account number for later processing, if needed. Both of these options could make merchant and processor computer networks less of a target because they would not store or transmit sensitive payment card information in forms that would be useful to hackers.

Barriers to improving card payment security

For the private market to find a socially optimal level of security, it must first overcome significant barriers (Roberds and Schreft 2009). Efforts to improve card payment security by one member of the network may benefit other members, just as one member's security breach may harm others. (22) But because one member of the network has no incentive to take account of the external benefits or costs of others, security for the network is less than optimal. Further, conflicts of interest can arise over the appropriate level of effort to enhance security. Some members will prefer relatively little effort, leaving the security of the entire network subject to its weakest links.

An answer to this dilemma is to pursue security efforts in a collective and comprehensive manner. Payment networks, for example, require membership to access network services. The threat of fines or expulsion makes members more likely to abide by rules regarding security and other operational matters (Braun and others).

Conflicts of interest can also complicate the development of security standards. Technically, standards would be more effective if members of the network determined them cooperatively. For example, security engineers recommend finding the most effective control points in the network to provide adequate security (Moore and others). But if each member of the payment network "goes it alone" and works only with its own control points, then it may be passing up effective security options that lie elsewhere in the network.

Research on standard-setting has found that governance is a key to success. Success is more likely if the governance structure includes all of the various interests in the network. The standards themselves need to be effective yet flexible enough to satisfy competitive interests. If done correctly, the process will promote compliance because all participants have a stake in the outcome (Steinfeld and others). Even then, the governance structure must also address issues such as intellectual property rights and provide a way to lessen the tendency of vested interests to block progress (Greenstein and Stango).

The International Organization for Standardization (ISO) uses a model of cooperation to coordinate international security standards for payments. In the United States, the affiliated American National Standards Institute's (ANSI) X9 committee is responsible for standards in the payments industry (Sullivan 2008). The PCI DSS and EMV standards are not developed in these standard-setting organizations. Instead, they use a centralized model controlled by the card issuers and networks. The centralized model may allow security standards to be developed rapidly, but perhaps at the expense of adoption. (23) Only half of the largest U.S. merchants met the PCI compliance deadline of September 30, 2007. (24) Similarly, many European retailers have been slow to achieve PCI compliance (Leyden).

Implementing the PCI DSS has also been controversial. Merchants and processors face significant costs of compliance and question the benefits they receive (Mott). (25) The standards themselves have been criticized because they do not address card network rules that require merchants to store card information to resolve disputed transactions or facilitate refunds. (26) In addition, some merchants who have been certified as compliant have still been the victims of successful security breaches, raising concerns about the quality of the standard. (27)

Considerations for policymakers

An important question concerns how well the payments industry as a whole can meet the challenge of protecting sensitive information. Policymakers can take some comfort that a significant amount of private sector activity is trying to find a solution to data breaches and associated payment fraud. By exploring several alternatives, the market may be able to sort out the most effective and efficient ways to protect sensitive card data.

Barriers to improving card payment security, however, may be higher in the United States than in many other countries. Coordination is particularly difficult, with over 18,000 federally insured depository institutions that offer deposit services and over 1 million retail establishments. In addition, the United States has a history of depending on paper checks for retail payments, which has a different security profile than electronic payments. The major shift to electronic payments is relatively recent, and developing appropriate security standards is in its first stages. The PCI Council is a framework for coordination, but it is too early to know whether its practices effectively balance the interests of cardholders, merchants, processors, and card issuers (box).

GOVERNANCE OF THE PCI COUNCIL

The PCI Council is owned by the five major credit card companies, and its executive committee consists of representatives from each of the companies. The executive director and chief technology officer of the council each have extensive experience in credit card companies. *

The council's membership consists of over 500 companies, including financial institutions, payments associations, merchants, equipment manufacturers, software developers, and payment processors. These members can vote for representatives on a board of advisors. But whether this broad membership provides meaningful influence is unclear. A letter sent by several merchant groups to the PCI Council in June 2009 that recommended several changes to the PCI DSS suggested that many merchants in the United States would like to have more influence on the design of card payment security standards. **

The PCI Council is a step forward because it has standardized security across the five major card companies. Whether it can also incorporate the interests of the wider payment community is unclear. The council is currently directing a revision to the PCI DSS (expected to be released at the end of September 2010). Participating organizations and stakeholders provided feedback on the current standard through October 31, 2009, which the council has been reviewing. The extent to which the PCI Council balances the interests of all stakeholders in the credit card industry will go a long way toward determining the success of the revised standard.

* See https://www.pcisecuritystandards.org/index.shtml for more information about the PCI Council.

** "Merchant Trade Groups Come Together to Advocate for Changes to Data Security Standards," Smart Card Trends, June 10, 2009.

Regardless of the reasons, several signs suggest that lack of coordination in the payments industry has impeded security improvements. First, once fully developed, end-to-end encryption, tokenization, and payment messages augmented by cryptograms may all provide more security. But, to the extent that they each make attacks on card networks less attractive, they appear to be redundant (Smart Card Alliance). If so, they are competing technologies that are expensive to develop and implement. The potential payoff to effective coordination of standard-setting is the ability to choose what may be the best option for all members of the payment network and to accomplish common goals before considerable investment is made in unneeded technology.

Second, slow adoption and disputes over the design of the PCI DSS suggest that development of the standard is one-sided, favoring issuers over merchants. This should concern policymakers because effective payment security has two parts: the security standard and its adoption. If members of the payments industry do not feel it is in their self-interest to adopt a new security standard, they may adopt it slowly, and thus overall protection of payments suffers.

Third, the rate of fraud on U.S. card payments is relatively high. Lower rates of card payment fraud have motivated the payments industry in other countries to take the major step of adopting payment smart cards. But a high rate of fraud has not led to U.S. adoption of payment smart cards. It may be that payment smart cards are not the best solution for U.S. fraud prevention, but an alternative, comprehensive, and coordinated solution is not being considered.

Finally, reining in payment fraud in the United States is hampered by a lack of detailed, consistent, and periodic data. In a time of profound changes to the retail payment system, such information is crucial. Existing data have quality issues and inconsistent availability, making it difficult to identify what strategies the industry and policymakers should pursue. Producing better statistics would require some effort and cost, but most of the basic data already exist in the information systems of payment providers. Set-up costs would be required to standardize reporting and to establish an entity to compile data and regularly report statistics. (28) Other countries have not found this system to be overly burdensome.

IV. SUMMARY

In the United States, fraud loss rates on debit and credit card transactions are higher than in Australia, France, Spain, and the UK. The main vulnerability is that fraudulent payments can be made with just a few pieces of information that the payment card industry uses in its payment approval process. Hackers have strong incentives to gather this information, leading to serious data breaches. The industry is moving to improve card payment security, but there are indications that their efforts could be more effective.

To guard against excessive fraud losses and to ensure confidence in card payments, policymakers need to monitor developments in card payment security. First, will card payment security continue to evolve without the benefit of industry-wide statistics on the level and sources of fraud losses? These statistics would help to determine whether the industry continues to tolerate a relatively high rate of fraud. Second, will the card payment industry move toward more coordination of security efforts? Such coordinated efforts have been successful in the Automated Clearing House system, another electronic payment system that has grown rapidly in recent years (Braun and others). If not, policymakers might consider a more active role to help the payments industry overcome barriers to effective coordination of security development.

APPENDIX: SOURCES AND METHODS

Calculation sources and details

The goal of the calculations is to obtain comparable estimates of fraud losses to all payment participants on payment cards issued by domestic institutions.

Australia:

Fraud rate = (ATM and debit card fraud losses+credit card fraud losses) / (ATM and debit card transaction value+credit card transaction value) .000239 = ($14.4 million+$85.3 million)/($186.3 billion+$230.7 billion) = 2.39 cents per $100 transaction value

Source:

Australian Payments Clearing Association (APCA) Media Release, "Payments Fraud in Australia," December 15, 2008.

France:

Fraud rate = Total fraud losses/Total transaction value (see table below) .000500 = 186.1 million [euro] / 372.5 billion [euro] =5.0 cents per $100 transaction value

Source:

Observatory for Payment Card Security (OPCS), Annual Report, 2006.

Scheme	Transaction type	Debit, ATM, and credit Fraud losses
Four party	French issuer, French acquirer	100,475,400 [euro]
Four party	French issuer, Foreign acquirer	73,835,500 [euro]
Three party	French issuer, French acquirer	9,147,180 [euro]
Three party	French issuer, Foreign acquirer	2,593,910 [euro]
Total		186,051,990 [euro]

Scheme	Debit, ATM, and credit Transaction value
Four party	331,270,000,000 [euro]
Four party	15,140,000,000 [euro]
Three party	24,340,000,000 [euro]
Three party	1,720,000,000 [euro]
Total	372,470,000,000 [euro]

Spain:

.000224=2.24 cents per $100 transaction value

Source:

ServiRed, Annual Report, 2007.

UK:

POS retailer fraud losses=total fraud losses in 2004 x (APACS fraud on POS transactions for 2006/APACS fraud on POS transactions for 2004) = 14 million [pounds sterling] x (72.1 million [pounds sterling]218.8 million [pounds sterling]) = 4.6 million [pounds sterling]

Online retailer fraud losses=total fraud losses in 2004 x (APACS fraud on CNP transactions for 2006/APACS fraud on CNP transactions for 2004) = 14.1 million [pounds sterling] x (212.7 million [pounds sterling]150.8 million [pounds sterling]) = 19.9 million [pounds sterling]

Fraud rate = (fraud losses reported by APACS + POS retailer fraud losses + Online retailer fraud losses) / (card purchase transaction value + value of ATM withdrawals) .000912= (427 million [pounds sterling] + 19.9 million [pounds sterling] + 4.6 million [pounds sterling])/(315.5 billion [pounds sterling] + 179.8 billion [pounds sterling]) =9.12 cents per $100 transaction value

Notes:

APACS reports only provide the value of fraud; the value of transactions is taken from separate reports on payment clearing and settlement. Levi, et al. (2007, p. 24) states that losses for transactions not fully authorized by card issuers are excluded from APACS data. They also report that in 2004 retail fraud losses not included in the APACS data amounted to 14.1 million [pounds sterling] for POS merchants and 14 million [pounds sterling] for CNP transactions.

Because of the transition to chip-and-PIN payment cards, POS merchant card fraud declined and CNP fraud increased from 2004 to 2006. To get an estimate for 2006, the 2004 figures are adjusted using APACS data (from 2004 and 2006) for fraud on face-to-face and CNP transactions.

Sources:

Association for Payment Clearing Services (APACS), "Quarterly Statistical Release," May 15, 2009.

APACS, "2008 Fraud Figures Announced by APACS," Press Release, March 19, 2008.

Michael Levi, John Borrows, Mathew H. Fleming, and Matthew Hopkins, "The Nature and Economic Impact of Fraud in the UK," Report for the Association of Police Officers' Economic Crime Portfolio, February 2007.

United States:

Card issuer losses on credit card transactions are the total value as reported by issuers. For other transactions, losses are calculated from loss rates on categories of payments (PIN debit, signature debit, and ATM transactions) multiplied by the total value of these transactions.

Card issuers:

Credit card losses: $1.24 billion

Debit and ATM cards: total losses=(PIN debit losses+signature debit losses+ATM withdrawal losses)

$762 million = (.000085 x $333 billion)+(.000505 x $666 billion) +(.000686 x $579 billion)

Total credit, debit and ATM card loss=$2.0 billion=$1.24 billion+$762 million

POS merchants:

total losses=(PIN debit losses+signature debit losses+credit card losses) x share of card payments on cards issued by domestic financial institutions

$0.829 billion = [(.0001 x $333 billion)+(.0003 x $666 billion)+ (.0003 x $2.1 trillion)] x 0.96

Internet, mail order, and telephone merchants:

Total losses=Total Internet, mail order, and telephone fraud loss x proportion of loss due to chargeback transactions

$0.9 billion=$183 billion x .014 x .35

Loss rate: (Fraud losses reported by card issuers+POS merchant fraud losses+Internet, mail order, and telephone merchant fraud losses) / total value of debit and credit card transactions

.000924= ($2.0 billion+$0.829 billion+$0.9 billion)/$3.1 trillion = 9.2 cents per $100 transaction value

Notes:

Loss rates are for actual debit and credit card fraud losses at domestic card-issuing financial institutions; at POS retail establishments; and at Internet, mail order, and telephone merchants. Issuer credit card losses are from "Credit Card Fraud--U.S.," (2007). Debit card losses are based on a survey of debit card issuers (Pulse 2008). Debit card loss rates are an average of statistics reported for 2005 and 2007. The loss rates are applied to estimates of the value of PIN and signature debit card transactions for the United States (Gerdes 2008) to obtain total losses.

Losses for Internet, mail order, and telephone merchants are found by applying a reported 1.4 percent loss rate on Internet sales (CyberSource 2007) to the overall sales for these merchants reported by the U.S. Census Bureau (2007). This results in $2.567 billion in payment fraud losses to Internet, mail order, and telephone merchants. The CyberSource loss rate includes sales that the merchants did not accept because the transactions were suspicious. To obtain actual losses, the author included 35 percent of the $2.567 billion, which represents the value of chargeback transactions. Losses for POS merchants are taken based on estimates of loss rates provided to the author by Steve Mott, the principal of BetterBuyDesign and an expert on payments who provides consulting services to merchants. Other sources of loss rate are similar but result in higher total losses than the rates provided by Mott (see McGrath and Kjos, footnote 22, p. 13; Mott 2007; and Taylor).

The estimates are for payment cards issued by domestic financial institutions, but some sales by U.S. merchants will be on payment cards issued by foreign financial institutions. According to the Bureau of Economic Analysis, foreign travelers in the U.S. spent $108 billion in 2006, which represents 4 percent of total card payments. Accordingly, the estimate for losses by POS merchants is reduced by 4 percent. This assumes foreign tourism and travel is purchased on payment cards and that the fraud rate for foreign and domestically issued cards is equal.

END NOTES AND SOURCES DELETED

Table 1

CHARACTERISTICS OF PUBLICLY DISCLOSED DATA

BREACHES IN THE UNITED STATES

Source

Outsiders	64%
Insiders-accident	21%
Insiders-malicious	7%

Type

Stolen laptop or computer	27%
Exposure on Internet or e-mail	17%
Hack	16%
Documents lost in mail or on disposal	9%
Scams and social engineering	8%

Notes: Statistics based on 2,318 incidents since 2000 tracked by the Open Security Foundation (datalossdb.org, accessed on March 25, 2010). The incidents compromised personally identifiable information such as credit card numbers, social security numbers, names and/or addresses, financial account information, financial information, date of birth, e-mail addresses, medical information, and miscellaneous.

Sources other than those listed above include insiders and unknown.

Types other than those listed above include lost media, stolen documents, lost tapes, lost documents, lost computer drives, stolen media, stolen computer drives, lost laptops, virus, disposal of computer tapes, missing laptops, disposal of computer drives, lost computers, disposal of computers, and unknown.

Table 2

FRAUD LOSSES ON DEBIT AND CREDIT CARD PAYMENTS UNITED STATES, 2006

	Billions	Share of total loss
Card issuers		
PIN debit	$0.028	
Signature debit	$0.337	
Credit cards	$1.240	
ATM withdrawals	$0.397	
Total issuer losses	$2.002	59%
Merchants		
POS	$0.828	
Internet, mail order, and telephone	$0.568	
Total merchant losses	$1.396	41%
Total losses	$3.718	

Note: See Appendix for sources and details.

Table 3

FRAUD LOSS RATES ON DEBIT AND CREDIT CARD

PAYMENTS, 2006

	Loss per $100
Australia	$0.024
France	$0.050
Spain	$0.022
UK	$0.086
U.S.	$0.092
U.S. card issuers only	$0.054

Note: See Appendix for sources and details.

Part II

OCCUPATIONAL CRIME AND AVOCATIONAL CRIME

3

Corruption in Asian Countries

Can It Be Minimized?

Jon S.T. Quah

ABSTRACT

The author discusses the history of political corruption in Asian countries and analyzes Asian governments' current attempts to thwart corruption. The effectiveness of anti-corruption laws, politicians' ability to maintain employment despite their history of corrupt practices, and ineffective anti-corruption strategies used by past governments are analyzed.

Can corruption be combatted? Yes, but only under certain circumstances! That appears to be the experience of Asian countries where corruption is ubiquitous with the exception of Singapore--a country that proved to be the only success story with a strong political leadership and better pay sales. Can this experience be replicated?

Three decades ago, Gunnar Myrdal (1968, 938-939) identified the taboo on research on South Asian corruption as one of the factors inhibiting the research of his book, Asian Drama. However, this taboo no longer exists, judging from the increasing amount of research on corruption in Asian countries in recent years. According to the Far Eastern Economic Review, corruption was the biggest story of 1996, the Year of the Rat, as a great deal of "newsprint and television time was devoted to reports and discussions on corruption

Corruption in Asian Countries: Can It Be Minimized? (Statistical Data Included) Jon S.T. Quah. Public Administration Review Nov 1999 v59 i6 p483 (8660 words)

41

in government" (Ghosh et al., 1997, 18). Furthermore, the financial crises in Thailand, South Korea, Malaysia, and Indonesia in 1997 have highlighted the problems of corruption, cronyism, and nepotism on one hand, and the need for more accountability and transparency in government and banking operations in these countries on the other hand.

Why is corruption such a serious problem in Asian countries? Is it possible to control or to minimize corruption in these countries? This paper contends that the extent of corruption in Asian (and other) countries depends on two factors: (1) the nature of the causes of corruption in these countries; and (2) the degree of effectiveness of the measures initiated by political leaders to combat corruption. In order to curb corruption in Asian countries, the causes of corruption must first be correctly diagnosed so that political leaders can take appropriate action to minimize, if not eliminate, such causes. Asian countries like Singapore and Hong Kong, which observe this logic of corruption control, are more successful in combatting corruption than other countries (Quah, 1995).

This paper is divided into three sections. In the first section, the different levels of corruption in Asian countries are discussed. Section two describes the anticorruption strategies employed in several Asian countries. The concluding section focuses on Singapore's experience, demonstrating that, while it is difficult to curb corruption, it is nonetheless possible to do so if a country's political leaders have the commitment or will to impartially implement effective anticorruption measures.

LEVELS OF ASIAN CORRUPTION

In September 1974, the Far East Economic Review featured the cover story "Corruption: The Asian Lubricant," which surveyed corruption in 10 Asian countries. The article concluded that:

> If you want to buy a Sherman tank, a Red Cross blanket, or simply speed up the installation of a telephone, there is probably no easier place in the world in which to do just that than in Asia--if you are willing to part with some cash, that is. With pathetically few exceptions, the countries in this region are so riddled with corruption that the paying of "tea money" has become almost a way of life (Far East Economic Review, 1974, 3).

This picture of pervasive corruption in Asia is supported by individual portraits of corruption in such countries as Bangladesh, the People's Republic of China, Hong Kong, India, Japan, Laos, Pakistan, Taiwan, and Thailand (Far East Economic Review, 1974, 22-31).

As it is not possible to measure the actual extent of corruption in a country, scholars usually rely on the reported extent of corruption. Lancaster and Montinola (1997, 16) have observed that students of political corruption use written documents (press reports, judicial records, and records from anticorruption agencies) and survey data to measure corruption. As these instruments are not problem-free, they have recommended the use of the Corruption Perception Index (CPI), published by Transparency International in 1995 and updated in 1996 and 1997, because it is a "robust" index that "captures more than a single indicator" and "combines several measures of political corruption for each country" (Ibid., 27-28).

According to Transparency International, the CPI is "an attempt to assess the level at which corruption is perceived by people working for multinational firms and institutions as impacting on commercial and social life" (TI Newsletter, 1996, 5). The Business International Index (BII) is based on surveys of experts or consultants conducted during 1980-1983 by Business International, which is now a subsidiary of the Economist's Intelligence Unit. The BII ranks countries from 1 to 10 according to "the degree to which business transactions involve corruption or questionable payments" (Wei, 1998, 3).

Unlike the CPI and BII, the Global Competitiveness Report Index (GCRI) is based on a 1996 survey of firm managers, who were asked questions about different aspects of competitiveness in the host countries where they invest. Specifically, 2,381 firms in 58 countries were asked to rate the level of corruption on a one-to-seven scale according to the extent of "irregular, additional payments connected with import and export permits, business licenses, exchange controls, tax assessments, police protection or loan applications" (ibid., 4).

Table 1 shows the levels of corruption in 13 Asian countries according to the three indices, the BII, CPI, and GCRI. Singapore is perceived to be the least corrupt Asian country by all three indices. This perception is confirmed by the Hong Kong-based Political and Economic Risk Consultancy Ltd., whose 1996 survey showed that Singapore "maintained its reputation as a `corruption-free' haven in a region in which shady practices are all too common" (Straits Times, 1996, 3). Conversely, Indonesia and Thailand were perceived as the most corrupt Asian countries on the BII. The CPI ranked Bangladesh as the most corrupt Asian country, and the GCRI identified Indonesia and the Philippines as the two Asian countries with the highest levels of corruption.

Table 1: Perceived Levels of Corruption in Asian Countries

Country	BII (1-10 scale)(*)	CPI97 (1-10 scale)(*)
Singapore	1.00	2.34
Hong Kong	3.00	3.72
Japan	2.25	4.43
Taiwan	4.25	5.98
Malaysia	5.00	5.99
South Korea	5.25	6.71
Thailand	9.50	7.94
Philippines	6.50	7.95
People's Republic of China	NA	8.12
India	5.75	8.25
Indonesia	9.50	8.28
Pakistan	7.00	8.47
Bangladesh	7.00	9.20

Country	GCR197 (1-7 scale)(*)
Singapore	1.24
Hong Kong	1.52
Japan	2.07
Taiwan	3.22
Malaysia	3.97
South Korea	4.34
Thailand	5.55
Philippines	5.56
People's Republic of China	4.10
India	5.11
Indonesia	5.56
Pakistan	NA
Bangladesh	NA

[Graphic omitted] Source: Wei, 1998, 5.

(*) According to Wei, the original BII, CPI, and GCRI were re-scaled so that higher scores imply more corruption. Thus, for all three indices, a higher score means a higher level of corruption.

Table 1 also indicates the different levels of corruption in 13 Asian countries. What accounts for the variations in the extent of corruption in these countries? To answer this question, it is necessary to examine the anticorruption strategies employed by seven of these countries to ascertain whether they have observed the logic of corruption control.(1)

ANTICORRUPTION STRATEGIES IN ASIAN COUNTRIES

The consequences of corruption can be minimized if government has an effective anticorruption strategy and implements it impartially. Specifically, the more effective anticorruption measures are, the greater their impact on the society in terms of reducing the negative effects and the level of corruption. The effectiveness of anticorruption measures depends on two factors: (1) the adequacy of the measures in terms of the comprehensiveness of their scope and powers; and (2) the level of commitment of political leaders to the goal of minimizing corruption. In other words, for anticorruption measures to be effective, they must be properly designed (to attack the causes of corruption), and they must be sponsored and upheld sincerely by political leaders. In short, the most elaborate and well-designed anticorruption measures will be useless if they are not enforced by the political leadership (Quah, 1982, 174-175).

By juxtaposing these two variables, the adequacy of anticorruption measures and the commitment of political leadership, a matrix of anticorruption strategies can be obtained (see Table 2).

Table 2: A Matrix of Anticorruption Strategies

Commitment of political leadership

	Anticorruption Measures	
	Adequate	**Inadequate**
Strong	Effective strategy	Ineffective strategy 2
Weak	Ineffective strategy 1	"Hopeless" strategy

Source: Quah, 1982, 175.

Table 2 shows four strategies for combatting corruption, depending on the adequacy of the anticorruption measures employed and the strength of political leaders' commitment. This matrix of anticorruption strategies can be used to analyze the anticorruption efforts of several Asian countries.

To be effective, anticorruption strategies must minimize--if not eliminate--the causes of corruption. In his comparative study of the control of bureaucratic corruption in Hong Kong, India, and Indonesia, Leslie Palmier (1985, 271) identified three important causes of corruption in these countries: opportunities (which depended on the extent of civil servants' involvement in the administration or control of lucrative activities), salaries, and policing (that is, the probability of detection and punishment). According to Palmier,

> [B]ureaucratic corruption seems to depend not on any one of the [three] factors identified, but rather on the balance between them. At one extreme, with few opportunities, good salaries, and effective policing, corruption will be minimal, at the other, with many opportunities, poor salaries, and weak policing, it will be considerable (emphasis added). (272)

Following Palmier's hypothesis, effective anticorruption strategies should reduce or remove opportunities for corruption, raise the salaries of civil servants, and ensure a high degree of policing.

"Hopeless" Anticorruption Strategy

Given the perceived high levels of corruption of Asian countries as indicated in Table 1, it is not surprising that the "hopeless" anticorruption strategy has been used in countries such as China, Indonesia, and Bangladesh; corruption in these countries has been institutionalized, as their anticorruption measures are inadequate and their political leaders are not at all concerned about minimizing corruption.

People's Republic of China: ,The high level of corruption in the People's Republic of China (PRC) can be attributed to the low wages of civil servants, the many opportunities for corruption during the last two decades of Deng Xiaoping's modernization policy, and the lack of political will in implementing anticorruption measures against senior party officials. Indeed, although bribery exceeding 100,000 Yuan is a capital offense, the death penalty has not been imposed on senior party officials found guilty of accepting such bribes.(2)

[Graphic omitted] Several public opinion polls conducted during the late 1980s in the PRC indicated that the public had identified corruption as "the most prevailing social crime" and confirmed its resentment of corruption (Gong, 1994, 135). In fact, the corruption issue was an important catalyst for the student demonstrations in the spring of 1989 as "the students' anticorruption banner appealed strongly to the public." After the Tiananmen Square incident, the Chinese media "dramatically increased the exposure of corruption cases to highlight the party's determination and efforts to repress corruptions" (ibid., 137). The Chinese Communist Party sought to clear its image by introducing new anticorruption rules designed to (1) strengthen centralized control over certain commodities and production materials; (2) forbid such "unhealthy practices" as gift giving in public affairs and squandering public funds; and (3) punish offenders through the stipulation of disciplinary penalties for embezzlement (ibid., 139-140).

In 1982, the Central Discipline Inspection Commission (CDIC) was reestablished to deal with discipline and anticorruption work. Five years later, the Ministry of Supervision (MOS) was also reestablished "in part to curb corruption and maladministration within the civil service." Even though the MOS had received more than 700,000 reports in 1993, both the CDIC and MOS could not stem the problem of corruption because the "authorities appear[ed] to lack the political will to handle corruption cases among more senior party members" (Burns, 1994, 57-58).

So far, only two senior party officials have been convicted of corruption in recent years. In 1994, Li Yiaoshi, former Vice-Minister of the State Science and Technology Commission, was sentenced to 20 years in jail for corruption (ibid., 58). On July 31, 1998, the former Beijing party chief, Chen Xitong, became the highest-ranking party member to be jailed for corruption when he was sentenced to 16 years for graft of 555,000 Yuan and dereliction of duty. As corruption is a capital offense in the PRC, Chen's sentence is lenient; more junior party cadres have been sentenced to life imprisonment or even death for corruption involving smaller sums over 100,000 Yuan (Straits Times, 1998, 14). The death penalty is imposed on officials who accept bribes exceeding 100,000 Yuan, or US$ 12,000 (Wang, 1998, 5). In short, party officials in the PRC can "short-circuit corruption investigations by appealing to their protectors in the party hierarchy" (Root, 1996, 752).

Indonesia: In Indonesia, corruption was a serious problem during the Dutch colonial period, as it was rife among the Dutch East India Company's personnel because of their low salaries. However, this traditional tolerance for corruption was eroded during the postwar period, when corruption was viewed more critically as the enhanced role of the public bureaucracy had increased opportunities for bureaucratic corruption (Quah, 1982, 154-155). Corruption became endemic during President Sukarno's rule because his "disastrously inflationary budgets eroded civil service salaries to the point where people simply could not live on them and where financial accountability virtually collapsed because of administrative deterioration" (Mackie, 1970, 87-88).

Corruption remained a serious problem and became institutionalized during the 32 years of Suharto's term of office. According to Hanna (1971, 1), corruption in Indonesia has "become so institutionalized" that "its eradication ... might mean the critical dislocation of the whole shaky national structure." Indeed, Suharto and his family had "extensive business interests" and "benefited from what appears to be privileged access to government contracts" (Girling, 1997, 56).

The Indonesian government's first attempt to curb corruption occurred after the 1955 election; it resulted in the arrests of those involved, including civil servants and a minister. In June 1968, Suharto assigned the task of tackling corruption cases to the Team Pemberantasan Korupsi (Corruption Eradication Team), which was, however, ineffective because its efforts were blocked by influential men in the regime (Quah, 1982, 170). Student protests in January 1970 and press criticism of government corruption resulted in the appointment of a special Commission of Four elder statesmen (Komisi IV) by President Suharto to review the problem of corruption within the civil service and to make recommendations for improvement.

This commission presented seven reports on those agencies and areas that were judged to be vulnerable to corruption to President Suharto from February to June 1970. Perhaps the most important consequence of these reports was the passing of the Prevention Against Corrupt Criminal Acts Bill in 1971; previously, corruption was dealt with as a crime under the penal code. Suharto accepted the commission's recommendation that civil servants should submit an annual return of their personal assets, and he published an instruction in 1970 requiring all officials to conform accordingly. However, civil servants ignored this regulation for nine years, and it was only in 1979 that 90 percent of the officials submitted their annual returns (Palmier, 1970, 12). This example illustrates clearly that laws in Indonesia are not always implemented, especially anticorruption laws, as the implementation of such laws would prevent corrupt officials from continuing their practices.

In June 1977, the task of combatting corruption was transferred by presidential instruction from the Commission of Four to the National Security Agency (Kopkamtib), which launched

Operation Orderliness (Operasi Tertib or Opstib) by making
"lightning visits" to government departments known for corruption,
dismissing officials caught red-handed on the spot. Even though
Kopkamtib had taken action against corrupt officials, its major
handicap was "its inability to take action against those generals and
senior government officials involved in corrupt practices" (Quah,
1982, 171).

"The family business," or the corruption involving Suharto's
family, grew without restraint during the 1980s and 1990s. Toward
the end of Suharto's term, especially during the late 1990s, public
criticism of his family's involvement in corrupt practices mounted,
culminating in his relinquishment of power in May 1998. As the
system of corruption in Indonesia has become "deeply ingrained"
during the past 32 years of Suharto's rule, it will be difficult for his
successor, President B.J. Habibie, to eradicate corruption. In other
words, even though Suharto is no longer in power in Indonesia today,
his legacy of widespread corruption will remain for a long time.
Indeed, according to Shari and Einhorn (1998, 33), "the qualities that
rank the country as the world's most corrupt after Nigeria won't be
erased with a change of presidency [as] ... the bureaucracy runs on
miserably low salaries, so until civil servants make a living wage,
bribery will remain."

Bangladesh: In Bangladesh, a 1997 national household survey
on corruption conducted for Transparency International Bangladesh
confirmed the country's perceived high level of corruption, as
revealed by the following findings:

> 41% of households paid a "donation" and 3.6% a direct
> payment for the admission of children into schools, while
> 36% of households made payments to or through hospital
> staff or other "influential persons" to secure admission into
> hospitals. 65% had bribed land registrars for recording a false
> lower sale price when registering a land transaction, while
> 54% had bribed either bank employees or "influential
> persons" to secure bank loans. 33% paid money to obtain
> electricity connections, while 32% paid less for water "by
> arrangement with the meter reader." 47% were able to reduce
> the holding tax assessment on house and property "by
> arrangement with municipal staff on payment of money,"
> while 65% found it impossible to obtain trade licenses without
> money or influence. 63% of those involved in litigation had
> paid bribes to either court officials or the opponents' lawyers,
> 89% of those surveyed being of the view that judges were

corrupt. 97% thought the police service was corrupt. (Quoted in Jayawickrama, 1998, 3)

Similarly, businessmen in Bangladesh have complained that "their high costs are due to the payoffs they have to make to government officials for sanctions, bank loans, and permits" (Kochanek, 1993, 199). Indeed, according to one businessman, "I get sick in my stomach whenever I have to see a government official" (Quoted in Kochanek, 1993, 199).

The politics of patronage and corruption have plagued all governments in Bangladesh since 1971, but the Ershad government has been described by one businessman as "the most centralized and corrupt in the country's history" (Kochanek, 1993, 264-265). Under General Ershad, corruption was pervasive and included petty corruption, project corruption, and programmatic corruption (Kochanek, 1993, 259). These three forms of corruption "led to a massive gap between policy and implementation," as under Ershad, "law and policy had little meaning" as "decisions were made on an arbitrary basis with little accountability or appeal" (Kochanek, 1993, 266-267).

In his analysis of bureaucratic culture in Bangladesh, Mohammad Mohabbat Khan (1998, 35) identified corruption as a dominant component, as it has been institutionalized in the public service during the last 25 years. He attributed Bangladesh's high level of corruption to four factors:

> First, bureaucrats involved in corrupt practices in most cases do not lose their jobs. Very rarely they are dismissed from service on charges pertaining to corruption. Still rarely they are sent to prison for misusing public funds. They have never been compelled to return to the state their ill-gotten wealth. Second, the law-enforcing officials including police personnel are extremely corrupt. They are happy to share the booty with other corrupt bureaucrats. Third, the people have a tendency not only to tolerate corruption but to show respect to those bureaucrats who made fortunes through dubious means.... Fourth, it is easier for a citizen to get quick service because he has already "paid" the bureaucrat rather than wait for his turn. (Khan, 1998, 36)

The lack of commitment by Bangladesh's political leaders is first manifested in the fact that "many elected officials, including members of parliament and ministers, are known to be involved in large-scale corruption" (Khan, 1998, 36). A more important manifestation of the lack of political will in fighting corruption is the transfer of the director-general of the Bureau of Anti-Corruption to the Ministry of Education because of his "crusade against corruption" and his unwillingness to stop the probe against four ministers, many members of Parliament, and several senior civil servants in May 1995. Khan (1998, 37) concludes pessimistically, but correctly, that the "bureaucratic and political elite will [not] start a campaign against corruption in public life as it adversely affect their individual, group and coterie interests."

Ineffective Anticorruption Strategies

The second and third cells of the matrix of anticorruption strategies in Table 2 represent two types of ineffective anticorruption strategies (strategies 1 and 2). Ineffective strategy 1 occurs when anticorruption measures are adequate but the political leadership's commitment is weak, thus resulting in the nonenforcement of anticorruption measures. This lack of political will can be seen in the ineffective anticorruption strategies adopted in the Philippines, South Korea, and Thailand.

The third cell of ineffective strategy 2 is possible but unlikely in reality, as political leaders who are strongly committed to eradicating corruption will probably improve inadequate anticorruption measures, instead of being satisfied with inadequate anticorruption measures. None of the 13 Asian countries listed in Table 1 fall into this category.

The Philippines: Corruption was introduced into the Philippines during the Spanish colonial period, when graft and corruption prevailed because civil servants were paid low salaries and had many opportunities for corrupt behavior (Corpuz, 1957, 129). In contrast, the bureaucracy of the American colonial period (1898-1913) was less corrupt, as "the bureaucrats received higher salaries and corrupt officials were promptly prosecuted" (Quah, 1982, 159). However, graft and corruption flourished in the Philippines after World War II, and the bureaucracy suffered from "low prestige, incompetence, meager resources, and a large measure of cynical corruption" (Corpuz, 1957, 222-223).

Bureaucratic corruption was a serious problem during the 1950s, especially during the administration of President Elpidio Quirino (1948-1953); during his tenure, corruption "permeated the entire Philippine bureaucracy" (Al filer, 1979, 323). Accordingly, Quirino created the Integrity Board in May 1950 to investigate complaints of graft and corruption against civil servants. However, the Integrity Board was dissolved five months later, as it did not receive public support.

When Ramon Magsaysay won the presidential election in 1953, he established the Presidential Complaints and Action Commission (PCAC) to reduce inefficiency and dishonesty in the civil service. However, Magsaysay's death in 1957 gave rise to the Garcia administration (1957-1962), which abolished the PCAC and replaced it with the Presidential Committee on Administration Performance Efficiency and the Presidential Fact-Finding Committee in 1958 to implement the government's anti-graft campaign. In February 1960, Garcia created a third anti-graft committee, known as the President's Anti-Graft Committee (ibid., 331-337).

Garcia's successor, Diosdado Macapagal, established the Presidential Anti-Graft Committee. In 1965, Macapagal was replaced by Ferdinand Marcos, who abolished that committee and formed the Presidential Agency on Reforms and Government Operations (PARGO) in January 1966. Three other agencies, the Presidential Complaints and Action Office, the Complaints and Investigations Office, and the Special Cabinet Committee in Backsliding, were later created to assist the PARGO in its task of weeding out corruption (ibid., 339-346).

According to Varela (1995, 174), "graft and corruption reached its all time high during the martial law regime under Marcos," as corruption "had permeated almost all aspects of bureaucratic life and institutions which saw the start of the systematic plunder of the country." Indeed, the tremendous amount of "official corruption" that was practiced by Marcos, his family, and friends during his two decades in power was only discovered after his downfall in February 1986. The plundering of the country's wealth by the former first family was revealed by Pedrosa:

> The documents [discovered by the investigators for the Aquino government] outlined the Marcoses' formula for systematic plunder. They had amassed their wealth through bribe-taking and kickbacks from crony monopolies; through the diversion of government loans and contracts; through the profits from over-priced goods and construction; through unaudited government revenue, usually raised from taxes; and through the expedient of taking over businesses by decree and the diversion of yet more funds from government-controlled entities. Nothing was spared ... [The Marcoses had stolen] a

staggering $15 billion, more than half of the entire national debt of the Philippines (emphasis added). (1987, 221-222)

When President Corazon Aquino took over in February 1986, "there was high expectation that the end of the culture of graft and corruption was near" (Varela, 1995, 174). She created the Presidential Commission on Good Government (PCGG) to identify and retrieve the money stolen by the Marcos family and their cronies. Unfortunately, Aquino's "avowed anti-graft and corruption" stance was viewed cynically by the public after two of her Cabinet members and her relatives were accused of corruption. The PCGG also became a target for charges of corruption, favoritism, and incompetence; by mid-1988, five PCGG agents faced graft charges and 13 more were under investigation. In May 1987, Aquino established the Presidential Committee on Public Ethics and Accountability in response to increasing public criticism. However, this committee was hindered by a shortage of staff and funds (Timberman, 1991, 233-234). In short, as Carino has indicated, Aquino's "honesty has not been matched by the political will to punish the corrupt" (Quoted in ibid., 235).

In his study of the consequences of low salaries on the prestige of the Philippine Civil Service, Padilla (1995, 195-202) found that civil servants augmented their low wages by vending within the office, holding a second job, teaching part-time, practicing their profession after office hours, and engaging in research and consultation projects. On the other hand, civil servants could also augment their low salaries by resorting to petty corrupt practices (ibid., 206). Indeed, as long as civil service salaries remain low in the Philippines, it will be extremely difficult to minimize corruption. Unfortunately, Aquino's successor, Fidel Ramos has failed to minimize corruption, too, as the salaries of civil servants have not been increased and he did not demonstrate his political will in fighting corruption)

South Korea: Corruption has been a serious problem in South Korea since the sixteenth century, when the participation of the king's family in politics led to "increasing nepotism and corruption in administration" (Rahman, 1986, 119). As a result of corruption scandals in recent years, South Korea has been described as "a ROTC (Republic of Total Corruption) by the people and mass media"(Kim, 1994, 215).

The fight against corruption began with President Park Chung Hee, who assumed office in May 1961 after ousting the government of Chang Myon because of its involvement in corruption, its inability to defend the country from communism, and its incompetence in initiating economic and social change (Han, 1989, 273). Park formed the Board of Audit and Inspection (BAI) in 1963 to act as a "direct check on the economic bureaucracy" (Hart-Landsberg, 1993, 54). In other words, the BAI was the first de facto anticorruption agency in South Korea. In March 1975, Park introduced the Seojungshaeshin (General Administration Reform) Movement to curb corruption in the civil service (Oh, 1982, 324); the number of civil servants prosecuted for corruption increased from 21,919 in 1975 to 51,468 in 1976 (Rahman, 1986, 122).

Park's assassination in October 1979 led to the assumption of power a year later by his successor, Chun Doo Hwan, who reaffirmed his government's anticorruption stance by purging corrupt public officials and introducing ethics laws to reward honest officials and to enhance the structures for civil service reform (Jun, 1985, 63). However, Chun's government lacked legitimacy because of opposition by rival political parties, student leaders, intellectuals, and progressive Christians (Han, 1989, 283-284). Chun's unpopularity led to his retirement in February 1988 at the end of his seven-year term. He, his two brothers, and his wife's family were accused of massive corruption, and on November 23, 1988, Chun and his wife apologized for their misbehavior and returned 13.9 billion Won (US$20 million) to the government.

Chun's successor, Roh Tae Woo, was plagued by the "long-festering problem of political corruption," with six legislators found guilty of extorting funds from the business community. The 1992 Hanbo scandal shocked the country when Chung Tae Soo, chairman of the Hanbo Construction Company, was accused of contributing substantial funds to ruling and opposition political parties for favors involving land development ("Korea-South," 1992, 138). However, Roh himself was not immune: in October 1995 it was discovered that he had received almost $600 million for his private political fund from individuals and major business conglomerates (Macdonald and Clark, 1996, 159-160).

When Kim Young Sam assumed power in February 1993, he voluntarily declared his personal assets of 1.7 billion Won (US$2.1 million) and gave up golf, which "had become a symbol of corporate-government cronyism and the exchange of corrupt gifts." He issued a presidential decree in August 1993 that Koreans must use their real names for all financial transactions, especially bank accounts, as the "anonymous or false-name account had been the backbone of the black economy and massive fraud, corruption and tax evasion schemes" (Sheridan, 1997, 13-15). More importantly, Kim strengthened the BAI, which became the first de jure anticorruption agency in South Korea. He created the Commission for the Prevention of Corruption, an advisory body of private citizens formed to assist the BAIs chairman in fighting corruption. In March 1993, the government formed a team of 100 special inspectors within the BAI to implement Kim's anticorruption campaign. By August 1993, the BAI had 776 officials involved in audit and administrative inspection. Article 24 of the BAI Act empowers the BAI to conduct anticorruption activities by examining civil servants' behavior.

President Kim's anticorruption campaign confirmed that corruption is a way of life in South Korea and exposed its pervasiveness in the country. However, Young Jong Kim (1994, 207) has lamented the lack of political will in South Korea's efforts to curb corruption, especially under the regimes of Presidents Rhee, Park, and Chun. Although Kim's anticorruption drive was hindered by the May 17, 1997, arrest of his son for bribery and tax evasion in the Hanbo loan scandal and his sentencing to three years' imprisonment five months later, Kim has clearly demonstrated his commitment to eliminating corruption by not obstructing the legal arrest and sentencing of his son. Nevertheless, the Hanbo scandal and his son's arrest and imprisonment seriously undermined Kim's legitimacy and jeopardized the continued success of his anticorruption drive. Whether Kim's commitment to curbing corruption will be continued by his successor, Kim Dae Jung, remains to be seen.

Thailand: Like South Korea, the origins of corruption in Thailand can be traced to the sixteenth century, when civil servants withheld revenue collected for the king for themselves, as they were not paid regular salaries, and sent only a small amount to the king (Chai-Anan, 1977, 1, 4). The Board of Inspection and Follow-up of Government Operations was established as the first de jure anticorruption agency in September 1972. It was ineffective, however, as its five members were guilty of corruption themselves and the group was dissolved after the October 1973 revolution.

In May 1974, Prime Minister Sanya appointed a Counter Corruption Committee to investigate charges of corruption against civil servants and to report its findings. This committee was required to prepare an anticorruption draft bill to supplement the inadequate penal code. The Cabinet approved the draft bill and in December 1974 sent it to the National Legislative Assembly. The Assembly passed the bill, and the Counter Corruption Act (CCA) was enacted in February 1975. The CCA changed the Counter Corruption Committee to the Commission of Counter Corruption (CCC), which consists of a chairman and between five and nine members.

The CCC set out to investigate allegations of corruption against civil servants and submits to the cabinet proposals for preventing corruption and for revising administrative practices. However, the CCC was ineffective for three reasons. First, according to Mulder (1996, 173-174), "the idea of corruption, meaning that the external world should not be exploited for personal gain because it constitutes the public interest" was "so baffling [to the Thais] that it lames all Anti-Corruption Commissions at the outset." Second, the CCC could not curb corruption because of the constant conflict between the Cabinet and bureaucracy (Dalpino, 1991, 66). Finally, the CCC was viewed by its critics as a "paper tiger" without real teeth, as "it could only send reports to the prime minister and the Cabinet" since it lacked "direct authority to punish public officials." Consequently, very few civil servants have been punished for corruption.

The CCC's ineffectiveness led to the CCA's amendment in 1987 to give it more power (Amara, 1992, 240). In spite of this amendment, the CCC still cannot take action against politicians, and it "only has the power to investigate a bureaucrat following a complaint." Officials found guilty by the CCC are usually reprimanded or disciplined within the department, as the public prosecutor does not use the evidence collected by the CCC to initiate new investigations (Pasuk and Sungsidh, 1994, 180-181).

Thailand's anticorruption strategy was described as "hopeless" by Quah (1982, 175-176) 16 years ago, as the country's anticorruption measures were inadequate and its political leaders unconcerned about minimizing corruption. Indeed, most Thai political leaders (with a few exceptions, such as prime ministers Anand Panyarachun and Chuan Leekpai) have not been committed in the fight against corruption. However, the situation has improved recently after Chuan Leekpai replaced General Chavalit Yongchaiyudh as prime minister in November 1997. Furthermore, the Constitution promulgated on October 11, 1997, or the "People's Constitution," is concerned, among other things, with making elected politicians and public officials accountable by introducing several measures to curb corruption. Specifically, codes of conduct for politicians and civil servants have been formulated to prohibit conflicts of interest. They are also required to declare their assets, liabilities, and their income tax returns (and those of their dependents) to the CCC when they assume and leave office and one year after leaving office. The CCC has been strengthened to "enable it to bring cases to court and to cover the cases of political officials" (Prudhisan, 1998, 275-276).

In short, Thailand's anticorruption strategy has been transformed from a hopeless strategy to an ineffective one as its current prime minister, Chuan Leekpai, is concerned about minimizing corruption. The new Constitution has introduced additional anticorruption measures, including the empowerment of the CCC. However, whether Thailand's anticorruption strategy can be transformed into an effective one will depend on how long Chuan Leekpai remains prime minister and the extent to which the new anticorruption measures are actually implemented.

Effective Anticorruption Strategy

The final anticorruption strategy is the effective strategy, which occurs when adequate anticorruption measures are in place and political leaders are strongly committed to eradicating corruption. Of the 13 countries listed in Table 1, only Singapore and Hong Kong, the two least corrupt Asian city-states, come under this category. Both have adequate anticorruption measures (Prevention of Corruption Act and the Corrupt Practices Investigation Bureau in Singapore, and the Prevention of Bribery Ordinance and the Independent Commission Against Corruption in Hong Kong); both are blessed with political leaders who are determined to remove the problem of corruption in their countries (Quah, 1995).

The final section of this paper will discuss Singapore's effective anticorruption strategy, with the aim of showing how corruption can be minimized when political leaders are sincerely committed to this task by impartially implementing comprehensive anticorruption measures.

LEARNING FROM SINGAPORE'S EXPERIENCE

As Table 1 indicates, Singapore is the least corrupt country in Asia today according to the three indices. However, the situation was quite different in Singapore during the British colonial period, when corruption was a way of life. The 1879 and 1886 Commissions found that bribery and corruption were prevalent among the Straits Settlement Police Force in Singapore. Indeed, an analysis of the Straits]rimes from 1845 to 1921 shows that 172 cases of police corruption were reported during this period (Quah, 1979, 24). Corruption was also widespread during the Japanese occupation (1942-1945), as rampant inflation made it difficult for civil servants to live on their low salaries. The situation deteriorated during the postwar period, and in his 1950 Annual Report, the Commissioner of Police revealed that graft was rife in government departments in Singapore.

When the Peoples Action Party (PAP) leaders assumed office in June 1959, they realized that corruption had to be curbed to ensure that the Singapore Civil Service attained the country's development goals. They also realized that they could not continue the British colonial government's incremental anticorruption strategy if their intention was to minimize corruption. Accordingly, the PAP government's immediate tasks were twofold--to minimize corruption and to change the public perception of corruption as "a low-risk, high-reward" activity to "a high-risk, low-reward" activity. In 1960, a comprehensive anticorruption strategy was introduced with the enactment of the Prevention of Corruption Act and the strengthening of the Corrupt Practices Investigation Bureau (CPIB). Because corruption is caused by both incentives and opportunities to become corrupt, the new comprehensive strategy was based on the "logic of corruption control," as "attempts to eradicate corruption must be designed to minimize or remove the conditions of both the incentives and opportunities that make individual corrupt behavior irresistible" (Quah, 1989, 842).

Reducing the Opportunities for Corruption

Singapore was a poor country in 1960, with per capita gross national product of S$ 1,330, or US$443 (Republic of Singapore, 1986, ix). As such, the PAP government could not afford to combat corruption by raising the salaries of its civil servants. It was left with the alternative of strengthening the existing legislation to reduce the opportunities for corruption and to increase the penalty for corrupt behavior. Corruption was first made illegal in Singapore in 1871 with the introduction of the Penal Code of the Straits Settlements. The first specific anticorruption law was introduced on December 10, 1937, when the Prevention of Corruption Ordinance (POCO) was enacted. The POCO was amended in 1946 to increase the penalty for corrupt offenses from two to three years and/or a fine of S$10,000, and to enable the police to arrest corrupt individuals without warrants.

The Prevention of Corruption Act (POCA) was enacted on June 17, 1960, and included five important features to eliminate the POCO's deficiencies and to empower the CPIB to perform its duties. First, the POCA's scope was increased to 32 sections, in contrast to the POCO's 12 sections.(4) Second, corruption was explicitly defined in terms of the various forms of "gratification" in section 2, which also identified for the first time the CPIB and its director. Third, to enhance the POCA's deterrent effect, the penalty for corruption was increased to imprisonment for five years and/or a fine of S$10,000 (section 5). The amount of the fine was further increased to

S$100,000 in 1989. Fourth, a person found guilty of accepting an illegal gratification would be fined the amount of the bribe, plus any other punishment imposed by the court (section 13). Finally, the fifth and most important feature of the POCA was that it gave the CPIB more powers and a new lease on life. It provided CPIB officers with powers of arrest and search of arrested persons, and it empowered the public prosecutor to authorize the CPIB's director and senior staff to investigate "any bank account, share account or purchase account" of anyone suspected of having committed an offense against the POCA. Section 18 enabled the CPIB officers to inspect a civil servant's banker's book and those of his wife, children, or agent, if necessary (Quah, 1978, 10-13).

To ensure the POCA's effectiveness, the PAP government amended it as necessary or introduced new legislation to deal with unforeseen problems. In 1963, the POCA was amended to empower CPIB officers to require the attendance of witnesses and to question them. This amendment enabled CPIB officers to obtain the cooperation of witnesses to help them in their investigations. In 1966, two important amendments were introduced to further strengthen the POCA. First, section 28 stated that a person could be found guilty of corruption even if he did not actually receive the bribe, as the intention on his part to commit the offense constituted sufficient grounds for his conviction. The second amendment (section 35) was directed at those Singaporeans working for their government in embassies and other government agencies abroad: Singapore citizens could be prosecuted for corrupt offenses committed outside Singapore and would be dealt with as if such offenses had occurred within the country. In 1981, the POCA was amended for the third time to increase its deterrent effect by requiring those convicted of corruption to repay the money they received in addition to facing the usual court sentence. Those who could not make full restitution would be given heavier court sentences.

On December 14, 1986, then-Minister for National Development Teh Cheang Wan committed suicide, 12 days after he was interrogated for 16 hours by two senior CPIB officers regarding two allegations of corruption against him by a building contractor. Teh was accused of accepting two bribes amounting to SSI million in 1981 and 1982 from two developers to enable one of them to retain land which had been acquired by the government, and to assist the other developer in purchasing state land for private development. An important consequence of the Commission of Inquiry that followed was the enactment on March 3, 1989, of the Corruption (Confiscation of Benefits) Act 1989, which concerned the confiscation of benefits derived from corruption; it stipulates that if a defendant is deceased, the court may issue a confiscation order against his estate.

The CPIB is the anticorruption agency responsible for enforcing the POCA's provisions. It has grown in size by nine times, from eight officers in 1960 to its current establishment of 71 officers, comprising 49 investigators and 22 clerical and support staff. The CPIB performs three functions: (1) to receive and investigate complaints concerning corruption in the public and private sectors; (2) to investigate malpractices and misconduct by public officers; and (3) to examine the practices and procedures in the public service to minimize opportunities for corrupt practices (CPIB, 1990, 2).

Reducing Incentives for Corruption

The PAP government was able to implement only the second prong of its comprehensive anticorruption strategy--the reduction of incentives for corruption by improving salaries and working conditions in the civil service--in the 1980s long after it had achieved economic growth. The improvement of wages began in March 1972, when all civil servants were given a 13-month nonpensionable allowance comparable to the bonus in the private sector. This allowance was not aimed at curbing corruption, but enhancing working conditions in the civil service in comparison to the private sector.

Perhaps the best justification for the PAP government's approach to combatting corruption by reducing or removing the incentives for corruption by improving political leaders' and senior civil servants' salaries was provided by the former Prime Minister Lee Kuan Yew in Parliament on March 22, 1985, when he explained why the wages of the Cabinet ministers had to be raised. He contended that political leaders should be paid the top salaries that they deserve in order to ensure a clean and honest government. If they were underpaid, they would succumb to temptation and indulge in corrupt behavior. According to Lee, Singapore needed a corruption-free administration and an honest political leadership to preserve its most precious assets. He concluded that the best way to deal with corruption was by "moving with the market," which is "an honest, open, defensible and workable system" instead of hypocrisy, which results in duplicity and corruption (Straits Times, 1985, 14-16).

Apart from reducing the incentives for corruption, the PAP government had to improve the salaries and working conditions in the civil service to stem the "brain drain" of competent senior civil servants to the private sector by offering competitive salaries and fringe benefits to reduce the gap between the two sectors. Accordingly, the salaries of civil servants in Singapore were revised upwards in 1973, 1979, 1982, 1989, and 1994 to reduce the drain to the private sector and the salary gap in the two sectors. As a result of these salary revisions, senior civil servants in Singapore earn perhaps the highest salaries in the world compared with their counterparts in other countries. For example, the basic monthly salary of the highest grade (staff grade V) is S$38,799, or US$25,866 (Straits Times, 1993, 28); this is much higher than the top monthly salary for the United States Federal Service, which is US$7,224, or SS 11,631 (Wright and Dwyer, 1990, 6).

Singapore's experience demonstrates that it is possible to minimize corruption if there is strong political will. Conversely, if such political will is lacking, the situation is hopeless, as political leaders and senior civil servants or military officers will pay only lip service to implementing anticorruption measures. On the other hand, it might be difficult for other countries to replicate and transplant Singapore's experience in curbing corruption for two reasons: Singapore's unique policy context differs from that of other countries; and the prohibitive economic and political costs of paying political leaders and civil servants high salaries and reducing the opportunities for corruption.

Jon S. T. Quah is a professor of political science at the National University of Singapore. He has published widely on public administration in Singapore and other Asian countries, with emphasis on administrative reform, anticorruption strategies, and human resource development. He is a member of Transparency International's Governance Council.

NOTES

(1.) As space limitations and limited access to data do not permit a discussion of all the 13 countries, only the anticorruption strategies of the PRC, Indonesia, Bangladesh, the Philippines, South Korea, Thailand, and Singapore will be analyzed in this paper.

(2.) A great deal of research has been done on corruption in the PRC in recent years. See, for example, Gong (1994), Gong (1997), Kwong (1997), and Mulvenon (1998).

(3.) For a recent treatment of corruption in the Philippines, see Coronel (1998).

(4.) The POCA now has 37 sections as a result of subsequent amendments.

REFERENCES DELTED

4

Cracking Down on Corporate Crime

Russell Mokhiber

AUTHOR'S ABSTRACT

*`Cracking down on crime', is the top priority of most governments.
Billions are spent annually on tackling criminals, but of those
billions, little if any is spent on bringing corporate criminals to
justice. Although it is corporate crime which most fundamentally
affects society, transnational corporations are allowed to get away
with murder.*

Only the most myopic of observers would deny the obvious:
that large, undemocratic corporations are the dominant
institutions of our time and are inflicting a kind of damage on
society that individuals acting alone could not conceive of
inflicting.

From the destruction of inner city rail transit (General Motors
was convicted of this crime in the 1950s and paid a $5,000 fine) to
unprosecuted and perhaps unprosecutable mass occupational
homicide (125 workplace-related deaths an hour worldwide),
pollution, corruption and the unconscionable tampering with life
through engineering -- the list is endless.

And yet the dominant voices of society deny the evidence and
proclaim the opposite: that individual criminals inflict more damage
on society than corporate criminals.

Charles Krauthammer, a Washington Post columnist and a
corporate conservative has written, for instance, that "crime is
generally an occupation of the poor." Richard Cohen, a Washington

*Cracking down on corporate crime. Russell Mokhiber. The Ecologist July 1999 v29 i4
p247(2).*

Post columnist and a corporate liberal believes that "young black males commit most of the crimes in Washington, D.C." James Glassman, another Washington Post columnist writes that the rich "don't commit the violent crimes that require billions to be spent on law enforcement."

And the American people, fed an unending stream of such garbage, are likely to agree.

Ask any American to name a crime and most likely he or she will say: burglary, robbery or theft. Most likely he or she will not say: corporate fraud, pollution, corporate homicide, price-fixing, or corruption of the government regulators.

Every year, the US Justice Department puts out a big fat book-length compilation of crimes statistics. It's called: "Crime in the United States". But by "Crime in the United States," the Justice Department means "Street Crime in the United States".

The Justice Department has no equivalent publication called "Corporate Crime in the United States". This despite the fact that there is an emerging consensus among corporate criminologists that corporate crime and violence inflict far more damage on society than all street crime combined.

The Federal Bureau of Investigation (FBI) estimates, for example, that burglary and robbery -- street crimes -- cost the nation $3.8 billion a year. Compare this to the hundreds of billions of dollars stolen from Americans as a result of corporate and white-collar fraud.

Health care fraud alone costs Americans $100 billion to $400 billion a year. The savings and loan fraud -- which former Attorney General, Dick Thornburgh, called "the biggest white collar swindle in history" -- cost them anywhere from $300 billion to $500 billion. And then you have your lesser frauds: auto repair fraud. $40 billion a year securities fraud: $15 billion a year -- and on down the list.

Recite this list of corporate frauds and people will immediately say to you: but you can't compare street crime and corporate crime -- corporate crime is not violent crime.

But in fact, corporate crime is often violent crime.

The FBI estimates that 19,000 Americans are murdered every year by street criminals. Compare this with the 56,000 Americans who die every year at work or from occupational diseases. On-the-job deaths are often the result of criminal recklessness. They are sometimes prosecuted as homicides or as criminal violations of federal workplace safety laws. Environmental crimes often result in death, disease and injury.

And, the vast majority of corporate crime and violence goes undetected or unprosecuted for a number of reasons. Firstly, corporations tend to `win' (with the help of generous research grants and the promise of endless job opportunities) the backing of most government and university scientists, and it is they who are charged with legitimising (often unsafe) products. Secondly, unlike all other criminal groups in the US, major corporations have enough power to define the law under which they live and to influence prosecutors not to bring criminal charges.

This point has been made over and over again, most recently in the book, Toxic Deception: How the Chemical Industry Manipulates Science, Bends the Law and Endangers Your Health by Dan Fagin, Marianne Lavelle and the Centre for Public Integrity (Common Courage Press, 1999), where the authors show how the chemical industry has overpowered the lawmakers and the police (euphemistically known here as "regulators") and forced dangerous chemicals onto the market.

Here's a case in point: The chemical companies are required by federal law to make any scientific findings available to the government if a chemical already on the market is found to pose a "substantial risk of injury to health or to the environment." Toxic Deception found that the industry frequently acted in "bad faith" in this regard. In 1991 and 1992 the despairing Environmental Protection Agency, knowing that there was little they could do to enforce the law, offered amnesty from big-money fines to any manufacturer that turned in health studies they should have provided under the law. In response chemical corporations turned over more that 10,000 studies showing that their products already on the market pose a substantial risk. In this way, corporations were able to avoid crippling fines.

Weak law, weak law-enforcement, no "crime."

There is a debate now raging among activists in the United States: what to do about an ever-expanding wave of unprosecuted corporate crime and violence? There are those activists who engage in battles against individual corporate predators, who seek to leverage power to change the ways of individual corporations, who seek to get regulatory reform legislation, who meet with corporations, who praise them when they do good and condemn them

66

when they do bad. This has been the de facto model of activism for the past 30 years.

But there is a new breed of activist roaming the land. These activists believe that there is something fundamentally wrong with the large corporation itself. These activists believe that it is not what multinational corporations do wrong that is the problem -- it is corporations that are the problem.

These activists believe large corporations as they exist today are fundamentally undemocratic and cannot be reformed. These activists question whether corporations should be considered legal persons with the same rights of you and me and other living human beings. They question the very nature of the corporation.

Hope for re-igniting a democratic campaign against dehumanising corporate power lies with this second camp led by Richard Grossman and his colleagues at the Program on Corporations, Law and Democracy.

For the past couple of years, Grossman and his colleagues have been travelling the country, encouraging activists of all stripes to begin asking fundamental questions about citizen control of corporations, to research the history of corporations, and to begin to question corporate control over the citizenry.

Grossman and his colleagues believe that instead of focussing on one corporate crime at a time, we must begin to question the legitimacy of the corporate form.

In each state where they are organised they are digging through the history books and finding that at the beginning of the corporate era more than 150 years ago we the citizens controlled corporations.

Through the corporate charter, citizens imposed full liability on shareholders for corporate wrongdoing (today, shareholder liability is limited), we limited the life span of corporations (today, they have unlimited life), and we revoked their charters when they did things we told them they couldn't (today, the corporate elites laugh at the possibility or corporate charter revocation).

And back at the turn of the century, we understood the corporation to be fundamentally different from you and me -- not something deemed to have the legal rights of a human citizen.

Here is Williams Jennings Bryan speaking to the 1912 Constitutional Convention in Columbus, Ohio. Ask yourself: Who today would speak in such a manner? (And Bryan was not alone -- he reflected a healthy cultural distaste for corporate power.)

"The first thing to understand is the difference between the natural person and the fictitious person, called the corporation. They differ in the purpose in which they are created, in the strength which they possess, and in the restraints under which they act. Man is the handiwork of God and was placed upon earth to carry out a divine purpose. The corporation is the handiwork of man and was created to carry out a moneymaking policy. There is comparatively little difference in the strength of men. A corporation may be one hundred, one thousand, or even one million times stronger than the average man. Man acts under the restraints of conscience, and is influenced also by a belief in the future life. A corporation has no soul and cares nothing about the hereafter."

The corporate culture is a century or more in the making. It will take a while before we figure out how we got ourselves into this soup -- from a situation where we controlled corporations, to where corporations are controlling us.

It will take a while longer to figure how to get out of it.

Russell Mokhiber is the editor of Corporate Crime Reporter, a legal weekly based in Washington D.C. He is co-author, with Robert Weissman of Corporate Predators: The Hunt for Mega-Profits and the Attack on Democracy (Common Courage Press, 1999).

Part III

STATE-CORPORATE CRIME AND CRIMES OF GLOBALIZATION

5

White Collar Crime

The Worldwide Rise in Corruption Monitoring

Hergüner Bilgen Özeke Attorney Partnership

A s a result of the increasing international focus on the fight against corruption, more and more countries are joining multinational treaties and introducing strict domestic anti-corruption regulations. Similarly, compliance with and enforcement of the US Foreign Corrupt Practices Act ("FCPA") has become more important for US and non-US companies alike, especially in the past five years. Globalized commerce and the development of global markets have induced even small companies to list themselves internationally, and subjected more companies than ever to the FCPA's restrictions.

International sensitivity to the fight against corruption - as evident from the level of overseas implementation and effect of the FCPA and international treaties such as the OECD Convention on Combating Bribery of Foreign Public Officials in International Business Transactions ("OECD Convention") - has deeply affected Turkey's approach to and treatment of corruption issues.1 White collar crimes regulated under the Turkish Penal Code ("TPC") - after amendments in 2005 in line with the OECD Convention - can be listed mainly as follows: bribery; fraud in tender; fraud in performance of obligations; laundering of the proceeds of an offense; abuse of trust; using a valueless bond; theft and qualified theft by deception; bankruptcy by deception and reckless bankruptcy; disseminating false information about companies or co-operatives; forgery of official documents; forgery of private documents;

White Collar Crime: The Worldwide Rise in Corruption Monitoring. By Hergüner Bilgen Özeke Attorney Partnership, May 5, 2010.

establishing crime organizations in order to commit offenses; failure to disclose criminal activity; alteration, concealment or destruction of evidence; disclosure of confidential documents or information relating to commerce, banking or private customers; restriction of supply of goods and services; and offenses concerning data processing systems. In Turkey, tougher penalties and more leniency options are being introduced, encouraging not only whistleblowing but also self-disclosure, leading to a race between the accomplices to crime - legal entities and their employees - to self-disclose. Leniency for some offenses listed above (such as bribery, laundering of the proceeds of an offense, bankruptcy by deception and reckless bankruptcy, etc.) is a novelty that the newly enacted TPC introduces.

Despite Turkey's newly introduced laws, regulations, and legislative amendments in line with the OECD Convention, as the OECD Working Group's Report2 noted, no corruption case has yet to be discovered through whistleblowing in Turkey. The OECD Working Group also commented that private and public sector employees receive insufficient training in the detection of foreign bribery in Turkey.

The FCPA is in many ways similar to the OECD Convention, mainly prohibiting bribery of foreign officials and introducing preventive measures to accomplish this end. The FCPA's anti-bribery provisions basically prohibit both US companies and foreign companies listed on a US stock exchange - and any officer, director or employee thereof - from underhandedly paying or offering to pay, directly or indirectly, money or anything of value to a foreign official, or any foreign political party or official thereof, to obtain or retain business or direct business for any person. The FCPA does not define the term "anything of value." However, in practice it is interpreted broadly, and depending on the subjective elements of each specific case, cash payments, gifts, meals, drinks, discounts and even transportation fees can be construed as "of value." The FCPA's "Books and Records and Internal Control Provisions" mainly require companies to keep their books, records and accounts accurate.

In Turkey, neither legislation nor legal precedent specifies any permissible value for the gifts, meals or other benefits that a government official may receive. A benefit that is intended to persuade the government official to perform or not perform an action in violation of his official duties will be deemed bribery. In this respect, if the desired action is intended to facilitate or speed up an action that is legal, and that the official should perform as part of his official duties, then there is no crime of bribery. The Regulation on Ethical Conduct of Government Officials,3 by contrast, provides some examples of lower-value benefits which would not fall within the scope of the prohibition. In the event of any dispute, courts decide whether the aim of the benefit or meal is to persuade the government official to carry out actions that - within the scope of his duties - he should not, or whether the benefit affects the government official's duties in some other way.

As seen from some recent high-profile examples - the Siemens and Deniz Feneri cases, as well as the older examples of Enron, Worldcom, etc. - such discovery may trigger investigations, not only in such entity's main jurisdiction, but in multiple jurisdictions worldwide. As observed from last year's experience alone, the increase in white collar crime-related matters - including corruption-related practice - signals the urgent need for companies in various sectors to obtain greater and more sophisticated legal assistance on the compliance of their market activities with the rules and standards of not only Turkish laws and regulations but also others, such as the FCPA and similar statutes.

FOOTNOTES

1. Turkey accepted the OECD Convention on 26 July 2000 and the related implementing legislation in Turkey came into force on 11 January 2003 with Code No. 4782, published in the Official Gazette dated 11 January 2003 and numbered 24990.

2. Working Group on Bribery in International Business Transactions, 7 December 2007 (Country Reports on Implementation of the OECD Convention).

3. Regulation on Ethical Conduct of Government Officials, published in the Official Gazette dated 13 April 2005, numbered 25785.

The content of this article is intended to provide a general guide to the subject matter. Specialist advice should be sought about your specific circumstances.

6

The Globalization of Crime

R Team of Futurists Examines the Ways in Which Crime Has Become Globalized and How the Worlds of Legitimate and Illicit Finance Intertwine

Stephen Aguilar-Millan; Joan E. Foltz; John Jackson;
Rmy Oberg

The nature of crime has changed significantly in a single generation. Just 20 years ago, crime was organized in a hierarchy of operations. It was "industrial" in that it contained the division of labor and the specialization of operations. This structure extended internationally, as organized crime mirrored the business world.

Then, just as it happened in the business world, the vertical and horizontal hierarchies of organized crime dissolved into a large number of loosely connected networks. Each node within a network would be involved in any number of licit and illicit operations. Networked systems spanned the globe. An event in one place might have a significant impact on the other side of the world. In short, crime became globalized.

Organized crime involves the illicit flow of goods and services in one direction and the flow of the proceeds of crime in the other.

The Futurist by WORLD FUTURE SOCIETY. Copyright 2008 Reproduced with permission of WORLD FUTURE SOCIETY in the format Textbook via copyright clearance Center.

Just as the business world has benefited from globalization, so has organized crime.

CRIME AS A GLOBALIZED ACTIVITY: AN OVERVIEW

In many ways, it is helpful to consider crime as a special form of business activity, affected by the same trends as other business activities.

Globalization--including the globalization of crime--can be said to have started with the fall of the Berlin Wall, the collapse of the Soviet Union, and the attempts by Western thinkers to offer economic prescriptions and organize international affairs along the lines of Western capitalism.

In practice, Western capitalism consisted of a belief in free markets for the allocation of resources, free flows of goods and services across international borders, and the free movement of labor and capital to harness the demand created by the free market. For globalization to take hold, two further revolutions were needed--the growth of low-cost mass-transit facilities and the growth of international telecommunications (i.e., the Internet).

The transportation revolution facilitated the mass movement of goods and people across the globe, and the Internet revolution has allowed the development of global service infrastructures, such as banking and financial services. It's also enabled global operations to be monitored and controlled remotely from anywhere in the world that has Internet access.

As these revolutions--the freeing of markets, the transportation revolution, and the Internet revolution--were taking place, the way in which the world works was also changing. In global business especially, the world shifted from being one of hierarchies to being one of networks. The rise of the networked organization laid the foundation for two features of modern life--outsourcing (where key roles are undertaken outside of the formal organizational structure) and offshoring (where, thanks to the transportation and Internet revolutions, key roles can be undertaken anywhere in the world). Needless to say, such encouragements of lawful trade proved to be a boon for illicit trade as well.

From a commercial perspective, the key to the flow of illicit goods--be they narcotics, people, counterfeit goods, or human transplant organs--is logistics: How do you move the goods from the point of origin to the point of consumption? The revolution in transportation lowered the cost of freight and increased the number of routes available. The need to secure these routes for illicit flows of goods has also led to the growth in the arms trade--especially of personal weapons of a relatively small caliber.

From the perspective of the law enforcement agencies, the problem with policing such activities is jurisdiction, which has led to the increase in cross-border police cooperation. The key to success in halting the flow of illicit goods is to have good intelligence, so law enforcement agencies (usually the police and customs agencies) are cooperating more closely with the military services (particularly military intelligence and the naval arm). In effect, law enforcement agencies have globalized in order to respond to the globalization of criminal gangs.

Meanwhile, some illicit activities have moved from the corporeal world to cyberspace. For example, the development of the Internet has allowed much pornographic activity to migrate to the virtual world. Initially, this was restricted to the transmission of images, but the development has taken on new forms with the rise of online worlds such as Second Life.

Online, the confusion of legal jurisdictions creates new problems. For example, in the case of online gambling, firms in the United Kingdom were engaged in the provision of gambling activities that were legal under European Union law but illegal in the United States. Alternatively, Second Life is alleged to host pedophile rings whose activities are contrary to EU law but take protection from the First Amendment in the United States. There has been some harmonization in legal codes, but this process is far from complete. What is needed is the globalization of legal codes to complete the process.

The flow of illicit goods in both the corporeal and the virtual worlds is aided by illicit services, particularly banking and financial services. The development of the Internet has greatly assisted global criminal networks in laundering their money. Preventing money laundering is likely to become even harder as new forms of money and financial instruments emerge. Just imagine a Rotterdam cocaine futures market!

The nature of banking is also changing. As we see with the development of payments through cell-phone transfers, it will become harder for the monetary authorities to police the monetary system. We can reasonably expect the flow of illicit goods to increase if the globalization trend continues. Some of the flows will

78

be diverted from the corporeal world to the virtual world. New crimes will develop within the virtual world as people exercise their inventiveness, and more illicit services will be invented to channel the proceeds of crime into lawful investment assets.

In the years ahead, national law enforcement agencies are likely to cooperate more, and there may also be greater involvement of military assets for law enforcement purposes. However, this is unlikely to be entirely successful without the political willingness to harmonize legal codes and to deploy international resources to where they have the greatest impact. This point is best demonstrated in the area of white-collar crime.

THE HIGH STAKES OF WHITE-COLLAR CRIME

The profile of white-collar criminals is changing as the possibility of enormous payouts increases the high stakes of the game. The $1-trillion illicit trade market is being fueled not just by organized groups, but also by individuals who are lured by the opportunities rising from the globally integrated financial systems. The rapid advancement of wireless technology enables financial transactions in every region in the world, so opportunities for white-collar crimes are proliferating as fast as the criminal landscape is changing.

Organized crime has long been involved in money laundering, fraud, and currency counterfeiting for self-benefit. More recently, governmental agencies are concerned about how the magnitude of those activities and other white-collar crimes could threaten national security and global financial markets. White-collar crime also includes intellectual property crime, payment card fraud, computer virus attacks, and cyberterrorism.

Corporate fraud has become a priority of the FBI, which has pursued cases involving more than $1 billion in losses to individuals, as well as securities and commodities fraud that amounts to approximately $40 billion worth of corporate losses per year.

The sophistication of the schemes is growing and the frequency of events is accelerating as improving technology eases the transfer of money across international borders and gives criminals access to more identities that may be stolen. With a growing amount of corporate and financial records, there is more potential opportunity for manipulation--and that threat has expanded to global proportions.

The spread of capitalism promotes open markets and aims to maximize opportunity but blurs the line between what is considered

© 2012 Cengage Learning. All Rights Reserved. May not be scanned, copied or duplicated, or posted to a publicly accessible website, in whole or in part.

creative money management and what is considered criminal behavior. The increasing opportunities for white-collar crimes and their potential payoff is extremely enticing to individuals who do not fit the typical criminal profile.

Social attitudes toward money and finances are also changing worldwide, and as yet there is no accepted global definition of white-collar crime. Some cultures don't consider certain activities involving corruption, corporate malfeasance, and stock manipulation even to be criminal. White-collar crime is not always a clear-cut act of deviance and is often intermingled with legitimate behavior that is spread out over a number of incidents. Meeting the goals of capitalism requires tough competition, which promotes attitudes and behaviors that may blur ethical lines. What behaviors should be rewarded? What should be penalized?

Electronic funds transfer systems handle more than $6 trillion in wire transfers daily, and the growing speed and interconnectivity of those transactions adds to the difficulty of tracing money transfers, particularly across borders into regions where regulations are not enforced. To combat the problem, more countries will participate in international organizations to regulate and control fraudulent financial activity, perhaps spurred by the proliferation of money laundering of funds for terrorist activities. International agencies such as Interpol also work closely with technology providers to develop security controls for tracking and preventing financial and high-tech crimes. But even the most advanced security systems and coordinated enforcement cannot prevent targeted attacks on international financial systems.

Daily international transfers of $2 trillion via computer communications pass through conventional banks, Internet banking, mobile banking, and e-commerce transactions. Many transactions cross borders going not through financial institutions, but rather through professional services, such as real estate agents and accountants facilitating transactions that exchange cash for purchases to mask ownership of originating funds. Offshore corporations and relatives also offer assistance transferring funds via mobile phones and Internet payment services such as PayPal.

The same technologies that make criminal activities possible-- rapid financial transactions via mobile devices or the Internet, for instance--also make transborder e-commerce more transparent and secure. Authorities can more easily track investment transactions. However, rogue traders and terrorist groups may continue to manipulate currencies and stocks and threaten to infiltrate financial systems, so countries, companies, and individuals must increasingly weigh the opportunities for fast and easy money versus regulation and security.

As competition and opportunities are sought by more players in a larger global market, more creative financial instruments and structured deals set up an environment where payoffs and lack of controls allow fraud and corruption. Without guidelines and a definitive identification of what constitutes punishable criminal activity, new business models will be created that stretch the systems and threaten economic stability, such as the subprime lending debacle.

Super-capitalism will drive a push for new financial instruments and schemes in other areas of corporate fraud, such as "pumping and dumping" stocks to set deceptive market prices or using Ponzi schemes. Such activities jeopardize not only personal portfolios, but also the stability of the global investment community. In 2006, the FBI investigated 1,165 cases of securities and commodities fraud that amounted to $1.9 billion in restitutions and $62.7 million in seizures.

The growth of unethical business practices that impact free markets will compel international regulatory bodies to define white-collar crime and to establish globally supported tracking systems and venues for prosecution. The challenge is to regulate criminal activities operating in a virtual space of global industries that are becoming more disconnected from national jurisdictions. This will require not only international cooperation, but also the sharing of information among law enforcement agencies and the ability to seize assets.

Efforts to deter money laundering and terrorist activities are gaining international cooperation, but going after corporate and securities fraud is another matter. Cooperation in battling these white-collar threats to global financial systems is unlikely until a significant disruption impacts all members of the global free market and until all governments understand that weak systems and corruption impair regional economic development.

COOPERATION AGAINST GLOBAL CRIME

One of the flaws in market-based capitalism is that it is open to corrupt influences and encourages undesirable behavior by providing a profit for meeting a demand. As long as there is a demand for narcotics, human servitude, and other illicit goods and services, there will be a market in human misery.

A glimmer of hope may be found in the fact that many of these global criminals desire respectability. They are victims of the system that they exploit, and they are exploited by those operating in the financial world, for whom they provide commissions, fees, and retainers. The point at which dirty money is laundered clean is the point at which those who operate in the world of organized crime wish to enter the mainstream world. This is the Achilles' heel of global organized crime.

Given the global nature of the monetary system that is being used, one would expect an international effort to harmonize the regulation of the global monetary system. By and large, this is happening, but we have not reached a harmonious point just yet, because a wide agreement will entail the sacrifice of some national interests. These national interests are not readily conceded in international negotiations, but progress is being made.

When we look to the future, we can see a greater degree of international cooperation in dealing with globalized crime. Military establishments may offer more support for policing efforts. Modern terrorism has blurred the boundary between war and peace, and modern organized crime has blurred the distinction between law enforcement activities and military operations.

The process of globalization is not yet complete. As an integrated system of trade and finance, it has become very developed. The problems that we currently face with globalization as a process are the result of a system of trade and finance that has developed faster than the regulatory framework in which trade occurs. As we move into the future, we can expect to see the regulatory framework catch up with the new reality of trade and finance. We would hope that this is bad news for organized crime.

ABOUT THE AUTHORS

Stephen Aguilar-Millan is the director of research for The European Futures Observatory, 6 Greenways Close, Ipswich, Suffolk IP1 3RB, United Kingdom. E-mail stephena@eufo.org.

Joan E. Foltz is a principal of Alsek Research in Chandler, Arizona, a socio-economic analyst of global development and market behavior and publisher of Alsek's Not-So-Daily Update. E-mail jfoltz@cox.net.

John Jackson is a sergeant with the Houston Police Department. E-mail johnajackson@cityofhouston.net.

Amy Oberg is a corporate futurist with the Kimberly-Clark Corporation in Wisconsin. E-mail future_in_sight@yahoo.com.

This article draws from the authors' paper, 'The Globalization of Crime," in the World Future Society's 2008 conference volume, Seeing the Future Through New Eyes edited by Cynthia G. Wagner. 444 pages. Paperback. $29.95 ($24.95 for members). Order online at www.wfs.org/wfsbooks.htm.

FEEDBACK: Send your comments about this article to letters@wfs.org.

7

Internet War Crimes Tribunals and Security in an Interconnected World

Sharon R. Stevens

I.   INTRODUCTION

II. CRITICAL INFRASTRUCTURE IS VULNERABLE DUE TO
     INTERNET
     A.   The Internet is Ruled by Transparency and is Resistant to
          Regulation
     B.   The Internet is Connected to Everything
     C.   Internet Attacks are Varied and Frequent
     D.   The Internet is a Great Place to Hide
     E.   Estonia Claims that a Recent Cyber Attack was an Act of War

III. INTERNATIONAL LAWS OF WAR FAIL TO GIVE SUFFICIENT
     GUIDANCE
     A.   The U.N. Charter Does Not Fit the Needs of Cyber Security
     B.   Do Cyber Attacks Constitute "Use of Force"?
     C.   Cyber Attacks May Have Some Benefits

IV. THE POLITICAL AND LOGISTIC CHALLENGES TODAY
     PLAGUE ALL ATTEMPTS TO CURB INTERNET ATTACKS
     A.   Could Changes to the Structure of the Internet Stop Cyber Attacks?
     B.   Can the ICJ or the ICC Provide Solutions?
     C.   Will the Cybercrime Convention Stop Cyber Attacks?
          1.   Universal Jurisdiction
          2.   Sovereign Immunity and State Prosecutions of Foreign
               Officials

*TRANSNATIONAL LAW AND CONTEMPORARY PROBLEMS by UNIVERSITY OF
IOWA. Copyright 2009 in the format Textbook via Copyright Clearance Center.*

I. INTRODUCTION

Imagine that the year is 2015 and some unknown person or group has used the Internet to attack the computer system for air traffic control at London's Heathrow Airport. This attack does not shut down computers; it feeds the controllers misinformation. The resulting confusion causes several near collisions. Before the airport can be shut down, two planes collide, killing hundreds of people. One of the fatalities is the Prime Minister of Israel, who is traveling to Europe to participate in peace talks. The British and Israeli governments scramble to trace the source of the attack. Within days, a source is identified, and Great Britain and Israel launch an Internet version of a reprisal, attacking the computers identified as the source of the Heathrow attack. These computers are located in China and operated by the Chinese military. The British/Israeli reprisal infects the Chinese computers with a virus that makes them inoperable. The Chinese respond in kind, and so begins a cyberspace skirmish that involves Internet attacks on critical infrastructure such as power grids, water treatment plants, the financial sector and other vital services. In the end, a terrorist group headquartered in the Middle East claims responsibility for the Heathrow attack, announcing that its hackers were able to make it appear that the attack originated in China.

Now, imagine that the Heathrow computer attack occurs and creates the same havoc and loss of life, but instead of resorting to self-defense, the British and Israeli governments launch a criminal investigation. This investigation is based upon an international agreement that identifies certain acts as Internet war crimes, and provides procedures for the investigation and prosecution of the criminals. With the assistance of the Chinese government, the culprits are identified and arrested. The accused stand trial before an international ad hoc tribunal, they are found guilty, sentenced, and punished.

The foregoing represents the worst- and best-case scenarios concerning cyber attacks and highlights the potential for future achievements in international law regarding the Internet. The technology exists today to execute these kinds of attacks. The question then becomes: what law applies to both public and private actors who use this technology? This Article will describe the technology, focusing on the Internet in general and cyber attacks in particular. It will outline existing international law concerning the use of force and describe the approaches advocated by various commentators on the subject of cyber warfare. Last, this Article will argue that current international law is insufficiently developed to properly address cyber attacks and that new law should be created through international cooperation. An international agreement is necessary to clearly identify what is forbidden as a war crime in cyber attacks and what cyber activities are allowed by the military during a time of war.

II. CRITICAL INFRASTRUCTURE IS VULNERABLE DUE TO INTERNET INTERCONNECTIVITY

In order to understand the need for new law on the subject of cyber attacks, it is important to understand some of the history and functions of the Internet and to see the scope of the interconnections and vulnerabilities of modern civilization. The Internet was born, so to speak, of the U.S. military. (1) Its initial purpose was not to function as a weapon (2) but to facilitate communication. (3) In fact, the Internet was meant to assist researchers who, in the 1960s, were competing against the Soviet Union for technological superiority in a variety of contexts, including the space race. (4) The agency overseeing this work was called the Advanced Research Projects Agency ("ARPA"). (5) ARPA needed a vehicle that would allow researchers to share access to these larger computers. (6) These researchers were spread throughout the country. Many of them were teaching at universities, and not all of them had access to powerful computers. (7) The researchers conceived of a network that would link the ARPA researchers together, pooling their resources. (8) The realization of this vision came in 1969 with the ARPANET original four-node network, connecting four universities in California and Utah into a single network. (9)

The early ARPANET used a principle still employed today called "packet switching," which breaks all communication into packets, sends them through the Internet via different routes, and reassembles them at their destination. (10) This allows for faster travel speeds, a higher volume of information, and permits the system to withstand additional stresses. (11) During the 1970s, the ARPANET began to interface with other "nets," the ALOHANET and the SATNET. (12) The popularity of these networks grew once the Transmission Control Protocol ("TCP") technology was developed, allowing for complete consistency between the packets of information, making it possible for these different nets to interface. (13)

A. The Internet is Ruled by Transparency and is Resistant to Regulation

The capacity of the Internet to interface is sometimes called "transparency" or referred to as the "end-to-end principle." (14) As Lawrence Solum describes this architectural function of the Internet, "[i]n short, the principle calls for a 'stupid network' and 'smart applications.' The network simply forwards or routes the data packets and does not--and cannot by its architecture--discriminate or differentiate traffic generated by different applications." (15) Thus, the information, whether in the form of an e-mail, web page, or MP3 file, is broken up into packets that, to the Internet, all look the same. The only apparent difference between these packets is where they originated and where they are going. The content of a packet while en route is meaningless because it has no software application attached to it and is only a portion of the whole. This aspect of the Internet's architecture is analogous to the system used by transport carriers that use transport containers hauled by trucks, ships, or railroads. Because these containers have a standard size and shape, the transport is relatively simple, even though the contents of the containers can be very different. Similarly, the Internet simply transports the information packets with complete disregard for content.

Two important characteristics that contributed to the early Internet's popularity were packet-switching and the capacity to interface. By 1990, a large number of networks had linked about 200 sites. (16) At that time, the ARPANET program was disbanded, and the networks that replaced it represented universities, research institutions, and colleges in several different countries. (17) These networks were not government-run. (18) In fact, the creators of these networks and technology used surprisingly libertarian guiding principles to operate the networks. "[T]he initial topology of the Internet corresponded with a libertarian bias against governmental intervention. This ideology was in turn reflected by a network 'architecture [that] has embedded rules for information flow that advance self-regulation and free market choice over public decision-making.'" (19) This self-regulating network of researchers initially eschewed the participation of commercial enterprises. (20) This changed in the 1990s with the creation of HTTP technology (allowing for the creation of websites) and with major upgrades enhancing network capacity. (21) By 1994, cyberspace saw its first commercial website. (22)

B. The Internet is Connected to Everything

In less than fifteen years, the United States has gone from having a single commercial website to a nation that has integrated the Internet into virtually every important aspect of its infrastructure, both critical and mundane. It is crucial to account for the integration of the world's critical infrastructure into the Internet in order to assess the risks of cyber attacks. According to the U.S. Department of Homeland Security ("DHS"), the level of integration is high:

> Our economy and national security are fully dependent upon information technology and the information infrastructure. At the core of the information infrastructure upon which we depend is the Internet, a system originally designed to share unclassified research among scientists who were assumed to be uninterested in abusing the network. It is that same Internet that today connects millions of other computer networks making most of the nation's essential services and infrastructures work. These computer networks also control physical objects such as electrical transformers, trains, pipeline pumps, chemical vats, radars, and stock markets, all of which exist beyond cyberspace. (23)

Thus, the pervasive interconnection between critical infrastructure and the Internet create security risks because the Internet utilizes an open architecture based on the free flow of information. Any Internet user is potentially vulnerable, including "electrical transformers, trains, pipeline pumps, chemical vats, radars, and stock markets." (24)

The Internet's open architecture also makes it very difficult to impose content regulations or controls on the flow of information through the system. (25) This includes information whose content is malicious in nature. (26) It is impossible to "scan" for content within the Internet until the information has reached its destination. (27) As a result, the Internet itself cannot police for hackers, Internet aggressors, or even viruses. (28) Firewalls scan packets, but the information they scrutinize is the information sent along with the packet itself, such as "protocol, source and destination addresses and ports." (29) Firewalls can do much to determine a packet's trustworthiness, but they are not good at detecting viruses. (30) Virus scanning is done once information has been accepted into the computer or network. (31) Thus, viruses cannot be prevented; they can only be cured.

Other security measures available to users include intrusion-detection systems to thwart hacking and the use of "honey pots," which are highly vulnerable computers deliberately put into a network to lure and detect hackers. (32) Complex computer networks are built with computer security in mind, created to cordon hackers into discrete portions of networks. (33) Thus, if a hacker gains access to one portion of a system, that hacker will not have access to the whole. The computer industry has worked to create the technology and structures that meet the demand for cyber security, but according to the U.S. government, more must be done. (34)

The question remains, of course: how safe is the Internet? The answer to this question is highly disputed. To get a sense of the scope of this issue, it is important to understand more about the threats, Internet aggressors, and their means of attack.

C. Internet Attacks are Varied and Frequent

Computers or computer networks may, of course, be attacked with conventional weapons, such as bombs. This kind of physical act, as opposed to conduct in cyberspace, is referred to as a "kinetic" act or attack. (35) This Article discusses attacks via cyberspace but not kinetic attacks or attacks utilizing electronic warfare. Attacks utilizing electronic warfare involve high charges of electricity meant to physically damage computers and software. (36)

The type of cyber attacks (37) at issue in this Article are conducted through the Internet using malicious code:

> Malicious code can be used to create a cyber attack, or computer network attack (CNA), directed against computer processing code, instruction logic, or data. The code can generate a stream of malicious network packets that can disrupt data or logic through exploiting a vulnerability in computer software, or a weakness in the computer security practices of an organization. This type of cyber attack can disrupt the reliability of equipment, the integrity of data, and the confidentiality of communications. (38)

Thus, this mode of an Internet attack directs malicious code against the computer or network of another. (39) The attackers may be children, governments, criminals, or terrorists. Their intentions run along a spectrum from computer vandalism to effectuating catastrophic damage and death. This wide spectrum of actors and intentions has made it difficult to parcel out definitions of "cyber crime" or "cyber terrorism." (40) Cyber attacks in general, however, encompass all of the above actors and intentions.

The weapons used in cyber attacks include viruses, worms, Trojan horses, bombs, and web-jacking:

> Virus--A virus is a program that is intentionally written and launched. Viruses' most common traits are their ability to (1) attach themselves to a host program and execute when the host is operated and (2) replicate themselves. Their authors intend them to impact the data or integrity of the computer without the owner's knowledge. ...

> Worms--A worm is a computer program that breaks into vulnerable computers, replicates itself, and then spreads to other computers, repeating the process through a spread algorithm. They are self- executing and do not require human action, such as clicking on an attachment. Worm payloads an install backdoors, deface websites, conduct distributed denial of service attacks and delete or corrupt code.

> Trojan Horse Programs--Trojans, unlike viruses, do not replicate. They hide inside another program and when that program runs, the Trojan is launched and performs undesirable actions to the system and/or data.

> Bombs and Droppers--Bombs are pieces of software that activate malicious program, such as a virus. Droppers are programs that transport or install viruses.

> Web-jacking results in the manipulation of websites and search engines to send unsuspecting users to other sites, ranging from irritating to criminal activities. (41)

Another powerful tool available to cyberspace aggressors is the "botnet," which involves the hijacking of third-party computers on a massive scale to form a network of "drones." (42) The hijacker then gives these drones commands from a remote location. (43) It is estimated that by May 2007, the Internet contained approximately three million such drones. (44) As a result of the proliferation of these weapons, cyber attacks are on the rise. (45) Appendix A of this

Article describes the huge increase in cyber attacks between the 1990s and 2002. (46)

D. The Internet is a Great Place to Hide

It is important to note several elements regarding the use of these tools. First, cyber weapons can spread to or use other computers, (47) and second, they can operate after the attacker has "left the scene." (48) These dynamics make it difficult to track computer aggressors after damage has been detected. (49) The attack itself might be effectuated by attaching the malicious software to something as innocuous as an e-mail or as hostile as hacking (50) into another computer or computer network. (51) Cyber aggressors use methods calculated to provide secrecy and to cause profound impacts. (52)

Internet attacks on the United States' critical infrastructure are a national security risk. According to a recent report issued by the General Accounting Office, there is reason for concern:

> There is increasing concern among both government officials and industry experts regarding the potential for a cyber attack on a national critical infrastructure, including the infrastructure's control systems. The Federal Bureau of Investigation has identified multiple sources of threats to our nation's critical infrastructures, including foreign nation states engaged in information warfare, domestic criminals, hackers, and virus writers, and disgruntled employees working within an organization...Federal and industry experts believe that critical infrastructure control systems are more vulnerable today than in the past due to the increased standardization of technologies, the increased connectivity of control systems to other computer networks and the Internet, insecure connections, and the widespread availability of technical information about control systems...Reported attacks and unintentional incidents involving critical infrastructure control systems demonstrate that a serious attack could be devastating. (53)

As the above excerpt shows, the integration of the Internet during the last fifteen years into modern society also extends to key elements of infrastructure that could be attacked through cyberspace. Some authors suggest that the risk of such an attack is low. (54) However, the DHS concludes that the technical sophistication required to carry out this type of attack is very high. (55) A recent cyber attack in Estonia sheds some further light on this issue.

E. Estonia Claims that a Recent Cyber Attack was an Act of War

In late April and early May 2007, Estonia was subjected to a massive cyber attack that it deemed was an act of war. (56) The mode of attack appears to be quite simple. Beginning with government websites and later extending to newspapers, universities, hospitals, and banks, the cyber aggressors flooded Estonia's websites with data requests. (57) These requests overwhelmed the websites, shutting them down. (58) The aggressors used botnets to accomplish the attack. (59) In the end, more than a million computers took part in this attack, in the form of botnet drones hijacked from innocent third parties. (60) The targets of the attack included paramedic and fire services, as well as Internet service providers and hospitals. (61) Unlike other attacks, the attack in Estonia lasted for weeks. (62)

The attack had profound economic and political consequences. Estonia's largest bank was forced to suspend online services for more than an hour and eventually barred foreign access to its servers. (63) Other sites followed suit. (64) This isolation of Estonia from the rest of the world interfered with its ability to "[make] its case to the world." (65) The effects of the cyber attack and a larger international issue involving Russia left Estonia in crisis. (66) Estonia had decided to move a Soviet era war memorial from a prominent location in its national capital to a location of lesser visibility. The Russian government strenuously and vocally opposed the decision, and Estonia felt a need to counter Russia's "propaganda." (67) The cyber attack left Estonia with fewer tools to explain its position to the world.

Estonia blamed Russia for the cyber attack and Russia denied involvement. (68) According to Estonia's Defense Minister, the attack "cannot be treated as hooliganism, but has to be treated as an attack against the state." (69) NATO did not treat the attack as an act of war, but it did take action to investigate the incident. (70) Some observers saw the cyber attack as a criminal act because it resulted in neither terror nor debilitating disruption; other observers looked to the level of disruption and equated it with the effect of conventional weapons. (71)

In the end, it has been difficult for Estonia to firmly establish who was behind the attacks. (72) Some experts believe that Estonia's attack was not state-sponsored:

> After some investigation, network analysts later concluded that the cyber attacks targeting Estonia were not a concerted

attack, but instead were the product of spontaneous anger from a loose federation of separate attackers. Technical data showed that sources of the attack were worldwide rather than concentrated in a few locations. The computer code that caused the DDOS attack was posted and shared in many Russian language chat rooms, where the moving of the war memorial was a very emotional topic for discussion. These analysts state that although access to various Estonian government agencies was blocked by the malicious code, there was no apparent attempt to target national critical infrastructure other than Internet resources. ... (73)

In some ways, the true identity and nature of the Estonian attackers may be less relevant than the story this experience tells the world. Estonia concluded that it was under siege from an enemy who had perpetrated an act of war. (74) It might have chosen to go to war with this enemy, using conventional weapons; other countries have waged war on less evidence. Estonia's forbearance in this instance may be more attributable to the political realities at that time than to Estonia's own inclinations. Yet, if the attack against Estonia had been executed by conventional means, international law would have provided the tools necessary to determine whether that attack was lawful or unlawful (thus justifying a military response). (75) That international law could not provide an answer to Estonia is troubling. Additionally, recent events indicate that Estonia is unlikely to be the sole victim of cyber attacks. Before and during Russia's attack on Georgia in August 2008, Georgia was subjected to cyber attacks that involved its government, banks, transportation services, and communications systems. (76) The international community (77) must do more to give the next victim of an Estonian style attack the vital answers it will need to determine if war is justified.

III. INTERNATIONAL LAWS OF WAR FAIL TO GIVE SUFFICIENT GUIDANCE

The international community has built the rules of warfare upon the use of conventional weapons and conventional modes of aggression. (78) These rules of warfare are based on well-established notions of jus ad bellum and jus in bello, the principles guiding when states may declare war and how they may exercise military aggression. (79) International law effectuates these principles through international agreements such as the U.N. Charter and the Hague and Geneva Conventions. The historical background to these agreements provides a better understanding of the modern law of warfare.

International legal scholars believe that the Treaty of Westphalia created the modern nation state in 1648. (80) The notion of the "modern nation state" relates in large part to the growing importance of state sovereignty in the relations between countries. (81) After the Treaty of Westphalia, states considered themselves to be entitled to rule their territories without interference from other nations. (82) Such interference could constitute an act of war and justify a military response. (83) Prior to Westphalia, states evaluated questions of morality or justness in deciding whether to wage war. (84) In modern times, the sole issue has become legality, and that legality was measured by a state's justification for its actions as expressions of sovereign authority. (85) If a state possessed authority to act, it could do so under international law. (86) As such, the doctrine of jus ad bellum was limited to questions of legality, not morality. The question of the morality of warfare is crucial to the understanding of current international law regarding the use of military force.

In the late 19th Century, advancements in warfare technology led to the brutality of the American Civil War, renewing the world's interest in the morality of warfare. (87) In 1899 and 1907, nations came together to address the moral issues raised by modern warfare, creating the Hague Convention Protocols to regulate the manner in which war was waged. (88) Specifically, these Conventions included what is now known as the "Martens Clause." (89) This clause provides that the signatory states are restricted by principles of humanity in their conduct. (90) Despite these attempts at forbearance, World War I resulted in casualties on a scale that was previously unknown to the world. (91)

In response to World War I, nations agreed to settle international disputes through arbitration, adjudication, or a mediated settlement regulated by the Council of the League of Nations. (92) The political realities of the day frustrated this attempt at restricting war. (93) Without U.S. participation, the League of Nations lacked the political clout to be effective. (94) Nonetheless, the international community continued to express its disapprobation for the use of warfare to resolve international disputes. (95) In 1928, the Kellogg-Briand Pact outlawed warfare as a legal method of dispute resolution. (96) Again, despite its illegitimacy, World War II broke out, and once again, war shocked the conscience of the world. (97)

A. The U.N. Charter Does Not Fit the Needs of Cyber Security

The horrors of World War II inspired the international community to build a framework to regulate international conflicts. (98) It did so with the U.N. Charter, which outlawed warfare in its entirety and created a structure of international law that tightly regulates any use or threats of force by nations. (99) The U.N. Charter and humanitarian law treaties, such as the Geneva Conventions, contain rules regulating when states may use military force, how states may exercise that force, and how states and their militaries must treat soldiers, civilians, and prisoners of war. (100) States enjoy few options under this structure to use force legitimately. (101) More important to this Article, this structure fails to address the vital issues of Internet security, such as the impact of cyber attacks on critical infrastructure, attacks by non-state actors, and the blurred lines between soldiers and civilians in the age of cyberspace. To understand the law relating to use of force and how it impacts cyber attacks, it is important to discern how the U.N. system works and how cyber attacks do not fit its structure. Finally, it is important to examine other mechanisms that could restrain Internet aggressors in order to judge whether critical infrastructure can be made more secure and whether international law can hold Internet aggressors accountable.

The basis of the philosophy motivating the U.N. Charter's framers is the notion that the world will maintain international peace and security collectively by preventing aggression or breaches of the peace. (102) As such, it seeks to eradicate warfare. (103) International law recognizes the U.N. Charter as providing the legal framework to determine whether a state may use aggression in the international sphere.

The U.N. Charter, coupled with the Statute of the International Court of Justice ("ICJ Statute"), forms the framework for the regulation of international disputes. (104) The U.N. Charter created the International Court of Justice ("ICJ"). (105) The court's power to act and hear cases is detailed in the ICJ Statute. That statute identifies the authoritative sources of international law as treaties, international custom, and general principles of law recognized by civilized nations. (106) Thus, the U.N. Charter and the ICJ Statute together form a whole. The ICJ Statute proclaims that international treaties are a valid source of international law, and the U.N. Charter, as an international treaty, regulates how states will legally affect aggression in the international sphere. (107)

The U.N. Charter provides very little leeway for states to settle disputes violently:

> Article 2(4) of the Charter of the United Nations was the coup de grace for the theory and practice of the jus ad bellum, that recognized the right of states to resort to war. This article requires all Member States to 'refrain in their international relations from the threat or use of force against the territorial integrity or political independence of any state. . .' The Charter clearly outlaws the aggressive use of force while recognizing a state's inherent right of individual and collective self-defense in Article 51 and the Security Council's obligation under Article 39 to maintain or restore international peace and security. (108)

As a result, in the context of international law, states no longer speak of going to war. War is unlawful. The proper inquiry under the U.N. Charter is whether the actions constitute a lawful or unlawful "use of force." (109) As the above excerpt shows, the sole basis for the lawful use of force by an individual state is the exercise of self-defense or authorization by the Security Council. (110) This right of self-defense is mentioned, but not defined, in Article 51 of the U.N. Charter: "Nothing in the present Charter shall impair the inherent right of individual or collective self-defense if an armed attack occurs against a Member of the United Nations, until the Security Council has taken the measures necessary to maintain international peace and security. ..." (111)

Accordingly, because the U.N. Charter does not define "self-defense," under the ICJ statute one must look to treaties, custom, and general principles of law to determine the meaning of the term. (112)

International law regarding the use of self-defense was fairly well established even prior to the adoption of the U.N. Charter. (113) Customary international law regarding this issue was articulated the Caroline Dispute:

> [To invoke the doctrine of self-defense, a state must show a necessity that is] instant, overwhelming, leaving no choice of means, and no moment for deliberation. It will be for it to show, also, that the [aggressors]. . .did nothing unreasonable or excessive; since the act justified by the necessity of self-defence (sic), must be limited by that necessity, and kept clearly within it. It must be strewn that admonition or remonstrance. . .was impracticable, or would have been

unavailing; it must be strewn that daylight could not be waited for; that there could be no attempt at discrimination, between the innocent and the guilty; . . .that there was a necessity, present and inevitable, for attacking. ... (114)

Similarly, a state employing the right of reprisal under the U.N. Charter must have an immediate necessity; it must make a demand for satisfaction, or such demand must be impractical or unavailing, and the response must be proportionate. (115) Since the signing of the U.N. Charter, international agreements have circumscribed the manner in which a state may exercise a reprisal. (116) The state must limit its attacks to military targets. (117) Consequently, if a state is attacked by force, it may respond to protect its citizens only if it has a legitimate military target to attack. (118)

The theory of "preemptive self-defense" has caused dispute about the law governing self-defense. (119) This theory focuses on the dangers posed by external threats. (120) Essentially, the theory proposes that in the modern world of weapons of mass destruction and other modes of mass killing, a nation cannot afford to suffer a debilitating blow before it may act in self-defense. (121) Thus, the level of threat justifies a preemptive act of aggression. (122) The former U.S. President Bush has been an ardent proponent of this doctrine, and it is sometimes called "the Bush Doctrine:"

> The United States has long maintained the option of preemptive actions to counter a sufficient threat to our national security. The greater the threat, the greater is the risk of inaction--and the more compelling the case for taking anticipatory action to defend ourselves, even if uncertainty remains as to the time and place of the enemy's attack. To forestall or prevent such hostile acts by our adversaries, the United States will, if necessary, act preemptively.

> The United States will not use force in all cases to preempt emerging threats, nor should nations use preemption as a pretext for aggression. Yet in an age where the enemies of civilization openly and actively seek the world's most destructive technologies, the United States cannot remain idle while dangers gather. (123)

The Bush Doctrine is hotly disputed in scholarly circles. (124) Yet in practice, states have embraced it to one degree or another. (125) In the end, the international community may be forced to choose between the collective model of peacekeeping envisioned by the U.N. Charter and a more unilateral approach as exemplified by the Bush Doctrine. To date, the international community has combined these two antithetical theories within the U.N. Security Council.

The Security Council, as an arm of the U.N. Charter system, may authorize collective military action by states to maintain or restore international peace and security. (126) At the behest of the Security Council, these types of police actions provide states with the option to use aggression legitimately in circumstances in which self-defense is not justified. Consequently, international law has cobbled together humanitarian notions of peacekeeping through collective regulation with more belligerent inclinations to use force as a tool of foreign policy. This balance of opposing theories is merely a modern reflection of the long-time tension between jus ad bellum and sovereignty. The international community may continue to feel this tension in the foreseeable future.

Despite the above balance between conflicting inclinations toward collective and unilateral actions by states, the resulting effect on international law is to provide two lawful justifications for the use of force in the international sphere. States may legitimately use or threaten to use force against another state when: (1) the Security Council authorizes force; or (2) the state is acting in self-defense after "an armed attack." (127) An armed attack relates to the use of military force, not economic or political coercion. (128) While this definition appears to be understandable in the context of conventional warfare, the distinctions blur when it is applied to cyber attacks. It becomes clear that Article 2(4) does not give the international community discernable rules concerning the legitimacy of cyber attacks under the U.N. Charter.

B. Do Cyber Attacks Constitute "Use of Force"?

Legal scholar Duncan Hollis uses three approaches to apply the Article 2(4) "use of force" doctrine to cyber attacks. The first is called the "instrumentality approach." (129) Under this traditional analysis, a cyber attack cannot constitute an "armed attack" under Article 2(4) because it lacks the physical characteristics of a traditional military attack. (130) To support this claim, its advocates point to U.N. Charter Article 41, which exempts interruptions of communications as "measures not involving use of armed force." (131) Since the object of many cyber attacks is to effectuate just that purpose, more or different forms of aggression must be shown in order to constitute an "armed attack" under the U.N. Charter.

The second approach, called the "target-based" approach, focuses on the nature of the target. (132) Whenever cyber attacks are aimed at critical national infrastructure, regardless of the scale of damage, an "armed attack" has occurred. (133) The problem with this approach is its broad stroke. Hollis points out that the target-based approach suffers from over-inclusion:

> [Cyber attacks] can produce wide-ranging effects, from merely informational (distributing propaganda) to inconvenient (disrupting systems temporarily via denial-of-service attack) to potentially dangerous (implanting a logic bomb doing no immediate harm but with the potential to cause future injury) to immediately destructive (disabling a system permanently via a virus). (134)

Notions of proportionality and fairness militate against allowing for a reprisal attack, either through cyberspace or by using more conventional means, when the damage is less harmful than a kinetic military attack. As a consequence, because the target-based approach would authorize military or cyber reprisals for any cyber attack on critical infrastructure, it is too inclusive. This response conflicts with the U.N. Charter's stated purpose of maintaining international peace and security. (135)

The final approach, the "consequentiality approach," focuses on the effects of the attack. (136) If the cyber attack causes the same kinds of effects as a kinetic attack--death or destruction of property-- it triggers the Article 51 authorization for using self-defense. (137) Yet, the lack of physical effects may not account for the real effect to a country. A cyber attack that shuts down any part of a nation's critical infrastructure may have an effect that is much more debilitating than a traditional military attack. The threat in such a situation may be more terrorizing and harmful than a traditional armed attack. Certainly, a country that is unable to use its banking system, or whose power grid has gone off-line due to a cyber attack, possesses legitimate claims for reparation, justice, and security. Because the consequentiality approach focuses on the same type of physical damage caused by a kinetic attack, it does not sufficiently protect critical infrastructure.

Commentators also identify additional weaknesses in applying the U.N. Charter's use of force doctrine to cyber attacks. The Charter only applies to the acts of nations in relation to each other. (138) Terrorists and other non-state groups are not covered. (139) The wisdom of the U.N. system made sense before the Internet and before the age of terrorism. In this earlier time, it was improper and illegal for nations to use military force against civilians. (140) In today's world, non-state actors may inflict damages tantamount to a state-sponsored military attack. Non-state aggressors may also gain sophisticated technological skills that parallel the type of attack that Estonia faced in 2007. (141)

This area of international law simply fails to meet the needs of the international community when it comes to Internet attacks. International law should help deter cyber attacks and help obtain justice for a country that has suffered an Internet attack by terrorists or other non-state actors. The international community would benefit from creating a standard that specifically applies to cyber attacks in order to clarify the law and provide a vehicle for justice and security that fits the circumstances.

C. Cyber Attacks May Have Some Benefits

The use of force doctrine under the U.N. Charter also presents a nation with a catch-22 dilemma when it has reasons to employ cyber attacks offensively as part of a military campaign. Any country that is authorized pursuant to the U.N. Charter to engage in the use of force may seek to employ Internet attacks as one weapon during its military campaign. These types of attacks, when compared to traditional kinetic methods, are likely to spare lives and physical infrastructure. Taking down a power grid or shutting down a transportation system through a cyber attack may be preferable to bombing the power station or blowing up trains and planes transporting people. In comparison to the grisly business of traditional warfare, cyber warfare may be more humane. (142)

The United States had this option in Kosovo during the Kosovo War. The U.S. military decided that it could not use cyber attacks against Serbian networks to disrupt military operations and civil services. (143) The United States was concerned that such attacks might constitute war crimes. (144) Thus, current international law prohibits states from using cyber attacks in situations where the interests of humanity may argue in their favor. Yet, international law forbids states from taking action against non-state actors who attack them through the Internet. (145) If a nation launched a cyber attack against another state, the law is unclear concerning what types of cyber attacks, if any, would allow the victim state to respond through a reprisal. (146) This state of the law does not suffice.

IV. THE POLITICAL AND LOGISTIC CHALLENGES TODAY PLAGUE ALL ATTEMPTS TO CURB INTERNET ATTACKS

Because the use of force regime does not attend to the international community's needs regarding cyber attacks, the international community must create new international rules to deal with cyber attacks. The international community must look to other mechanisms that may provide security for critical infrastructure and hold Internet aggressors accountable. Commentators suggest alternative solutions to deal with the problem of Internet attacks, such as changing the structure of the Internet itself to address cyber attack problems, (147) using the International Criminal Court ("ICC") or the ICJ to adjudicate claims, (148) or depending on individual states to police Internet aggressors under the Cybercrime Convention. (149) As this Article will show, these suggestions are either logistically or politically impractical. It is nonetheless helpful to understand their strengths and weaknesses in order to comprehend both the challenges in this area and the necessary elements to construct new rules for cyber attacks. The following approaches reveal the challenges that the Internet itself poses and the pitfalls that the current legal system struggles to avoid.

A. Could Changes to the Structure of the Internet Stop Cyber Attacks?

The open architecture of the Internet presents great obstacles to building safeguards within the Internet to stop hackers and saboteurs. The principles embedded in the very code used to build the Internet fortify its function as a free-flowing highway of information without regard to content. They reflect a libertarian, countercultural philosophy that views the Internet as a vehicle to empower individuals. Steven Wozniak, co-founder of the Apple Computer, expresses it this way:

> We were meeting at our Homebrew Computer Club right there at SLAC (Stanford Linear Accelerator Center) in Menlo Park and were surrounded by a lot of the old hippie thinkers from the counterculture movement, basically trying to apply the same internal drives and passions into the use of technology to get us to that better, good world where people were equal and not so subject to the major corporations of the time, having all the power. The guy who knew how to program a computer was going to be the most important person in the company, more important than the CEO. It was so tied in with empowering the normal low-level people. (150)

This idea of equality, so important to the founders of the Internet, (151) is also reflected in the way that the Internet treats information. As explained above, the Internet uses packet-switching and the end-to-end principle to make information conveyance more efficient. The power of the Internet is in part derived from its ability to transport information without regard to content. Yet, its power is also its weakness because the Internet itself cannot discriminate. Without the power to discriminate, the Internet cannot discern what is worthy, dangerous, illegal, or beneficial. It simply cannot provide the means to make these judgments because its basic building blocks forbid it.

As a result, calls to alter the Internet to deal with the problems of cyber security simply address fringe aspects, such as attempting to ban "bad actors" from the Internet. (152) In part, this would be done by blacklisting effectuated through "naming and shaming" Internet perpetrators. (153) Law enforcement could assist in the expulsion of Internet aggressors as well, if given additional investigatory tools such as access to private information stored by Internet Service Providers. (154) These methods are worthy of debate and may be implemented to assist in providing cyber security in general. However, they seem insufficient to meet the needs of defending against an attack on the scale of the 2007 assault against Estonia.

Others suggest that the government disengage from the Internet by constructing its own insular computer network that does not interface with the Internet. (155) While such an approach might protect government computers, it does nothing to protect critical infrastructure. The private sector owns 85 percent of the critical infrastructure in the United States. (156) It is this critical infrastructure that must be protected against cyber attacks.

Furthermore, this tactic is unlikely to prevent hackers from accessing such a government network. That network would be as vulnerable as the current system because, in part, the government uses commercial software with vulnerabilities known to hackers. (157) The hacker community regularly discovers vulnerabilities in commercial software and distributes this information by publishing it on the Internet or selling it at auction. (158) Thus, hackers who gain access to this government network would have the same advantages in attacking government sites as they enjoy under the current system.

Consequently, attempts to provide additional safety through Internet innovations have not proven to be sufficiently fruitful. These approaches only emphasize the power of the Internet as either boon or danger, and the Internet's impotence to defend itself from those who wish to abuse it. While the notion of direct prevention through technology seems engaging, the more likely solution to the cyber-security problem may lie in deterrence.

B. Can the ICJ or the ICC Provide Solutions?

Criminal sanctions provide deterrence to criminals and malefactors. Some commentators suggest that the ICJ or the ICC provide the proper mechanisms to cope with cyber attacks on infrastructure. (159) Yet, the logistical and political obstacles to using these courts are high. First, both courts lack the proper jurisdiction to hear all such cases. Second, neither court possesses the political authority to enforce its judgments. Without the de jure and de facto authority to pass on these issues, both the ICJ and the ICC lack the legitimacy needed to cope with cyber attacks.

The ICC, like the ICJ, is a creature of statute. It was created by an international treaty, the Rome Statute of the International Criminal Court, signed in July 1998, and effective in July 2002. (160) Approximately 42 percent of the world's countries are members of the ICC. (161) Significantly, the United States, China, Russia, and India are not among them. (162) The Rome Statute authorizes jurisdiction for the ICC in specific circumstances: where the defendant is a citizen of one of the member states, the crime occurred in the territory of a member state, a non-member state accepts jurisdiction of the court, or the case is referred by the U.N. Security Council. (163)

The ICC prosecutes genocide, war crimes, crimes against humanity, and crimes of aggression. (164) The definitions of these crimes are largely taken from the Geneva Conventions and Protocols as well as the Hague Rules. (165) The definitions are general and expansive. Under the Rome Statute, a crime against humanity is "any of the following acts [murder, extermination and enslavement, etc.] when committed as part of a widespread or systematic attack directed against any civilian population, with knowledge of the attack." (166) The section further states, "'Attack directed against any civilian population' means a course of conduct involving the multiple commission of acts referred to in paragraph 1 against any civilian population, pursuant to or in furtherance of a State or organizational policy to commit such attack. ..." (167)

Anomalously, the Statute also provides, "The definition of a crime shall be strictly construed and shall not he extended by analogy. In case of ambiguity, the definition shall be interpreted in favour (sic) of the person being investigated, prosecuted or convicted." (168) Thus, these broadly defined crimes must be construed strictly. As a general rule, the crimes against humanity all appear to involve some kind of direct physical assault. (169) As such, they would not apply to situations in which a cyber attack takes down a power grid or cripples a state's financial system. Oddly, as broad and general as the definitions of these crimes are, they would not reach cyber attacks.

The provision relating to war crimes may be more to the point. Article 8(2)(b) of the Rome Statute lists "other serious violations of the laws and customs applicable in international armed conflict, within the established framework of international law." (170) Five of the activities listed are potentially relevant to the issue of cyber attacks: (1) directing attacks against a civilian population; (2) directing attacks against civilian, non-military objects; (3) launching attacks that will cause incidental injury or damage to civilians or civilian objects; (4) attacking undefended and nonmilitary objectives such as towns, villages, homes, or buildings; and (5) destroying or seizing the enemy's property in a manner that is unnecessary for the prosecution of war. (171) These acts seem to pinpoint some of the evils inherent to cyber attacks.

It is easy to understand how these acts, if committed by a terrorist or other non-state actor through a cyber attack, might seem like a war crime. Yet, the Rome Statute does not clearly establish that the ICC may prosecute such acts. War crimes under the Rome Statute are limited to "[g]rave breaches of the Geneva Convention." (172) The Geneva Convention only applies to the acts of nations, not individuals. (173) On the other hand, Article 27 of the Rome Statute provides, "This Statute shall apply equally to all persons without any distinction based on official capacity." (174)

Yet, because war crimes under the Geneva Convention are limited to actions of government officials and members of the military, Article 27 cannot render acts of non-state actors amenable to prosecution. (175) Article 27 of the Rome Statute may remove distinctions based on the governmental chain of command in war crimes prosecutions, but it does not reach non-state actors. (176) Additionally, the Geneva Conventions are implicated in situations involving "armed conflict." (177) Whether a cyber attack constitutes an armed conflict is highly disputed under international law, as explained supra. As a result, ICC prosecutions would not address some of the real problems with cyber attacks.

Furthermore, regarding state use of cyber attacks during a time of war, the Rome Statute goes too far. A cyber attack against civilians during a time of war might be a preferred mode of warfare to the slaughter resulting from a conventional bomb, missile, or gun. International law should encourage nations, rather than prohibit them, in choosing alternatives that restrict damage to economic rather than physical targets. Neither the Geneva Convention nor the Rome Statute was created to address cyber attacks. As a result, they should be inapplicable.

Similarly, the ICJ cannot resolve the problem of cyber attacks because it was created to deal with other issues. The ICJ has jurisdiction to hear cases between states and cannot hear cases involving individual people. (178) Davis Brown argues that such cases before the ICJ between states would be based upon the theory of original responsibility if states agree to refer the cases to the ICJ:

> The ICJ would then have the power to adjudicate not only questions regarding the interpretation and application of the proposed convention, but also claims for injury to states that are victims of information war crimes. While individuals would not be held accountable under this means of enforcement, the delinquent state would be held liable to the injured state in law for the actions of both its employees and agents under the theory of original responsibility, and possibly also for those of noncombatants under its jurisdiction, depending on the degree to which the delinquent state endorsed the acts or failed to take reasonable measures to prevent and punish the acts. (179)

This approach provides a creative solution to the problems that sovereignty presents in the international sphere. However, would powerful states such as the United States make an agreement to refer cyber attack cases to the ICJ, allowing that court to pass judgment on its acts? Recent events militate against such a conclusion. As Brown points out, the United States has rejected participation in the ICC. (180) Without U.S. participation, the ICC will not provide a useful mechanism to combat cyber attacks. (181) The same result is likely if the United States rejects outright the use of the ICJ for that purpose. The ICJ also faces the additional problem of enforcement. Some states abide by ICJ decisions, but no mechanism forces them to do so. (182)

In fact, states do not always abide by the ICJ. The Nicaragua Case provides a good example of this problem. (183) On April 9, 1984, Nicaragua sued the United States in the ICJ. (184) Nicaragua alleged that the United States had mined its harbors, used unlawful force, and intervened in Nicaragua's internal affairs. (185) The initial proceedings before the ICJ related to the court's jurisdiction to hear the matter. (186) The United States argued that the ICJ lacked jurisdiction to hear the case because Nicaragua had failed to essentially "sign up" with the court by perfecting its signature of the Protocol. (187) It argued that because Nicaragua had never formally granted the court jurisdiction, the court did not possess that jurisdiction. (188)

Nicaragua contended that its prior conduct exhibited an intention to submit to the jurisdiction of the court. (189) In November 1984, the court determined that it had jurisdiction to hear the merits of the case based upon a prior treaty between Nicaragua and the United States. (190) In a letter dated January 18, 1985, the United States announced that, "with great reluctance, it has decided not to participate in further proceedings in the case." (191) The U.S. government refused to acknowledge that the ICJ possessed authority over it. (192) The ICJ later heard the merits of the case, and it found that the United States had violated international law in absentia and concluded that the United States had a legal obligation to pay reparations to Nicaragua. (193) The United States never paid reparations, and it instead withdrew its grant of compulsory jurisdiction to the ICJ and blocked the enforcement of the judgment through the U.N. Security Council. (194) In short, the Nicaragua Case revealed the ICJ's lack of political authority. Without the capacity to control powerful states, the ICJ lacks both the power and the legitimacy to meet the needs of this problem.

Both the ICJ and the ICC suffer from this weakness. As Brown points out, the United States has taken "painstaking" efforts to exempt its military from the ICC. (195) He concludes:

> For political reasons alone, a convention expressly granting ICC jurisdiction over information war crimes would probably lose the signatures of the United States and China. Without the support of all of the major powers of information warfare, any set of rules governing it would be significantly weaker. Simply put, a treaty norm lacking the support of states most affected by it necessarily loses its normative legitimacy. (196)

Unfortunately, the same weaknesses that Brown so eloquently highlights regarding the ICC also apply to ICJ. In both cases, without the political clout of states like the United States and China behind them, these courts lack the power to address the problems of cyber attacks in the international sphere. This is particularly true because many cyber cases are likely to implicate the United States in some manner for three reasons. It is a third-party transit country for more network traffic than any other country, hosts more hackers than any other country, and hosts the largest number of information systems and Internet sites than any other country. (197) Thus, until the United States manifests an intention to submit to the jurisdiction of either court, it is unlikely that either will provide sufficient solutions.

C. Will the Cybercrime Convention Stop Cyber Attacks?

Unlike the ICC and ICJ, the Cybercrime Convention has gained the favor of the U.S. government. In 2001, the Council of Europe adopted the Convention on Cybercrime. (198) The United States ratified the Convention in 2006, and it took effect in January 2007. (199) The strength of the Convention regarding cyber attacks is that it was specifically created with the Internet in mind. (200) Its weakness is that substantive regulation and jurisdiction for imposing restrictions are based on the domestic laws of the member states. (201) The use of these domestic laws carries three drawbacks: (1) it relies on the current international system of potentially conflicting domestic criminal laws; (2) these domestic laws carry jurisdictional limitations on their extraterritorial application in the international sphere; and (3) because of sovereign immunity, these criminal laws cannot reach the acts of foreign officials. An examination of the Convention and how it may apply to cyber attacks shows why it cannot satisfy the needs of cyber security.

The Convention identifies five main purposes: (1) harmonization of substantive criminal law on cybercrime; (2) harmonization of criminal procedure; (3) facilitating mutual legal assistance; (4) codifying international law, with an emphasis on territory-based jurisdictional rules; and (5) providing for a legal framework to enable development and understanding of the issues related to cybercrime. (202) The Convention focuses on creating international mechanisms that will effectuate domestic law enforcement of domestic criminal law. (203) It seeks to give a uniform voice to the cyber community regarding Internet norms. (204) It also assists law enforcement on difficult legal issues regarding jurisdiction, privacy, and extraterritorial process. (205)

In essence, the purpose of the Cybercrime Convention was to create a vehicle that would facilitate the creation of uniform domestic laws relating to Internet crime. (206) The interest in harmonizing cyber laws stemmed from the chaotic and impossible dilemma presented to anyone intending to do international business via the

Internet. The web of varied and conflicting criminal sanctions was overwhelming and burdensome. Not only was it difficult to understand what law applied to a given situation, but even if one could manage that feat, in order to act lawfully, that actor would have to sink to the lowest common denominator, i.e., to follow the most restrictive law in the world. (207) This situation was unfair and too restrictive on the Internet itself.

As a result, the Council of Europe created a plan that uses the same approach as the EU Directive. (208) The Cybercrime Convention gives direction concerning what types of laws states should enact domestically, but it leaves each state free to draft and enact the particulars. (209) To be sure, the Convention was a needed tool. The creator of the "Love Bug" virus, which "caused an estimated U.S. $10 billion of damage globally," was found and apprehended in part because of this Convention. (210) He could not be prosecuted, however, because local law in the Philippines did not prohibit his conduct. Limitations on the extraterritorial application of domestic laws precluded nations that suffered the effects of the virus from holding its creator criminally liable. (211)

An added layer of complexity is found in the rules that each nation uses to judge its extension of jurisdiction outside of its physical territory. Although the United States evaluates jurisdictional issues based on due process and fairness to the defendant, other countries premise jurisdiction on questions of territoriality. (212) These differing jurisdictional rules create much of the confusion in the international sphere regarding Internet norms. The Cybercrime Convention does little to alleviate this confusion since Article 22(2) allows states to reserve the right to exempt its jurisdictional rules from the Convention regime. (213) As such, it is important to understand the challenges of conflicting jurisdictional rules under the current state of affairs in the international legal arena.

In the United States, due process limits the power of courts to hear cases without sufficient contacts with the jurisdiction. (214) In contrast, courts in countries like France will hear cases in which a citizen has suffered harm, whether or not the defendant has intentionally connected herself with the jurisdiction or even takes part in the court case. (215) Under such a situation, it is difficult to know which law to follow. The Cybercrime Convention establishes jurisdiction over offenses committed either in the territory of the nation-party or by one of its nationals. (216) Although this may assist to some degree in harmonizing jurisdictional rules pursuant to Article 22(2), the Convention cannot force countries like the United States to change their constitutional rules that restrict jurisdiction, and it

108

cannot force countries like France to limit bases of extraterritorial jurisdiction. (217)

Additionally, the Cybercrime Convention does not protect states from extraterritorial collateral consequences from a cyber attack. Although U.S. law reaches conduct that is targeted toward U.S. territory, it does not reach all conduct that affects the United States. (218) A good example of this dilemma is found in the hypothetical provided at the beginning of this Article. If the President of the United States was killed in a cyber attack abroad, would U.S. courts possess jurisdiction to prosecute? It appears that under U.S. constitutional law, the answer to that question is no. (219) Yet, the United States would have a tangible interest in seeing the perpetrators brought to justice. The global reach of the Internet brings global consequences. This globalizing effect of the Internet creates a demand for international law to provide security and accountability for extraterritorial effects from warlike acts of aggression via cyberspace.

Another option open to the members of the Cybercrime Convention would be to change the Convention to impose universal jurisdiction in cybercrime cases. (220) Of course, this drastic step would in all likelihood require a constitutional amendment in the United States, (221) but even more importantly, universal jurisdiction carries serious drawbacks that militate against its use by domestic courts.

1. Universal Jurisdiction
The issue of universal jurisdiction is currently at the center of a great global debate. Amnesty International gives a working definition of the notion:

> There is, however, an all inclusive form of jurisdiction called universal jurisdiction which provides that national courts can investigate and prosecute a person suspected of committing a crime anywhere in the world regardless of the nationality of the accused or the victim or the absence of any links to the state where the court is located. (222)

Thus, universal jurisdiction is the idea that a state may make laws that apply to all the people of the world. (223) There are no requirements of contacts with the prosecuting jurisdiction, notice to the defendant, or even presence of the accused at the trial or court proceedings. (224) It allows for an all-encompassing authority to exercise jurisdiction in a "universal" manner. (225)

As states exert the authority of their laws within the international legal arena, commentators around the world argue the pros and cons of the issue. (226) In 2001, Foreign Affairs provided a forum for two such commentators to air their ideas. (227) These two articles highlighted the policy concerns that underlie the battles over the merits of universal jurisdiction. In the first article, former U.S. Secretary of State Henry Kissinger weighed in, leaving no doubt concerning his position. (228) The article begins, "In less than a decade, an unprecedented movement has emerged to submit international politics to judicial procedures. It has spread with extraordinary speed and has not been subjected to systematic debate, partly because of the intimidating passion of its advocates." (229) Kissinger clearly disfavors universal jurisdiction. He gives his own definition of the concept:

> The doctrine of universal jurisdiction asserts that some crimes are so heinous that their perpetrators should not escape justice by invoking doctrines of sovereign immunity or the sacrosanct nature of national frontiers. Two specific approaches to achieve this goal have emerged recently. The first seeks to apply the procedures of domestic criminal justice to violations of universal standards, some of which are embodied in United Nations conventions, by authorizing national prosecutors to bring offenders into their jurisdictions through extradition from third countries. The second approach is the International Criminal Court (ICC), the founding treaty for which was created by a conference in Rome in July 1998 and signed by 95 states, including most European countries. (230)

In the article, Kissinger's criticisms center on American-style concerns for due process and distrust for governmental authority (in this case, in the hands of the prosecutor and the judge). (231) In particular, he worries that without sufficient procedures, clear evidence against the accused, and proper restraints on prosecutor, such cases could become vehicles for political agendas rather than attempts to obtain justice. (232) Kissinger's most persuasive arguments center on the political maneuvering possible under such a wide exercise of jurisdiction. (233) He gives the example of the Arab-Israeli conflict, arguing that universal jurisdiction would permit these political enemies to "project their battles into the various national courts by pursuing adversaries with extradition requests." (234)

Kissinger's other concern relates to external pressure on states implementing national reconciliation procedures. (235) These "truth commissions" became popular in the 1980s in Africa and Latin America as a method to ease political tensions through limited grants of immunity for wrongdoing during violent and repressive regimes. (236) Kissinger fears that external second-guessing or meddling by other countries attempting to prosecute such individuals will harm the domestic process of prosecution or reconciliation. (237) He sees such a dynamic as a politically motivated action rather than one instituted for the purpose of seeing justice done. (238) In his distrust for universal jurisdiction, Kissinger is willing to sacrifice justice for the procedural fairness of the system, arguing that "a universal standard of justice should not be based on the proposition that a just end warrants unjust means, or the political fashion trumps fair judicial procedures." (239)

Human Rights Watch Executive Director Kenneth Roth is not so quick to discount the value of accountability for those guilty of atrocities. He argues that"[b]ehind much of the savagery of modern history lies impunity. Tyrants commit atrocities, including genocide, when they calculate they can get away with them. Too often, dictators use violence and intimidation to shut down any prospect of domestic prosecution." (240) And with this beginning to his article, Roth gives his most persuasive rejoinder to Kissinger: the "fair" procedures that Kissinger touts are not fair at all--at least when it comes to countries run by tyrants and malevolent dictators. (241) He contends that the prospect of future prosecution may mitigate the savagery of tyrants by giving them reason to "think twice" before engaging in barbarity. (242)

Roth places great emphasis on the international human rights agreements signed by the United States and other nations of the world. (243) He exhorts readers to remember the commitments made by the signatories to both the principles and the promises contained in the documents. (244) According to Roth, signatories agreed to hunt down and prosecute violators of the Geneva Conventions. (245) Thus, to Roth, neither the concepts of human rights nor the principles of universal jurisdiction are new concepts to the world. (246) In his estimation, the new development is that countries are finally willing to live up to those promises and hold high-placed politicians accountable. (247) He concludes that the use of universal jurisdiction has become commonplace in recent years and names examples of war crimes trials in the international sphere. (248) He states that "it has come to the point where the main limit on national courts empowered to exercise universal jurisdiction is the availability of the defendant, not questions of ideology." (249)

In countering Kissinger's complaints concerning procedural depravations, Roth downplays the lack of jury trials, abuse by prosecutors, and vague descriptions of crimes Kissinger disparaged. (250) In essence, Roth points to contexts outside criminal prosecutions using such procedures and infers that the ICC procedures suffice. (251) In addition, he points to the war crimes tribunals for Rwanda and Yugoslavia as examples of fair procedures, claiming that the jurists involved utilized "scrupulous regard for fair trial standards." (252) In the end, it is clear that Roth trusts institutions such as the ICC, and Kissinger does not.

The primary question essential to the discussion of universal jurisdiction is this: Can it be trusted? Both Roth and Kissinger praise the war crimes tribunals for Rwanda and Yugoslavia. (253) Yet these courts are vastly different from prosecutions by individual states. The U.N. Security Council created the Rwandan and Yugoslav courts to adjudicate matters of international law, which by its very nature is universally applicable. (254) The same cannot be said about the domestic laws of individual countries. Furthermore, Kissinger's concern about show trials is well founded. In the context of Cybercrime Convention prosecutions of cyber war crimes, the danger of a single nation or a group of states applying universal jurisdiction is great. The political motive for retribution would be high in prosecuting an alleged perpetrator of a cyber attack. In such a case, the prosecuting jurisdiction would have little reason to concern itself with the rights of the defendant or the impact on his or her home forum. In order for the Cybercrime Convention to sufficiently deal with the issues raised by cyber attacks, it would have to employ universal jurisdiction for the individual criminal laws of member states. This is neither wise nor just. Because the application of universal jurisdiction by the Cybercrime Convention is unwarranted, it is an insufficient vehicle for providing justice in the realm of cyberspace and critical infrastructure.

The additional problem under the Cybercrime Convention, when applied to Internet attacks, is that it cannot deter the acts of states. Although issues of sovereignty argue against universal jurisdiction for individual states, sovereignty also blocks prosecution of government officials by individual states under the doctrine of sovereign immunity. (255) This doctrine prevents states from prosecuting the misconduct of other states' officials. (256) The ICJ's decision relating to sovereign immunity in the context of war crimes highlights the problem in using the Cybercrime Convention to police cyber attacks.

2. Sovereign Immunity and State Prosecutions of Foreign Officials

Under the doctrine of sovereign immunity, a state cannot prosecute the officials of foreign countries for official acts. (257) In 2002, the ICJ addressed this issue in a case between Belgium and the Democratic Republic of the Congo ("DRC") called the Arrest Warrant Case. (258) This case shows that international law prohibits unilateral action by one country to impose criminal liability on the officials of another country.

The Arrest Warrant Case relates to Belgium's issuance of an international arrest warrant in an attempt to prosecute the incumbent Foreign Minister for the DRC, Abdoulaye Yerodia Ndombasi ("Yerodia"). (259) The Belgian charges related to Yerodia's 1998 statements to the Congolese people, encouraging them to kill members of a rebellion against the government. (260) The rebels were primarily ethnic Tutsis. (261) Yerodia's statements were made in the DRC, to the Congolese people. (262) Belgium did not contend that Yerodia had aimed these statements at Belgian citizens or that Belgium was directly harmed in any way. (263)

Belgium based the charges on its Universal Jurisdiction Law. (264) This law was adopted in 1993 to try persons accused of genocide, crimes against humanity, and war crimes. (265) It allowed anyone to institute the criminal action, and permitted prosecution without proof of a connection to the forum or victim. (266) The Belgian government brought the case in Belgium in 2000. (267) Belgium issued an international arrest warrant and sent it to the Congolese government and Interpol. (268) In October 2000, the DRC filed an application with the ICJ, requesting relief from the Belgian arrest warrant, claiming that Belgium lacked jurisdiction to issue such a warrant and that a criminal proceeding against Yerodia violated international norms of sovereign immunity. (269) In February 2002, the ICJ rendered its decision. (270)

Although the underlying basis of the claim relates to the propriety of the 2000 arrest warrant, much of the case before the ICJ concerned the legal maneuverings of the parties and, in part, the court. Two facts were important to the case at the time the final submissions were made. First, Yerodia was no longer serving as an employee of the Congolese government. (271) Second, the DRC abandoned its objection to universal jurisdiction, and based its sole claim on sovereign immunity. (272) This placed the court in a bind because Belgium argued that the DRC could not litigate the claims of private citizens. (273) If the DRC wanted to do so, it had to proceed under diplomatic immunity, and it had not fulfilled the prerequisites of that claim. (274) Belgium contended that when Yerodia left office, the court's jurisdiction vanished. (275) Secondly, Belgium asserted that if the court were to reach the merits of the case, it should pass on the issue of universal jurisdiction because that issue was not properly before the court. (276)

The ICJ rejected Belgium's first claim and accepted the second with conditions. (277) Regarding the court's ability to hear the case, the ICJ disagreed with Belgium concerning the effect of the changed circumstances. (278) The court determined that Belgium's allegation that a change in circumstances affected the court's power to hear the case was incorrect. (279) According to the court, this was a mootness issue, not a jurisdictional issue. (280) The court invoked the rule that the facts would be restricted to those the DRC originally pled and decided the case as if Yerodia were still in office. (281) This limited the holding in the case to questions of sovereign immunity for officials who were currently serving in the government. (282)

The court agreed with Belgium's claim that it could not reach the merits of the universal jurisdiction question because the final submission did not make that claim. (283) Regarding the merits of the sovereign immunity claims, the court found in favor of the DRC, stating:

> The Court has carefully examined State practice. . . It has been unable to deduce from this practice that there exists under customary international law any form of exception to the rule according immunity from criminal jurisdiction and inviolability to incumbent Ministers for Foreign Affairs where they are suspected of having committed war crimes or crimes against humanity. (284)

Thus, a state may not prosecute in its national courts a serving member of a foreign government, even if that person is accused of committing the most abhorrent of crimes. (285) The court provided an outline for sovereign immunity in the international sphere. Nations must abide by traditional sovereign immunity rules in claims against serving members of foreign governments. (286) This is a telling conclusion for the prospect of the Cybercrime Convention and its ability to deter state actors from attacking other states through the Internet. According to the holding in this case, a country could not prosecute a member of a foreign government for a cyber attack under the Cybercrime Convention or any other provision, regardless of any resulting damage or death.

114

This does not answer the question of a state's power to prosecute such an official after he or she has left office. The court in the Arrest Warrant Case went on to address this very issue. (287) In doing so, the court struck a balance between the needs of sovereignty and the demands of human rights. The court stated that "the immunity from jurisdiction enjoyed by incumbent Ministers for Foreign Affairs does not mean that they enjoy impunity in respect of any crimes they might have committed, irrespective of their gravity." (288) In so stating, the court found equilibrium between the sovereignty rights under sovereign immunity and the humanitarian demands that impunity to commit war crimes will not be tolerated.

As the Roth article shows, this notion of "impunity" typifies for the human rights movement the kind of power no leader should be allowed to exercise. The new norm under international law is that rulers who violate the Geneva Convention with impunity should be punished. (289) The challenge to the court in the Arrest Warrant Case was to create a framework that balances sovereignty with the ability to punish leaders who had previously enjoyed impunity for their crimes:

> Immunity from criminal jurisdiction and individual criminal responsibility are quite separate concepts. While jurisdictional immunity is procedural in nature, criminal responsibility is a question of substantive law. Jurisdictional immunity may well bar prosecution for a certain period or for certain offenses; it cannot exonerate the person to whom it applies from all criminal responsibility. (290)

Consequently, the court set out four ways in which a government official could be prosecuted: (1) the official's state could prosecute; (2) the official's state could waive immunity; (3) after the official has left office, a foreign court could prosecute acts carried out in a private capacity or done before or after his or her tenure in office; (291) or (4) the official could be prosecuted by one of "certain international criminal courts, where they have jurisdiction." (292) Examples of such international criminal courts are the International Criminal Tribunal for the former Yugoslavia, (293) the International Criminal Tribunal for Rwanda, (294) and the ICC. (295) National courts, therefore, are limited to prosecuting foreign officials for non-official acts after they have left office.

The Special Court for Sierra Leone, a hybrid domestic and U.N.-authorized ad hoc international court, used these principles to find that sovereign immunity rules did not apply to it because it was an international court under the auspices of the United Nations, not a domestic court:

> Be that as it may, the principle seems now established that the sovereign equality of states does not prevent a Head of State from being prosecuted before an international criminal tribunal or court.... We hold that the official position of the Applicant as an incumbent Head of State at the time when these criminal proceedings were initiated against him is not a bar to his prosecution by this court. The Applicant was and is subject to criminal proceedings before the Special Court for Sierra Leone. (296)

These cases provide ideal examples of the challenges posed to individual nations in policing the conduct of other governments. Principles of sovereignty, recognized through the doctrine of sovereign immunity, prohibit interference by one state in the government of another. (297) These cases show that individual states will have a very circumscribed area within which to prosecute former officials of foreign states. It is likely that the types of acts involved in planning and carrying out a cyber attack would constitute official acts under sovereign immunity and thus prevent prosecution. Without a waiver of immunity by the home state, the victim of the cyber attack would be left with no domestic remedy under the Cybercrime Convention. As a consequence, the use of the Cybercrime Convention to deter cyber attacks seems unlikely. Because of sovereign immunity, the Cybercrime Convention suffers from jurisdictional roadblocks and limitations like other international instruments.

As previously established, the ICJ and ICC suffer from similar insufficiencies of jurisdiction and political authority. In addition, the Internet itself cannot stop cyber attacks because it cannot discriminate valuable information from the malicious. Like the application of the U.N. Charter use of force analysis, these three approaches fail to meet the needs of the international community because they were not created with cyber security in mind. The proper approach gives states the authority to validly exercise universal jurisdiction and to allow prosecution without the restraints of sovereign immunity. To effectuate this result, the international community must create a new set of rules that apply specifically to cyber attacks, and these rules should be enforced by a mechanism that uses universal jurisdiction that is not limited by sovereign immunity principles. International ad hoc tribunals satisfy these requirements.

V. AD HOC TRIBUNALS PRESENT A VIABLE SOLUTION

A little over fifteen years ago, the world saw its first commercial website. (298) At approximately that same time, the world also saw the first U.N.-authorized criminal court. This type of court was an entirely new creation, a creature of statute and authorized by the U.N. Security Council. (299) In May 1993 and November 1994, the International Criminal Tribunals for the former Yugoslavia ("ICTY") and Rwanda ("ICTR") came into being. (300) The Security Council, acting pursuant to Chapter VII of the U.N. Charter, issued Resolutions 827 and 955. (301) These Resolutions outlined the scope of jurisdiction, the law to be applied, the scope of criminal responsibility for persons charged, the courts' relation to domestic courts, and the procedures to be used in the organization and proceedings of the courts themselves. (302) In essence, these Resolutions created entire court systems that enjoy limited life spans. These courts came into being for the sole purpose of judging issues of human rights violations in connection to acts occurring in "the territory of the former Socialist Federal Republic of Yugoslavia ... [for] a period beginning on 1 January 1991" (303) and "the territory of Rwanda ... [for] a period beginning on 1 January 1994 and ending on 31 December 1994." (304) These fascinating judicial creatures are an entirely new phenomenon.

The 1994 Report of the Secretary General to the Security Council regarding the ICTY shows that in creating these ad hoc tribunals, the Security Council walks a fine line between human rights and sovereignty. The Report indicates that an international court could be created by treaty. (305) This would be in keeping with traditional expressions of international law. Yet, a treaty would not have served the needs of expediency and universality required by the situation. In concluding that the creation of the ad hoc tribunal would be legal, the Report argues that widespread violations of humanitarian law "constitute a threat to international peace and security" (306) and that the Security Council has precedent to establish subsidiary organs for the purpose of restoring and maintaining international peace and security. (307) These statements relate to U.N. Charter Chapter VII, which allows the Security Council to take action to maintain or restore international peace and security. (308) This shows the connection between the scope of power for the Security Council and the sovereignty rights of member states. The Security Council's authority comes from the grant of power by the nations of the world in signing the U.N. Charter. (309)

The Security Council depends on this grant of power in order to take action.

Nonetheless, the Secretary General makes clear that the Security Council has no power to legislate for member states. (310) The function of the ad hoc tribunal is merely to give effect to existing humanitarian law, which exists as part of the body of international law and binds all the nations of the world. (311) The report states:

> It should be pointed out that, in assigning to the International Tribunal the task of prosecuting persons responsible for serious violations of international humanitarian law, the Security Council would not be creating or purporting to 'legislate' that law. Rather, the International Tribunal would have the task of applying existing international humanitarian law. (312)

Nor would the tribunal be subject to the political demands of the Security Council; as a judicial instrument, it necessarily would be independent. This organ would, of course, have to perform its functions independently of political considerations; it would not be subject to the authority or control of the Security Council with regard to the performance of its judicial functions. (313)

In articulating the basis for this new type of court, the Secretary General wrestles with the need for expediency under principles of humanitarian law, the legal conscripts regarding universal application of jurisdiction, and the limitations on the Security Council's authority to infringe upon the sovereignty rights of the member states. (314)

These sovereignty rights are not mere legal buzzwords, but are instead firmly rooted in the U.N. Charter itself:

> Article 2
>
> The Organization and its Members, in pursuit of the Purposes stated in Article 1, shall act in accordance with the following Principles.
>
> 1. The Organization is based on the principle of the sovereign equality of all its Members. ...
>
> 7. Nothing contained in the present Charter shall authorize the United Nations to intervene in matters which are essentially within the domestic jurisdiction of any state or shall require

the Members to submit such matters to settlement under the present Charter; but this principle shall not prejudice the application of enforcement measures under Chapter VII. (315)

Thus, the Security Council cannot intervene in domestic matters. It may take action regarding matters that are international in nature and that further its Chapter VII mandate of maintaining or restoring international peace and security. (316)

This is the scope of authority within which the international ad hoc criminal tribunals must operate. They cannot act, as domestic courts do, merely to procure justice and protect the populace. (317) Their aim is to protect international peace and security through the enforcement of international humanitarian law. (318) The unspoken premise beneath this extension of Security Council authority is that grave breaches of international humanitarian law constitute depravations of the general peace and security of the world itself. (319) This conclusion is not, however, immediately apparent. Rather, it only becomes clear when viewing the nature of the evidence that the prosecution must present to justify its case:

> The factual allegations are usually that entire cities and towns have been devastated, their populations murdered, imprisoned, or forcibly removed. The sheer scale and severity of these factual circumstances are never encountered in national prosecutions. The aim before international criminal courts is not to try 10,000 murder cases, but to conduct crimes against humanity and war crimes' trials. (320)

Thus, ad hoc tribunals prosecute the crimes of waging illegal war and other acts that are so severe and horrific that they threaten the security of humanity itself. This distinction is vital in determining how to implement future ad hoc tribunals. They must work to protect the interests of the world at large and to maintain or restore international peace and security. A further limitation on future ad hoc tribunals is that they must enforce current international law. (321) This is the limited scope within which ad hoc tribunals operate.

A. Internet War Crimes Tribunals Bring Certainty and Security to the Internet

Within these limitations lies an opportunity for the international community to come together to create positive international rules regulating Internet conduct. Those rules would tell the world what is allowed and what is not. For states engaged in the lawful use of force, those rules would identify what types of Internet attacks are sanctioned. The rules would also prohibit acts that are out of bounds--those so repugnant as to threaten the security of the people around the world.

As explained above, the international community possesses a strong incentive to encourage the use of Internet attacks as a viable weapon for states engaged in the lawful use of force. Some Internet attacks may be used in lieu of kinetic military attacks. The advantage is that Internet attacks greatly lessen the threat to life and property while still disrupting and even debilitating their target. It is more humane to shut down a power plant through an Internet attack than it is to bomb it and its occupants. Another advantage available to the framers of these rules is the opportunity to reevaluate the standards regarding military targets. Under current international law, the military cannot lawfully target civilians or their property. Such conduct is considered immoral and illegal. Yet, if the attack created inconvenience, economic damage, loss of productivity, and general disorder, would that attack, even if aimed at civilians, be immoral? The experience of Estonia in 2007 provides an example.

Recall that in early May 2007, Estonia experienced a series of Internet attacks aimed at both government and private entities. (322) The attacks lasted for weeks. (323) They inflicted serious economic losses, served to isolate Estonia from the world, and resulted in major inconvenience and chaos. (324) Estonia viewed the attack as an act of war. (325) Estonia had reason to judge itself threatened, as it may have sustained economic losses that equaled or surpassed the effects of a kinetic attack. Yet, the world essentially ignored the situation. The attacks were certainly illegal, certainly wrong, but probably not as immoral as traditional kinetic alternatives. Interestingly, Estonia's experience shows that the civilian populace feels the direct effect of such attacks. In the context of modern use of force, that might be desirable if it prevents the escalation of kinetic military engagement and further loss of life.

At the time of the creation of the Hague Rules and the Geneva Conventions, most combatants in warfare were soldiers. (326) Nations felt the effect of wars in the loss of their sons, husbands, or brothers, or in the physical devastation of property. This horrible price of war provided a strong deterrent to states. War today is more sanitized. This is not to downplay the immense sacrifices made by the men and women in today's armies, or those of their families; however, soldiers and their families must pay a horrendous price while much of the rest of the public is distanced and mollified. Changes in military operations now allow for this type of disconnect.

Technology allows modern armies to operate with fewer soldiers. Perhaps more importantly, many of today's soldiers are paid contractors. In the Iraq war, the United States employs over 160,000 (327) private contractors. (328) Many of these contractors perform functions that resemble our traditional notions of soldiers, such as communications, security, interrogation, and transport. (329) The incorporation of private contractors into military operations eases political tensions, allowing politicians more leeway to engage in unpopular military campaigns.

Thus, the price we pay today for aggression comes more and more from the pockets of our citizens, not our hearts or our homes. Yet, who should feel the effects of the decision to use our military? Should it not be those who have the power to affect policy and choose more peaceful methods of dispute resolution? Comparison to the field of immunology explains the benefit of expanding potential targets to include economic damage through cyber attacks.

Within the field of Internet technology, Romero contends that Internet security threats are an overall benefit. Scholars like Romero see the Internet from an immunological point of view, comparing it to a biological organism. (330) The Internet, like a biological organism, becomes stronger when attacked because it creates new defenses and ways to deal with the attacks, they contend. (331) As a result, the stress of the attack results in a better overall system because technology must change and advance to meet the new threat. (332) According to this immunological approach, a populace feeling the economic effects of a cyber attack may respond with intelligence and innovation, finding new ways to resolve differences and realizing that aggression is a less palatable option. From this point of view, it behooves the international community to reassess the Hague and Geneva Conventions in light of Internet attacks and to reassess the appropriate targets while exercising the lawful use of force. It may be appropriate to create international rules to allow for attacks that reach civilians and civilian property, if those attacks are economic in nature and do not create physical harm.

As much as the international community would benefit from allowing certain types of Internet attacks during the lawful use of force, there are other types of Internet attacks that should be per se illegal, attacks which intend to create the kinds of devastation and horrific loss of life that the Geneva Conventions seek to prohibit. A cyber attack that intentionally causes a dam to open and flood areas, killing people and devastating towns must be considered a war crime or a crime against humanity and punishable before an international ad hoc tribunal. (333) Thus, the international community should seize the opportunity to create an addendum to the current jus in bello regime specifically dealing with the Internet. Because the Internet brings a different dynamic to issues of use of force, specific rules are necessary.

At the same time, the international community should address jus ad bellum law, prohibiting the preemptive use of cyber attacks by states. As explained above, international law gives no definite answer concerning the legality of a state-sponsored Internet attack. Some would say that a cyber attack does not fall within the definition of the use of force because it is not an armed attack pursuant to Articles 2(4) and 41 of the U.N. Charter. (334) Others would look to the effects of the attack or the critical nature of the target to determine the lawfulness of the attack. (335) Nonetheless, the current framework of the U.N. Charter gives uncertain results.

The law should be clear on this matter. Preemptive cyber attacks provide a tempting and powerful weapon against adversaries. They can be used insidiously. Hidden attacks can wage a war of attrition on a computer network that over time can seriously threaten the utility of an organization's system. Use of such preemptive or unprovoked measures hardly fortifies international peace and security, nor does their use comport with any civilized person's notion of fair play or decency. States like Estonia should have the support of clear international rules that proclaim that, in the event an Internet aggressor is traced to officials of another state, such an attack is illegal. (336)

International law should also clarify its position regarding non-state actors. International law currently cannot define the legal status of non-state aggressors who use kinetic technology to inflict massive death and destruction. It certainly will do no better in the case of an Internet attack. Some cyber attacks may be domestic in nature and would be handled under domestic criminal law and the Cybercrime Convention where applicable. (337) Other attacks that threaten international peace and security through their heartless and horrific effects should constitute war crimes, whether the actor is a public official or a private citizen. Those acts should be punishable before ad hoc war crimes tribunals, and Internet aggressors should know of their potential fate before they choose to act.

B. The Design of New International Sanctions for Cyber Attacks

The acts referred to above, implicating international peace and security and prosecutable in ad hoc international tribunals, should be written with the same specificity as domestic criminal statutes. This Article will refer to these crimes as Internet war crimes. The international agreement should identify the elements of the offenses of Internet war crimes in clear terms.

There are many reasons supporting the need for specificity. Not the least of these is that international law requires it. The following international agreements proclaim that nations may not prosecute individuals for acts that were not identified as crimes at the time of the alleged offense: the Universal Declaration on Human Rights, the International Covenant on Civil and Political Rights, the American Convention on Human Rights, the African Charter on Human and People's Rights, and the European Convention on Human Rights. (338) In addition, codification of international criminal provisions for cyber attacks adds to the efficacy and fairness of those rules. The clarity brought by codification creates greater deterrence because actors will know what is forbidden. (339) Similarly, the legitimacy gained by codification increases their deterrence value. (340) In other words, people are more likely to follow rules that carry the authority of legitimacy.

Also, the clarity brought by codification will make future international prosecutions less vulnerable to attack by defendants challenging the fairness of the prosecution. (341) The current system of humanitarian law bases prosecutions on norms of international law. (342) Because these norms are not codified and are based largely on international treaties meant to bind states and not intended to police the acts of individuals, their usefulness as the basis of a criminal prosecution is highly problematic:

> The drafters of the [ICCTY and ICCTR] Statutes drew on a range of prohibitions in the laws of armed conflict and other branches of humanitarian law found in fundamental sources, such as the Geneva Conventions. . . The prohibitions and standards in these conventions and in the body of international humanitarian law generally, although plainly established as part of the international legal framework, were directed principally to setting standards and prohibitions which bind States. They include little of the specificity necessary for the application of a prohibition as a criminal law which binds individuals in their personal capacity, with potentially penal consequences. (343)

For example, Article 3(e) of the Geneva Convention prohibits rape but does not identify the elements of rape. (344) As a result, this vagueness forced the ad hoc tribunals to rely on general principles found in domestic state practice or domestic statutory or case law to define the elements of the crimes themselves. (345) Some prosecutions failed due to a lack of applicable substantive law. (346) This weakness should not be imported into the international sanctions for Internet war crimes. Rather, the international agreement should state the elements of the offenses clearly and not rely on domestic law for predicate offenses or assume that the court can discern which international norms to apply to cases.

In addition, because Internet war crimes prosecutions might require proving that the effects are felt in many jurisdictions, not just one, there might not be a single jurisdiction that could provide the elements of a predicate offense. (347) Furthermore, unlike traditional war crimes or crimes against humanity, the international legal system has not established international norms governing criminal offenses for these types of cyber attacks. Certainly, the Cybercrime Convention was created because of the lack of uniformity in cybercrime laws. (348) Consequently, the international system criminalizing Internet war crimes should provide a strong and fair structure, clearly stating the elements of the offenses.

Author Davis Brown provides a starting point for creating this international agreement. He has created the Draft Convention Regulating the Use of Information Systems in Armed Conflict. (349) This draft convention is reproduced in its entirety in Appendix B of this Article. While this Article challenges Brown's preference for enforcement through the ICJ, his approach is important because it develops the law of jus in bello regarding cyber attacks. (350) It identifies what states should and should not be allowed to do in waging "information warfare." (351) The draft convention begins with definitions that identify the types of attacks at issue and the status of the actors involved. (352) Like the current international regime, the draft convention creates two categories of actors relating to aggression: combatants and noncombatants. (353) States, through the use of combatants, are allowed to engage in cyber attacks in certain circumstances. (354) Noncombatants are not. (355)

In many ways, the draft convention tracks the jus in bello provisions of the Geneva Conventions in prohibiting perfidy, attacks on medical or religious facilities, or attacks creating severe damage to the natural environment. (356) In others, the draft convention is tailored with the Internet in mind. For example, in certain circumstances, it prohibits the use of malicious code or the alteration of images or sounds. (357) The draft convention also prohibits identity theft, fraudulent commercial transactions, and attacks on personal finances as viable means of information warfare. (358) Many of these suggestions are on point and should be incorporated into the international rules regulating cyber warfare.

The weakness of Brown's draft convention is that it is incomplete. First, it fails to address questions related to jus ad bellum. (359) Additionally, the draft convention fails to provide for noncombatant liability for Internet war crimes. (360) Third, it fails to identify the potential penalties for violations of its provisions. (361) Because it is limited to the actions of states, the remedies available would be monetary damages. (362) This does not address, however, issues of humanitarian law and its applicability to the individuals responsible for war crimes or crimes against humanity. Although the draft convention prohibits these types of acts, it says nothing about the consequences for individuals in committing those acts. (363) Furthermore, the draft convention fails to identify the specific elements of particular offenses. Finally, the draft convention limits information warfare to military targets and leaves few options open for states to use cyber attacks as an economic pressure on a populace to end a military conflict. As explained above, allowing cyber attacks to create economic pressure on the populace to end its support for a war may be instrumental in ending military conflicts. Thus, Brown's suggestions on the whole are very worthwhile, but they are just the beginning.

Regarding jus ad bellum, the international agreement regulating cyber warfare should provide that a cyber attack by one state cannot be used in anticipatory self-defense. A cyber attack should never be allowed as a first strike. It is too easy to start wars this way, and retaliation can be just as easy, just as quick, and just as reckless as traditional warfare. Additionally, many types of cyber attacks are insidious and may not be detected for years. (364) After-the-fact justifications for this type of attack would be difficult to muster in the face of a bright line rule prohibiting first-strike cyber attacks. Furthermore, use of cyber attacks in retaliation for kinetic or Internet attacks should be proportional. The drafters of this international agreement will find it challenging to provide sufficient guidance on this issue.

To some degree, comparing cyber attacks to kinetic attacks is like comparing apples to oranges. The framers of the agreement should adopt some method of comparison, whether based on estimates of monetary losses, disruption, or military advantage. In any event, the agreement should make clear that a limited military attack by one state will not justify a retaliatory cyber attack that cripples portions of the enemy's critical infrastructure.

Additionally, the international agreement should create specific statutory offenses for Internet war crimes that apply to both combatants and noncombatants. These war crimes should be aimed at prohibiting cyber attacks that result in physical injury to civilians, or that result in large-scale destruction of nonmilitary targets and that are calculated to create terror in the populace. The crimes should identify not only the elements of the offenses, but also the penalties that will apply to violators. Finally, the agreement should indicate that an Internet war crime will be enforced by an application made by a complaining state to the U.N. Security Council for the authorization of an ad hoc tribunal to prosecute the crime. In the event that the Security Council grants the application, it will provide the enacting legislation that outlines the procedural rules and the situs of the tribunal. (365)

Finally, the agreement must address the issue of cyber attacks by states that result in economic losses or inconvenience to civilians. Certainly, this kind of attack will create pressure on the populace and, presumably, on the heads of state to find solutions to end a military conflict. Nonetheless, this type of attack also carries risks. Economic attacks could be used by an enemy country to target certain ethnic groups, gain economic advantage in international trade, or influence international exchange rates. Similarly, cyber attacks whose effects are felt only by a nation's lower-income citizens seem inordinately burdensome and unjust. This Article does not attempt to provide solutions to these issues, but recognizes that they must be faced and debated. There are good reasons to provide allowances for economic attacks, and reasons for caution as well. Ultimately, the framers of the agreement must decide this issue.

This agreement, constructed to address issues of cyber attacks by state and non-state actors, will provide guidance to the international community concerning what is allowed on the Internet and what is not. Such an agreement will deter those who would use the Internet as a tool for aggression and allow the system to have greater security and legitimacy through clear rules and a structure for enforcement. In realizing these goals, the agreement will facilitate the benefits we all gain from the Internet's free flow of information.

VI. CONCLUDING THOUGHTS ABOUT THE GLOBAL MOVEMENT TOWARD DECENTRALIZATION

The past fifteen years have seen an accelerated melding of the global system. The Internet and the movement toward supranational mechanisms such as international courts are both the causes and results of this globalization. (366) These changes affect the personal lives of the world's population by changing the civilian's relationship with sovereign nations. From a broader perspective, it becomes clear that globalization and technology are pushing the world toward a decentralization of power that goes in two directions. The power that the sovereign traditionally has held since the Peace of Westphalia is being redistributed into the hands of individuals, international mechanisms, and organizations. (367) This movement has been well documented. (368)

From the perspective of many political scientists, sovereignty is waning. "[A] basic assumption shared by many thinkers. is that the sovereignty of the nation-state is under threat, if not already seriously undermined." (369) The power previously held by national governments is being redistributed:

> [t]he sovereignty of the nation-state is redirected in two opposite directions; into 'network states' such as the European Union, or into identity groups such as the environmental groups, cults, survivalist movements, virulent forms of nationalism that do not correspond to states, ethnic groups and so on. The state still performs its functions, but more and more of these occur at an international level, enabled by networked communications. (370)

According to these authors, the cause of this change in sovereignty is the globalization of the world's economy, effectuated by the rise in and capacity of information and communications technologies. (371) The second cause is "identity politics," i.e., changing allegiances from the nation to other groups. (372)

Other authors provide powerful empirical evidence of this phenomenon. Thomas Friedman presents tangible examples of the "flattening" of the world. (373) A flat world to Friedman is a world in which economic power and opportunity is exercised through horizontal, not vertical, means. (374) This dynamic of flattening is occurring because of the Internet, computer technology, and the events brought about by the end of the Cold War, including China's decision to join the WTO. (375) This reshapes the flow of creativity, (376) allowing individuals to "participate and make their voices heard." (377) These changes also enable outsourcing at every level and increase the flow of goods across the world. (378) A flat world is one in which everyone has the same access to information. (379) Friedman quoted Russian-born Google cofounder Sergey Brin: "[i]f someone has broadband, dial-up, or access to an Internet cafe, whether a kid in Cambodia, the university professor, or me who runs this search engine, all have the same basic access to overall research information that everyone has. It is a total equalizer." (380)

A flat world is also one that is wireless. (381) This wireless world is "'digital, mobile, virtual, and personal,' as Carly Fiorina, former HP CEO, put it." (382) New technologies push the world toward individualization and the unbounded flow of information and creativity, as well as its fruits. (383) Thus, as the boundaries of the Cold War dissolved and the "Iron Curtain" came down, the technology of the computer and the Internet emerged to intricately connect the world through entirely new networks of relationships and systems of engagement.

The world population is now interconnected through a complex web of technology and is more interdependent than ever before. (384) Yet, international law does not reflect this intermingled, interdependent world; it is running to catch up, and its drill command is twofold: "sovereignty" and "morality." (385) These two themes run throughout the U.N. Charter, and the tension between these themes is apparent in the framework of our international legal system.

The international community must find a compromise between the necessities of these demands for sovereignty and morality in order to bring security to the Internet. It must facilitate the good that is to be gained from the Internet and its promise of a "world without borders." At the same time, the international community must work to protect the security and values of an individuated world. This world of the individual no longer complacently permits torment and ruination dealt by any source--whether that source is a state, a group, or a movement. (386) The rise of the human rights movement and its accompanying panoply of courts demonstrate this.

Nonetheless, international law cannot accommodate a truly borderless legal system. The world is not "flat" enough for that. The real world has changed, to be sure, but the process of "flattening" has yet to be realized. The world still hosts powerful states and states that have yet to find their power in the international arena. This second variety of states is protected by their rights to sovereign power. (387) International lawmakers must continue to learn and create new ways of balancing these competing needs. One way, in the context of Internet security, is to formulate specific rules regarding Internet conduct. The fairness and good that flow from such rules would provide security and guidance to the world at large. These rules should give due accord to the interests of sovereignty and allow all nations the opportunity to establish their capacity to rule their dominion where capable and appropriate. At the same time, these rules have great capacity to spur new, more humane modes of resolving international disputes. As such, the international community should be quick to embrace this sorely needed good.

The opportunity, therefore, is not just to readjust the rules of international conflict, but also to codify international criminal law relating to Internet attacks. This process of codification must occur through an international agreement because the Security Council cannot legislate for the world. Yet, the deterrent effect of clear and concise rules, telling states and non-state actors alike what is allowed and what is not, will provide a vehicle for Internet security. In creating such clear rules, the international community will embrace the good that the Internet offers while deterring its dangerous elements. The issues before the framers of such rules are complex. Not all states possess the same technological capacity. Not all states possess the same technological defenses. In creating a fair system, the creators of the new rules will have to balance these dynamics. Yet, to choose to do nothing is a poor option. The international community can instead respond to the harbinger of the Estonia attack and give fair rules to the world--to do nothing seems like an invitation of the worst kind. The world demands more, and the international community right now holds the tools to create a fair and safe system. The challenge to the international community is to create rules that provide the certainty of specific criminal provisions, the security of legitimate mechanisms of enforcement, and the flexibility needed to deal with future advances in technology.

Sharon Stevens is a practicing attorney. She received her JD and LLM at The University of Iowa College of Law. She specializes in criminal and international law.

NOTES AND APPENDICES DELETED

Part IV

FINANCE CRIME

8

Financial Institutions Fraud

Twenty-Fifth Edition of the Annual Survey of White Collar

Sara A. Hallmark and Megan L. Wolf.

ANNUAL REVIEW OF SOCIOLOGY Copyright 1997 by ANNUAL REVIEWS, INC..
Reproduced with permission of ANNUAL REVIEWS, INC. in the format Textbook via
Copyright Clearance Center.

I. INTRODUCTION

This article reviews the development and application of three federal criminal statutes that govern offenses by or against financial institutions. Section II analyzes the Bank Fraud Statute ("BFS"), (1) which targets fraud against financial institutions. Section HI reviews the Financial Institutions Reform, Recovery, and Enforcement Act of 1989 ("FIRREA"), (2) which regulates the conduct of officers, directors, and third-party fiduciaries who fraudulently managed financial institutions. Section IV examines the Bank Secrecy Act ("BSA"), (3) which prohibits deceptive financial transactions designed to evade certain reporting requirements.

II. BANK FRAUD STATUTE

This Section examines the Bank Fraud Statute ("BFS"), 18 U.S.C. [section] 1344. Specifically, this section addresses the purpose and broad scope of [section] 1344; delineates its five statutory elements; discusses several defenses to a charge of bank fraud; and presents the sanctions associated with the statute.

A. Purpose and Scope

The purpose of the BFS is to protect the interests of the federal government as an insurer of financial institutions. (4) The driving force behind the legislation was the Supreme Court's decision in Williams v. United States, (5) where the Court held that the crime of making false statements to financial institutions did not encompass check-kiting schemes. (6) Congress passed [section] 1344 in reaction to this ruling primarily to give the government the ability to prosecute check-kiting. (7) The BFS also criminalized a variety of other schemes intended to defraud federally insured financial institutions. (8)

The BFS covers a variety of offenses against financial institutions, including check-kiting, (9) check forging, (10) false statements and nondisclosures on loan applications, (11) stolen checks, (12) unauthorized use of automated teller machines ("ATMs"), (13) credit card fraud, (14) student loan fraud, (15) bogus transactions between offshore "shell" banks and domestic banks, (16) automobile title frauds, (17) diversion of funds by bank employees, (18) submission of fraudulent credit card receipts, (19) false statements intended to induce check cashing, (20) and mortgage fraud. (21) Thus, [section] 1344, as enhanced by the Financial Institutions Reform, Recovery, and Enforcement Act of 1989 ("FIRREA") (22) and the Crime Control Act of 1990, (23) has become the basic provision for prosecuting bank fraud offenses.

Although broadly written, [section] 1344 fails to reach all crimes relating to financial institutions. For example, money laundering, (24) bribery of bank officials, (25) fraud committed by a bank on its customers, (26) and schemes to pass bad checks (27) fall outside of the scope of [section] 1344. Similarly, [section] 1344 does not protect a bank customer against "pigeon drop" schemes, (28) where funds are legally withdrawn from an account by the customer and are no longer under the custody or control of the institution when the fraud occurs. (29)

B. Elements of an Offense

To obtain a conviction under [section] 1344 the government must show that the defendant: (i) knowingly, (ii) executed or attempted to execute, (iii) a scheme or artifice, (iv) to either (a) defraud, or (b) through false or fraudulent pretenses, representations, or promises, obtain the monies or other property of, (v) a financial institution. (30)

1. Knowledge

The knowledge element of the BFS requires the government to prove that the defendant had the intent to defraud a financial institution. (31) Such intent "cannot be inferred from the mere presence of a defendant at the scene of the crime or association with members of a criminal conspiracy." (32) However, intent can be adduced from the totality of the evidence, (33) including evidence of prior similar acts (34) and other circumstantial evidence. (35) Further, the defendant need not conceal his actions from bank employees to find intend to defraud. (36) If the government proves the defendant had such fraudulent intent, it need not demonstrate either that the defendant received personal benefits (37) or contemplated harm to the bank. (38)

The knowledge element of [section] 1344 also does not require the government to prove that the defendant knowingly made direct misrepresentations to the financial institution. (39) Whether the defendant knew the financial institution was federally insured is irrelevant to establishing knowledge. (40) Instead, the question turns on what the defendant actually knew about the status of the accounts used. (41) Finally, a showing of "reckless indifference" (42) or "conscious avoidance" (43) to a scheme to defraud can also support an inference of knowledge.

2. Executes or Attempts to Execute

Under the BFS, the government must prove that the defendant either executed or attempted to execute a scheme to defraud a financial institution. (44) Where an indictment includes both the "execute" and "attempt to execute" language, a jury must unanimously find the defendant guilty on only one alternative to convict; that is, find that the defendant either executed or attempted to execute a scheme to defraud a financial institution. (45)

Section 1344 does not specifically define "execution." Thus, courts consider the following factors in determining whether a scheme has been executed: (i) the ultimate objective of the scheme, (ii) the nature of the scheme, (iii) the benefits intended, (iv) the interdependence of the acts, and (v) the number of parties involved. (46) Since it is possible to have more than one execution of the same criminal scheme, courts often must determine if separate acts are independent executions or simply acts in furtherance of one execution. (47) An act constitutes a separate execution if it is intended to put the financial institution at a "separate, distinguishable financial risk from the risk it already undertook." (48)

Actions subsequent to the fraud do not affect consideration of whether a person executed or attempted to execute a scheme. A person who knowingly defrauds a financial institution of capital on false pretenses is violating [section] 1344 even if the money is eventually returned. (49)

3. Scheme or Artifice

Section 1344 further requires a "scheme" or "artifice" to defraud a financial institution. (50) The courts have liberally construed this language to include "any plan, pattern or [course] of action ... intended to deceive others to obtain something of value." (51)

In Neder v. United States, (52) the Supreme Court unanimously held that materiality is an element of a scheme or artifice to defraud under [section] 1344. (53) A representation is material if it has "a natural tendency to influence, or [is] capable of influencing, the decision of the decision-making body to which it was addressed," (54) but need not induce actual reliance. (55) The Court explicitly stated that, "under the rule that Congress intends to incorporate the well-settled meaning of the common-law terms it uses, we cannot infer from the absence of an express reference to materiality that Congress intended to drop that element from the fraud statutes." (56) Therefore, materiality is required under [section] 1344, but reliance is not; the scheme "need not have exerted actual influence, so long as it was intended to do so and had the capacity to do so." (57)

Several circuits require that the defendant expose a financial institution to an actual risk of loss to find the scheme to defraud element. (58) However, other circuits have chosen to consider risk of loss as a relevant, but non-essential, element in the determination of a scheme to defraud. (59)

4. To Defraud or Obtain Monies By False or Fraudulent Pretenses

The fourth statutory element, to defraud or obtain monies by false or fraudulent pretenses, comprises two alternative parts. The government may seek a conviction under either [section] 1344(1), implementing a scheme or artifice to defraud, or [section] 1344(2), employing false pretenses or promises to obtain property owned, held, or controlled by a financial institution. (60) An indictment that refers generally to [section] 1344 may refer to either clause. Because the clauses are treated independently, an act may be criminal under [section] 1344 by falling under either prong. (61)

There are two important distinctions between subsections (1) and (2) of [section] 1344. First, subsection (1) does not require false or fraudulent misrepresentations, a requirement under (2). (62) Second, subsection (1) does not require the defendant to deprive the financial institution of monies or property, whereas subsection (2) does. (63)

a. Defrauding a Financial Institution

Courts have broadly construed the phrase "a scheme or artifice to defraud" using the mail and wire fraud statutes (64) as a guide. (65) Section 1344(1) requires that the defendant attempt to obtain something of value from the financial institution, though it need not be through false or fraudulent pretenses. (66) Thus, crimes involving no false representations to a financial institution, such as check-kiting, can be prosecuted under [section] 1344(1). (67) Additionally, [section] 1344(1) encompasses crimes where the scheme defrauds a financial institution of "the intangible fight of honest service." (68) The principle of "honest service" developed out of the doctrine that the withholding of "the honest and faithful discharge of ... fiduciary duties can constitute a scheme to defraud" even without the loss of money or property. (69)

b. False or Fraudulent Pretenses

The false or fraudulent pretenses prong of [section] 1344 covers a wide range of actions, including forging sale documents, falsifying appraisals, and failing to repay bank loans. (70) Misrepresentations may be explicit or implicit, (71) and need not be made prior to a transfer or transaction. (72) However, merely presenting checks that were knowingly drawn on insufficient funds may not be covered by the language of [section] 1344(2) because, "technically speaking, a check is not a factual statement at all, and therefore cannot be characterized as 'true' or 'false." (73)

5. Financial Institution

The final element of the BFS requires that the victim or intended victim be a federally insured financial institution. (74) Without proving that the financial institution was federally insured, the government cannot obtain a conviction. (75) While the amended statute does not define "financial institution," the government applies the definition found in [section] 20(1) of Tire 18. (76)

Under [section] 1344, a financial institution is considered a victim of bank fraud if it is an actual or intended victim, and the bank need not be the immediate victim of the fraud. (77) Courts typically find banks to be victims of fraud if the bank had "custody or control" of the funds in question, thereby exposing the bank to a risk of loss or civil liability. (78)

A scheme to defraud a third party of money held in a bank account constitutes a violation of [section] 1344. (79) A conviction under [section] 1344 will not stand, however, unless the defendant's scheme to defraud the third party also intended to defraud a federally insured financial institution. (80) Fraudulent ATM transactions, which simultaneously defraud the legal account holder and the financial institution from which the funds are withdrawn, are commonly prosecuted under [section] 1344. (81)

C. Defenses

While opposing prosecution under BFS, the following defenses have been asserted: (i) the financial institution did not have "custody or control" of the assets in question; (ii) the defendant was acting in good faith; and/or (iii) the indictment was multiplicitous. This part will examine these defenses and their respective limitations.

1. Custody or Control

As a defense to [section] 1344, defendants can argue that the assets were not "under the custody or control" of a federally insured financial institution at the time of the alleged fraud. (82) A defendant will not succeed on this defense, however, by merely showing that the bank's funds were not directly at risk; as long as the funds involved were under the custody or control of the financial institution, actual loss to the bank is not required. (83) It is also important to note that the "custody or control" requirement has been interpreted broadly to find defendants guilty of bank fraud where a financial institution has any property interest in the funds targeted by the scheme. (84)

2. Good Faith

A second potential defense under [section] 1344 is to attack the government's evidence of knowledge and intent by demonstrating the defendant's good faith. (85) Good faith is a complete defense to bank fraud because it is inconsistent with finding intent to defraud. (86) However, it is important to note that a defendant is not considered to have acted in good faith when an illegal act is performed with a belief that the act was legal. (87) Further, the good faith defense does not apply in situations where the defendant made a deliberate and conscious effort to avoid discovering the details of suspicious activity, (88) or had a belief that the collusion of the defrauded bank's officers in the scheme removed the fraudulent component. (89)

3. Multiplicity of the Indictment

A multiplicitous indictment is one that charges a single offense in multiple counts. (90) Such an indictment creates the risk that a defendant will be punished twice for "the same conduct, in violation of the Constitution's guarantee against double jeopardy. (91) When a defendant charged with multiple counts under [section] 1344 and other statutes raises a double jeopardy defense, courts examine whether the various counts require proof of different elements or factors. (92)

The circuits that have addressed multiplicity in the context of bank fraud have generally agreed that the BFS only imposes punishment for each "execution" of the scheme, unlike the mail and wire fraud statutes, which punish each "act" undertaken in furtherance of a scheme to defraud. (93) Thus, the critical inquiry is whether a defendant executed a "scheme." (94) The answer to that question is often obscure (95) and highly fact-specific. (96) Some courts utilize a definition of "execution" that closely parallels the definition of "acts in furtherance of a scheme" as applied in the mail and wire fraud statutes. (97) Other courts employ a definition that characterizes several acts in aid of a single scheme as a single execution. (98) One commentator has noted that, to eliminate the confusion and inconsistency surrounding the term "execution," Congress must strike the term from the statute or the Supreme Court must clarify its specific meaning. (99)

To find a middle ground between these two extremes, an increasing number of circuits have held that a single scheme can be executed several times, giving rise to multiple counts. (100) Prosecutors can avoid the multiplicity defense by carefully crafting bank fraud indictments to allege only one execution. (101)

D. Penalties

Sentences for violations of federal criminal laws are determined with reference to the United States Sentencing Guidelines ("Guidelines"). (102) In 2005, the Supreme Court severed the provision that made the Guidelines mandatory, rendering them "effectively advisory." (103) The Guidelines are one among a number of factors--including the purposes of punishment and the nature and circumstances of the offense, and the history and characteristics of the defendant--to be considered in imposing federal sentences. Accordingly, the Guidelines remain highly relevant despite their advisory nature.

Violators of [section] 1344 face maximum penalties of one million dollars in fines or thirty years imprisonment, or both, (104) and are sentenced under section 2B 1.1 of the Guidelines. (105) The base offense level under the Guidelines is seven. (106) If the loss at issue exceeds five thousand dollars, the offense level is increased by an amount indicated in the loss table. (107) In situations where the wrongdoer's gross receipts from the crime exceed one million dollars, the court should apply a level increase of two, (108) unless the fraud "substantially jeopardized the safety and soundness of a financial institution," in which case a level increase of four is warranted, regardless of the amount of gross receipts, (109) If the offense level remains below twenty-four after this increase, then the offense level will be adjusted upward to twenty-four. (110)

The Guidelines also provide for an increase in offense level by two for fraudulent schemes (1) "committed through mass-marketing"; (111) (2) committed from outside the United States; (112) (3) relocated to another jurisdiction to evade prosecution; (113) or (4) that "involved sophisticated means." (114) In these cases, if the offense level is less than twelve after the two-level increase, it increases to twelve. (115) Additionally, some courts allow for a two-level sentence reduction, specified within the Guidelines, when a defendant accepts responsibility for his offense. (116)

In applying the Guidelines, courts may find the facts necessary to calculate the appropriate range, (117) and are not bound by an overly strict standard when calculating the damage done by a defendant. (118) While courts must use accurate information in applying the Guidelines, they are not required to rely on exact figures. (119)

III. THE FINANCIAL INSTITUTIONS REFORM, RECOVERY, AND ENFORCEMENT ACT

Congress passed the Financial Institutions Reform, Recovery, and Enforcement Act of 1989 ("FIRREA") (120) in the wake of the widespread savings and loan association failures of the 1980's. (121) This statute restructured the federal depository insurance system, abolishing the insolvent Federal Savings and Loan Insurance Corporation ("FSLIC"), and shifting its regulatory responsibilities to the Federal Deposit Insurance Corporation ("FDIC"). (122) Additionally, FIRREA created the Office of Thrift Supervision ("OTS"), an office within the Department of the Treasury headed by a director with "extremely broad regulatory powers to 'provide for the examination, safe and sound operation, and regulation of savings associations.'" (123) Because the savings and loan crisis was caused, in part, by fraud and insider abuse, (124) FIRREA amended the Federal Deposit Insurance Act ("FDIA") to improve supervision, enhance enforcement powers, and define and expand the direct civil and criminal liability for financial institutions and personnel that do not employ safe and sound banking practices. (125)

A. Purpose and Scope

FIRREA was passed with the intention to "both clean up the savings and loan mess and prevent future disasters." (126) FIRREA liability reaches all "institution-affiliated parties" ("IAPs") who breach fiduciary duties, violate any law or regulation, or employ unsafe or unsound practices likely to cause an adverse effect on the insured depository institution. (127) FIRREA enhanced the enforcement powers of banking regulatory agencies to include the authority to: require restitution, reimbursement, indemnification, or guarantee against loss; restrict the institution's growth; dispose of any loan or asset; rescind agreements or contracts; require the employment of qualified personnel; and take other actions deemed necessary. (128) It also establishes a tiered schedule of increased civil money penalties for violations by insured financial institutions and IAPs, (129) a criminal penalty for participating in the affairs Of a bank holding or saving and loan holding company by individuals prohibited from engaging in the affairs of a financial institution, (130) and enhances criminal penalties for certain financial institution offenses. (131) Additionally, FIRREA authorizes increased appropriations for the Department of Justice to investigate and prosecute financial institution-related offenses, and for the Federal courts system to adjudicate. (132)

B. Civil Sanctions for Insider Fraud

The federal government instituted various civil sanctions as supplemental enforcement mechanisms to combat banking fraud. All of the federal bank regulatory agencies, including the FDIC, OTS, and the Office of the Comptroller of the Currency ("OCC"), have administrative authority to protect federally insured institutions after exposure to fraud. Section 1818 of Title 12 (133) authorizes civil penalties (134) and the removal and prohibition of insiders and other affiliated parties from participating in the affairs of an insured institution. (135) The sanctions apply not only to insured institutions, but also to all IAPs. (136)

The OCC's Fast Track Enforcement Program supplements these efforts to prevent insiders guilty of low level violations from remaining employed in the banking industry. (137) The program enables the agency to investigate improper activities by IAPs to seek restitution for losses caused by insider fraud, and to prohibit certain IAPs from serving in financial institutions. (138) The program selection criteria include: (i) subject must be a bank employee, officer, director or principal shareholder of a national bank; (ii) subject has engaged in "a criminal act involving dishonesty or breach of trust" against said institution; (iii) "unqualified evidence" of the offense at issue exists, or the subject admits responsibility; (iv) at least $5,000 was lost by the bank or involved in the transaction; and (v) "prosecution of the person was declined by federal law enforcement agencies" or the subject has entered a pre-trial diversion program. (139) If the "criteria are not met in only a minor way, the OCC is required to see if additional information would allow the criteria to be met." (140)

1. Applicable Law in Civil Cases under FIRREA: Atherton v. FDIC

The administrative actions taken by the FDIC have lead to significant questions concerning conflicts between federal and state common law. In Atherton v. FDIC, (141) the Supreme Court resolved a circuit split over whether federal or state law supplies the rules of decision in civil prosecutions brought by the FDIC against former principals of failed federally chartered financial institutions. (142) The Court in Atherton held: (i) federal common law does not provide a standard of care for officers and directors of federally insured savings institutions, and (ii) the relevant federal statute, (143) which requires gross negligence for the director and officer liability, does not preclude states from enacting stricter standards making principals liable under a lesser standard of negligence. (144)

The Supreme Court addressed two questions: (i) whether the federal interest in a FIRREA prosecution is sufficiently strong to justify application of a federal common law tort standard, (145) and (ii) how to reconcile the differences between the statutory standard and the controlling state common law standard. (146)

On the first question, the Court held the FDIC's interest in defining the standard of liability in a FIRREA prosecution did not present one of the "few and restricted instances" warranting a federal override of the standards of care established by state common law. (147) In the Court's opinion, state law posed no significant conflict with, or threat to, a federal interest in this situation. (148)

With respect to the second question--the effect of [section] 1821(k)'s gross negligence standard on the common law duty of care borne by bank officers and directors--the Court characterized the provision not as a displacement of common law standards, but rather as a statutory floor. (149) On this point, the Third Circuit had expressed concern that if the gross negligence standard of [section] 1821(k) (which applies after a bank has entered receivership) displaced the common law ordinary negligence standard, bank principals could effectively shield themselves from the consequences of negligent behavior by allowing their banks to go insolvent. (150) The Supreme Court allayed this concern by reading the statute's standard of care as "only a floor--a guarantee that officers and directors must meet at least a gross negligence standard. It does not stand in the way of a stricter standard that the laws of some states provide." (151) Section 1821 (k) further provides that "[n]othing in this paragraph shall impair or affect any right of the corporation under other applicable law," (152) which the Court read to embrace state law as well as other federal statutes. (153) Thus, state law provides the duty of care owed by principals of federally chartered institutions, provided it is not more lenient than [section] 1821 (k). (154)

2. Federal Common Law Post-Atherton: "No-Duty" Rule

The Court in Atherton resolved the question of the standard of care owed by principals of federally chartered institutions; however, the decision left unresolved the issue of whether the duty of care owed by the FDIC following receivership is controlled by federal common law in the face of conflicting state law.

In FDIC v. Healey, (155) the district court rejected the bank principals' affirmative defenses (permitted by Connecticut state law) of contributory negligence and failure to mitigate damages--both based entirely on post-receivership conduct of the FDIC--on the ground that federal common law permits no duty of care to be placed on the FDIC following receivership of a failed financial institution. (156) In response to the contention that Atherton does not allow federal common law to control where state law supplies a standard of care, the court distinguished Atherton both factually and in terms of legal principle. First, the court noted that Healey concerns post-receivership conduct of the FDIC, while Atherton concerns pre-receivership conduct of bank officials; bank failure and receivership present a wholly different legal landscape in which the Atherton analysis is not appropriate. (157) Second, within that post-receivership landscape are federal interests of a type not present in Atherton, which "require deference to the discretionary actions of the FDIC." (158) In light of these countervailing federal interests as to the regulation of federally chartered institutions, to allow "state-law affirmative defenses would assail the discretionary acts of the FDIC [and] would present a significant conflict between federal policy and state law." (159)

Another district court, however, arrived at the opposite conclusion. In Resolution Trust Corp. v. Massachusetts Mutual Life Insurance Co., (160) the court allowed the defendant institution to assert contributory negligence and failure to mitigate damages (affirmative defenses permitted by New York state law) by the FDIC post-receiversliip. (161) The court rejected the federal common law "no-duty" rule, stating that the Supreme Court's decision in O'Melveny & Myers v. FDIC (162) had effectively ended the use of federal common law in cases governed by FIRREA. (163) Also, the court noted that provisions of FIRREA explicitly incorporated state standards of law, and that Atherton had affirmed such incorporation. (164) Finally, although the court acknowledged that FIRREA vests discretion in the FDIC acting in receivership, the court also stated FIRREA "contains no provision that insulates the FDIC from state law affirmative defenses regarding the FDIC's post-receivership conduct." (165)

3. Federal Common Law Post-Atherton: D'Oench Doctrine
The Court's decisions in O'Melveny and Atherton sparked a debate in the circuits over whether another area of federal common law, the D'Oench doctrine, survived the adoption of 12 U.S.C. [section] 1823(e). (166) The D'Oench doctrine states that in defending against the FDIC's attempt to collect on a bank note, the borrower or guarantor of the note is estopped from using a secret side agreement (or representation by the bank) that would misrepresent the financial status and obligations of the institution to creditors or regulatory agencies. (167)

The Eleventh Circuit ruled in Motorcity of Jacksonville, Ltd. v. Southeast Bank, N.A. (168) that the federal common law D'Oench doctrine survives Atherton. In Motorcity, the court relied on D'Oench to reject a debtor's proffer of an unwritten side agreement with a failed bank as a defense against FDIC collection. (169) At issue on appeal to the Supreme Court was "whether Congress intended FIRREA to supplant the previously established and long-standing federal common law D'Oench doctrine." (170)

After Atherton, the Supreme Court remanded Motorcity for further consideration. On remand, the Eleventh Circuit affirmed its earlier holding, distinguishing Atherton on two grounds. First, since Atherton held that state common law, not [section] 1821, supplied the controlling legal standard, the case provides no support for the contention that the federal common law D'Oench doctrine had been superseded by federal statute. (171) Second, unlike the common law principle offered by the government in Atherton, the establishment of the D'Oench doctrine came after the creation of the Erie doctrine (172) because it presented one of the "few and restricted" instances where there is "a significant federal interest and policy which warranted the creation of a federal common law rule." (173)

The Eleventh Circuit does not stand alone in its view of the D'Oench doctrine. The Fourth Circuit, acknowledging that [section] 1823 "substantially codified" the common law D'Oench doctrine, also held that it does not preempt it. (174) The Fifth Circuit also continues to recognize the D'Oench doctrine. (175)

A number of circuits disagree with the view that D'Oench survives the Court's decision in Atherton. Relying on O'Melveny, (176) the Third Circuit held in FDIC v. Deglau (177) that the D'Oench doctrine does not survive [section] 1823. (178) Finding that the statute is "detailed and comprehensive," the Court held it does not need D'Oench to supplement it. (179) Similarly, both the Eighth and D.C. Circuits have held that the D'Oench doctrine is preempted by [section] 1823. (180) The Ninth Circuit has limited D'Oench's applicability to cases involving the FDIC, but has declined to go as far as to hold that D'Oench was overruled by Atherton and O'Melveny. (181)

The Tenth Circuit has taken a more moderate approach to the D'Oench debate. This circuit views [section] 1823 simply as a codification of the D'Oench doctrine, and applies virtually the same standards under either controlling authority. (182) The Second Circuit applies a similar approach. (183)

C. Criminal Penalties Under 12 U.S.C. [section] 1818(j)

As noted above, 12 U.S.C. [section] 1818(e) provides for the administrative removal of institution-affiliated parties ("IAPs") and prohibits any further participation in the affairs of the institution by those parties. (184) After an IAP has been served with a removal or suspension order under the civil provisions of FIRREA, [section] 1818(j) criminalizes the further participation of IAPs in the affairs of an FDIC-insured institution, absent prior written approval from the FDIC. The criminal penalty applies regardless of whether the underlying offenses, standing alone, would subject the offender to administrative sanctions only. (185)

1. Scope

The criminal penalties in [section] 1818(j) apply to bank officers, employees, controlling stockholders as well as appraisers, attorneys and accountants who: (i) cause financial loss to an FDIC-insured institution; (ii) prejudice the interests of the bank's depositors; or (iii) receive financial gain or other benefit from the violation. (186)

Before FIRREA, IAPs could escape prosecution by resigning before the federal regulator began removal proceedings. (187) Consequently, Congress closed this legislative loophole by including a provision in FIRREA that allows banking regulators to initiate enforcement of penalties against individuals for six years after the date of their termination of employment. (188)

2. Elements

The elements of a [section] 1818(j) criminal violation require that the defendant (i) knowingly participates in the conduct of the affairs of any insured financial institution; (ii) is subject to an order which prohibits such participation; and (iii) has not received written approval from a regulatory agency prior to such participation. (189)

3. Penalties

Section 1818(j) provides that any violator shall be fined not more than $1,000,000, imprisoned for up to five years, or both. (190)

D. Double Jeopardy

As mentioned above, FIRREA provides for both criminal and civil sanctions for violations by financial institutions and IAPs. (191) Because the FDIC has the authority to enforce both types of penalties, this dual role has occasionally produced double jeopardy concerns. (192)

1. The Dual Functions of the FDIC

The enabling legislation of the FDIC endows it with dual roles: (i) governmental regulator of federally-insured financial institutions, and (ii) receiver of failed institutions. (193) In the latter role, it stands in the shoes of the bankrupt institution, acting as a private party vindicating private interests. (194) When an FDIC-insured institution enters receivership the agency will act as both regulator and receiver for the same institution. (195)

2. Hudson v. United States

The Supreme Court dispensed with the argument that the Double Jeopardy Clause constituted a barrier to future prosecution by the FDIC acting in its capacity as receiver in Hudson v. United States. (196) The Court stated that the Fifth Amendment's Double Jeopardy Clause only protected defendants from successive criminal punishments, and that sanctions imposed by the FDIC post-receivership are civil. (197) The Court abrogated its previous holding in United States v. Halper, (198) where it bypassed the threshold question of whether the successive punishments were criminal and instead focused on whether the sanction was so grossly disproportionate to the harm caused to be deemed punishment. (199) Although Hudson acknowledged that a civil sanction might constitute criminal punishment when the "clearest proof" indicates that it is so "punitive in purpose or effect as to transform what was clearly intended as a civil remedy into a criminal penalty," (200) the Court concluded that such a determination of the sanction's criminal nature must first be established before implicating the Double Jeopardy Clause. (201) The Court also determined that, when a civil sanction has been designed to serve as a deterrent, a deterrence purpose alone does not alone transform civil sanctions into criminal punishment. (202) Thus, prior civil proceedings, resulting in sanctions that fall to rise to Hudson's standard for criminality, fail to trigger the Double Jeopardy Clause.

IV. THE BANK SECRECY ACT

This Section addresses the Bank Secrecy Act's statutory rationales, examines its record-keeping requirements, and discusses its reporting requirements and analyzes structuring offenses.

A. Purpose

In 1970, Congress enacted the Currency and Foreign Transactions Reporting Act, commonly referred to as the Bank Secrecy Act (203) ("BSA"), out of concern for the increasing use of financial institutions to launder unreported income and obtain funds illegally.

(204) The BSA requires that financial institutions maintain "certain reports or records where they have a high degree of usefulness in criminal, tax, or regulatory investigations or proceedings, or in the conduct of intelligence or counterintelligence activities, including analysis, to protect against international terrorism." (205) This enhanced documentation of the deposit, transfer, and exchange of currency can be used to uncover illegal concealment and thus improve the effectiveness of law enforcement. (206)

The increased interest in and importance of the BSA is due to the recognition of the global scale on which illicit funds enter the flow of commerce through legitimate financial institutions. The illegal drug trade and global terrorism groups rely heavily on these financial institutions to integrate and move such funds. (207)

The BSA, as amended, (208) requires financial institutions (209) to keep certain account records of currency transactions over indicated dollar amounts, to report currency transactions of more than $10,000 into or out of a financial institution, and to disclose certain accounts that United States citizens and residents hold at foreign financial institutions. (210) The BSA imposes civil and criminal penalties on financial institutions, non-financial trades, and businesses. (211)

In response to the terrorist attacks of September 11, 2001, Congress enacted the USA Patriot Act of 2001. (212) This legislation amended several provisions of the BSA, including broadening the definition of "financial institution" under the BSA; (213) expanding requirements for financial and certain non-financial trade or business institutions with respect to recordkeeping; reporting, due diligence, anti-money laundering programs, "Know Your Customer" standards, (214) and correspondent accounts with foreign shell banks; and increasing the civil and criminal penalties for certain BSA offenses. (215) Title III of the USA Patriot Act is the International Money Laundering Abatement and Anti-Terrorist Financing Act; its purposes include: preventing, detecting, and prosecuting international money laundering and the financing of terrorism; providing a clear national mandate for subjecting those foreign jurisdictions and financial institutions that pose particular, identifiable opportunities for criminal abuse to special scrutiny; and ensuring that all appropriate elements of the financial services industry are subject to appropriate requirements of reporting potential money laundering transactions to the proper authorities. (216)

B. Title I: Record-Keeping Requirements

Provisions of the BSA authorize the Secretary of Treasury to promulgate regulations requiring banks, securities brokers and dealers, and certain uninsured financial institutions to maintain adequate records of customers' transactions that can be used in criminal, tax, or regulatory investigations and proceedings. (217) Any person who willfully or through gross negligence falls to maintain the requisite records or causes a violation of any of the requirements under the BSA or those prescribed by the Secretary of the Treasury ("Secretary") can be subject to civil (218) and/or criminal penalties. (219) The record-keeping requirements facilitate law enforcement investigations and proceedings as well as "the conduct of intelligence and counterintelligence activities ... to protect against domestic and international terrorism." (220)

Each financial institution must retain for a period of not less than five years the records of: (i) certain transactions that exceed $10,000; (221) (ii) the sale or issuance of bank checks, cashier's checks, traveler's checks, or money orders that equal or exceed $3,000; (222) and (iii) funds transfers and transmittals that equal or exceed $3,000. (223) Additional record-keeping requirements apply specifically to banks, securities brokers and dealers, casinos, and currency dealers and exchangers. (224)

1. Additional Records to Be Retained by Banks

The regulations promulgated by the Secretary set forth several record-keeping requirements specifically for banks. (225) Every bank is required to obtain the taxpayer identification number of the customer involved, or of a person having a financial interest in the certificate where there are two or more customers, "[w]ith respect to each certificate of deposit sold or redeemed ... [and] each deposit or share account opened." (226) The Secretary is also required to prescribe regulations establishing minimum standards for financial institutions and their customers regarding the verification of the identity of the customer opening of an account. (227) In response, the Federal Reserve Board, Federal Deposit Insurance Corporation, Financial Crimes Enforcement Network ("FinCEN"), (228) National Credit Union Administration, Office of the Comptroller of the Currency, Office of Thrift Supervision, and the United States Department of the Treasury issued a rule requiring covered institutions to institute a written Customer Identification Program ("CIP"). (229) Each CIP must at minimum: (1) provide for a system of internal controls to assure ongoing compliance; (2) provide for independent testing to assure ongoing compliance; (3) designate individuals responsible for coordinating and monitoring ongoing compliance, and; (4) provide training for appropriate personnel. (230) Treasury has promulgated similar customer identification rules governing futures commission merchants and introducing brokers (231) as well as mutual funds and investment companies. (232)

In addition, a bank must maintain records covering a wide range of business transactions, including checks, money orders drawn, or deposits in amounts in excess of $100 and foreign financial transactions in excess of $10,000. (233) Finally, the bank must retain signatory cards for each account-holding customer. (234) These documentation requirements facilitate the identification of customers and the transactions in which they engage to decrease the incidence of fraudulent banking activity.

2. Additional Records to Be Retained by Brokers and Dealers in Securities

A broker or dealer in securities must secure and maintain the taxpayer identification numbers of customers within thirty days of the date a brokerage account is opened. (235) The broker or dealer in securities must also retain the original copies of the following: (i) a signature card or grant of trading authority; (ii) each record required by the Securities Exchange Commission under 17 C.F.R. [section][section] 240.17a-3(a)(1)-(3), (5)-(9); (iii) a record of each remittance or transfer of funds, or of currency, checks, other monetary instruments, investment securities, or credit of more than $10,000 to a person, place, or account outside the United States; and (iv) a record of each receipt of currency, checks, other monetary instruments, investment securities, or credit of more than $10,000 received on any one occasion directly from any person, place, or account outside the United States. (236)

3. Additional Records to be Retained by Casinos (237)

Casinos, in addition to what is required by virtue of being included in the definition of financial institution, (238) are subject to several additional record keeping requirements. (239) Casinos must verify and record the name, social security number, and permanent address of each person who has a financial interest in funds deposited with an account opened by, or credit extended by the casino. (240)

In addition, for each account, casinos must retain records of: (i) each receipt of funds, (241) bookkeeping entry, (242) statement, ledger card, or other account record; (243) (ii) all credit extension exceeding $2,500, including the terms and conditions, and repayments; (244) (iii) advice, requests, or instruction received or given by the casino regarding foreign transactions; (245) (iv) all records that would be needed to reconstruct a deposit or credit account; (246) (v) all records required under local regulations; (247) and (vi) all records used to monitor a customer's gaming activity. (248) Casinos must also log certain transactions involving checks in the amount of $3,000 or more. (249)

4. Additional Records to be Retained by Currency Dealers and Exchangers

Currency dealers and exchangers must secure within thirty days the name, address, and taxpayer identification numbers of each person opening an account or receiving a line of credit, (250) and of each person who presents a certificate of deposit for payment into that account. (251)

In addition, currency dealers and exchangers must maintain a system sufficient to prepare an accurate balance sheet and income statement (252) and retain records of the following: (i) bank statements; (253) (ii) daily work records needed to reconstruct currency transactions with customers and foreign banks; (254) (iii) exchanges of currency in excess of $1,000; (255) (iv) signature cards; (256) (v) transfers exceeding $10,000 to a person, account, or place outside the United States; (257) (vi) receipts of funds exceeding $10,000; (258) and (vii) information needed to reconstruct an account and trace a deposited check in excess of $100. (259) These requirements do not apply to banks that offer currency services to their customers as an adjunct to their regular service. (260) These record-keeping requirements promote transactional transparency among banks, brokers and dealers in securities, casinos and currency dealers and exchangers.

5. Enforcement and Penalties

Overall enforcement of record-keeping requirements is delegated to the Assistant Secretary (Enforcement) of the Treasury. (261) Authority to examine financial institutions to determine compliance is delegated according to the nature of the institutions. (262) Authority to investigate criminal violations is delegated to the Commissioner of Internal Revenue, (263) and authority to impose civil penalties is delegated to the Assistant Secretary (Enforcement) of the Treasury and, in the Assistant Secretary's absence, the Deputy Assistant Secretary (Law Enforcement) of the Treasury. (264)

A willful or grossly negligent violation of any recordkeeping requirement under Chapter 21, Title 12 of the United States Code is punishable by a civil penalty of up to $10,000. (265) A willful violation is also punishable by a criminal penalty of a fine of up to $1,000 and imprisonment for up to one year, or both. (266) If the willful violation is committed in furtherance of the commission of a violation of Federal law punishable by imprisonment for more than one year, the violation is punishable by a fine of up to $10,000 or imprisonment for up to five years, or both. (267)

A willful violation of any recordkeeping requirement under Subchapter II, Chapter 53, Title 31 of the United States Code is punishable by a civil penalty of "not more than the greater of the amount (not to exceed $100,000) involved in the transaction (if any) or $25,000." (268) A negligent violation is punishable by a civil penalty of up to $500, (269) and a pattern of negligent violations is punishable by an additional civil penalty of up to $50,000. (270) A willful violation is also punishable by a criminal penalty of a fine of up to $250,000 or imprisonment for up to five years, or both. (271) If the willful violation is committed while violating another United States law or as part of a pattern of any illegal activity involving more than $100,000 in a twelve month period, the violation is punishable by a fine of up to $500,000 and imprisonment for up to ten years, or both. (272)

A willful violation of any recordkeeping requirement under Part 103, Chapter I, Subtitle B, Title 31 of the Code of Federal Regulations is punishable by a civil penalty of up to $1,000. (273) A negligent violation is punishable by a civil penalty of up to $500. (274) A willful violation is also punishable by a criminal penalty of a fine of up to $1,000 and imprisonment for up to one year. (275) If the willful violation is committed in furtherance of the commission of any violation of Federal law punishable by imprisonment for more than one year, the violation is punishable by a fine of up to $10,000 and imprisonment for up to five years, or both. (276)

C. Title II: Reporting Requirements

1. Money Services Businesses

Under Title II of the BSA, (277) all money services businesses must register with the Secretary and maintain a list of authorized agents in compliance with Treasury regulations. (278) The phrase "money services businesses" (279) encompasses currency dealers and exchangers; (280) check cashers; (281) money transmitters; (282) and any issuer, seller, or redeemer of traveler's checks, money orders, or stored value. (283) All money services businesses were required to register with the Secretary by December 31, 2001, and re-registration is required every two years thereafter. (284) Registration includes the information required under Title II of the BSA and any additional information as required by the Treasury Secretary. (285)

In addition, each January 1, a money services business must update the information on a list of its agents, (286) including each agent's name, address, telephone number, and types of services provided; (287) the name and address of any depository institution where the agent has a transaction account; (288) and the months of the previous year in which the agent's gross transaction amount exceeded $100,000. (289) This list must be made available upon request to FinCEN or any appropriate law enforcement agency. (290) Failure to comply with any requirement can result in a $5,000 civil penalty per day of violation, (291) a civil action to enjoin the violation, (292) and criminal penalties that may include fines and imprisonment. (293) Under this disclosure and registration scheme, the Secretary has a database of information detailing money services businesses' accessibility and the type of business to make available to law enforcement.

2. Currency Transaction Reports

Under Title II of the BSA, (294) domestic financial institutions must report transactions involving the payment, receipt, or transfer of United States currency in excess of $10,000. (295) The Currency Transaction Report ("CTR") is the primary reporting mechanism for financial institutions other than casinos. (296) The Treasury also requires certain other reports. (297)

a. Domestic Currency Transactions

Under 31 U.S.C. [section] 5313, financial institutions, other than casinos, are required to "file a report of each deposit, withdrawal, exchange of currency or other payment or transfer by, through, or to such financial institution which involves a transaction in currency of more than $10,000." (298) Under certain circumstances, transactions that individually are less than $10,000 but in aggregate total more than $10,000 during any single business day are treated as a single transaction. (299) Banks do not have to report the transactions of "exempt persons," (300) including other banks, (301) government agencies and entities, (302) and entities and their subsidiaries listed on the New York Stock Exchange, the American Stock Exchange, the NASDAQ Stock Market, or any of these markets' subsidiaries. (303) Banks also do not have to report certain payroll withdrawals, (304) or any transaction with a commercial enterprise that meets specified criteria. (305)

Casinos are required to "file a report of each transaction in currency, involving either cash in or cash out, of more than $10,000." (306) Multiple transactions are treated as a single transaction if "the casino has knowledge that they are by, or on behalf of, any person and result in either cash in or cash out totaling more than $10,000 during any gaming day." (307) A casino is deemed to have knowledge if any employee of the casino, acting within the scope of his or her employment, has knowledge either directly or through review of casino records. (308)

A violation of [section] 5313 is punishable by up to five years' imprisonment and a fine of up to $250,000, (309) or by ten years' imprisonment and up to a $500,000 fine where the offender commits the violation while violating another federal law or as part of a pattern of illegal activity involving more than $100,000 in a twelve-month period. (310) In addition, the unreported cash or monetary instrument is subject to civil (311) or criminal (312) forfeiture. Only willful violations are punishable under [section] 5322, and the government must therefore show that the defendant had knowledge of the legal duty to report and "acted with knowledge that his conduct [to avoid reporting] was unlawful." (313)

b. Foreign Currency Transactions

Banks and other depository institutions as well as non-banking enterprises in the United States must file periodic reports (314) "with respect to specified claims and liabilities positions" in foreign countries. (315) Non-banking enterprises must file reports on deposits and certificates of deposit with foreign banks as well as monthly and quarterly reports on "specified claims and liabilities positions with unaffiliated foreigners." (316) Both banks and non-banking enterprises must report on "domestic and foreign long-term securities or other financial assets with foreign residents." (317) The civil and criminal penalties imposed for violations of other sections of the BSA do not apply to foreign currency transactions. (318) Instead, the penalty provision for proscribed foreign currency transactions limits the civil penalty to $10,000. (319)

c. Transactions with Foreign Financial Agencies

A foreign resident or citizen doing business in the United States who engages in any transaction with any person associated with a foreign-based financial agency must keep records and file reports that include the identities of the participants, their legal capacities, the real parties in interest, and descriptions of the transactions. (320) Furthermore, persons having a financial interest in a foreign-based financial account must report those interests on their annual federal income tax returns. (321)

3. International Transportation of Currency and Monetary Instruments Reports

Under 31 U.S.C. [section] 5316, a person who "transports, is about to transport, or has transported" currency or monetary instruments exceeding $10,000 out of, into, or through the United States "at one time," (322) or who receives such an amount from abroad, (323) must file a Report of International Transportation of Currency or other Monetary Instruments ("CMIR"). (324) Failure to file a CMIR can result in a criminal penalty, as well as forfeiture of the amount transported. (325)

a. Elements of the Offense

The elements of a CMIR criminal offense under [section] 5316 are: (i) a legal duty to file a CMIR; (ii) knowledge of the reporting requirement; and (iii) willful failure to file the CMIR. (326)

i. Legal Duty to File

The regulations impose reporting requirements on any person receiving or transporting currency or other monetary instruments exceeding $10,000 at one time out of, into, or through the United States. (327) The report must contain the "amount, the date of receipt, the form of monetary instruments, and the person from whom received." (328) The regulations exempt certain entities from filing a report when transporting currency in excess of $10,000. (329) The Secretary's definition of "at one time" includes attempts to structure the transaction so as to avoid reporting requirements. (330) The division of money among several people to avoid triggering reporting requirements is also prohibited. (331)

The legal duty to report attaches at the time of entry or departure or within 15 days of receipt of funds from abroad. (332) A violation occurs upon failure to report and is determined on a case-by-case basis. (333) The offense of bulk cash smuggling is triggered when a person knowingly conceals more than $10,000 of currency or other monetary instruments on his person or in luggage with the intent to evade a currency reporting requirement under [section] 5316 (334) by transporting or transferring such currency or monetary instruments. (335) One district court, eliciting a general principle from the holdings of various circuit court cases, stated, "the 'time of departure' from the country is reached when one is reasonably close, both spatially and temporally, to the physical point of departure itself, and manifests a definite commitment to leave." (336)

ii. Knowledge

Knowledge of the reporting requirement forms an essential element of a [section] 5316 violation. (337) The government may prove knowledge by showing that the government placed travelers on sufficient notice of the reporting requirements. (338) Notice is sufficient where the government has posted signs near the areas of departure, (339) where stated orally by Customs officers, (340) and where the defendant has previously reported transporting monetary instruments. (341) Proficiency in the English language is not required where the government has taken steps to provide notice to those of limited English competency. (342)

The knowledge requirement may be difficult to meet where the defendant either enters or leaves the United States without passing through an established port of entry or departure. (343) Courts may infer knowledge, however, from the surrounding facts and circumstances. (344)

iii. Willful Violation of the Reporting Requirement

Only willful violations are criminally punishable under [section] 5316. (345) The government must therefore show that the defendant had knowledge of the legal duty to report and "acted with knowledge that his conduct [to avoid reporting] was unlawful." (346) The structuring prohibition has been extended by [section] 5324 (including conduct calculated to avoid the reporting requirements of [section] 5316), [section] 5325 (requiring banks to report sales of bank checks and other instruments of $3,000 or more), and [section] 5326 (authorizing the Secretary to promulgate additional reporting requirements for certain domestic currency transactions). (347) The government is not required to demonstrate that the defendant acted willfully for [section] 5324 structuring offenses. (348)

b. Enforcement and Penalties

Enforcement of [section] 5316 is delegated by the Secretary to the Commissioner of Customs. (349) As with violations of other provisions of Title II, a [section] 5316 violation is punishable by up to five years' imprisonment and a fine of up to $250,000, (350) or by ten years' imprisonment and up to a $500,000 fine where the offender commits the violation while violating another federal law or as part of a pattern of illegal activity involving more than $100,000 in a twelve-month period. (351) In addition, the unreported cash or monetary instrument is subject to civil (352) or criminal (353) forfeiture.

c. Defenses

Convictions for [section] 5316 violations generally have withstood Fourth and Fifth Amendment challenges. Courts have uniformly held that warrantless searches authorized by [section] 5317(b) (354) are constitutional under the Fourth Amendment. (355) Searches of persons entering or leaving the United States fall within the border search exception to the Fourth Amendment. (356) Moreover, the reporting requirement does not violate the individual's Fifth Amendment protection against self-incrimination. (357) The imposition of criminal (358) or civil forfeiture under 31 U.S.C. [section] 5317(c) in connection with a [section] 5316 violation,

however, is vulnerable to challenge under the Eighth Amendment's
Excessive Fines Clause (359) and possibly under the Fifth
Amendment's Double Jeopardy Clause. (360)

i. Excessive Fines

In United States v. Bajakajian, (361) the Supreme Court held that
imposition of a criminal forfeiture (362) in a [section] 5316
conviction was punitive and, therefore, constituted an illegitimate
Eighth Amendment fine. (363) In its first application of the
Excessive Fines Clause, (364) the Court adopted the standard of
"gross disproportionality" to determine whether a punitive forfeiture
is constitutionally excessive. (365) Applying this standard, the Court
found the magnitude of the $377,144 forfeiture grossly
disproportional to the gravity of the defendant's offense. (366) The
Court noted that the offense was solely one of reporting; the violation
was "unrelated to any other illegal activities"; the defendant did not
"fit into the class of persons [money launderers, drug traffickers, tax
evaders, etc.] for whom the statute was principally designed"; the
forfeiture greatly exceeded the maximum the defendant could have
been fined; and the harm caused by the defendant's action--depriving
the government of information--was minimal. (367)

Civil in rem forfeiture pursuant to [section] 5317 can
constitute impermissible punishment under the Eighth Amendment.
(368) Civil in rem forfeitures traditionally had been viewed as
nonpunitive because they were not punishments against an individual
for an offense; however, the Bajakajian Court, while distinguishing
criminal from nonpunitive, civil in rem forfeiture, noted that:

> It does not follow ... that all modem civil in rem forfeitures
> are nonpunitive and thus beyond the coverage of the
> Excessive Fines Clause ... [A forfeiture] is a 'fine' for Eighth
> Amendment purposes if it constitutes punishment even in
> part, regardless of whether the proceeding is styled in rem or
> in personam. (369)

Although forfeiture of property as an instrumentality of a
crime may also serve a remedial, non-punitive statutory purpose,
(370) the Court rejected this characterization of unreported currency
because it does not "bear any of the hallmarks of traditional civil in
rem forfeitures." (371) The Bajakajian Court, finding that the
forfeiture did not serve a remedial purpose by compensating the
Government for a loss, affirmed the Ninth Circuit's reasoning that the
currency did not facilitate the commission of a crime and was
"merely the subject of the crime of failure to report." (372) "Cash in a

suitcase does not facilitate the commission of that crime as, for example, an automobile facilitates the transportation of goods concealed to avoid taxes," thus, the currency was not an instrumentality of the drug-related offense. (373)

ii. Double Jeopardy

The rejection by the Bajakajian Court of the claim that currency forfeiture for a [section] 5316 offense acted as a remedy (374) may have made [section] 5317(c)(2) regarding civil forfeiture more vulnerable to challenge as punitive in effect, thus violating the Double Jeopardy Clause when imposed in conjunction with criminal penalties. Under the Court's analysis in United States v. Ursery, (375) the most significant factor in determining whether a nominally civil forfeiture proceeding is punitive and criminal in effect for double jeopardy purposes is whether the statute serves non-punitive, remedial goals. (376) However, courts thus far have held that imposition of a [section] 5317(c)(2) civil forfeiture in addition to criminal penalties does not violate the Double Jeopardy Clause. (377)

The courts are likely to treat a [section] 5317(c)(1) criminal forfeiture imposed for a [section] 5316 offense differently. Although Bajakajian expressly invalidated the contested criminal forfeiture under the Excessive Fines Clause, (378) the Court's reasoning strongly suggests that the forfeiture can be challenged under the Double Jeopardy Clause. In holding that a criminal forfeiture neither serves a remedial purpose nor applies to the instrumentality of a crime, the Court indicated that the statutorily-directed imposition of this criminal forfeiture upon a person convicted of a [section] 5316 violation would constitute double jeopardy. (379) Post-Bajakajian jurisprudence contains no case in which a court has faced such a claim.

4. Structuring Transactions to Avoid Reporting Requirements

The BSA (380) makes it a criminal offense to: (i) "cause or attempt to cause" a report not to be filed; (381) (ii) cause or attempt to cause a report to be filed with "a material omission or misstatement of fact;" (382) or (iii) structure or assist in structuring financial transactions to avoid or attempt to avoid reporting requirements. (383) Structured transactions are those involving monetary instruments that, when acquired or deposited individually, are less than $10,000 but that, in aggregate, total over $10,000. (384)

a. Elements

To prove a structuring offense, the government must establish that the defendant (1) engaged in acts of structuring, (2) did so with the knowledge of the reporting requirements of financial institutions under [section] 5324, and (3) intended to evade those reporting requirements. (385) For example, if a defendant deposited $8,000 into each of two or more banks with the intent to avoid the reporting requirements, the defendant would be guilty of a criminal structuring offense under [section] 5324, despite neither bank alone having a duty to report the transaction. (386) Proving the defendant acted for the purpose of evading the reporting requirements necessarily entails evidence of the defendant's knowledge of those requirements. (387) While structuring alone is not sufficient to prove a purpose of evasion of the reporting requirements, (388) the method of the structuring can be significant in evincing an intent to evade. (389) Although currently a mere showing of the defendant's intent to evade the reporting requirement may establish the requisite mental state, courts apply the law in force at the time of the alleged offense. (390)

b. Enforcement and Penalties

A structuring offense is punishable by fines under Title 18, maximum imprisonment of not more than five years, or both. (391) A person who violates the structuring statute "while violating another law of the United States or as part of a pattern of any illegal activity involving more than $100,000 in a twelve-month period" is subject to enhanced penalties such as double fines and/or imprisonment for up to ten years. (392) Property involved in or traceable to a structuring offense for which a conviction has been obtained is subject to criminal forfeiture. (393)

c. Defenses

Before the Money Laundering Suppression Act of 1994 (MLSA), good faith reliance on the advice of counsel functioned as a complete defense to the willfulness requirement. (394) Congress foreclosed this defense by removing the willfulness requirement.

Although the MLSA removed the willfulness requirement of the structuring offense, [section] 5324 still contains an implied scienter requirement of knowingly engaging in unlawful conduct. (395) Because the government must continue to prove the defendant's knowledge of the reporting requirements, [section] 5324 most likely will continue to be upheld against vagueness challenges. (396) Additionally, the statute has withstood Fifth Amendment self-incrimination challenges. (397)

To combat fraudulent transactions with financial institutions, including banks, brokers or dealers in securities, casinos and currency dealers and exchangers, Congress has increased the burden on these institutions with respect to customer identification, record-keeping, verification and disclosure. (398)

NOTES DELETED

9

The Savings and Loan Debacle, Financial Crime, and the State

K. Calavita; R. Tillman; H.N. Pontell

AUTHOR'S ABSTRACT

The savings and loan crisis of the 1980s was one of the worst financial disasters of the twentieth century. We argue here that much financial fraud of the sort that contributed to this debacle constitutes "collective embezzlement," and that this collective embezzlement may be the prototypical corporate crime of the late twentieth century. We further argue that the state may have a different relationship to this kind of financial fraud than to manufacturing crime perpetrated on behalf of corporate profits. In the conclusion, we suggest that an understanding of the relationship between financial fraud and state interests may open up new regulatory space for the control of these costly crimes. Our data come from a wide variety of sources, including government documents, primary statistical data on prosecutions, and interviews with regulators.

INTRODUCTION

The savings and loan (S&L) crisis of the 1980s was one of the worst financial disasters of the twentieth century. Experts gauge its cost to US taxpayers over 30 years to be approximately $500 billion, including interest payments on the government bonds sold to finance the industry's bailout (US General Accounting Office, cited in Johnston 1990:1; National Commission

ANNUAL REVIEW OF SOCIOLOGY Copyright 1997 by ANNUAL REVIEWS, INC. Reproduced with permission of ANNUAL REVIEWS, INC. in the format Textbook via Copyright Clearance Center.

on Financial Institution Reform, Recovery and Enforcement
[NCFIRRE] 1993:4). Reliable estimates of the percentage of losses
due to criminal wrongdoing range from 10% to 44% (Office of Thrift
Supervision 1990, Resolution Trust Corporation 1992, Akerloff &
Romer 1993, NCFIRRE 1993).

The savings and loan scandal was by no means an isolated
phenomenon in the high-flying 1980s. Insurance fraud, junk bond
manipulation, insider trading, and securities fraud took their place
alongside the thrift debacle in the headlines and on the nightly news.
By the end of the decade, Charles Keating, Michael Milken, and Ivan
Boesky had become household words, their names synonymous with
corporate wrongdoing. Besides this ill-gotten notoriety, and the vast
wealth accruing from their legitimate and illegitimate activities, these
offenders had something else in common. Unlike much of the
corporate crime of earlier decades addressed by so much of the
scholarly literature - for example, the electrical company conspiracy,
the Pinto scandal, unsafe practices in the pharmaceutical industry,
and occupational safety and health violations (Geis 1967, Cullen et al
1987, Braithwaite 1984, Carson 1981) - their crimes had nothing to
do with production or manufacturing but instead entailed the
manipulation of money.

In this case study of the savings and loan disaster, we argue 1.
that much financial fraud of this sort constitutes a specific form of
corporate crime, what we call "collective embezzlement;" 2. that this
collective embezzlement may be the prototypical corporate crime of
the late twentieth century in the United States, in that it corresponds
to the shift away from manufacturing or industrial capitalism to
finance capitalism; 3. that the state may have a different relationship
to collective embezzlement than to manufacturing crime perpetrated
on behalf of corporate profits; and, 4. that by examining this change
in the nature of corporate crime, and exploring the state's reaction to
these offenses, we may be able to delineate with more precision the
relationship between the state and economic activity and more
generally to advance state theory. In the conclusion, we suggest that
an understanding of the relationship between financial fraud and state
interests may open up new regulatory space for the control of these
costly crimes.

The data for this paper come from a wide variety of sources.
In addition to secondary data such as government documents,
regulators' reports, and other published accounts of the S&L crisis,
we have gathered two kinds of primary data. The first consists of
interviews with 105 government officials who were involved in
policymaking, regulation, prosecution, and/or enforcement, in

Washington, DC, and in field offices in California, Texas, and Florida, where the bulk of thrift(1) fraud took place. These unstructured, open-ended interviews provide substantial background information on techniques of fraud and the state response. Second, we have assembled several statistical data sets on the nature of thrift crime and the government's prosecution effort. These data were compiled from the statistics provided us by three federal agencies: the Resolution Trust Corporation (RTC, the federal agency created to manage and sell assets from seized thrifts); the Office of Thrift Supervision (OTS, which after 1989 took over from the old Federal Home Loan Bank Board the task of examination and enforcement); and the Executive Office of the US Attorneys (which made prosecutorial decisions). These statistical data provide detailed information on criminal referrals, indictments, convictions, and sentencing.

Of course the picture is far from complete and our data are necessarily imperfect. For one thing, we can never be sure how much crime goes undetected, nor whether the crimes that do come to light are representative of thrift crime in general. While this is a concern in all criminological research, it is particularly acute in the area of white-collar crime where fraud is often disguised within ordinary business transactions (Katz 1979), proving fraudulent intent is problematic, and potentially criminal wrongdoing consequently is not prosecuted. Using the "criminal referral" as our indicator of fraud goes partway in addressing this "front end" problem in white-collar crime research.

Criminal referrals, usually filed by examiners or regulators or by whistle-blowers at the institution itself, describe suspected crimes, name individuals who may have committed crimes, and estimate dollar losses. These referrals are sent through the regulatory field office to the FBI and the US Attorney's Office for investigation, where in a relatively few cases they result in indictments. The accuracy of these referrals as a measure of thrift crime - like the accuracy of statistics on "crimes known to the police" as an indicator of street crime - is limited by the existence of a "dark figure of crime," that is, the significant number of crimes that are never detected or reported. We use criminal referrals here to gain some sense of the incidence and patterns of thrift crime, with the understanding that they do not cover the entire population of fraud.(2)

The following section draws on these data to describe the basic forms of thrift fraud. As we will see, despite their apparent complexity, many of these frauds were variations on a fixed number of themes. As one of our informants put it, "It was as if someone had found a cookie cutter" (personal interview).

TYPES OF S&L FRAUD: HOT DEALS, LOOTING, AND COVERING UP

Corporate crimes of the sort involved in the savings and loan scandal are among the most complex white-collar offenses ever committed, leading one journalist to complain that when "regular people" tried to figure it out, they got "hopelessly bored and confused, as though they'd fallen a month behind in their high-school algebra class" (O'Rourke 1989:43). The concerned layperson is helped considerably by the fact that there are a limited number of basic formulas for abusing thrifts. Before describing these basic formulas, we need to note that our discussion is focused on insider abuse, by which we mean those frauds in which thrift owners and/or managers were central players, either alone or in collaboration with outsiders.

While some have implied that the industry's problems in the 1980s were brought on by outsiders who victimized thrifts (Lewis 1989, Lowy 1991), the schemes at the heart of the scandal required the participation of insiders. Our RTC data,(3) which allow us to identify the organizational positions of those cited in criminal referrals, confirm that high-level insiders were participants in the majority of these frauds. Of the 2265 criminal referrals in this data set, insiders were listed as suspects in 1294 or 63%. Far from a case of naive insiders being victimized by slick con artists, most thrift fraud at these institutions was self-inflicted.

At the most general level, we can decipher three types of insider abuse, called here hot deals, looting, and covering up. All involved one or more violations of federal bank fraud statutes, including prohibitions against "kickbacks and bribes" (18 USC Section 215); "theft, embezzlement, or misapplication of funds" (18 USC Sections 656,961c); "schemes or artifices to defraud federally insured institutions" (18 USC Section 1344); "knowingly or willfully falsifying or concealing material facts or making false statements" (18 USC Section 1001); "false entries in bank documents with intent to injure or defraud bank regulators, examiners..." (18 USC Section 1005); and/or "aiding and abetting and conspiracy" (18 USC Sections 2, 371). The following sections describe hot deals, looting, and covering up, and outline their contribution to the thrift debacle.

Hot Deals

These investment frauds were the sine qua non of insider abuse, providing both the cash flow from which to siphon off funds and the transactional medium within which to disguise it. Four kinds of transactions were central in these deals. As Senate Banking Committee staff members Alt & Siglin (1990:3-5) explain, these transactions include such schemes as land flips, nominee loans, reciprocal lending, and linked financing. Land flips involve selling a property back and forth among two or more partners, inflating the price each time and refinancing the property with each sale until the value has increased many times over. Alt& Siglin (1990:4) use the following example:

A sells a parcel of real estate to B for $1 million, its approximate market value. B finances the sale with a bank loan .... B sells the property back to A for $2 million. A finances the sale with a bank loan, with the bank relying on a fraudulent appraisal. B repays his original loan and takes $1 million in 'profit' off the table, which he shares with A. A defaults on the loan, leaving the bank with a $1 million loss.

While the flip technically could be achieved without the lending institution's participation, thrift insiders were often collaborators. For one thing, insiders were sometimes business associates of the corrupt borrowers, who at a future date would exchange the favor. In addition, while the lending institution was left with an overpriced property on its hands, in the short-term, it made upfront points and fees from the huge loans, from which executive bonuses could be drawn.

It was not unusual in the mid-1980s for partners to sit down and in one afternoon flip a property until its price was double or triple its original market value, refinancing with each flip. The playful jargon for this was "cash-for-trash," and the loans were "drag-away loans," because the intention from the beginning was to default, dragging away the proceeds. Don Dixon at Vernon Savings and Loan in Texas (nicknamed by regulators "Vermin") reportedly "flipped land deals [like] pancakes" (O'Shea 1991:76). He and associates like (fast Eddie) McBirney at Sunbelt Savings and Loan in Dallas (nicknamed by regulators "Gunbelt"), and Texas developer Danny Faulkner used land flips among other schemes to develop hundreds of miles of condominiums on I-30 northeast of Dallas. Officers at nearby Empire Savings and Loan financed the land flips to inflate the value of the land and provide the rationale for making the condo development loans despite an already glutted Dallas real estate market (personal interviews). Faulkner and his partners hosted weekend brunches at Wise's Circle Grill in the I-30 corridor. Invited guests included officials from Empire Savings and Loan, investors, appraisers, and increasingly, politicians who drew huge campaign contributions from the events. Over breakfast, properties quickly changed hands and millions of dollars of phony profits were made in a few hours (O'Shea 1991:32; personal interviews).

Nominee loans were often used in conjunction with land flips. Nominee lending used a straw borrower to circumvent loan-to-one-borrower regulations or restrictions on insider borrowing. One costly nominee loan partnership involved former dentist Duayne Christensen and real estate broker Janet McKinzie in Santa Ana, California. Christensen opened North American Savings and Loan in 1983. In partnership with McKinzie, Christensen used the thrift to make loans to his own real estate projects and to participate in multiple land flips, through a company owned and controlled by McKinzie. In one typical scheme, straw borrower David Morgan purchased property brokered by McKinzie's real estate company and financed by North American. He then resold the property at an inflated value to his own holding company. Fees and commissions poured into McKinzie's real estate brokerage. North American made upfront points and fees but apparently never saw the proceeds from the resale of any of the properties (US Congress, House Committee on Government Operations, Subcommittee on Commerce, Consumer, and Monetary Affairs 1987a:304-9). The thrift was closed in 1988, at a loss of $209 million.

Reciprocal lending was another way of circumventing restrictions against insider borrowing. Instead of making a loan directly to oneself, which would have sounded the alarm among regulators, two or more insiders at different thrifts made loans to each other. Making loans to each other is not in itself illegal, but making loans contingent on a reciprocal loan is fraud (Alt & Siglin 1990:5). These "daisy chains" often involved multiple participants, and unraveling them sometimes took investigators far afield of the original institution and exposed the complex conspiratorial quality of thrift fraud. One investigation in Wyoming in 1987 revealed a single daisy chain of reciprocal loans among four thrifts that by itself resulted in a $26 million loss to taxpayers (US Congress, House Committee on Government Operations, Subcommittee on Commerce, Consumer, and Monetary Affairs 1987b:79-80, 129-130). A Texas network included at least 74 daisy chain participants and involved all the insolvent thrifts in the state (US Congress, House Committee on Banking, Finance and Urban Affairs 1990:799-872).

Similar in logic to reciprocal lending arrangements, linked financing involves depositing money in a thrift, with the understanding that the depositor will receive a loan in return. Loan broker Mario Renda specialized in setting up linked financing deals, even advertising in the Wall Street Journal, the New York Times, and the Los Angeles Times: "MONEY FOR RENT: BORROWING OBSTACLES NEUTRALIZED BY HAVING US DEPOSIT FUNDS WITH YOUR LOCAL BANK: NEW TURNSTYLE APPROACH TO FINANCING" (quoted in Pizzo et al 1991:127). Renda placed large brokered deposits in thrifts, for which he received a finder's fee, in return for which borrowers with credit "obstacles" received a generous loan from the thrift. Response to Renda's ads was overwhelming; according to his own court testimony, Renda brokered the deposits for hundreds of linked financing schemes.

Investigators and regulators report finding variations of land flips, nominee loans, linked financing, and reciprocal lending arrangements over and over in their autopsies of seized thrifts. Many hot deals combined elements of all four transaction frauds. So-called "ADC" (acquisition, development and construction) lending is a good example. ADC lending was a form of direct investment by thrifts in the 1980s, in which thrifts provided up to 100% of the financing for a speculative development project, reaping proceeds (and collecting on the loan) only if the development turned a profit. Points, fees, and several years of interest payments were often included in the loan, so that it appeared on paper to be in good standing, and the thrift recorded income from the self-funded points and fees. Fraudulent ADC lending was at the core of the S&L debacle in Texas and helps explain continued investment in Texas commercial real estate when the market was already glutted. As the National Commission on Financial Institution Reform, Recovery and Enforcement (1993:48) explains, "ADC loans were an attractive vehicle for abuse. They bound up in one instrument many of the opportunities available." A land flip might provide inflated collateral for a generous ADC loan; the loan then might be to a straw borrower who shared the proceeds with thrift insiders (nominee lending); thrift managers might make the loan contingent on a deposit or other investment (linked financing); and/or, thrift insiders might exchange loans to finance development projects with each other (reciprocal lending arrangements). As Texas S&Ls were pumped up with these huge development loans, they reported unprecedented paper profits from which thrift insiders extracted generous bonuses and dividends - one major form of "looting."

Looting

Looting refers to the siphoning off of funds by thrift insiders and is thus more like traditional forms of crime than are the business transactions involved in hot deals. Because thrift management was doing the looting, it took different forms from a typical bank robbery or embezzlement by a lower-level employee. The most straightforward, but probably least common, way to loot was simply to remove deposits from the thrift and stash them away. Probably more common were shopping sprees with thrift funds, and excessive bonuses or other forms of compensation.

David Paul bought CenTrust Savings Bank in Miami in 1983 and quickly turned it into a megathrift with $9.8 billion in assets (Pizzo et al 1991:404-5; Lowy 1991:152-53). Paul used over $40 million of CenTrust money for a yacht, a Rubens painting, a sailboat, Limoges china, and Baccarat crystal (Lowy 1991:152). In addition, he built the 47-floor Miami CenTrust skyscraper at a cost of $170 million (Mayer 1990:77; Pizzo et al 1991:405; Lowy 1991:152-53). When CenTrust collapsed, it was the largest S&L failure in the Southeast, costing taxpayers $1.7 billion. For his part in the insolvency, David Paul was convicted of 97 counts of racketeering and fraud and sentenced to eleven years in prison (Los Angeles Times 1994:D2).

Excessive compensation schemes were another way for insiders to loot their institutions. The US General Accounting Office (GAO)(1989:21) defines "compensation" as "salaries as well as bonuses, dividend payments, and perquisites for executives." A federal regulation limits permissible compensation for thrift personnel to that which is "reasonable and commensurate with their duties and responsibilities" (GAO:21). At the most expensive failures, executives typically paid themselves exorbitant bonuses and dividends, even as their thrifts were collapsing (GAO 1989:21). For example, Don Dixon and his top executives at Vernon took more than $15 million in bonuses between 1982 and 1986, at a time when the thrift was already deeply insolvent (O'Shea 1991:217-18). During the six years that David Paul was driving CenTrust into the ground, he paid himself $16 million in salary and bonuses, $5 million of it coming in 1988 and 1989 when the thrift was piling up losses from its junk bond investments (Pizzo et al 1991:406).

Of the 26 most costly failed thrifts studied by the US General Accounting Office (GAO)(1989:21), shopping sprees and excessive compensation had occurred in the vast majority. A large proportion of prosecutions have been for such looting, probably because of the relative ease of building a convincing body of evidence for these more straightforward frauds compared to the complex business transactions involved in hot deals (personal interviews). In any case, hot deals and insider looting went hand-in-hand: The deals provided the cash flow and reported income with which to finance shopping sprees and excessive compensation - indeed the ability to siphon off phony "profits" provided the incentive for hot deals and the rapid growth they fueled.

Covering Up

As savings and loans teetered on the brink of insolvency, broken by hot deals and looting, their operators struggled to hide both the insolvency and the fraud. In some cases, the cover-up came in the form of deals whose primary purpose was to produce a misleading picture of the institution's state of health. US Attorney Anton R Valukas describes a number of such cover-up deals:

> In the prosecuted cases of Manning Savings and Loan, American Heritage Savings and Loan of Bloomingdale and First Suburban Bank of Maywood, when the [nominee] loans became non-performing the assets were taken back into the institution, again sold at inflated prices to straw purchasers, financed by the institution, in order to inflate the net worth of the bank or savings and loan. The clear purpose was to keep the federal regulatory agencies ... at bay by maintaining a net worth above the trigger point for forced reorganization or liquidation" (quoted in US Congress, House Committee on Government Operations, Subcommittee on Commerce, Consumer, and Monetary Affairs 1987b:99-100).

Insiders also could simply doctor their books to shield their thrift from regulatory action. At one S&L studied by the GAO (1989:41), three sets of books were kept - two on different computer systems and one manually. At another, $21 million of income was reported in the last few days of 1985 in transactions that were either fabricated or fraudulent, allowing the thrift to report a net worth of $9 million, rather than its actual negative $12 million (GAO 1989:44-45). McKinzie and Christensen at North America S&L prepared bogus documents when challenged by regulators. When the thrift was finally taken over, examiners found evidence of fake certificates of deposit, forged bank confirmation letters, and other cover-up materials (US Congress, House Committee on Government Operations, Subcommittee on Commerce, Consumer, and Monetary Affairs 1987a:308).

Relative Frequency of Hot Deals, Looting, and Covering Up: The Dallas OTS Files

For a more detailed picture of the part these insider frauds played in the thrift crisis, we can look at a subsample of Category 1 criminal referrals in one state, Texas. Here we rely on data from files in the Dallas Office of Thrift Supervision (OTS). This OTS office maintained computer files on all criminal referrals for thrift fraud in Texas. We selected a 20% sample from this list of 1210 criminal referrals filed between January 1985 and March 1993, by choosing every fifth referral. We then examined the actual referral forms for each of the 241 cases in our sample, as well as the numerous supporting documents that accompanied these referrals. For each case, we coded the type of suspected violation, whether insiders were involved, and the estimated loss from the suspected crime.

Our main objective was to obtain a better sense of the crimes being reported at thrift institutions. Based on a careful perusal of these referral files, we developed 11 specific categories of insider fraud (including, for example, insider loans, land flips, kickbacks, falsification of documents, etc). While many of these categories overlapped in practice, since these frauds were usually complex and often contained several layers of deception, we made distinctions according to what the primary offense or central ingredient of the suspected misconduct was. We then sorted these offenses according to whether they constituted hot deals, looting, covering up, or some other broad category of fraud. For example, insider loans and land flips are hot deals, kickbacks are a form of looting, and falsification of documents is a method of cover-up.

Of the 241 cases of suspected misconduct, 193 involved insider fraud, as opposed to victimization by outsiders, which is consistent with the RTC data discussed above. More important here, all but three of the 193 insider fraud cases involved some form of hot deals, looting, or covering up. The most common form of fraud was hot deals, with various types of such deals comprising almost 68% of these suspected frauds and contributing by far the highest price tag - over $1.08 billion out of the total $1.6 billion in estimated losses.

Hot Deals and Looting as "Collective Embezzlement"

In discussing different forms of white-collar crime, Sutherland (1983:231) described embezzlement: "The ordinary case of embezzlement is a crime by a single individual in a subordinate position against a strong corporation." Cressey, in Other People's Money (1953), focused on the lone white-collar embezzler, stealing from his or her employer. Traditionally, then, embezzlement has been thought of as an isolated act of an individual employee who steals from the corporation for personal gain.

Criminologists have typically drawn a sharp distinction between this "embezzlement" by individuals against the corporation and "corporate crime," in which fraud is perpetrated by the corporation on behalf of the corporation. For example, Wheeler & Rothman (1982:1405) speak of two distinct types of white-collar crime: "Either the individual gains at the organization's expense, as in embezzlement, or the organization profits regardless of individual advantage, as in price-fixing." Similarly, Coleman (1987:407) argues, "The distinction between organizational crimes committed with support from an organization that is, at least in part, furthering its own ends, and occupational crimes committed for the benefit of individual criminals without organizational support, provides an especially powerful way of classifying different kinds of white-collar crime."

Neglected in this dichotomy is the possibility of organizational crime in which the organization is a vehicle for perpetrating crime against itself, as in the hot deals and looting described here. This form of white-collar crime represents a hybrid between traditional corporate crime and embezzlement - crime by the corporation against the corporation - and might be thought of as "collective embezzlement." Unlike Sutherland's and Cressey's embezzlers, these "collective embezzlers" were not lone, lower-level employees but thrift owners and managers, acting in networks of coconspirators inside and outside the institution. Indeed, this embezzlement was often company policy. In some cases, it was the very purpose of the organization to provide a vehicle for fraud against itself. Wheeler & Rothman (1982:1406) have pointed to "the organization as weapon" in white-collar crime: "[T]he organization ... is for white-collar criminals what the gun or knife is for the common criminal - a tool to obtain money from victims." In the collective embezzlement of the thrift industry, the organization was both weapon and victim.

COLLECTIVE EMBEZZLEMENT AND LATE TWENTIETH CENTURY CAPITALISM

As we approach the twenty-first century, the US economy - and those of other advanced capitalist countries - is compared to a "casino" (Bates 1989:D1, Business Week 1985:78-90). In this casino economy, the largest profits are made from placing a clever bet, not making a better mousetrap. Unlike in industrial capitalism where goods and services are produced to make a profit, in finance capitalism - where the "means of production" are currency trades, corporate takeovers, loan swaps, and futures trading - profits come from "fiddling with money" (Trillin 1989). Nobel Prize winner Maurice Allais underscores the magnitude of this shift from an economy based on the circulation of goods to one circulating money itself, pointing out that "more than $400 billion is exchanged every day on the foreign exchange markets, while the flow of commercial transactions is only about $12 billion" (quoted in Bates 1989:D1).

Beginning in 1980, the futures market, in which investors gamble on the future price of hogs, grain, tobacco, and other commodities, rapidly outpaced the production of the goods whose prices were being bet on. In 1983, US futures trading totaled $7 trillion, or $28 billion a day, and by 1985, futures trading was growing at a rate ten times the rate of industrial production (Harrison & Bluestone 1988:54). The US financial market was so active that in 1984, over $4 trillion in trades came through a single investment banking firm - First Boston Corp. - more than equaling the national GNP for that year (Plotkin & Scheuerman 1994:59).

As the management of money and financial speculation outstrip production as the greatest sources of profit, this finance capitalism spawns vast new opportunities for fraud such as the hot deals and looting discussed above. Further, there are relatively few constraints or risks associated with these lucrative opportunities. Unlike corporate criminals in the industrial sector who generally commit crime to advance corporate profits and are constrained by concern for their corporation's long-term survival, collective embezzlers in the casino economy have little to lose. With no long-term investment in the infrastructure of production, their main concern is to get in and out of the house with as much of the pot as possible. The effect of their crimes on the health of the casino, or even its long-term survival, are unimportant to these financial high-flyers. Business Week (1985:90) describes "all the games the casino society plays": "The object ... is to get rich today, come what may." Collective embezzlement, in which highly placed insiders loot their own institutions, may be the prototypical form of white-collar crime in this context, much as violations of fair labor standards or consumer protections are to the industrial production process.

COLLECTIVE EMBEZZLEMENT AND THE STATE

Sociologists have long made a distinction between "social" regulations (such as occupational safety and health standards), which are aimed at controlling production processes, and "economic" regulations (such as insider trading restrictions), which regulate the market and stabilize the economy (Barnett 1981, Cranston 1982, Snider 1991, Yeager 1991). While the former protect workers and consumers against the excesses of capital - and tend to cut into profits - the latter regulate and stabilize the capital accumulation process and historically have been supported by affected industries.

This distinction is consistent with a structural approach to the state, which emphasizes the "objective relation" (Poulantzas 1969) between the state and capital (see also Althusser 1971, O'Connor 1973). This objective relation guarantees that the capitalist state will operate in the long-term interests of capitalists independent of their direct participation in the policymaking process or mobilization of resources. Central to this objective relation under capitalism, the state must promote capital accumulation because its own survival depends on tax revenues derived from successful profit-making activity, as well as the political stability that is contingent on economic growth. In addition, it must actively pursue "political integration" (Friedland et al 1977), "legitimation" (O'Connor 1973), or "the cohesion of the social formation" (Poulantzas 1969) in the interest of political survival and the economic growth upon which it depends.

In this structuralist rendition, the state enjoys relative autonomy in its efforts to realize these potentially contradictory functions. In direct contrast to the instrumentalist model espoused by Domhoff (1967, 1979) and others (Kolko 1963, 1965, Miliband 1969), structuralists argue that state managers are not captive to individual capitalists' interests and indeed are capable of violating those interests in order to pursue the broader and more long-term interests of capital accumulation and political legitimacy. Nonetheless, its autonomy is "relative." While the state may be free from the manipulation of individual capitalists or even of the business community as a whole, it is by no means autonomous from the structural requirements of the political economy within which it is embedded and which it must work to preserve (see Poulantzas 1969).

Regulation scholars who borrow from this perspective have generally focused on social - rather than economic - regulation. This literature addresses the lax enforcement of social regulations and ties that laxity to the capital accumulation function of the state and the perceived costs of interfering with profitable industry (Barnett 1981, Calavita 1983, Snider 1991, Yeager 1991). These scholars also note that the legitimation mandate of the state periodically requires that it respond to political demands to shore up worker safety, reduce environmental hazards, or enforce labor standards. The point, however, is that active enforcement of social regulation occurs primarily in response to public pressure and legitimation concerns, and it recedes once political attention has shifted elsewhere and state legitimacy is no longer threatened (Barnett 1981, Carson 1982, Walters 1985, Calavita 1983, Gunningham 1987, Yeager 1991).

In contrast, when the goal is economic regulation, the state tends to assume a more rigorous posture. Despite occasional protest from the individual capitalists at whom sanctions are directed, the state rather vigorously enforces regulations that stabilize the market and enhance economic viability. Unlike social regulations that are implemented primarily in response to on-again/off-again legitimation needs, economic regulations are integral to the capital accumulation process and are thus more consistently and urgently pursued (Barnett 1981, Snider 1991, Yeager 1991). While case studies are far fewer in this area, some excellent research has focused on the US Securities and Exchange Commission (SEC). As Yeager (1991) and Shapiro (1984) have shown, although the SEC is by no means omnipotent in the face of its powerful Wall Street charges, nonetheless it rather routinely seeks criminal sanctions and stiff monetary fines for elite offenders.

Extensive empirical research documents this enforcement discrepancy. Clinard et al's (1979) comprehensive analysis of enforcement actions against the 582 largest corporations in the United States during 1975 and 1976 found a strong relationship between level of enforcement and type of violation. While over 96% of "manufacturing violations" (involving social regulations concerning such things as product safety and food and drug standards) were handled entirely at the administrative level, only 41.5% of "trade violations" (involving economic regulations controlling bid-rigging and other unfair trade practices) were disposed of administratively. Further, while over 21% of trade violations were processed criminally, fewer than 1% of manufacturing violations were criminally processed, and no labor standard violations were prosecuted criminally. Clinard et al (1979:147) conclude, "Corporate actions that directly harm the economy were more likely to receive the greater penalties, while those affecting consumer product quality were responded to with the least severe sanctions. Although over 85 percent of all sanctions were administrative in nature, those harming the economy were most likely to receive criminal penalties" (see also Barnett 1981).

Based on these empirical findings and the structural theory with which they are consistent, the lenient treatment of corporate offenders documented by Sutherland over 40 years ago and reaffirmed by subsequent white-collar crime scholars may be a function of the state's relationship to capital. It may be, however, that this documentation of leniency is related to the fact that the primary focus in this literature is on violations of social regulations that cut into profits.

But, what of the collective embezzlement described above? If the structural logic is valid, then the state should have an altogether different relationship to collective embezzlement in the thrift industry than to traditional corporate crimes in the manufacturing sector. For one thing, the structural model would predict - and the empirical literature reviewed above supports this prediction - that the state would take violations of economic regulations quite seriously. Further, we would expect that enforcing banking regulations, which lie at the very heart of the economic system, would be among the state's highest priorities and would thus be a showcase for enforcement.

In addition, remember that collective embezzlement is aimed not at enhancing corporate profits, but at personal profit-making at the expense of the institution. In the S&L context, this "crime by the organization against the organization" not only decimated individual institutions, but threatened the demise of the whole industry, and with it the financial stability of the US economy. As a senior staff member of the Senate Banking Committee put it, "This [thrift] industry is very close to the heart of the American economy. We teetered on the edge of a major, major problem here. Well ... we got a major problem, but we teetered on the edge of a major collapse.... All these financial industries could bring down the whole economy" (personal interview). For the state whose functions include capital accumulation and long-term economic stability, we would expect that containing this collective embezzlement would have been a top priority.

Instead, extensive evidence indicates that the state not only failed to avert the crisis but was complicitous in shielding thrift offenders from detection (Calavita & Pontell 1990, Calavita et al 1997, US Congress, House Committee on Standards of Official Conduct 1989, National Commission on Financial Institutions Reform, Recovery and Enforcement 1993). In the remainder of this paper, we argue that a close look at the evolution of the thrift crisis and the role of government in delaying its resolution suggests the need to go beyond the reductionism of current state theory, toward a more synthetic model of state activity.

PUSHING THE LIMITS OF STATE THEORY

At first blush, the S&L debacle seems to reaffirm the instrumentalist notion of a state captured by monied interests in the form of campaign contributions and other less subtle forms of "honest graft" (Jackson 1988). Indeed, implicit or explicit collusion of government officials with thrift offenders seems to have played a significant role in thwarting regulation and thereby exacerbating the crisis. At the lowest level of field inspectors and examiners - those with front-line responsibility for detecting and reporting fraud - there were occasional instances of cooptation by fraudulent thrift operators. One strategy of thrift executives was to woo examiners and regulators with job offers at salaries several times higher than their modest government wages (Pizzo et al 1991, personal interviews).

More important than these relatively infrequent forms of outright collusion by regulators and examiners were close connections between thrift industry executives and elected officials. The powerful US League of Savings and Loans, the thrifts' major lobbying group in Washington and generous donor of campaign funds, was a significant force in deflecting regulatory scrutiny, under-funding regulatory agencies, and generally postponing the closure of insolvent and fraud-ridden thrifts.(4) While the "Keating Five" - the five Senators who challenged San Francisco regulators on behalf of Charles Keating - provide the most visible example of Congressional attempts to rein in regulators, they were not alone. Congressman Fernand St Germain, Chair of the House Banking Committee and cosponsor of the deregulatory legislation in the early 1980s that set the stage for the thrift crisis, was a frequent recipient of US League of Savings and Loans largesse. Having been observed regularly dining out in Washington on the US League's expense account, St Germain was investigated by the Department of Justice for conflict-of-interest violations. The Justice Department concluded that there was "substantial evidence of serious and sustained misconduct" by St Germain in his connections with the thrift industry. A House Ethics Committee investigation came to the same conclusion. No formal prosecution was initiated, and St Germain was voted out of office in 1988. He is currently a lobbyist for the thrift industry (Jackson 1988, Pizzo et al 1991).

House Speaker Jim Wright was particularly adept at intervening on behalf of his thrift benefactors and often called Federal Home Loan Bank Board (FHLBB) Chair Ed Gray to task for his attempts at aggressive thrift regulation. On several occasions, documented in the independent counsel's report to the House

Committee investigating Wright's alleged conflicts of interest (US Congress. House Committee on Standards of Official Conduct 1989, see also the National Commission on Financial Institutions Reform, Recovery and Enforcement 1993), the Speaker of the House from Texas asked the chief regulator to back off of Texas thrifts and advocated on behalf of specific thrift owners who had contributed generously to his campaign fund.

This complicity of government officials is exactly what instrumentalists would predict, and it sharply contradicts the structuralist notions of relative autonomy and the priority placed on economic regulation and long-term financial stability. The fact that state officials shielded the collective embezzlement of thrift operators at the expense of economic stability adds substantial credibility to the instrumentalist model of the impact of raw economic power and influence-peddling.

However, there is more to it than this. While it is true that the US League of Savings and Loans and its individual members exerted considerable influence in Congress, at the same time a vitriolic struggle between members of Congress and the FHLBB raged behind the scenes (Black 1994, Waldman 1990, US Congress. House Committee on Standards of Official Conduct 1989). By all accounts, Ed Gray and his staff at the FHLBB were stunned by the escalating thrift crisis in Texas and elsewhere, and they approached their assignment with urgency. Gray was said to have had his "Road to Damascus experience" (Black 1994:9) watching a homemade videotape of miles of abandoned condominiums east of Dallas financed by the insured deposits of Empire Savings and Loan. He spent the rest of his tenure at FHLBB attempting to reregulate thrifts and encountering resistance from the industry, the White House, and Congress. One investigative reporter described the attack on Gray and his dogged persistence: "If Gray's reign as the bank board's chairman had been a fight ... they would have stopped it.... He stood in the middle of the ring ... taking repeated blows. But he never fell to the canvas" (Binstein 1987:48).

This clash between regulators who were alarmed at the pending disaster and key members of Congress who shielded their thrift benefactors refutes not only the structural notions of uniform state purpose and relative autonomy, but instrumentalists' depiction of state actors as simply lackeys of monied interests. It suggests instead that relative autonomy may vary across the institutions that together comprise the state. Members of Congress, whose political careers depend on a steady influx of campaign funds, may be particularly susceptible to the demands of those with the resources to make large contributions. Civil servants in regulatory agencies, while certainly not immune to such political and financial pressures, may for structural reasons be less susceptible to them and periodically may take a more rigorous enforcement approach in the interests of economic stability.

This account of the evolution of the thrift crisis suggests the need for a synthetic model of state action. As we have seen from the literature cited above, the state is capable of concerted action and rigorous regulation in the interest of financial stability, consistent with structural theory. On the other hand, as we have seen in the savings and loan crisis, the real-life political actors who comprise the state have their own political and career interests and are susceptible to a variety of external influences. Thus, while the state has a structural interest in economic stability and therefore in containing collective embezzlement, instrumental influences on state actors can - and periodically do - neutralize that structural interest and derail the regulatory agenda.

DISCUSSION

We have argued here that much of the insider fraud in the S&L industry in the 1980s constituted variations on "hot deals," "looting," and "covering up," and that some of these financial crimes can be thought of as collective embezzlement. Distinct from the corporate crime in the manufacturing sector first documented by Edwin Sutherland (1983), this collective embezzlement is motivated entirely by personal - not corporate - gain and erodes the institution's financial health.

We have also argued that the state's relationship to such collective embezzlement is quite different than to that of crimes perpetrated on behalf of the corporation. As a number of scholars have noted, the structurally based interest of the state in advancing corporate profits - or at least not interfering with them - helps explain the lenient treatment of corporate crime upon which the white-collar crime literature has generally focused. But to the extent that collective embezzlement undermines corporate profit-making and jeopardizes long-term economic stability, the structural restraints on enforcement do not apply; indeed, structural imperatives would dictate a quick and rigorous response.

However, as we have seen here, the US government response to the first signs of S&L fraud in the mid-1980s was conflicted and contributed to the crisis. Close examination of this response reveals that the savings and loan industry and its individual members were able to shield themselves temporarily through effective lobbying of key members of Congress and other officials. With regard to state theory, this pattern of government collusion in the crisis and intrastate struggle over regulation suggests the need for a more synthetic model, the beginnings of which we have sketched above.

This analysis, however, also has policy implications. First, in contrast to the regulatory catch-22 surrounding the enforcement of social regulations, the state has an unequivocal interest (both long-term and short-term) in containing collective embezzlement. The recognition of this new form of fraud for what it is, and the understanding of its objective relationship to the state and economic stability, might open up new regulatory space for deterrence and rigorous sanctions. After all, the looting described above - and its relationship to the state - is different from bank robbery only in its magnitude and its destabilizing effect on the whole economy. As the former Commissioner of the California Department of Savings and Loans told a Congressional committee, "The best way to rob a bank is to own one" (quoted in US Congress, House Committee on Government Operations 1988:34).

More broadly, this analysis suggests the need to revisit the role of monied interests in the political process, not just for the sake of political democracy but to shore up financial stability in this age of global economic transformation. For, while structural relations between the state and capital may allow - even dictate - a strict response to collective embezzlement, this response is subject to sabotage by those with the resources to woo policymakers with hefty campaign contributions. As one S&L regulator told us,

"It was always the worst S&Ls in America that were able to get dramatically more political intervention.... If you know you are engaged in fraud, what better return is there than a political contribution" (personal interview).

In concluding, we urgently call for more research in this emerging area. While neither collective embezzlement nor its regulatory neglect are new, the epic proportions of these financial crimes and the increasing dominance of the finance capitalism on which they are based are unprecedented. Future research should build on the rich white-collar crime and state theory traditions to explore further the theoretical and policy implications of these important changes.

178

ACKNOWLEDGMENTS

The research reported here was supported under award 90-1J-CX-0059 from the National Institute of Justice. Points of view expressed in this document are the authors' and do not represent the official position of the US Department of Justice.

1 We use "savings and loans" and "thrifts" interchangeably here to refer to federally insured savings institutions that have as their primary historical function the provision of home mortgage loans. See Calavita & Pontell (1990, 1991, 1993) for a discussion of the regulatory changes in the early 1980s that freed these institutions to make direct investments, that effectively altered their function as home-mortgage lenders, and that provided extensive opportunities for fraud.

2 There may be some cases in which referrals were filed in the absence of actual criminal misconduct. However, our conversations with regulators, investigators, and prosecutors, and our perusal of the detailed referrals to which we gained access, suggest that these forms were by no means filed frivolously. Because of the amount of information required on these forms, and because the reputation of the agency that filed a referral was at stake, they were likely to be limited to the most egregious cases of suspected misconduct, particularly as caseloads bogged down in the late 1980s. See Calavita et al (1997) for a description of the triage-like prosecutorial decisions that resulted in indictments in only one case out of every seven criminal referrals in Texas, and one in four in California.

3 As part of its mandate to manage the assets of seized thrifts, the RTC collected data on criminal referrals through its Thrift Information Management System (TIMS). This system recorded and tracked criminal referrals at all RTC institutions (that is, those institutions that had been declared insolvent and taken over by the RTC). The TIMS data referred to here summarize the contents of "Category 1" (suspected thrift fraud of $100,000 or more) criminal referrals filed by the RTC or other federal agencies through May, 1992.

4 For a detailed discussion of the role of government corruption in the S&L debacle, see Calavita & Pontell (1994) and Calavita et al (1997).

REFERENCES DELETED

Part V

ENTERPRISE CRIME, CONTREPRENEUTRAL CRIME, AND TECHNOCRIME

10

Computer Crimes

Twenty-Fifth Edition of the Annual Survey of White Collar Crime

Jessica L. McCurdy

Computer crimes. Twenty-Fifth Edition of the Annual Survey of White Collar Crime Jessica L. McCurdy. American Criminal Law Review Spring 2010 v47 i2 p287(43). Reprinted with permission of the publisher, American Criminal Law Review (c) 2010.

I. INTRODUCTION

This Article discusses federal, state, and international developments in computer-related criminal law. This Section defines computer crimes. Section II covers the constitutional and jurisdictional issues concerning computer crimes. Section III describes the federal approaches used for prosecuting computer crime and analyzes enforcement strategies. Section IV examines state approaches to battling computer crime. Lastly, Section V addresses international approaches to regulating computer crimes.

A. Defining Computer Crime

The U.S. Department of Justice ("DOJ") broadly defines computer crime as "any violations of criminal law that involve a knowledge of computer technology for their perpetration, investigation, or prosecution." (1) Because of the diversity of computer-related offenses, a narrower definition would be inadequate. While the term "computer crime" includes traditional crimes committed with the use of a computer, (2) the rapid emergence of computer technologies and the exponential expansion of the Internet (3) spawned a variety of new, technology-specific criminal behaviors that must also be included in the category of "computer crimes." (4) To combat these new criminal behaviors, Congress passed specialized legislation. (5)

Experts have had difficulty calculating the damage caused by computer crimes due to: the difficulty in adequately defining "computer crime;" (6) victims' reluctance to report incidents for fear of losing customer confidence; (7) the dual system of prosecution; (8) and the lack of detection. (9) In 2006, DOJ's Bureau of Justice Statistics and the Department of Homeland Security's National Cyber Security Division conducted a joint effort to estimate the number of cyber attacks and the number of incidents of fraud and theft of information. (10) It found that nearly 67 percent of businesses reported at least one incident of computer crime the past year. (11)

B. Types of Computer-Related Offenses

1. Object of Crime

DOJ divides computer-related crimes into three categories according to the computer's role in the particular crime. (12) First, a computer may be the "object" of a crime. (13) This category primarily refers to theft of computer hardware or software. Under state law, computer hardware theft is generally prosecuted under theft or burglary statutes. (14) Under federal law, computer hardware theft may be prosecuted under 18 U.S.C. [section] 2314, which regulates the interstate transportation of stolen or fraudulently obtained goods. (15) Computer software theft is only included in this category if it is located on a tangible piece of hardware because the theft of intangible software is not prosecutable under 18 U.S.C. [section] 2314.

2. Subject of Crime

Second, a computer may be the "subject" of a crime. (16) In this category, the computer is akin to the pedestrian who is mugged or the house that is robbed, it is the subject of the attack and the site of any damage caused. These are computer crimes for which there is generally no analogous traditional crime and for which special legislation is needed. This category encompasses spam, viruses, worms, Trojan horses, logic bombs, sniffers, distributed denial of service attacks, and unauthorized web bots or spiders. In the past, malice or mischief rather than financial gain motivated most offenders in this category. Now, many crimes are driven by personal profit or malice. (17) These types of crimes were frequently committed by juveniles, disgruntled employees, and professional hackers as a means of showing off their skills. (18) Disgruntled employees are widely thought to pose the biggest threat to company computer systems. (19) In sentencing juvenile offenders, courts have had a particularly difficult time in finding appropriate penalties. (20) However, in recent years, more of these crimes have been committed for financial gain. (21)

a. Spam
Spam is unsolicited bulk commercial email from a party with no preexisting business relationship. (22) Spam is so common that in 2009 over 97 percent of all emails sent over the Internet were unwanted. (23) Additionally, hackers often use spare as a way of distributing viruses, spyware, and other malicious software. (24)

b. Viruses
A virus is a program that modifies other computer programs, causing them to perform the task for which the virus was designed. (25) It usually spreads from one host to another when a user transmits an infected file by e-mail, over the Internet, across a company's network, or by disk. (26)

c. Worms
Worms are like viruses, but they use computer networks or the Internet to serf-replicate and "send themselves" to other users, generally via e-mail, while viruses require human action to spread from one computer to the next. (27) Worms have far more destructive potential than viruses because they can spread so much faster. (28)

d. Trojan Horses
Trojan horses are programs with legitimate functions that also contain hidden malicious code. (29) Like its namesake, a Trojan horse dupes a user into installing the seemingly innocent program on his or her computer system and then activates the hidden code, which may release a virus or allow an unauthorized user access to the system. (30) Hackers use Trojan horses as the primary way they transmit viruses. (31)

e. Logic Bombs

Logic bombs are programs that activate when a specific event occurs, such as the arrival of a particular date or time. (32) They can be destructive but software companies commonly use them to protect against violation of licensing agreements by disabling the program upon detection of a violation. (33)

f. Sniffers

Sniffers, also known as network analyzers, can read electronic data as it travels through a network. (34) Network administrators use them to monitor networks and troubleshoot network connections. (35) Sniffers can help network administrators find and resolve network problems. (36) However, a hacker can break into a network and install a sniffer that logs all activity across a network, including the exchange of passwords, credit card numbers, and other personal information. (37)

g. Denial of Service Attacks

In a denial of service attack, hackers bombard the target website with an overwhelming number of simple requests for connection, thus rendering the site unable to respond to legitimate users. (38) In distributed denial of service attacks, hackers use the networks of innocent third parties to overwhelm Websites and prevent them from communicating with other computers. (39) After breaking into several network systems, the individual makes one system the "Master" system and turns the others into agent systems. (40) Once activated, the Master directs the agents to launch a denial of service attack. (41) The use of third party "agents" makes it particularly difficult to identify the culprit. (42)

h. Web Bots & Spiders

"Web bots" or "spiders" are data search and collection programs that can create searchable databases that catalogue a website's activities. (43) Although seemingly innocuous, too many spiders on the same web site can effectively be a denial of service attack. In addition, they can steal data from the websites that they search. (44)

3. Instrument of Crime

Third, a computer may be an "instrument" used to commit traditional crimes. (45) These traditional crimes include identity theft, (46) child pornography, (47) copyright infringement, (48) and mall or wire fraud. (49)

II. GENERAL ISSUES

A. Constitutional Issues

This Section addresses general constitutional issues with computer crimes. Specific constitutional issues with federal and state statutes are discussed in the relevant Sections of this article. Constitutional issues related to computer crimes usually fall under either the First Amendment or the Fourth Amendment. There are also some federalism issues. In particular, there is a question as to how much the federal government can regulate intrastate behavior under the Commerce Clause. This is discussed in the following Section on federal jurisdiction.

1. First Amendment

The First Amendment (50) protects the same forms of speech in cyberspace that it does in the real world. Hate speech and other forms of racist speech receive the same protection on the Internet as they have always received under traditional First Amendment analysis. (51) The guarantee of the First Amendment extends well beyond personally held beliefs to include speech that advocates conduct, even when that conduct is illegal. (52) Racist speech is also probably protected on the Internet, as it is not likely to fit within the "fighting words" exception to the First Amendment. (53)

There is an exception to this general free speech principle for "true threats," (54) such as sending threatening e-mail messages to a victim or even a public announcement on the Internet of an intention to commit an act that is racially motivated. (55) A similar exception exists for harassment on e-mail or the Internet, as long as it is sufficiently persistent and malicious as to inflict, or is motivated by desire to cause, substantial emotional or physical harm (56) and is directed at a specific person. (57) Child pornography is not protected either, but finding a sufficiently narrow description to prevent its spread on the Internet has proven difficult. (58)

In 2008, the Virginia Supreme Court struck down a Virginia statute, which criminalized the falsification of identifying transmission information in unsolicited bulk e-mail messages (spam), as overly broad and infringing on the First Amendment fight to engage in anonymous speech. (59) The court emphasized that the statute in question did not distinguish between commercial and non-commercial unsolicited e-mails, including those expressing political and religious messages. (60) Therefore, the statute could not survive strict scrutiny because it was not narrowly tailored to the compelling state interests, as laid out in the federal CAN-SPAM Act, (61) of preserving the efficiency and convenience of e-mail. (62)

2. Fourth Amendment

A number of difficult Fourth Amendment (63) issues inhere in computer crimes. The Fourth Amendment prohibits unreasonable searches and seizures by the government. (64) However, what constitutes a search or seizure with respect to computers is not always clear. There is disagreement as to whether there should be a special approach created for computer-related searches and seizures, or whether it is adequate to draw comparisons from traditional Fourth Amendment analysis. (65) This section will examine how courts have defined a Fourth Amendment search and applied the warrant requirement in the context of computers.

The Supreme Court has held that a search occurs within the meaning of the Fourth Amendment when government actions violate an individual's legitimate or "reasonable" expectations of privacy. (66) Generally, a person has a reasonable expectation of privacy in a computer they own in their home, but this is less clear-cut in the workplace. (67) Fourth Amendment issues may also arise when law enforcement intercepts address information on the Internet, such as e-mail addresses and website addresses. Before 2001, the FBI routinely searched similar information on Internet communications without much mention of constitutional issues. (68) The Ninth Circuit has held that obtaining Internet address information by installing a surveillance program at the Internet Service Provider's ("ISP") facility is "constitutionally indistinguishable" from the use of a pen register and, therefore, Internet users have no expectation of privacy in such information. (69) The Fourth Circuit has similarly held that a criminal defendant has no reasonable expectation of privacy in the information he provides to his ISP. (70)

The use of investigative tools devised for eavesdropping on Internet communications may present additional Fourth Amendment questions. (71) The use of a keystroke logger system appears to be constitutional. (72) The constitutionality of other techniques, however, will likely be tested as the government discloses more information about both the nature of its capabilities and the frequency of their application.

Although the Fourth Amendment generally requires specificity in search warrants, broad search warrants have been upheld when addressed to computer crimes. (73) Broad searches have been justified as "about the narrowest definable search and seizure reasonably likely to obtain the [evidence]." (74) There is a circuit split as to whether law enforcement agents with a warrant may search and seize computer files even though doing so might cause seizure of contents having no relation to the crime being investigated. (75) There is also a split as to how the plain view exception (76) should apply to computer files. (77)

Another relevant Fourth Amendment issue is the doctrine of staleness, (78) which "applies when information proffered in support of a warrant application is so old that it casts doubt on whether the fruits or evidence of a crime will still be found at a particular location." (79) The durability of data and graphics stored on computer hardware has drastically extended the period after which the staleness doctrine applies. For example, the Ninth Circuit upheld the validity of a search warrant even though ten-month-old information supported it. (80)

In executing a warrant, agents may seize and search a disk, even if its label indicates that it is not within the scope of the warrant. (81) Agents may also search computer hardware and software when they have reason to believe that those items contain records covered by the warrant. (82) They may even remove the hardware and software from the owner's premises to conduct their examination. (83) They may not, however, seize peripheral items, such as printers, to assist them in their review of the seized items. (84) State courts have split on extending this principle to their search and seizure jurisprudence. (85)

B. Jurisdiction

1. Federal Jurisdiction

The majority of federal computer crimes statutes have been enacted under Congress' power "to regulate Commerce ... among the several States." (86) As the Internet is considered to be both a channel and instrumentality of interstate commerce, it falls under the Commerce Clause's broad power. (87) Most courts have held that the courts should treat jurisdictional components of federal statutes as meaningful restrictions. (88) Therefore, they must judge whether the activity in question implicates interstate commerce on a case-by-case basis. (89) This analysis has centered on there being a sufficient nexus between the offending activity and interstate commerce. Where there has been movement of people or materials in interstate commerce in furtherance of the offending activity, (90) or where the Internet has been employed, the application of the statute has been held constitutional. (91) However, a serious question remains as to whether the statute can reach purely intrastate activity. (92) Under the Supreme Court's holding and reasoning in Gonzales v. Raich, (93) courts considering the question have answered "yes." (94)

2. State Jurisdiction

A significant challenge to state officials in prosecuting computer crimes is one of jurisdiction. (95) Jurisdictional problems arise for state prosecutors when the acts are committed out of state (96) because the jurisdictional rules of criminal law require the prosecutor to prove that the defendant intended to cause harm within his state. (97) As a result, many states have broadened their jurisdictional rules to address the new concerns that arise from the global nature of the Internet. (98) For example, Wisconsin's criminal statute permits jurisdiction even when no result occurs in the state. (99) Alabama, California, and South Dakota have statutes providing for jurisdiction where an offense begins outside the state and "consummates" within the state. (100)

C. Other Issues

In addition to constitutional obstacles, federal laws may interfere with computer crime statutes at both the federal and state level. Several laws intended to protect privacy have implications in computer crimes as well. For example, Title III applies to both the government and civilians in situations in which there are Fourth Amendment issues. (101) Title III applies to state actors as well and states may not legislate lower standards for interception, although they may set higher ones. (102)

Another complication arises as a result of additional protection for computer records provided by the Privacy Protection Act of 1980. (103) The statute requires police to obtain a subpoena prior to searching or seizing work product or other materials reasonably believed to pertain to public communications such as newspapers. (104) This protection does not include child pornography. (105) The Privacy Protection Act still applies to other material that may be public communications.

III. FEDERAL APPROACHES

This Section explores the major federal statutes, enforcement strategies, and constitutional issues regarding computer related crimes. The government can charge computer-related crimes under at least forty different federal statutes. (106) There are also a number of traditional criminal statutes whose application to computer crime is unclear. (107) In addition, the federal government has sometimes used the United States Sentencing Guidelines ("Guidelines") to enhance sentences for traditional crimes committed with the aid of computers. (108) This Section discusses the role of the Sentencing Guidelines in general, key federal statutes in the prosecution of computer crimes, and relevant enforcement efforts. Although the focus of this Article is the federal government's approach to prosecuting criminal computer offenses, past litigation has also sought civil remedies. (109)

A. Sentencing Guidelines

The Guidelines supplement the federal computer crime statutes and help determine how much of the maximum sentence a perpetrator should serve. (110) The Guidelines treat most computer crimes as economic crimes sentenced under [section] 2B1.1. (111) The Guidelines also dictate "special skills" enhancements for particular crimes including computer crimes. (112)

B. Federal Statutes

Since 1984, Congress has pursued a dual approach to combating computer crime. The Counterfeit Access Device and Computer Fraud and Abuse Act of 1984 (113) and subsequent amending acts (114) address crimes in which the computer is the "subject." This line of statutes culminated in the Computer Fraud and Abuse Act ("CFAA"), (115) which is discussed in detail in Section 2. The federal government's other approach to regulating computer crime has been to update traditional criminal statutes to reach similar crimes involving computers. (116)

1. Child Pornography Statutes

Federal child pornography statutes have not fared well under the First Amendment. In Reno v. American Civil Liberties Union, (117) the Supreme Court gave an unqualified level of First Amendment protection to Internet communications. (118) Under Reno, legislation will not withstand scrutiny if it requires web surfers or Internet content providers to estimate the age of those with whom they communicate or to tag their communications as potentially indecent or offensive, prior to engaging in "cyberspeech." (119) The Court found that less regulation is necessary to protect children on the Internet compared to television or radio because users rarely come across content on the Internet accidentally and warnings often precede sexually explicit images. (120) The global nature of the Internet also renders it difficult, if not impossible, for users to predict when their potentially offensive communications will reach a minor. (121) Consequently, Reno requires courts to apply unqualified First Amendment scrutiny to speech restrictions affecting the Internet.

(122) Note that "unqualified" protection does not cover obscenity or child pornography, which the government may ban. (123) Under this standard, parts of several federal child pornography laws discussed below and all of the Child Online Protection Act of 1998 ("COPA"), (124) have been found unconstitutional. (125)

a. Communications Decency Act of 1996

The Communications Decency Act of 1996 ("CDA"), or Title V of the Telecommunications Act of 1996, (126) originally prohibited the transmission of "indecent," (127) "patently offensive," (128) or "obscene" (129) material to minors over the Internet. In Reno v. American Civil Liberties Union, (130) the Supreme Court struck down those portions of the statute that banned "indecent" (131) and "patently offensive" (132) images as being unconstitutionally vague and overbroad. (133) The rest of [section] 223(a), banning transmission of obscene speech to minors, remains in effect. (134)

Under [section] 223(a), knowing transmission of obscene speech or images to minors is punishable by a fine, imprisonment of up to two years, or both. (135) The Guidelines set a base offense level of ten for transportation of obscene matter, which is automatically increased by five levels if the obscene matter is transmitted to a minor. (136) A seven-level upward adjustment is mandated if the distribution was intended to convince a minor to engage in prohibited sexual conduct. (137) The base level of the offense can be raised no less than five levels if the offense is related to distribution of material for pecuniary gain. (138) If the material involved in the offense portrays sadistic, masochistic conduct, or other depictions of violence, the offense level increases by four. (139)

b. Child Pornography Prevention Act of 1996

In 1996, Congress passed the Child Pornography Prevention Act (140) ("CPPA"), which criminalized the production, distribution, and reception of computer-generated, sexual images of children. (141) Thus, CPPA sought to prohibit computer transmission of erotic photographs of adults doctored to resemble children. (142) However, in April 2002, the Supreme Court held two provisions of the statute, prohibiting pornography that appeared to depict minors, but in actuality depicted young-looking adults or virtual child pornography, unconstitutionally vague and overbroad. (143)

In response, Congress passed the Prosecutorial Remedies and Other Tools to End the Exploitation of Children Today Act of 2003 ("PROTECT Act"). (144) The PROTECT Act included a provision prohibiting advertisement, distribution, and solicitation of pornography in such a way to reflect a belief or induce others to believe that the material depicts real children. (145) After a number of circuit courts questioned the constitutionality of this provision under the reasoning of Ashcroft v. Free Speech Coalition, (146) the Supreme Court upheld the statute. (147)

2. Computer Fraud and Abuse Act

18 U.S.C. [section] 1030, (148) which many courts refer to as the Computer Fraud and Abuse Act ("CFAA"), (149) protects against various crimes involving "protected computers." Because "protected computers" include those used in interstate commerce or communications, the statute covers any computer attached to the Internet, even if all the computers involved are located in the same state. (150)

a. Offenses Under the Statute

The CFAA prohibits seven specific acts of computer-related crime. (151) First, it is a crime to access computer files without authorization and to subsequently transmit classified government information if the information "could be used" to the injury of the United States. (152) Second, the CFAA prohibits obtaining, (153) without authorization, information from financial institutions, (154) the United States, or private computers that are used in interstate commerce. (155) Third, it proscribes intentionally accessing a United States department or agency nonpublic computer without authorization. (156) If the government or a government agency does not use the computer exclusively, the illegal access must affect the government's use. (157) Fourth, it prohibits accessing a protected computer, without authorization, with the intent to defraud and obtain something of value. (158)

The fifth prohibition, which addresses computer hacking, has two categories of offenses depending on whether there is intent to cause damage. The first category criminalizes knowingly causing the transmission of a program, code, or command, that intentionally causes damage to a protected computer. (159) This subsection applies regardless of whether the user had authorization to access the protected computer. Thus, company insiders and authorized users can be culpable for intentional damage to a protected computer.

The second category Of offenses prohibits intentional access without authorization that results in damage but does not require intent to damage. (160) The statute, however, does not define either "access" or "authorization." (161) The culpability for damage can be either reckless (162) or negligent. (163) This provision makes unauthorized users responsible even if the transmission was not intentional but was reckless (164) or negligent. (165) Damage under the statute is "any impairment to the integrity or availability of data, a program, a system, or information." (166)

Sixth, the CFAA prohibits someone from trafficking in passwords knowingly and with intent to defraud. (167) The passwords must either permit unauthorized access to a government computer or the trafficking must affect interstate or foreign commerce. (168) Finally, the CFAA makes it illegal to transmit in interstate or foreign commerce any threat to cause damage to a protected computer with intent to extort something of value. (169) Threats against protected computers only violate the CFAA if they intend to extort from individuals. (170)

b. Jurisdiction

The U.S. Secret Service has investigatory authority for all violations of the CFAA. (171) The FBI has express jurisdiction over offenses for obtaining national security information (172) that involve espionage, foreign counterintelligence, unauthorized access to national defense information or restricted data. (173) Certain offenses for obtaining national security information (174) and damaging a protected computer (175) are also included in the definition of "federal crime of terrorism," bringing them under the express jurisdiction of the Attorney General. (176)

c. Defenses

One defense to charges of accessing a protected computer without authorization is that the defendant simply did not "obtain anything of value." (177) The First Circuit interpreted the statutory language "obtain anything of value" to require something more than simply viewing information. (178) Instead, prosecutors must prove that the information was valuable to the defendant in conducting his fraudulent scheme. (179)

In order for the CFAA to apply, a defendant must not only access a protected computer and cause damage, but that damage must cause some additional injury. (180) The damage must be worth at least $5,000 over a one-year period, (181) or lead to potential injury or a threat to public health or safety. (182)

d. Penalties

The CFAA punishes attempts to commit an offense as if the offense had been successfully carried out. (183) The CFAA has lesser penalties for first-time than for repeat offenders. The CFAA defines recidivism as a subsequent violation of any of the subsections of the act. (184) Thus, a repeat offender can receive an enhanced sentence even if she commits a different type of computer fraud than before. Conviction includes any conviction under state law if the elements include unauthorized access to a computer. (185)

First-time offenders who obtain national security information or intentionally damage a protected computer are subject to a fine, imprisonment of not more than ten years, or both. (186) Subsections (a)(2), (a)(3), (a)(5)(A)(iii), and (a)(6) have penalties of a fine, imprisonment of not more than one year, or both, for first offenses. (187) First time offenders under (a)(4), (a)(5)(A)(ii), and (a)(7) are subject to a fine, imprisonment of not more than five years, or both. (188)

CFAA also differentiates between conduct that involves improper access and conduct in which the defendant uses access for pernicious purposes. It does so by increasing the maximum prison sentence for first time violations of (a)(2) to five years if the crime was committed for financial gain or commercial advantage, in furtherance of a criminal or tortious act, or if the value of the obtained information exceeds $5,000. (189) This is the same as the sentencing for first time offenders under (a)(4), (a)(5)(A)(ii), and (a)(7). (190)

Repeat offenders may receive much tougher sentences. Maximum sentences under (a)(2), (a)(3), (a)(4), (a)(5)(A)(ii), (a)(6), and (a)(7) rise to ten years for recidivists. (191) The maximum sentence goes up to twenty years for repeat offenders who obtain national security information or intentionally or recklessly damage a protected computer. (192)

Sentences also go up considerably if serious injury or death results from the violation. The maximum sentence is twenty years for anyone who "knowingly or recklessly causes or attempts to cause serious bodily injury" by intentionally damaging a protected computer. (193) The maximum sentence is life in prison for anyone who "knowingly or recklessly causes or attempts to cause death" by intentionally damaging a protected computer. (194)

The Guidelines set the base offense level for obtaining national security information at thirty-five if unlawfully accessed national defense information is top secret, and at thirty otherwise. (195) The offense levels for violations of the rest of the CFAA, except subsection (3), are largely dependent on the value of the loss suffered. Subsections (2), (4), (5), and (6) are covered by the Guidelines' section on theft, stolen property, property damage, fraud, forgery, and counterfeiting. (196) The section on trespass covers [section] 1030(a)(3). (197) And the section on extortion covers [section] 1030(a)(7). (198) Attempts to violate the CFAA, also a crime under the statute, are also covered by the Guidelines. (199)

3. Controlling the Assault of Non-Solicited Pornography and Marketing Act of 2003

Unsolicited commercial email or "spam" has been a growing problem in the United States for many years. (200) Congress has considered many proposed federal anti-spam bills since 1995, but did not enact a comprehensive statute until December of 2003. (201) The Controlling the Assault of Non-Solicited Pornography and Marketing Act of 2003 (202) ("CAN-SPAM") was enacted to establish a national standard for email solicitations. (203) The CAN-SPAM Act has several key provisions that affect persons or companies sending commercial solicitations via email. Section 1037 of Title 18 prohibits a number of well-known deceptive and/or fraudulent practices commonly used in commercial emails. (204) These techniques include using deceptive subject lines, providing false or misleading header information, and using another computer to relay email messages without authorization to prevent anyone from tracing the email back to its sender. (205) Section 7704 of Title 15 further prohibits similar deceptive practices, as well as requiring that a commercial email include a method for the recipient to "opt-out" of future solicitations and that the subject line warn if the email contains sexually oriented material. (206)

The CAN-SPAM Act has provisions for both fines and criminal penalties, which the FTC and the DOJ enforce. (207) A violator of the act is subject to a maximum fine of $11,000. (208) An individual who is found guilty of fraud or other intentionally deceptive violations of the Act could be sentenced to up to five years in prison. (209)

4. Copyright Statutes

Copyright violations are particularly harmful to computer software developers. (210) Software piracy presents unique challenges to law enforcement because of the various ways the crime can be committed, (211) the ease (212) and minimal cost of reproduction, (213) and the slight degradation in the quality of pirated software. (214) The difficulty of detection also exacerbates the problem of electronic infringement. (215) Many of these issues also apply to other media in digital form. (216)

a. Criminal Copyright Infringement in the Copyright Act

Persons who unlawfully copy and distribute copyrighted material by computer may be subject to punishment for criminal copyright infringement. (217) The criminal copyright infringement statute has four elements: (218) (i) existence of a valid copyright; (219) (ii) that the defendant willfully; (220) (iii) infringed; (221) and (iv) "either (1) for commercial advantage or private financial gain, (2) by reproducing or distributing infringing copies of works with a total retail value of over $1,000 over a 180-day period, or (3) by distributing a 'work being prepared for commercial distribution' by making it available on a publicly-accessible computer network." (222)

i. Defenses
Under the first sale doctrine, one who legally purchases a copy of a copyrighted work may freely distribute that particular copy. (223) The alleged copyright infringer bears the burden of proving that the first sale doctrine applies. (224) This defense does not apply to computer software copyright infringement if the software is distributed by licensing agreement. (225)

The fair use doctrine permits non-copyright holders to make use of copyrighted works for purposes such as criticism, comment, news reporting, teaching, scholarship, or research. (226) The "fair use" defense requires consideration of four factors: (227) (i) the purpose and character of the use; (228) (ii) the nature of the work; (229) (iii) the substantive amount of the portion used in relation to the work as a whole; (230) and (iv) the effect of the use upon the potential market for the work. (231)

ii. Penalties
Section 2319 of Title 18 sets forth the punishment for criminal copyright infringement. (232) Section 2319(c) provides variable prison terms and fines for copyright infringements through the reproduction or distribution of one or more copies or phonorecords with a total retail value of more than $1,000: (i) first-time offenders who reproduce or distribute more than ten copies or phonorecords of one or more copyrighted works that have a total retail value of $2,500 or more, face up to three years in prison; (ii) subsequent offenders face up to six years imprisonment; and (iii) those who reproduce or distribute one or more copies or phonorecords of one or more copyrighted works that have a total retail value of $1,000 or more face up to one year's imprisonment. (233)

Sentences for defendants convicted of criminal copyright infringement are determined considering [section] 2B5.3 of the Guidelines. (234) The base offense level is eight. (235) If the retail value of the infringing items (236) exceeds $2,000, then the offense level is increased by the corresponding number of levels from the table in [section] 2B 1.1 237

b. Digital Millennium Copyright Act

The Digital Millennium Copyright Act of 1998 ("DMCA") (238) generally prohibits tampering with any access control or copy control measures applied to digital copies of copyrighted works. (239) Section 1201 prohibits circumvention of technological measures used to protect copyrighted works. (240) "[A] technological measure 'effectively controls access to a work' if the measure, in the ordinary course of its operation, requires the application of information, or a process or a treatment, with the authority of the copyright owner, to gain access to the work." (241) "To 'circumvent a technological measure' means to descramble a scrambled work, to decrypt an encrypted work, or otherwise to avoid, bypass, remove, deactivate, or impair a technological measure, without the authority of the copyright owner." (242) No person may manufacture, import, offer to the public, provide, or otherwise traffic (243) in a technology, (244) product, service, or device (245) that is used to circumvent (246) such technological measures, if one of the following conditions is met: (i) the technology, product, service or device is primarily designed or produced to circumvent; (ii) it has only limited commercial use other than that prohibited by the statute; or (iii) it is marketed for use in circumventing. (247) A number of exceptions are available for research and other purposes. (248)

In Universal City Studios, Inc. v. Reimerdes, (249) the District Court for the Southern District of New York acknowledged that [section] 1201 is in tension with the fair use doctrine in section 107 of the Copyright Act. (250) Despite this tension, the court held that DMCA does not unduly frustrate the purpose of the fair use doctrine because DMCA provides exceptions for those uses it considers fair. (251) The court ruled that the fair use doctrine is unavailable as a defense under [section] 1201 because production of a technology circumvention measure does not qualify as a use of a copyrighted work; furthermore, the prohibition on circumvention does not extend to an individual who has already obtained an authorized copy of a copyrighted work. (252)

Section 1202 prohibits interference with the integrity of copyright management information. (253) "Copyright management information" includes: (i) the name of the work; (ii) the name of the author; (iii) the name of the copyright owner; (iv) the name and other identifying information about the author of a performance fixed, for example, on audio CD; (v) the name and other identifying information about the writer, performer, or director of a fixed audio-visual work; and (vi) terms and conditions of use. (254) Finally, "copyright management information" includes any information that the Register of Copyrights may require by regulation. (255)

Section 1202(a) prohibits knowing dissemination of false copyright management information, if done with the intent to induce, enable, facilitate, or conceal copyright infringement, while [section] 1202(b) prohibits the intentional removal of copyright management information and the dissemination of works from which the copyright management information has been removed. (256) The statute also prohibits tampering with the symbols that refer to this information, including Internet hypertext links to web pages containing copyright management information. (257)

The "safe harbor defense" provides a defense against contributory liability for ISPs whose services are used to violate the DMCA. (258) An ISP is exempt from liability if it: (i) did not know of the infringement or the facts making infringement apparent; (ii) received no material benefit from the infringement; and (iii) acted expeditiously to remove the offending sites once it was made aware of them. (259)

Violation of either of these sections is subject to a maximum fine of $500,000 or up to five years imprisonment, or both, for a first offense, and a maximum fine of $1,000,000 or up to ten years imprisonment, or both, for repeat offenses. (260)

5. Electronic Communications Privacy Act

The Electronic Communications Privacy Act of 1986 ("ECPA") (261) regulates crimes with no close "traditional crime" analog, such as hacking. Unlike CFAA, ECPA approaches such crimes by updating existing federal prohibitions against intercepting wire and electronic communications. (262) ECPA updated Tire III and created the Stored Communications Act ("SCA"). (263) ECPA attempts to curb hacking activities by fortifying the privacy rights of computer users (264) and enabling law enforcement officers to employ electronic surveillance in the course of investigating computer crimes. (265) The government has used ECPA to prosecute hackers, (266) although they generally rely on CFAA for such prosecutions. (267) Prosecutors have invoked ECPA, however, against piracy of electronically encrypted, satellite-transmitted television broadcasts. (268) Devices used to intercept cable television signals likewise fall within ECPA's purview. (269)

a. Stored Communications Act

Congress intended for the SCA to protect stored email and voicemail. The SCA prohibits any person from gaining (1) intentional access (2) without or exceeding authorization (3) to a facility that provided an electronic communication service and (4) using that access to obtain, alter, or prevent authorized access to a communication in electronic storage. (270)

There is a good faith defense available for parties who reasonably relied on a warrant, grand jury subpoena, or other exception to the SCA. (271) In addition, the SCA does not apply to ISPs reading stored communications on their own systems. (272) Nor does it apply if one of the parties to the stored communication gives permission to access. (273)

For violations of the SCA a first-time offender shall be fined under Title 18, imprisoned for not more than one year, or both. If the SCA is violated for purposes of private financial gain or malicious destruction or damage, a first-time offender shall be fined under Title 18, imprisoned for not more than five years, or both. (274) A repeat offender shall be fined finder Title 18, imprisoned for not more than ten years, or both. (275) A repeat offender shall be fined under Title 18, imprisoned for not more than five years, or both. (276) Additionally, the SCA's provisions for money damages can address governmental as well as private transgressions. (277)

b. Title III (Wiretap Act)

ECPA extended the prohibitions in Title III of the Omnibus Crime Control and Safe Streets Act of 1968 ("Title III") (278) on intercepting oral and wire communication to include electronic communications intercepted during transmission. (279) Title III was originally intended to protect privacy by codifying the Fourth Amendment standards for wiretapping and applying them to civilians. (280) Now, Title III prohibits any person from intercepting or attempting to intercept any "wire, oral, or electronic communication." (281)

Under Title HI, the government needs a court order for a wiretap. (282) The court may require a showing that normal investigative techniques for obtaining the information have failed or are likely to fail. (283) It may also require the government minimize the intrusion of any interception. (284) The application to the court must show, through a sworn affidavit, why the intercept is necessary as opposed to other less-intrusive investigative techniques. (285) It must also provide additional detail, including: whether there have been previous interceptions of the target's communications; the identity of the target (if known); the nature and location of the communication facilities; and, a description of the type of communications sought and the offenses to which the communications relate. (286)

Senior DOJ staff, the principal prosecuting attorney of a state, or an attorney for the government must approve the Title III application, depending on the circumstances. (287) The interception can last no longer than thirty days without an extension by the court. (288) Courts can also require that they receive progress reports. (289) In addition, DOJ has other procedures governing the use of Title HI surveillance including requiring approval from the Office of Enforcement Operations ("OEO") in the Criminal Division of the DOJ. (290)

i. Defenses

There is a good faith defense available for parties who reasonably relied on a warrant, grand jury subpoena, or other exception to Title III. (291) Title III also allows computer service providers who are victims of attacks by computer trespassers to authorize persons acting under color of law to monitor trespassers on their computer systems in a narrow class of cases without a court order. (292) A computer trespasser is a person "who accesses a protected computer without authorization and thus has no reasonable expectation of privacy in any communications transmitted to, through, or from the protected computer." (293) Notably, the law does not reach a person known to have an existing contractual relationship with the owner or operator for access to all or part of the protected computer. (294) Interception of an unscrambled satellite communication intended for retransmission to the public is also not punishable under this section. (295) Keystroke loggers may also be exempt under Title III. (296)

ii. Penalties

Remedies for violating Title HI include criminal sanctions, civil suit, and adverse employment action for law enforcement officials. (297) For repeat offenders, a violation of Title III can result in a fine, imprisonment for not more than five years, or both. (298) If first-time offenders violate the statute for purposes other than private financial gain, and the illegally received communication is not scrambled or part of a cellular telephone communication, punishment is limited to imprisonment of not more than one year, and a fine. (299)

Under the Guidelines, defendants convicted of intercepting communications or eavesdropping receive a base offense level of nine. (300) If the purpose of the conduct was to obtain direct or indirect commercial advantage or economic gain, the offense level is increased by three. (301) Additionally, if the purpose of the conduct was to facilitate another offense with a higher offense level, the guideline applicable to an attempt to commit that offense applies. (302)

Moreover, evidence seized in violation of Title III or the Fourth Amendment may be suppressed. (303) Additionally, Title III's provisions for money damages can address governmental as well as private transgressions. (304)

c. Statutory Issues

Effectively, Title III governs communications in transit, while the SCA governs communications in storage. However, it is not always obvious which ECPA provisions cover communications, such as electronic mail, that may be stored during transmission. In United States v. Councilman, (305) the First Circuit held that an interception of electronic communications took place even though the intercepted e-mails had been stored periodically during transmission. (306) The Court found that the legislative history shows that Congress only intended to include stored copies of the e-mail at the sender's location. (307)

This holding stands in contrast with the holdings of cases in the Third, Fifth, Ninth and Eleventh Circuits which found "that the Wiretap Act's prohibition on intercepting electronic communications does not apply when they are contained in electronic storage, whether such storage occurs pre-or post-delivery, and even if the storage lasts only a few mili-seconds." (308) Furthermore, the circuits, including one case from the First Circuit in 2003, have held that the definition of "intercept" "encompasses only acquisitions contemporaneous with transmission." (309) It is possible to distinguish the facts in Councilman from those in the other circuits, although the logical extension of the legal reasoning remains in conflict. For example, in Steve Jackson, (310) the Fifth Circuit found that unread e-mail in the recipient's mailbox is stored and therefore was not intercepted even though the recipient had not read it yet. (311) However, the interception in Councilman took place before the file reached the user's mailbox, (312) so the two cases can be reconciled by assuming that e-mail transmission ends at the user's mailbox, not when the user opens the e-mail. (313)

6. Identity Theft

Section 1028 of Title 18 prohibits the knowing transfer, possession, or use of a means of identification, such as names, social security numbers, and dates of birth, to commit a crime. (314) It prohibits the production, (315) transfer, (316) or possession, in certain circumstances, (317) of false (318) or illegally issued identification documents. (319) It further prohibits production, transfer, or possession of a "document-making implement," (320) specifically including computers, with the intent to use it in the production of a false identification document. (321) The term "transfer" includes making either false identification documents or the software or data used to make them available online. (322)

a. Penalties

Illegal possession, transfer, or use of a means of identification, possession of five or more stolen or false identification cards with intent to transfer, use of at least one stolen or false identification card to aid an illegal activity, or production, transfer or use of less than five stolen or false identification cards results in a fine, a maximum sentence of five years imprisonment, or both. (323) Illegal possession, transfer, or use of a means of identification that makes more than $1,000 in a year, or transfer or production of a false identification document or document-making implement, are punished by a fine, not more than fifteen years imprisonment, or both. (324) Up to twenty years imprisonment is prescribed for these crimes for recidivists, if the crime is intended to aid drug trafficking, or is committed in connection with a violent crime. (325) There is a maximum sentence of thirty years if the crime is committed to "facilitate an act ... of terrorism." (326)

The Guidelines ordinarily apply a baseline of six with upward departures based on the size of the monetary lOSS.327 Where the primary purpose of the offense is to violate, or assist in violating, immigration laws, different sections apply. (328) Furthermore, where the established schedule does not fully capture the harmfulness and seriousness of the conduct, an upward departure beyond that which the Guidelines recommend is permissible. (329)

7. Wire Fraud Statute

The federal wire fraud statute (330) prohibits the use of interstate wire communications to further a fraudulent scheme to obtain money or property. (331) Several cases have held that the wire fraud statute applies to computer crimes. (332) District courts have taken divergent positions as to whether the wire fraud statute reaches copyright infringement. (333) Congress later amended the Copyright Act to address this issue. (334)

Penalties for violation of the wire fraud statute can be severe. Violations of the wire fraud statute are punishable by fines, imprisonment of up to twenty years, or both. (335) If the violation affects a financial institution, the punishment is a fine of not more than $1,000,000, imprisonment of not more than thirty years, or both. (336) Violation of the wire fraud statute is also a predicate offense for RICO and money-laundering charges. (337)

Defendants convicted of wire fraud are subject to punishment for deprivation of the intangible right to the honest services of government officials. (338) The base offense level is fourteen, and is increased if the loss to the government or the value gained by a public official exceeds $5,000. (339) If the offense involves an elected official or one holding a decision-making or sensitive position, the offense level increases by four. (340) Otherwise, the base offense level is six and increases according to the table in that provision if the gain or loss exceeds $5,000. (341)

C. Enforcement

Computer crimes are notoriously difficult to prosecute due to both the nature of the technology itself and the relative unfamiliarity of law enforcement with the technology. For example, people may encrypt data so that even if law enforcement seizes or intercepts the data, they will be unable to understand its contents or use it as evidence. The nature of the Internet allows people to engage in criminal conduct online with virtual anonymity. (342) With respect to computer crimes such as hacking, a victim may never realize that anyone attacked her. Further impeding law enforcement, many private and commercial entities that do detect an intrusion are afraid to report offenses due to the potential for negative publicity. (343)

The FBI and DOJ have created numerous programs and deployed new technologies to aid in the investigation and prosecution of computer crime. In 1998 the FBI launched a new division, the Cyber Division, dedicated to investigating computer crimes. (344) The Cyber Division is designed to act as a central coordinator for the FBI divisions that address computer crimes. (345) Specifically, the Cyber Division is responsible for criminal investigations of intellectual property, high-tech, and computer crimes. (346) The Cyber Division also has jurisdiction over investigations of online child pornography through the Innocent Images National Initiative ("IINI"). (347) Between fiscal years 1996 and 2007, there was a 2062 percent increase in the number of IINI cases opened. (348) The FBI also investigates computer crimes through its Internet Crime Complaint Center ("IC3"), (349) which acts as an intermediary between law enforcement agencies and victims of computer fraud. In 2008, the IC3 received 275,284 complaints of Internet-based fraud and other crimes, a 33.1 percent increase over the previous year. (350)

DOJ's efforts to combat computer crime are centralized in its Computer Crime and Intellectual Property Section ("CCIPS"). (351) The CCIPS is responsible for prosecuting computer crimes, lobbying for strengthened penalties, and pushing for expanded coverage of the federal computer crime statutes. (352)

In March of 2004, the DOJ launched the Task Force on Intellectual Property to signal a renewed emphasis on combating intellectual property crime. (353) This became part of a multi-agency Strategy Targeting Organized Piracy ("STOP") initiative involving the Department of Commerce, Department of Homeland Security, and the Office of the United States Trade Representative. (354) The Task Force has called for an expansion of the Computer Hacking and Intellectual Property ("CHIP") program. (355) CHIP units within U.S. Attorney's offices work closely with the FBI and other agencies to establish relationships with the high-tech community and encourage them to refer cases to law enforcement. (356) In addition to investigating and prosecuting computer crimes, CHIP provides specialized training for law enforcement and businesses on preventing, detecting, and investigating breaches in cyber security. (357)

DOJ has also stepped up its enforcement of child pornography. Through its Child Exploitation and Obscenity Section ("CEOS"), DOJ provides training and assistance to law enforcement officers throughout the country. (358) In 2002, DOJ formed the High Tech Investigative Unit ("HTIU") within CEOS. (359) The HTIU is a multi-agency computer forensic and investigatory unit targeting child pornography and offenses against children that occur or are facilitated by the Internet. Prosecution of child pornographers appears to be increasing, despite the constitutional challenges to the various Federal Child Pornography statutes. (360)

Given the global nature of Internet-related crimes, CCIPS and CEOS must work with many other countries to achieve effective prosecution of cases involving organized Internet piracy and Internet-related child exploitation. (361) Even so, the proliferation of computer bulletin boards, peer-to-peer networking, and other online services has created an ongoing qualitative and quantitative challenge. (362)

IV. STATE APPROACHES

A. Overview of State Criminal Codes

In 1978, state legislatures began enacting computer crime statutes, beginning with Arizona (363) and Florida. (364) Since then, every state has enacted some form of computer-specific criminal legislation. (365) Approximately half of the states modeled their statutes on the 1977 or 1979 versions of the proposed Federal Computer Systems Protection Act, (366) while the remainder enacted comprehensive computer-assisted crime statutes less closely related to the proposed federal legislation. (367) The precise definitions and penalties in these specialized provisions offer significant advantages over general criminal codes by explicitly addressing the unique issues posed by computer crimes, thereby promoting computer security, enhancing deterrence, and facilitating prosecution. (368)

Like the federal statutes, many of the state statutes divide computer crimes into the same three categories: "crimes where a computer is the target, crimes where a computer is a tool of the crime, and crimes where a computer is incidental." (369)

Reforms in state computer crime statutes have included provisions expanding forfeiture of computer equipment used in crimes, allowing state authorities to seize property involved in computer crimes. (370) Some states have begun to respond to the growing concerns of online harassment by criminalizing online threats by including electronic communications under "unconsented contact" in anti-stalking statutes, (371) and incorporating computers and electronic communications devices into general telephone harassment statutes. (372) Other state statutes specifically address the problem of offenders whose target victims are minors. (373) These statutes, however, may face significant constitutional challenges on First Amendment grounds. (374)

One particularly widespread initiative among the states is the effort to thwart spam. Thirty-nine states have enacted anti-spam laws regulating the use of Internet communications to send unsolicited advertisements for the purpose of promoting real property, goods, or services for sale or lease. (375)

Other states have recognized that prevention may be less difficult than apprehending and prosecuting computer criminals. For instance, Nebraska's computer crime statute empowers potential victims to implement their own security measures. (376) Several states have enacted statutes that provide a civil cause of action for compensatory damages, (377) thereby encouraging victims of computer crimes to come forward.

In order to prevent the proliferation of "spyware," a type of software usually unknowingly installed that collects a computer user's private information or displays unsolicited advertisements to the user, many states have enacted "antispyware" laws, often with criminal penalties. (378) However, spyware companies are rarely, if ever, criminally prosecuted. (379)

In the absence of federal legislation, 23 states (380) have passed legislation protecting private personal information and setting requirements for the use and storage of such data. (381) Most of these statutes closely follow the provisions of the landmark statute passed by California in 2002. (382)

B. Enforcement

Prosecution of computer crimes under state law has been increasing. (383) In 2005, 60 percent of prosecutors' offices reported prosecuting either felony or misdemeanor computer-related crimes under their state's computer statutes. (384) In addition, 89 percent of offices serving populations of one million or more reported conducting such prosecutions. (385) While the prosecution of child pornography was the most popular charge, state prosecutors have also charged computer crimes ranging from credit card fraud, to unauthorized access to computers, to cyber stalking. (386)

V. INTERNATIONAL APPROACHES

Developing an international paradigm for addressing computer crime is difficult, given the global nature of the technology. This Section covers issues in international computer crime law and addresses solutions to these problems, as well as areas of convergence and cooperation among nations, international organizations, and private corporations.

A. Issues

All nations continue to struggle to define computer crimes and develop computer crime legislation applicable to both domestic and international audiences. (387) Purely domestic solutions are inadequate because cyberspace has no geographic or political boundaries (388) and many computer systems can be easily and surreptitiously accessed from anywhere in the world. (389) International financial institutions are common targets for computer fraud and embezzlement schemes. (390) In addition, the development of sophisticated computer technology has enabled organized crime and terrorist groups to bypass government detection and carry out destructive acts of violence. (391) Even when computer-specific criminal statutes are in place, however, the rules of evidence in several industrialized countries could continue to hinder prosecutions until they adapt them to computer crimes. (392)

Countries that restrict their political discourse face the problem that the Interact provides a source of "illegal" information that is difficult to regulate. (393) Moreover, what constitutes "acceptable" speech in the various countries on the information super-highway differs greatly. In Germany and France, the dissemination of Nazi propaganda and paraphernalia is illegal. (394) Such material, however, is easily accessible via the Internet. Countries observing strict Islamic law have similar problems. (395)

Solutions to freedom of expression issues on the Internet have varied widely. France and Germany initially tried to target ISPs. (396) Germany has since decided not to hold ISPs "liable for content they merely transmit." (397) China, on the other hand, has implemented regulations that criminalize the "distribution or consumption via the Internet of ... 'harmful information.'" (398) Cuba has addressed the problem by limiting Internet access, allowing only 200,000 of its some eleven million citizens to have access. (399)

Intellectual property crimes are also a serious problem in the international arena. International software piracy remains endemic. (400) Software piracy remains at around 41 percent worldwide. (401) In practical terms, this means that approximately 41 percent of all business software applications existing on PCs around the world continue to be unpaid-for, illegal copies.

B. Solutions

While "computer crime" remains loosely defined, most industrialized countries have amended their law to address four needs created by computer crimes: (i) protection of privacy; (ii) prosecution of economic crimes; (iii) protection of intellectual property; (402) and (iv) procedural provisions to aid in the prosecution of computer crimes. (403) Worldwide, national governments are adopting computerspecific criminal codes that address unauthorized access and manipulation of data similar to the CFAA. (404)

While a number of differences remain, there are significant areas of convergence in nations' legislation. (405) By defining specific new offenses and penalties, these codes avoid analytical difficulties that arise when general criminal laws are applied to computer crimes. There have also been two significant steps towards achieving a uniform transnational legal framework for addressing multinational computer-related crimes. First, thirty-nine countries have signed the Council of Europe's Treaty on Cybercrime. (406) The Treaty requires parties to: (i) establish substantive laws against cybercrime; (ii) ensure that their law enforcement officials have the necessary procedural authorities to investigate and prosecute cybercrime effectively; and (iii) provide international cooperation to other parties in the fight against computer-related crime. (407) The United States became a party to the Treaty on January 1, 2007. (408) Second, the United States participates in the Subgroup on High-Tech Crime at G-8's Lyon Group. (409) One accomplishment of the Subgroup is the development of a network that allows law enforcement authorities of member nations to contact each other for rapid assistance in investigating computer crime and preserving electronic evidence. (410)

In addition to increased multinational governmental cooperation, international organizations and private corporations are also working to combat international computer crimes by contributing to the drive to harmonize national legislation. (411) For example, the Business Software Alliance, a software industry trade group, has an international copyright enforcement program involving national software trade associations and law enforcement agencies. (412) Nonetheless, international efforts have been mixed.

11

Data Security, Privacy, and Identity Theft

The Economics Behind the Policy Debates

William Roberds and Stacey L. Schreft

INTRODUCTION AND SUMMARY

A by product of improved information technology has been a loss of privacy. Personal information that was once confined to dusty archives can now be readily obtained from proprietary data services, or it may be freely available (and, as Facebook users know, often voluntarily provided and accessible) through the Internet. While the increased collection and dissemination of personal data have undoubtedly provided economic benefits, they have also diminished people's sense of privacy and, in some cases, given rise to new types of crime.

Is this loss of privacy good or bad? Press accounts repeatedly argue the latter: Too much data are being collected in ways that are too easy for criminals to access. (1) But in a thought-provoking essay, Swire (2003) argues that a meaningful answer to this question requires some notion of efficient confidentiality of personal data--that is, of a degree of privacy that properly balances the costs and benefits of our newfound loss of anonymity. In this article, we explore the concept of efficient confidentiality, using some ideas from economic theory.

Data security, privacy, and identity theft: the economics behind the policy debates.
William Roberds, Stacey L. Schreft. Economic Perspectives Spring 2009 v33 i1 p22(9).

LOSS OF PRIVACY: THE COSTS ARE LARGE AND EASY TO FIND

The most dramatic consequence of the increased availability of personal information has been the emergence of a new form of payment fraud, identity theft. The 1998 U.S. Identity Theft and Assumption Deterrence Act (ITADA) defines identity theft as the knowing transfer, possession, or usage of any name or number that identifies another person, with the intent of committing or aiding or abetting a crime. Traditional varieties of identity theft, such as check forgery, have long flourished, but over the last decade, identity theft has become a major category of crime and a significant policy issue. (2)

Identity theft takes many guises, but it is divided into two general categories: existing account fraud and new account fraud. Existing account fraud occurs when a thief uses an existing credit card or similar account information to illicitly obtain money or goods. New account fraud (traditionally) occurs when a thief makes use of another individual's personal information to open one or more new accounts in the victim's name. Both types of identity theft depend on easy access to other people's data.

Today, identity theft is big business. A study conducted by the Federal Trade Commission (FTC), encompassing both new account fraud and existing account fraud, indicates that in 2006 identity thieves stole about $49.3 billion from U.S. consumers. (3) When the time and out-of-pocket costs incurred to resolve the crime are added in, identity theft cost U.S. consumers $61 billion in 2006 (Schreft, 2007). Even this is a conservative estimate, however, as it omits certain categories of identity theft and some types of costs that are not generally known to consumers. For example, an increasingly prevalent type of identity theft is fictitious or synthetic identity fraud, in which a thief combines information taken from a variety of sources to open accounts in the name of a new fictitious identity (Cheney, 2005; and Coggeshall, 2007). There is no single victim, in contrast to traditional types of identity theft, but retailers and ultimately consumers end up bearing the cost.

Much of the data used in identity theft is obtained through low-tech channels. In consumer surveys, victims who know how their identifying information was stolen commonly attribute identity theft to stolen wallets or mail or to personal acquaintance with the identity thief(Kim, 2008). In these same surveys, however, the large majority of identity theft victims are unable to pinpoint how the thief obtained their data. Available evidence suggests that much of these data are obtained through illicit access (called "breaches") of commercial or government databases.

Statistics on data breaches are available from information security websites, such as Attrition.org and the Identity Theft Resource Center (www.idtheftcenter.org). Certainly data breaches are numerous and increasing: Attrition.org lists 326 reported data breach "incidents" for 2007, leading to the compromise of 162 million records of personal data, as compared with 11 reported incidents and 6 million compromised records in 2003. (4) These numbers must be placed in perspective. A data breach does not necessarily lead to identity theft, and one reason for the upsurge in reported breaches is the spread of state laws that require consumer notification when a data breach occurs (Anderson, Durbin, and Salinger, 2008). Nevertheless, there is widespread recognition that data breaches promote identity theft. A strong demonstration of this can be found in the August 2008 indictment of an 11-person, global identity theft ring, responsible for the theft of 41 million credit card and debit card numbers, as well as hundreds of millions of dollars in fraud losses. (5)

THE BENEFITS OF LOSS OF PRIVACY: MORE SUBTLE, BUT SUBSTANTIAL

If identity theft costs the U.S. economy so much, are there offsetting benefits? To try and make sense of this question, we will employ a branch of economics known as monetary theory Broadly speaking, monetary theory seeks to understand how transactions are structured within an economy.

The classic model of monetary theory was proposed by Knut Wicksell (1935). Wicksell's model economy is depicted in figure 1 and consists of only three individuals: Andy, Bob, and Clyde (A, B, and C, for short). Andy can produce a good valued by Bob, Bob can produce a good valued by Clyde, and Clyde can produce a good valued by Andy. The point of Wicksell's model is that in real-world economies, transactions typically happen between people who cannot deal through simple barter. For example, when Andy and Bob meet, Bob would like to purchase Andy's good, but the good that Bob has available to trade is only valued by Clyde. How should exchange proceed?

One way to solve this problem is through the use of cash. Suppose that A and B meet on every Monday, B and C meet on every Wednesday, and A and C on Fridays. Then if everyone agrees that the goods they exchange are each worth $1, the economy can function perfectly well with a "money supply" of two dollar bills. (6) For example, Bob sells his good to Clyde on every Wednesday, earning a dollar that he uses to buy Andy's good the following Monday. Andy uses this dollar to buy a good from Clyde every Friday, and so on. This "Wicksell triangle" shows how cash can function as a sort of recordkeeping system for transactions within an economy; every dollar that someone spends is proof of an earlier sale by the same person. (7)

Cash has some well-known limitations, however--some of which appear even in the context of this simple model. For example, if Clyde gets sick or otherwise fails to show up one Wednesday, then Bob will have no money with which to make next Monday's purchase. In practice, cash has other drawbacks, including risk of counterfeit or theft, the inconvenience of finding an automated teller machine (ATM), limited usefulness in telephone and Internet transactions, and the fact that it does not pay interest.

The alternative to cash is credit. In Wicksell's model economy, cash would not be needed if A, B, and C could get together and agree that each individual would receive a good of their preferred type, so long as they had provided a good to someone else the previous week. That way, if an individual occasionally was unable to sell his good during one week, he could still purchase goods on the expectation that he would resume sales the following week. The value of this additional exchange of goods, beyond what would be possible if all transactions were only in cash, is known as a credit benefit. Paying by credit has other advantages, which are the "mirror image" of the disadvantages of cash: fewer trips to the bank, less liability in case of theft, ease in transactions at a distance, and the reduced need to carry non-interest-bearing cash. (8)

Any estimate of the total credit benefit in an economy is somewhat speculative, since it involves the comparison of the value of exchange in an actual economy to the value of exchange in a hypothetical economy where only cash is available for most transactions. (9) For a developed economy such as that of the U.S., however, this benefit is almost certainly quite large. For example, in 2006 (the year of the FTC identity theft survey), U.S. residents made about $3 trillion in purchases, using credit and debit cards. (10) If the credit benefit of these transactions alone (ignoring other types of credit transactions) amounted to, say, just 5 percent of their total value, the resulting benefit to the overall economy would be $150 billion--more than enough to outweigh the estimated costs of identity theft.

In the rest of this article, we will argue that some loss of privacy is central to the provision of this credit benefit.

IDENTITY: REAL AND TRANSACTIONAL

In Wicksell's model economy, there's no chance of identity theft. Andy, Bob, and Clyde are well known to one another, and as long as one of their mutual friends (say, Dave) can keep a tally of who's provided a good to whom, it would be easy to maintain a credit-based system of exchange. This system would be self-enforcing, since any shirking by one party would quickly be noted by Dave and immediately become apparent to the other parties. (11) Such informal credit systems are common among friends and families, in primitive societies, and in other settings with limited social interactions.

But most transactions in today's economy are either between 1) parties who are total strangers, and/ or 2) parties who feel no particular sense of obligation toward one another. Credit in such situations requires some system to control two types of risk. The first type of risk is credit risk--the risk that the purchaser may not repay the debt incurred. Overcoming credit risk requires a way to keep track of "credit histories," that is, a way to restrict the use of credit to people who habitually pay their bills. The second type of risk is fraud risk--the risk of deception by the purchaser. Overcoming fraud risk requires a way to associate transactors with credit histories: For example, I may have a spotless credit record, but somehow that information has to be conveyed to the grocery store before I'm allowed to leave the store with a bag of groceries. To be effective, both types of services require the accumulation, storage, and distribution of large amounts of personal data. But the data required by the second service concern a person's identity, and are bound to be of a more confidential and controversial nature. (12)

"Identity" in general refers to all the distinguishing attributes of an individual--potentially a very long list. The term personal identifying data (PID) is used to describe some portion of a person's identity--name, birth date, Social Security number, etc.--that is readily observable by others. In order to distinguish individuals, the credit bureaus, credit card companies, data brokers, and other parties in the credit industry have compiled large databases of PID. These subsets of a person's "real" identity that are stored by these parties and used in transacting can be thought of as transactional identities (Schreft, 2007). Once the relevant data have been verified, a person's transactional identity may be augmented by the creation of new, synthetic data unique to that person, such as a credit card number,

PIN (personal identification number), and so on (Kahn and Roberds, 2008).

A typical credit transaction--say, a purchase of a bag of groceries, using a credit or debit card--can be thought of as a merchant exchanging goods in return for two essential pieces of payment information corresponding to the types of risk described previously: 1) that the purchaser, based on his credit history, is likely to pay his bill (13) and 2) that the purchaser's transactional identity is genuine so that the consumer is not a fraudster.

TRANSACTIONAL IDENTITIES AS CLUB GOODS

All credit-based payments require systems for processing valuable information. We can think of this information (credit histories and transactional identities) as economic goods, or items having value in exchange. These goods have value, since they facilitate the exchange of other goods (say, groceries) that people want to consume. Electronic versions of payment data, once amassed, can be stored at a few locations and then shared among payment system participants at very low cost. The data used in credit-based transactions meet Varian's (1998) description of a digital good, a good that can be stored and transferred in digital form.

Digital goods are also nonrival goods, meaning that they are not diminished by successive use. This distinguishes them from rival goods, such as cars and cornflakes; one individual's consumption of a rival good diminishes or eliminates the possibility of another person consuming it. Other examples of digital (and also nonrival) goods are given by the electronic information that is incorporated into broadcast and cable television, computer programming, or recorded music and video: For instance, my consumption of an episode of American Idol does not diminish another's enjoyment of the same episode. The same holds true with payment data, including transactional identities: The fact that Wal-Mart knows that I am not a fraudster does not diminish the value of the same information to Home Depot.

Nonrival goods are classified as club goods or public goods. A club good is an excludable nonrival good--that is, one for which a group or individual can be excluded from consuming (for example, cable TV programming). (14) A public good is a nonexcludable nonrival good--that is, one for which access cannot be limited (for example, national defense or clean air). The club good classification is more appropriate for payment information, since access to this information can be controlled (to a greater or lesser degree).

The "nonrivalness" of electronic payment information is a tremendous source of economic efficiency. Turning the clock back several decades, in any retail situation involving credit, a merchant had to independently come by the information needed to assess a customer's creditworthiness. The high cost of this information meant that credit was impractical in many situations, for example, during travel or for small transactions. The development of the credit industry (the large databases of credit histories and transactional identities, credit and debit cards, electronic authorization procedures, and antifraud technologies) has meant that merchants can take advantage of economies of scale in managing this information, and has spread the costs of information management over a larger group of merchants (and, ultimately, consumers). (15) This has, in turn, increased the credit benefit available to society as a whole.

Of course, the transformation of payment information into a nonrival good has not occurred in isolation. All kinds of data (music, video, maps, encyclopedias, and celebrity gossip) have been widely digitized, and thanks to the essentially nonrival nature of digital goods, they are rapidly accumulated and widely disseminated.

THE DARK SIDE OF NONRIVALNESS

A central feature of any digital good is its quality. Recorded music or video, for example, is useless if the original is garbled. A potentially interesting website may seem less so if it is known to harbor computer viruses. Quality is especially critical for payment data because people using a payment system expect it to work flawlessly virtually 100 percent of the time. Contamination of a payment system's data through even a few errors or instances of fraud can quickly erode its value.

A "dark side" of the efficient production of payment information is that it can compromise quality; that is, it can facilitate fraudulent activity as well as legitimate use. Once a fraudster has assumed another person's transactional identity (through either new or existing account fraud), the fraudster becomes an apparently legitimate participant in one or more payment systems and, by extension, a legitimate participant in the eyes of many participants in those systems. This vulnerability means that payment data, as an economic good, will only have value in the presence of the complementary good "data integrity," which is the quality and reliability of the data incorporated into the payment system (Braun et al., 2008). (16) Data integrity, like the underlying payment data, is a nonrival (club) good: The assurance that a payment information database is secure against data breaches is not diminished by successive use.

Another widely recognized drawback of modern payment arrangements stems from the more difficult to measure, but nonetheless important, consequences of diminished privacy. That is, the digitization of personal data contained in transactional identities has made these data available to many more people than ever before, often with negative consequences. These may take the form of intangible, but undeniable, costs in terms of people's loss of a "sense of space" about their personal lives. Or, for victims of identity theft, these costs may assume a more concrete form, through harassment by bill collectors, misplaced civil lawsuits, or even criminal investigations.

Many current payments and credit practices can be interpreted as attempts to partly restore the sense of privacy that may have existed in earlier times. When someone makes a purchase with a credit card, for example, that purchaser must effectively reveal some information to the merchant concerning his transactional identity--at least in the form of a relatively anonymous credit card number. This "surrender" of information represents a compromise between the merchant's need to identify the purchaser and the purchaser's desire to preserve his own privacy. Ideally, the merchant obtains enough information about the purchaser to determine that the transaction is legitimate, but no more. Consumers themselves have also undertaken forceful actions to safeguard their privacy, removing their names from public directories and mailboxes, installing paper shredders in their homes, and only giving out personal information to the most trusted parties.

Ironically, these very attempts to restore privacy may have contributed to the rise of identity theft, according to LoPucki (2003). LoPucki points out that in earlier times, individuals' access to credit often depended on their public persona, that is, on their standing within a local community or circle of business associates. Those seeking access to credit had to sacrifice much of their privacy (say, by socializing with their neighbors on a regular basis or joining civic organizations) in order to gain a reputation as an upstanding and creditworthy individual. Modern information technology, by enabling "instant credit" between relatively anonymous parties, has reduced the need for a public persona, but it has also multiplied the potential for fraud.

EFFICIENT CONFIDENTIALITY: BEYOND SUPPLY AND DEMAND

Using the ideas outlined thus far, we can now look at the issue of efficient confidentiality. The term confidentiality has a specific meaning in our context, which is the likelihood that a person's transactional identity will not be observed by miscreants and put to inappropriate use. A person's confidentiality can be thought of an economic good, whose provision in the marketplace depends on two other economic goods: 1) the amount of PID incorporated into that person's transactional identity and 2) the level of security for these data, or the degree of data integrity applied to the person's transactional identity. An increase in the second good always improves confidentiality. An increase in the first good can improve confidentiality, up to a point. The more data that are collected (all else being equal), the more precise the identification of individuals is, and hence, the greater the availability of credit-based payment is throughout the economy. But increasing the amount of PID collected (again, all else being equal) reduces privacy and can also amplify the negative consequences that occur when such data are misused, eroding confidentiality.

How should we know if these two goods (data collection and data security) are being efficiently provided? Textbook economic theory says that for many goods, it is (conceptually, at least) easy to describe how that good can be efficiently provided: An efficient market exists for a good when its supply curve intersects with its demand curve. The demand curve for a good, in turn, is given by its marginal benefit to buyers, and the supply curve is determined by sellers' marginal cost of producing that good. In a competitive industry, if the price of a good is above (below) its marginal cost, producers enter (leave) the industry until efficiency prevails.

Unfortunately this familiar model doesn't work for digital goods, since their marginal cost is practically zero. Instead, a more typical pattern for digital goods is for there to be competition among a few large producers, which are able to take advantage of the extensive economies of scale in these goods' production (think of the computer software and entertainment industries). Prices remain above marginal costs, so as to defray the costs of production.

We see the same pattern in the construction of transactional identities by a relatively small number of large players such as credit bureaus, credit card networks, and card issuing banks. (17) Through the accumulation of large amounts of PID, these organizations attempt to meet the demand for transactional identities that exists in the market economy. Just as with other digital goods, such as computer software and recorded video, it is hard to know whether these data are being efficiently collected and priced. (18)

The situation is different when we turn to the issue of data integrity. Because payment data are only useful if they are communicated (in some form), these data must be touched by a large number of hands to be of any value. A real-world list of such hands would include consumers, merchants, credit bureaus, banks, and payment processors. In other words, efficient production of data integrity, a club good, requires the cooperative efforts of a large number of "club members."

Large clubs often promote efficiency because they allow for economies of scale in the production of a good. But within large clubs, conflicts of interest can arise as to the amount of the good that should be provided. This is especially true for goods such as data integrity, for which the "weakest link" or "flood control" model of a nonrival good is often applicable (Hirshleifer, 1983).

For a weakest link good, the total amount of the good provided to the club is equal to the lowest amount of the good supplied by a club member (the weakest link in a chain, or the lowest levee in a flood control system). The idea of a weakest link is consistent with many press accounts of identity theft, in which a data breach at a single retailer or payment processor leads to widespread fraud. There is a natural tendency to supply an inefficiently small amount of a weakest link good (Varian, 2004), which can arise from the following conflict: A club member with relatively little at stake will tend to put less effort into providing the club good than a club member with a lot at stake. This tension is present in many situations involving data security (Anderson and Moore, 2006).

Recent changes in the payments industry's security practices can be seen as a response to this problem. For example, a set of industry-wide data security standards--the PCI (Payment Card Industry) standards (www.pcisecuritystandards.org)--has been created as a way of strengthening the weakest links in the data security chain. Another development along these lines has been the increasingly common practice of merchants quickly disposing of payment data, rather than storing it for an extended period of time. (19)

An additional source of inefficiency comes from externalities (also called spillovers) across data security practices. An externality occurs when the consumption or production of a good by one party affects another's, conferring benefits or costs on the other party. A negative externality results when a party does not take into account the full cost of his action to others.

In the context of data security, the potential for negative externalities exists for at least two reasons. First, as noted previously, payment data often passes through many hands, so it is difficult to determine how an identity thief was able to access the necessary data. Second, under current U.S. and Canadian laws, recovering the costs of a data breach through the courts can be difficult (Schreft, 2007; and Chandler, 2008). Either way, if payment data are stolen from one party and used to commit identity theft with costly consequences for another, the first party may not expect to pay the full costs of the breach. Taken together, these complications suggest that there are obstacles to the efficient provision of data integrity in the marketplace. Because payment system participants may not fully take into account all of the costs associated with their security practices, this can lead to underprovision of data security. This would, in turn, imply an inefficiently low level of confidentiality in the marketplace, even if the market is collecting the "right" amount of PID.

In Roberds and Schreft (2008), we present a model that shows how this inefficiency could be exacerbated by the interaction between PID collection and data security. If some payment systems are not adequately securing their data and other payment systems are alerted to this, then each system's best safeguard against identity theft may be to increase the amount of PID it uses for transactional identities. Under these circumstances, gathering more PID can reduce fraud, but doing this is inefficient because it further reduces confidentiality.

ROLES FOR REGULATION

The previous discussion points to a role for public policy. If the markets for information on transactional identities are providing inefficiently low levels of confidentiality, there may be ways for well-designed policies to improve on market outcomes.

One policy implication that is not supported is government entry into the markets for payment information. As with other types of club goods, the excludability of payment information provides a profit incentive to motivate ongoing improvements in efficiency. But the production of club goods is rarely a straightforward business, and it is usually subject to extensive policy interventions. Electronic entertainment products, computer software, and various types of

Internet content, to name just three examples, are frequent subjects of public controversy, legislation, regulation, and litigation.

This same general pattern is found in the markets for payment information. Various pieces of legislation and regulatory efforts have sought to address the "weakest link" and "spillover" problems identified before, but have stopped short of trying to micromanage industry practices. For example, the Fair and Accurate Credit Transactions Act of 2003 (commonly known as the FACT Act) seeks to increase the industry standards for minimally acceptable security practices. The FACT Act requires banks and other creditors to develop procedures to respond to account activity that could reasonably be interpreted as evidence of identity theft ("red flags"), but does not specify the details of how this should be done. (20)

In the same vein, a number of state laws now require that consumers be notified whenever their data are breached. One motivation for this requirement is to enable quicker detection of identity theft by consumers. An equally important purpose for this requirement, though, may be to motivate better security practices by increasing the costs of a data breach (in terms of both dollars and reputation). A number of states have taken another tack, which is to allow consumers to limit or "freeze" access to their credit reports, that is, to limit access to information on their transactional identities.

A concern with this type of regulation is the cost of compliance. Since securing data is costly, perfect confidentiality of personal data cannot be an efficient outcome, and should not be a goal of sensible regulation. As outlined in this article, some amount of identity theft is inevitable given modern information technology. Eliminating identity theft entirely would not be possible without eliminating the efficient sharing of information at the heart of our modern credit and payment systems.

PUBLIC GOODS

Government intervention is traditionally viewed as beneficial when it yields public goods. One such good is "public security," as is provided by the criminal justice system. The ITADA and various state laws have sought to discourage identity theft by imposing severe criminal penalties--a form of deterrence not available to the private sector.

The nature of identity theft puts limits on the effectiveness of criminal sanctions, however. By stealing someone else's payment data, an identity thief gains that person's access to credit in largely anonymous situations, such as in purchases over the Internet. This same anonymity that benefits legitimate purchasers (in terms of access to credit with increased confidentiality) makes criminal prosecution of identity theft impossible in many cases--as when the identity thief is located in a different country from that of the victim.

Another noteworthy public good in this context is that of overall "confidence" in credit and payment systems. As discussed previously, people do not like to use payment systems without something close to 100 percent reliability. If incidences of identity theft and data breaches were to become sufficiently common, the result could be a loss of this public good--that is, a loss of confidence not only in the directly affected parties, but in credit-based payment more generally (Braun et al., 2008). One rationale for recent regulatory actions in the payments area is that, apart from the effects of any specific provisions, these laws and regulations demonstrate governments' commitment to maintain a reasonable standard for confidentiality of payment information.

CONCLUSION

In this article, we have looked at the issue of confidentiality of personal information from the standpoint of economic theory. Some loss of privacy is necessary for the credit benefit, which is a key advantage of modern payment systems. By consolidating personal information into transactional identities, information technology now allows people to enjoy this credit benefit in circumstances that would have been unthinkable a generation ago.

The sharing of information on transactional identities is vital to the operation of these payment systems. However, this information sharing can facilitate fraud in the form of identity theft. Information sharing can also create conflicts of interest that may not be easily resolved through the operation of the marketplace. Thoughtful public policy should be aimed at resolving these conflicts and providing public goods. The ultimate goal of regulation should not be absolute privacy of consumers or complete suppression of identity theft, but instead the promotion of efficient confidentiality of personal information.

REFERENCES AND NOTES DELETED

12

The CFO's Role in Managing Cyber Risk

Robert Gregg

Most organizations do less than they should to manage the risks associated with their handling of sensitive information. This can lead to data breaches and make companies susceptible to cybercrime. The key factors contributing to this growing problem, to a great extent, are due to archaic approaches to management structure and accountability for risks that are not aligned with today's environment.

The Obama Administration's May 2009 Cyberspace Policy Review found that American business losses due to cyber attacks had grown over the years to more than $1 trillion. And security software and services company Symantec Corp. found in its January 2010 internet Security Threat Report that new cyber threats on the Internet grew nearly 500 percent year-over-year from 2008 to 2009.

WHY DO ORGANIZATIONS SEEM UNABLE TO STEM THIS TIDE OF CYBERCRIME?

The Internet Security Alliance and the American National Standards Institute (ISA/ANSI) recently published The Financial Management of Cyber Risk, a report that explores the issue and makes concrete recommendations. These organizations brought together dozens of industry experts in cybercrime, security, privacy and risk management to look into these troubling trends and identify the underlying causes and develop practical solutions. The final report also describes the key role that the chief financial officer can and must play in addressing cyber risk.

Reprinted with permission from Financial Executive (Sept 2010) © Financial Executives International, 1750 Headquarters Plaza, West Tower, 7th Floor, Morristown, NJ 07960; 973 765-1000; www.financialexecutives.org.

WHY LOSSES DUE TO CYBER RISKS ARE GROWING

Several factors have contributed to the extraordinary growth in the financial losses to American businesses resulting from cyber attacks. Among them are the explosion in the number of attacks, the reduction in budgets for information security and failure to address cyber risks from an enterprise-wide strategic and cooperative perspective.

Cyber threats are doubling each year as a result of the global nature of cybercrime. Offshore organized crime efforts view this as a high leverage and profitable endeavor. The U.S. Secret Service estimated that there are between 40,000 and 50,000 hackers active in today's world who are developing their skills at a rapid rate to target vulnerabilities in corporate systems.

Cyber criminals are using social engineering to exploit the weaknesses of human and technical systems. Phishing attacks continue to grow and insidious malware has caused some of the largest and most costly data breach incidents during this past year.

Despite the active threat environment, a 2009 study by PricewaterhouseCoopers (Global Information Security Survey) revealed that 47 percent of enterprises are actually reducing their budgets for information security initiatives.

While this may seem perilous because of the level of financial exposure posed by cyber risks, the 2009 Center for Strategic & International Studies study, In the Crossfire: Critical Infrastructure in the Age of Cyber War states: "Making the business case for cyber security remains a major challenge because management often does not understand either the scale of the threat or the requirements for the solution."

The report notes that the most salient factor leading to the growth in cyber losses is that most organizations do not take a holistic, enterprise-wide management approach to quantifying and addressing cyber risks. It is common to consider this problem an "IT issue." By relegating the management of cyber risk to the information technology security team, organizations look at the problem too narrowly, without considering the larger costs and business issues they pose.

A 2008 Carnegie Mellon University study conducted by CyLab, Governance of Enterprise Security Study, concluded that less than half of U.S. companies have a formal enterprise risk management plan. Further, a study conducted last October by Deloitte, Information Security & Enterprise Risk, found that 65 percent of U.S. companies have neither a documented process to assess cyber risk nor a person in charge of the assessment process.

The Deloitte study also notes that 95 percent of U.S.-based corporate CFOs are not at all involved in the management of their company's information security risks, and that 75 percent also do not have a chief risk officer.

STEPS FOR ADDRESSING CYBER RISK

The good news in this high-risk environment is that the majority of data breaches are preventable. Testifying before Congress last year, Richard Schaffer of the National Security Agency stated: "Eighty percent of cyber attacks were preventable using existing standards, practices and technologies."

The ISA/ANSI paper mentioned above, representing some of the best thinking of dozens of experts from academia, government and industry, advises organizations how to address and manage cyber risks. It concludes that in order to effectively address cyber risk, organizations must follow the leadership of the CFO in owning and pursuing an enterprise-wide approach. It also outlines a set of key steps that every organization, led by their CFO, should follow.

- **Own the Problem.** Cyber risk must not be relegated to an IT issue. Senior executives with cross-departmental authority must take strategic and operational control of the cyber risk problem. The CFO in most organizations is the right individual to "own" and lead this effort.

- **Create a Cyber Risk Team.** Because of the breadth and complexity of cyber security issues, the responsible executive needs to form and lead a team that draws from relevant domain expertise across all functional areas of their organization.

- **Hold Regular Meetings.** Because of the unique and technical nature of cyber risk, meetings must be held regularly and ideally in person. It is often the case that such teams need to develop a common vocabulary to address issues, since often IT security people are used to "speaking a different language" than others.

- **Develop a Cross-Functional Cyber Risk Management Plan.** The adoption of a cyber risk plan by senior executive management will foster the proper level of visibility and understanding of the level of financial exposure inherent to cyber risk. In most organizations, it is the lack of risk awareness and appreciation that leads to inadequate management of the issue.

- **Create a Cyber Risk Budget.** The lack of appreciation for cyber risk by senior executives is partly because the financial exposure often is not quantified. It is recommended that the CFO quantify the organization's cyber risk, using a proposed model and then base the budget for managing cyber risk as a percentage of the exposure.

- **Implement and Audit Performance.** Cyber risk is a moving target. Once the plan is created to manage cyber risk and implementation is underway, the CFO must ensure that progress and performance is regularly assessed and periodically formally audited. In many industries--primarily financial services and health care-- this audit process is consistent with and will contribute toward regulatory compliance.

The CFO should be motivated to take these actions. If not, he or she is exposing their organization to huge risk of loss--financially as well as to the company's reputation and brand.

RELATED ARTICLE: A DATA BREACH SCENARIO

Data breaches are a fact of life for many organizations that maintain sensitive personal information on customers, clients, employees, partners, vendors and other individuals. Despite investments in security technology, data breach incidents are rising and exposing larger populations of individuals to risks of identity theft.

A recent example that illustrates both the attention being focused on cyber risk and the fallout that can result from a mishandling of a data breach incident is Health Net Inc. Health Net is one of the largest publicly traded managed-health organizations in the United States, insuring approximately six million customers in several states.

In May 2009, Health Net lost a computer hard drive that contained unencrypted records with protected health information (PHI) on more than 1.5 million of its members. PHI can contain sensitive patient information including health insurance identification numbers, doctors, medical services provided and diagnoses as well as other personal information such as name, birthday and social security number.

Under the Health Insurance Portability and Accountability Act of 1996 (HIPAA), organizations such as Health Net are responsible for maintaining the security and privacy of PHI.

Despite the company's belief it was compliant with the HIPAA security and privacy rules, this data breach was a significant violation that required notification to the affected individuals.

While Health Net became aware of this incident in May 2009, the company did not carry out the notification to insurance officials and the affected individuals until November--a full six months following the event. The delay was attributed to a detailed forensic investigation into the data contained on the laptop hard drive and the potential that it had been misused.

The delay led to a lawsuit filed by Connecticut Attorney General Richard Blumenthal charging Health Net with multiple violations of HIPAA privacy and security rules. The lawsuit alleged that the delay in notification to its members constituted an unfair trade practice under state law. Just recently, Health Net announced that it has settled this lawsuit with the Connecticut AG and will pay $250,000 in statutory damages. Health Net will also be liable for an additional $500,000 if misuse of the exposed information becomes detected in the future.

The settlement fees in this case are just the tip of the iceberg in terms of the financial implications of this data breach. Ponemon Institute research concludes that the costs associated with a data breach incident average $202 per affected individual. Using this rule of thumb, the costs to Health Net would be estimated at approximately $300 million.

Robert Gregg (bob.gregg@idexpertscorp.com) is CEO of ID Experts, a Portland, Ore.-based company that specializes in the prevention and remediation of privacy and security data breaches. He worked closely with the Internet Security Alliance and the American National Standards Institute on the recently published The Financial Management of Cyber Risk.

13

Riskiest Cities for Cybercrime

Findings, Better Business Bureau Statistics, Aging Population Puts UK Economy At Risk

Emily Holbrook

In this modern, electronic world, it is not surprising that cybercrime is on a constant rise. There are a frightening number of security breach incidents reported daily on DataLossDB.org, a database of breaches updated in real time. For instance, on the day of this writing, H&R Block reported a data breach involving 60 records, and the day before that, the Connecticut Office of Policy and Management reported a breach involving 11,000 records. The daily statistics are staggering.

But what are the riskiest cities for such a crime? Symantec, the largest maker of personal computer security software, including Norton AntiVirus, was wondering the same thing. So it partnered with Sperling's BestPlaces, an organization that analyzes data about various people and locations, to come up with the 50 riskiest cities for cybercrime. Seattle snagged the number one spot, followed by Boston and Washington, D.C. With more cyber-attacks and potential infections than any other city, along with widespread online behavior that exposes people to cybercrime (such as online shopping and banking online), Seattle rightfully earned the title of riskiest U.S. city for cybercrime. Boston and Washington came in second and third

Riskiest cities for cybercrime. Findings, Better Business Bureau statistics, aging population puts UK economy at risk Emily Holbrook. Risk Management May 2010 v57 i4 p44(2).

because, like Seattle, the cities experience a very high level of cybercrime, perhaps due in part to their large number of WiFi hotspots, as the study states. Rounding out the top ten were San Francisco; Raleigh, North Carolina; Atlanta; Minneapolis; Denver; Austin, Texas; and Portland, Oregon.

"With more people than ever relying on the internet to stay in touch, shop and pay their bills, feeling confident and secure in our information-driven world is vital," said Marian Merritt, Norton internet safety advocate. "This study highlights the cities most at risk of cybercrime and reminds individuals, families and businesses across the country of the hazards they face each time they go online."

Of the 50 major cities that were ranked, Detroit came in last as the least risky online city. Residents of the Motor City were found less likely to participate in risky online behavior compared to other cities in the study. Also ranking very low in cybercrime, access to the internet, expenditures on computer equipment and wireless internet access were Memphis, Tennessee, and El Paso, Texas, which came in 48th and 49th, respectively.

Part VI

STUDYING VICTIMS OF WHITE COLLAR CRIMES

14

Government of Canada Introduces Legislation to Stand Up for Victims of White-Collar Crime

The Honourable Rob Nicholson, P.C., Q.C., M.P. for Niagara Falls, Minister of Justice and Attorney General of Canada, and the Honourable Christian Paradis, Minister of Natural Resources, today announced that the Government re-introduced legislation to provide tougher sentences for fraud, to help combat white-collar crime.

"Our Government is standing up for victims of white collar-crime," said Minister Nicholson. "Our legislation would make jail time mandatory - at least two years for fraud over $1 million. It would toughen sentences further, by adding aggravating factors courts can consider."

These aggravating factors would include:

- the financial and psychological impact of the fraud on the victim, given the victim's particular circumstances, including their age, health and financial situation;

- the offender's failure to comply with applicable licensing rules or professional standards; and

- the magnitude, complexity, and duration of the fraud and the degree of planning that went into it.

"White-collar crime has a devastating impact on individuals and communities," said Minister Paradis. "Our government has listened to the concerns of victims of fraud. We are taking action to

Government of Canada Introduces Legislation to Stand Up for Victims of White-Collar Crime. Department of Justice Canada.

help them seek restitution and to ensure their voices are heard in sentencing those who have harmed them so profoundly."

The proposed legislation would require judges to consider demanding offenders make restitution to their victims in all fraud cases. It would permit the court to prohibit the offender from taking employment or doing volunteer work involving authority over other people's money. The court would also be permitted to receive and consider a Community Impact Statement that would describe the losses suffered as a result of a fraud perpetrated against a particular community, such as a neighbourhood, a seniors' centre or a club.

Standing Up for Victims of White-Collar Crime Fraud can include securities-related frauds such as Ponzi schemes, insider trading, and accounting frauds that overstate the value of securities. It also includes mass marketing fraud, mortgage and real estate fraud, and many other deceptive practices. There are always two elements that characterize fraud - deception or some other form of dishonest conduct, and depriving another person of their property or putting their property at risk.

Fraud can have a devastating impact on the lives of its victims, including loss of life savings and feelings of humiliation for having been deceived into voluntarily handing over their property. The Government of Canada is proposing to amend the fraud provisions of the Criminal Code by providing tougher sentences for those who victimize honest citizens.

SENTENCING

Sentencing-related measures have been proposed to better ensure that sentencing for large-scale fraud reflects the serious nature of the crime. These measures are aimed directly at shaping the sentence that can be imposed on the offender. These include:

- mandatory jail time of at least two years for fraud over $1 million regardless of the number of victims involved;

- additional statutory aggravating factors that can be applied tosentencing in fraud cases such as:

- the financial and psychological impact of the fraud on the victim, given the victim's particular circumstances, including their age, health and financial situation;

- the offender concealing or destroying records relating to the fraud or the disbursement of proceeds of the fraud;

- the offender failing to comply with applicable licensing rules or professional standards; and,

- the magnitude, complexity, and duration of the fraud and the degree of planning that went into it.

- requiring the court to indicate which statutory aggravating and non-mitigating factors it considered in determining the sentence, and;

- allowing the court to impose a prohibition order to prevent the offender from having employment or working in a volunteer capacity that involves having authority over other people's money.

RESTITUTION

Additional proposed measures are aimed at improving the responsiveness of the justice system to the needs of victims of fraud through restitution and community impact statements. These amendments are intended to increase the use of restitution orders in fraud cases by:

- requiring judges to consider restitution from the offender in all casesof fraud involving an identified victim with ascertainable losses. Judges would also be required to provide reasons if restitution is not ordered.

- requiring the Crown to advise the court what steps have been taken to allow victims to set out their readily ascertainable and quantified losses to the court so that restitution can be considered. This would ensure that sentencing does not proceed without any consideration of restitution or without any opportunity for victims to indicate to the Crown that they wish to seek restitution.

- developing a standard form for victims to indicate that they want the Crown to seek restitution from the offender and to set out their ascertainable losses.

COMMUNITY IMPACT STATEMENTS

A final measure proposed is with respect to Community Impact Statements. Currently, the Criminal Code requires the court to consider a Victim Impact Statement of an individual. This is a written statement made by the victim of a crime that describes the harm done to the victim and, more generally, the effect that the crime has had on his or her life. The statement is considered by the judge who is sentencing the offender.

In some fraud cases however, where a group of people have been targeted for fraud, direct victims and even others not financially affected may still suffer other impacts. The proposed amendments will include a provision to permit the court to receive a Community Impact Statement that would describe the losses suffered as a result of the fraud perpetrated against a particular community, such as a neighbourhood, an association or a seniors' group.

15

Government Whistleblowers

Crime's Hidden Victims

Carleen A. Botsko and Robert C. Wells.

Abstract

White-collar crime investigation presents several problems to whistleblowers. They may face protracted and tedious inquiries carried out by investigators who appear insensitive in their quest for facts. Whistleblowers may also initially feel guilty about turning in their employers, or for not reporting the crime when it first took place. In addition, they also face the risk of losing their jobs as the case is being investigated. As such, investigators should exhaust all means to protect the identities and alleviate the fear and anxiety often experienced by whistleblowers.

For the past 8 years, Tom has worked for the same Federal agency. He earns a good salary as a senior research analyst and owns a home in a quiet suburb. He and his wife have two children and a third is on the way. Although Tom is, by all accounts, a model employee, he is about to make a decision that will place his career, and eventually other aspects of his life, in jeopardy.

During the past several months, Tom has observed his supervisor taking routine lunches with a local contractor who does business with Tom's section. He also has learned from several knowledgeable sources that this same contractor paid for many of the frills included in his supervisor's recent Hawaiian vacation. While

Government whistleblowers: crime's hidden victims. Carleen A. Botsko, Robert C. Wells. The FBI Law Enforcement Bulletin July 1994 v63 n7 p17(5).

irritated by the apparent lack of judgment demonstrated by his supervisor, Tom did not wish to make waves in an otherwise ideal work situation.

Now, as his supervisor rummages through bids submitted by contractors for an upcoming project, Tom observes him dial the phone and ask for the contractor with whom he lunches regularly. In partial disbelief, Tom overhears his supervisor read off the bid totals.

Tom knows that this information must be reported to the appropriate authorities. While he has no interest in becoming involved in a lengthy Federal investigation, he does what he has been encouraged to do during numerous agency security awareness briefings--he dials his agency's hotline number.

Reluctantly, Tom has joined the ranks of an often-misunderstood circle referred to as government whistleblowers. Unfortunately, these potentially invaluable witnesses to serious criminal acts and breaches of public trust routinely must endure what Tom fears most--protracted and tedious inquiries carried out by investigators who appear insensitive as they methodically pursue "the facts."

This need not be the case. White-collar crime investigators can take steps to alleviate the fear and anxiety often experienced by whistleblowers. In doing so, they can successfully sustain these witnesses through the long and often-bewildering investigative/judicial process.

THE EMOTIONAL IMPACT OF CRIME

In white-collar crime investigations, the testimony provided by government whistleblowers may be the best evidence for proving a case. Investigators need to preserve the testimony of these important eye witnesses just as they would protect corporate financial records. An integral component of this effort includes understanding the emotional impact witnesses experience. Investigators must ensure that these emotional factors do not become barriers to the quality and quantity of information disclosed by these informers.

The Whistleblower as Victim

Traditionally, in many white-collar crime cases, the government is labeled as the victim. But what about individuals like Tom? In the months, or even years, ahead, his role will be that of a witness for the government. Still, his emotional response--including nervous distress caused by the retaliatory actions of his supervisor--closely parallels those of violent crime victims. In order to deal effectively with such witnesses, investigators must understand how the impact of crime affects an investigation.

A psychologist and former New York City police officer, Morton Bard, provided the first glimpse of the emotional impact of crime from the perspective of the victim. In a behavioral profile of victims and witnesses,(1) he identified three separate stages in the process of resolving the crisis brought on by their involvement in a crime. These three stages are impact, recoil, and reorganization.

Stage 1: Impact

The impact stage is characterized by disbelief, disorientation, disorganization/confusion, feelings of vulnerability, suggestibility, and difficulty in recalling details. In the case of whistleblowers, the impact stage begins when they report the crime and can last up to 72 hours.

Stage 2: Recoil

In the recoil stage, whistleblowers commonly exhibit intense anger, resentment, extreme fear, shame, or guilt, as well as phobic reactions to details of the crime, particular places, times of day, and kinds of people. This is the stage during which most white-collar crime investigators deal with witnesses. For whistleblowers, this stage begins several days after reporting the crime and continues until the investigation ends.

The recoil stage represents a particularly difficult period for most victims and witnesses. During this period, their thinking often focuses on understanding why the crime occurred or why they chose to get involved. Most will wake early each morning, as Tom did, thinking about the crime and mentally replaying the events in an attempt to understand it fully. During this period, some will take an emotional roller coaster ride. Moods will fluctuate between feelings of apathy and anger, resignation and rage, serenity and anxiety. Victims/witnesses may be obsessed with the crime one minute and deny such feelings the next.

In Tom's case, he became haunted by fears of reprisal at the hands of his supervisor. Because he experienced all of the emotional reactions common to the recoil stage, his family, friends, and coworkers noticed changes in his behavior. Once well-liked and well-respected, Tom no longer felt a part of the organization. He increasingly isolated himself from coworkers. Ultimately, his supervisor was able to exploit these changes in his behavior as justification for a series of negative job actions against him.

Stage 3: Reorganization

During the reorganization stage, feelings of fear and rage slowly diminish as the victim thinks and talks less about the crime. Like Tom, most victims, witnesses, or whistleblowers will be unable to achieve this stage of resolution while the criminal case is pending.(1)

White-Collar Crime Investigations

White-collar crime investigations should realize that criminal investigations may escalate the crisis experienced by whistleblowers. While Tom struggles with a disorienting assortment of emotional reactions, the justice system may add new elements to his ordeal.

In addition to the emotional reactions experienced in the impact, recoil, and reorganization stages, whistleblowers also face challenges brought on by the investigative process itself. Investigators should realize that these elements, often unique to white-collar crime cases, may affect an informer's ability to sustain the rigors of the investigative and judicial processes.

Perhaps the most profound of these factors is the time required to investigate and to prosecute a white-collar crime case successfully. Most citizens get their information concerning the workings of the criminal justice system from television. Of course, on television, cases move quickly--in sharp contrast to the slow, methodical process of investigating and prosecuting a case of fraud against the government. Whistleblowers should be informed from the outset that white-collar crime investigations may last 1 to 5 years.

The types of guilt experienced by whistleblowers may seriously affect their ability to provide information. Many whistleblowers will experience not one but two layers of guilt. As a whistleblower, the individual may initially feel guilty about "turning in" an employer, particularly one who has provided the employee with a "real" job or an opportunity to excel. Once the whistleblower resolves this layer of guilt, another often develops--guilt over not reporting the illegal activities when they first took place. Whistleblowers may believe that investigators view them as irresponsible for not reporting the incidents sooner. Investigators should reassure whistleblowers who place such undue pressure on themselves.

In addition, whistleblowers may fear losing their positions while the case is investigated. This fear results from the pressure of continuing to work within an environment that is under investigation. Whistleblowers often question whether their identity as the complainant has been disclosed. To allay these fears, investigators should assure whistleblowers that every effort will be taken to protect their identity.

DEALING WITH WHISTLEBLOWERS

To gather the most accurate information, investigators should first focus on the needs and concerns of whistleblowers. When whistleblowers sense a genuine interest in their welfare, they focus more energy on the needs of an investigation. Accordingly, investigators should learn more about the emotional reactions common to whistleblowers.(2)

Additionally, investigators should ask questions to find out whether informers are experiencing any emotional reactions. Are they getting along with coworkers, supervisors, spouses, children? Are they having trouble keeping focused either at home or at the office? Are they experiencing anger or guilt? Are they having difficulty sleeping?

If whistleblowers admit to a problem, investigators should discuss it with them. Most important, investigators should make sure that whistleblowers fully understand the process in which they are involved. Investigators may need to review whistleblowers' roles continually during the judicial process, depending on their emotional state and ability to deal with the situation.

It is important to give a whistleblower the opportunity to vent feelings of anger or fear before initiating any questioning. Investigators should ask how things are going and watch to see whether the whistleblower's body language and other nonverbal reactions match verbal responses. If the verbal response is positive while a frown forms on the subject's face, then investigators should understand that the whistleblower may not be emotionally prepared to cooperate fully.

Investigators should prompt whistleblowers to break down their resistance by eliciting questions from them before the inquiry begins. For example, they might consider saying, "We are going to be asking you a lot of questions, but before we do, do you have anything that you would like to ask?" A common response might be, "Yes, I have a question. How long is it going to take for the government to get this case to trial?" Such a question allows investigators to respond sympathetically, thus building trust and breaking down emotional barriers. A proper response would be, "You are right. We know this has not been easy for you. We would like to tell you where we are with the investigation."

Investigators should also acknowledge whistleblowers' agendas in order to help disarm the hidden anger that may develop toward the government. By letting whistleblowers know what to expect, investigators remove another barrier, allowing whistleblowers to devote more energy to recalling information, thus enhancing the investigation.

As part of this effort, investigators should also keep whistleblowers informed of the status of the investigation. Generally, it is best to keep them advised as major events unfold, such as possible indictment, arrest, or trial dates.

Finally, investigators should advise whistleblowers of their rights. Because these rights differ from State to State and among agencies, investigators must be fully aware of the laws, regulations, and court decisions that fall under their jurisdiction.

GETTING PAST EMOTIONS

Whistleblowers do not arrive for interviews bearing clear indicators of their emotional state or agenda. However, imagine if a whistleblower did arrive for an interview wearing a nametag complete with an emotional reading: Bob--angry. Investigators would first acknowledge, then help to diffuse, the anger. Likewise, investigators' reactions should be the same, even though they may have to prompt whistleblowers to reveal their true emotional state.

Consider the following example. For the past 6 months, an employee's marriage has been deteriorating. Because she fears her marital problems may interfere with her work performance, she decides to speak to her supervisor. As she haltingly begins to relate her problems, her supervisor interrupts--telling her that a report he had wanted at the end of the week will have to be on his desk by this afternoon.

Chances are that the supervisor will get the report. But how good will it be? The fact that the supervisor failed to address the employee's emotional concerns will directly affect the quality of the report.

For white-collar crime investigators, the same thing can occur if they ask for information before dealing with the emotional agenda of whistleblowers. Consider how much of their attention and energy remains focused on such concerns as job loss rather than on the questions being asked of them by investigators.

CONCLUSION

Effective management of witnesses represents one of the most challenging responsibilities for white-collar crime investigators. To overcome such barriers as anger and fear and to collect and preserve the most accurate testimony possible from government whistleblowers, investigators should focus on informers' emotional agendas.

Investigators must also remember that good information is best preserved by keeping the source of that information informed. In the final analysis, a whistleblower who knows what to expect from the investigative and judicial process is more likely to be an effective and credible witness when called upon to recall facts or to testify.

ENDNOTES

1 Morton Bard and Dawn Sangrey, The Crime Victim's Book, 2d ed. (New York: Brunner/Mazel Publishers), 1986.

2 To assist investigators, the Behavioral Science Division at the Federal Law Enforcement Training Center (FLETC) in Glynco, Georgia, developed a course to address these specific issues.

Ms. Botsko is a senior instructor in the Financial Fraud Institute, Federal Law Enforcement Training Center (FLETC), Glynco, Georgia.

Mr. Wells is a senior instructor in the Behavioral Science Division of FLETC.

16

But Doctor, I Still Have Both Feet!

Remedial Problems Faced By Victims of Medical Identity Theft

Katherine M. Sullivan

I. INTRODUCTION

When Lind Weaver starting receiving collections demands for a foot amputation she never had, she assumed it was a clerical error. (1) Unfortunately, the operation had been performed on someone pretending to be Weaver, causing Weaver's medical history to become entangled in the thief's. (2) Media reports about identity theft show Weaver's experience is far from unique. For example, a Chicago man was arrested after using his friend's identity to obtain $350,000 worth of cardiovascular surgery at a local hospital. (3) Hackers broke into the medical records of thousands of University of California students. (4) A staff member left a laptop containing records of patients of a local AIDS clinic on Boston public transportation. (5)

Further opportunities for thieves lurk in every unshredded envelope, online transaction or credit card purchase. Breaches of financial data, often the result of hacking or theft or loss of sensitive computer equipment are routine fixtures of the news cycle. (6) Consumers are encouraged to check their credit scores and monitor their accounts for any suspicious activity. (7) In sum, we are being

But doctor, I still have both feet! Remedial problems faced by victims of medical identity theft. Katherine M. Sullivan. American Journal of Law & Medicine Winter 2009 v35 i4 p647(35).

bombarded with warnings about the threat of identity theft. This media saturation focuses on the misuse of a data linked to a victim's identity to gain access to consumer credit tools such as credit cards and loans.

Yet, medical identity theft, what Lind Weaver experienced, lurks in the background. Medical identity theft consists of the misuse of personal information to gain access to healthcare. (8) A 2006 report by the Federal Trade Commission (FTC) estimated that there were at least 250,000 victims of medical identity theft for the period 2001-2006. (9) The actual number is likely even higher. (10) In a more recent survey of identity theft victims assisted in 2008 by the non-profit Identity Theft Resource Center, two thirds of the 100 victims surveyed reported being billed for medical services they did not receive. (11) To some extent the emergence of medical identity theft is not surprising. First, healthcare providers are the largest compilers of personal data (12) and are just as vulnerable to attack as the financial industry. (13) Second, the high cost of health care creates an incentive to steal the identity of someone with insurance in order to obtain needed health care services, to further drug-seeking behavior, or to defraud third-party payers. (14) In addition to financial harms such as being billed for services not rendered, medical identity theft can introduce inaccuracies into a victim's medical records, causing a cascade of clinical, insurance, and even reputational harms.

Unlike victims of financial identity theft who can use the credit reporting system to recover from financial identity theft, victims of medical identity theft lack similar statutory resources, and there are few available private remedies. Further, structural and regulatory features of the healthcare system, including those governed by the Health Insurance Portability and Accountability Act of 1996 (HIPAA) (15) make it extremely difficult for victims to discover and remedy the damage caused to their medical records by an identity thief. To put it simply, "[t]here is no single place individuals can go to locate and correct inaccurate medical information." (16)

Current regulatory focus on increasing privacy and security through technological improvement, such as the HITECH Act amendments to HIPAA and the push to develop electronic health records (EHRs) do nothing to address victims' access problems to their own medical records. Further there is no private incentive to develop resources for victims. Finally, new regulations requiring health care providers to prevent fraud and new data breach notification rules do not resolve the basic problem of access. This note will argue that, given the fragmented nature of the healthcare market, a new federal regulatory initiative modeled on what is available to victims of financial identity theft is necessary to give victims an effective means of protecting the integrity of their personal health records.

This note will examine the issues faced by victims of medical identity theft as follows. Part II explores the differences between medical and financial identity theft. Part III assesses the structural factors of the healthcare industry that make medical identity theft more difficult to detect and remedy than financial identity theft. Part IV evaluates the remedies available to victims of medical identity theft with those available to victims of financial identity theft. Part V examines potential avenues for better remedies for victims of medical identity theft and proposes a federal legislative solution modeled on extant remedies for victims of financial identity theft.

II. DEFINING THE PROBLEM: WHAT IS MEDICAL IDENTITY THEFT?

Medical identity theft is a crime that appeals to two groups of people--those that would not otherwise have access to the healthcare system, and those who seek to defraud third party payers for their own financial ends. Regardless of the motivation for medical identity theft, the consequences for individual victims are the same: inaccurate medical records and financial consequences similar to those of financial identity theft. This Part will discuss the how and why medical identity theft is committed and the consequences for both individual victims and for the healthcare industry as a whole.

A. Sources Of and Motivations for Medical Identity Theft

Medical identity theft shares with financial identity theft the concept of a financially motivated appropriation of another person's identity information, but differs in that the theft is limited to healthcare services. Essentially, the thief seeks to either appropriate another's healthcare benefits for their own use or to bill the victim's third party payer for services never rendered to anyone but attributed to the victim. In either case medical identity theft requires taking advantage of third party payers rather than defrauding merchants and financial institutions, as is the case with financial identity theft. Thus, while an identity thief with a stolen credit card number could use the credit card number to pay for medical services, this is not financial identity theft if the medical services rendered are attributed to the thief's own identity (or an assumed identity).

Medical identity theft generally takes two forms--individual medical identity theft and medical identity fraud. Both forms of medical identity theft corrupt the victim's medical records by causing entries unrelated to the victim to be associated with the victim's medical records. (17) Individual medical identity theft involves the compromise of an individual's medical records by a thief and is often assisted by social engineering techniques, (18) such as the lack of procedures in individual hospitals or clinics to adequately verify a patient's identity. This lack of verification, of course, can also harm the identity thief, since the victim's medical records may indicate a different blood type, drug allergies, or medical history than that of the thief, leading to incorrect care for either the thief or, subsequently, the victim, if the victim's medical history is altered to match that of the thief. (19)

The second form of medical identity theft is the theft of multiple medical identities in order to defraud third-party payers. This can be accomplished by billing a victim's insurance plan for services and procedures that were neither needed nor received by the victim. For example, a former administrator at Cedars Sinai Hospital in Los Angeles used hundreds of patient records to file false insurance claims. (20) Medical identity fraud can result in prosecutions for theft, criminal conspiracy, and even substantive violations of HIPAA. (21) Like individual medical identity theft, medical identity fraud causes incorrect information to become associated with the victim's medical records, and can result in adverse medical treatment for the victim going forward. (22) In contrast to individual medical identity theft, medical identity fraud can impact a large number of victims due to the actions of a single thief. It is generally the result of coordinated fraudulent access to medical health records, rather than the actions of an individual desperate for medical treatment or access to prescription medication. (23) Often, medical identity fraud is the result of theft by an employee of a medical service provider who then sells the identity information to others seeking to commit the fraud. (24) Third party benefits providers--companies that handle various aspects of medical claims processing, such as pharmaceutical benefits, are also vulnerable to medical identity fraud. (25) What individual medical identity theft and medical identity fraud have in common are the systemic, regulatory and legal roadblocks currently in place that prevent victims of medical identity theft from remedying their situation. Thus, given the similar impact on victims, both types of identity theft will be referred to as "medical identity theft" for purposes of this analysis.

B. Consequences of Medical Identity Theft

There are two types of victims in medical identity theft--primary and secondary victims. Primary victims are individuals who suffer from incorrect medical records, improper denial of insurance due to non-existent health conditions, and billing for services not received. (26) Secondary victims are institutional parties and businesses that are parties to healthcare transactions, such as healthcare providers, insurance companies, and local and national agencies and organizations that rely on the accuracy of medical records. (27)

For primary victims, medical identity theft can have impact that goes far beyond that of financial identity theft. First, the identity thief can cause incorrect information to be associated with the victim's health history. (28) Since health care providers rely on medical histories in diagnosing and treating patients, incorrect information can impair a provider's ability to treat the victim. (29) Association with some medical problems, if incorrect, could have serious patient safety repercussions for a victim. For example, an incorrect blood type or drug allergy entered into a victim's chart during the thief's treatment can have disastrous subsequent consequences for the victim, particularly in emergencies. (30) Likewise, treatment for conditions that the victim does not have, such as heart disease or diabetes, can impact subsequent rendering of medical care to the victim.

Adverse medical history associated with the identity thief can also impact the cost and availability of health and life insurance by making a victim appear to be more high-risk than he or she actually is. (31) Further, insurance companies may refuse to pay for medical care needed by the victim if the victim's records show that it has already been rendered to the thief, and services rendered to an identity thief can impact a victim's lifetime benefits cap or pre-existing conditions if they go undetected. (32) Additionally, time and effort spent by the victim to correct their records constitutes an additional cost of the theft beyond that of the value of the services rendered. There may also be repercussions for a victim's reputation if incorrect information regarding a victim's health status becomes public knowledge due to the theft. (33)

Finally, as in regular identity theft, the victim will be billed for services that were not received by the victim. In many instances, bills and collection notices for medical services may be a victim's first indication that their identity has been compromised. If a medical identity thief has also changed the address to which the bills are sent, however, a victim of medical identity theft often may not become aware that there is a problem unless unpaid bills show up on a credit report--and the victim has been diligent enough to monitor his or her credit reports. (34) Financial identity theft and medical identity theft thus converge in their potential impact on a victim's credit report, and the financial ramifications of medical identity theft are similar to the more common forms of identity theft.

For secondary victims of medical identity theft, the consequences are primarily financial and administrative. Fraudulent medical claims cost public and private insurers millions of dollars every year (35) due to the fact that an allegation of fraudulent medical charges by a victim will result in additional administrative costs on the part of the provider or third party payer. If the fraud is proven, the cost of the services rendered will have to be absorbed by the healthcare provider or by the insurer, and the cost may be passed on to consumers in the form of higher healthcare prices. Additionally, the inclusion of false information can change the loss history of a given data sample of insureds, increasing the premium prices of experience-rated insurance products. Inaccurate data could also result in incorrect epidemiological data, undermining research quality. Ultimately, the costs associated with all types of medical fraud are likely to be passed on to consumers.

Thus, even though an identity thief may be an individual desperate for access to the healthcare system or an individual with insider knowledge of medical billing procedures, the consequences of medical identity theft on victims, third party payers and the healthcare system as a whole are the same regardless of the thief's original motivation. By taking advantage of systemic inefficiencies within the healthcare system, a medical identity thief gains financial and health advantages and the costs are ultimately recouped in the form of more expensive healthcare for everyone else. The following Part will discuss the structural difficulties that prevent efficient remedy of inaccuracies introduced into a victim's medical record.

III. HEALTHCARE INDUSTRY PRACTICES MAKE IT DIFFICULT TO REMEDY MEDICAL IDENTITY THEFT

One of the major reasons why medical identity theft is more pernicious than financial identity theft is due to common payment and record-keeping payment and record-keeping practices in the healthcare industry. Unlike the financial services industry, which has historically taken advantage of improvements in billing and processing technology in order to increase profits, the incentives for uniform and efficient data transmission within the healthcare industry have been lacking. Health care stakeholders with enough influence to push for uniformity, such as third party payers, do not have a financial incentive to do so. This is because third party payers do not have an incentive to push for faster claims processing, since insurance premiums have already been paid. On the provider side, industry-wide uniformity does not result in a benefit to any individual provider, thus incentives to invest in streamlined processing are capped by the marginal cost of those improvements. Because there are no incentives to standardize industry practices, healthcare provider billing has developed organically, with each provider's system tailored to that provider's needs. Thus, the billing methodologies used in any given healthcare encounter will be unpredictable from a patient standpoint. As a result, healthcare providers tend to engage in discrete billing and record-keeping procedures that are not widely understood or accessible to healthcare consumers. This Part will explore how industry practices often frustrate victims in their attempts to recover from medical identity theft.

A. The Creation and Handling of Medical Records

Unlike a fraudulent loan or credit card transaction, a single fraudulent medical transaction can result in the creation of records from many different parties beyond that of the actual healthcare provider. As health care diagnostic technology has gotten more complicated, medical records have become disseminated beyond the physician-patient relationship. (36) For example, laboratory work, specialists, pharmacists and third-party diagnostic services all keep record of services rendered to an individual. In a simple transaction, such as a visit to a physician's office may generate a single record at the provider's office and a record with the patient's insurance provider. Additional records may be generated if diagnostic tests are performed or a prescription is written. However, even in this simple scenario, dozens of people may be involved as a claim for health benefits makes its way through the system. (37)

For a more complex health care encounter, such as a hospital stay, the number of people who may view a file multiplies substantially, since additional specialists and diagnostic services will likely be required. (38) The number of disclosures made of a victim's medical record in the normal course of business contributes to the difficulty in resolving medical identity theft claims. Multiple providers, for example, treating physicians and nurses, specialists, and administrative personnel such as billing and claims administrators, all receive access to a patient's health record in the normal course of providing care and may keep their own records of the encounter. (39)

If a claim is processed through third party benefits payer, it may be transmitted through numerous administrative contractors, all of which keep records of what services were provided. (40) Some private insurers also place health records obtained during underwriting in a central database called a medical information bureau (MIB) to which other insurance companies are allowed access, with the purpose of combating insurance fraud. (41) Ironically, this anti-fraud measure could potentially result in fraudulent claims associated with a victim's medical record impacting the availability of coverage with other insurance providers.

The extent of the damage to a victim's medical records caused by an identity thief can often depend on the way in which the victim's medical records were kept. For health care providers that choose to keep non-electronic records, a fraudulent service or diagnosis may not affect a large portion of an individual's medical files. Even electronic records may be difficult to track down, however, since they may be stored "be in multiple locations, poorly aggregated and identified by a different number or identification scheme in each place ..." (42) Thus, due to the way in which data is stored throughout the health care industry, a victim of medical identity theft may not be able to track down all of the erroneous records generated by an identity thief.

B. Financial transaction processing vs. Medical claims billing

In terms of payment processing, consumers of financial services enjoy a faster, more-standardized billing and processing arrangement. (430 Examining a purely financial transaction involving a consumer payment card transaction and one that involves billing for a routine medical claim (44) covered by medical insurance illustrates the differences in timing and traceability between financial transactions and health care transactions. The most important difference is that a credit transaction is completed within a matter of days, and the consumer receives notice of the transaction (via a bill from the card issuer) within a month, whereas it can be months before a consumer receives a notice of a medical claim, either as an explanation of benefits or a bill from a healthcare provider.

When a consumer purchases goods with a credit card, the transaction activates a string of electronic processing relationships between the merchant selling the goods, the bank that issued the card to the consumer, and the intermediaries that gave the merchant access to the credit card network (the "merchant acquirer") and process and settle the transaction on behalf of the bank. (45) These parties are governed by contractual relationships in which a portion of the purchase price is paid out in fees in exchange for processing services. (46) The transaction happens quickly--the amount charged is debited from the customer's credit limit when the transaction is authorized, and the payment from the bank moves through the intermediaries and to the merchant (minus processing fees) within days of the transaction.

In contrast, the first step in billing for medical services is the submission of the claim and request for payment to the third-party payer. This can be done either on paper or electronically. (47) The healthcare provider's billing department handles this request. It may be weeks or even months before a healthcare provider passes along a claim to an insurance company. For example, a 2006 study of insurance claims processing found that 29 percent of claims were received from health care providers more than 30 days after the date of patient service, and 15 percent of claims were received from providers more than 60 days after service was provided. (48)

Once an insurer receives a claim, it is usually processed within thirty days. (49) A lack of sufficient information or a denial of coverage may delay claims processing. (50) Eventually, the insurer will issue an explanation of benefits (EOB) to the consumer, explaining what portion of the health care claim was paid by the insurer. (51) Part of the long lag time between the receipt of healthcare and its billing may be that banks have traditionally not been facilitators between the various parties to the transactions the way they are with regard to credit cards. (52) Due to the long lag time between the theft, billing by the healthcare provider, and processing by the insurance company, victims of medical identity theft may not be notified of their loss in a timely manner. In instances where an EOB or other insurance notification is not sent to the victim, a victim's first notice may not be until the outstanding bill is turned over to a credit bureau or collection agency.

Thus, a health care transaction differs from a financial transaction in two key ways. First, the disparate entities involved in health care transactions can vary depending on the type of health care encounter in ways that are not at all obvious to a health care consumer, and all of these entities keep a record of the transaction.

Further, the dissemination of patient records to the various parties to the healthcare transaction makes it difficult or impossible for victims of identity theft to correct all of their health records after the theft has occurred. (53) Second, the large amount of lag time in medical claims billing prevents victims from being notified that medical identity theft has occurred until well after the fact. Both of these factors are the result of standard industry practice that has developed in the absence of incentives to process claims more efficiently. As discussed in the next Part, regulators have made some attempts to improve consumer access to medical records. However, in addition to being burdened by the cumbersome record-keeping and processing endemic to the health care industry, victims of medical identity theft lack the powerful remedial tools available to victims of financial identity theft.

IV. LEGAL REMEDIES CURRENTLY AVAILABLE TO VICTIMS OF MEDICAL IDENTITY THEFT

Given the complexity of the handling of medical records, it seems likely that victims of medical identity theft will need assistance from the government or the courts in order to successfully purge their medical records of erroneous information and dispute charges for medical services that were never rendered. Although there have been some regulatory changes that could be of use to victims of medical identity theft, current resources available to victims fall far short of creating a comprehensive solution. This Part will first examine the statutes and regulations that apply to medical records and which could provide resources for victims of medical identity theft. Next, various legal theories for recovery by victims of identity theft will be discussed. Finally, the resources available to victims of financial identity theft will be examined as a model for a potential legislative solution for victims of medical identity theft.

A. Regulatory Sources of Protection and Remedy

There are two primary federal agencies that have jurisdiction over the problem of medical identity theft: the Department of Health and Human Services (HHS) and the Federal Trade Commission (FTC). HIPAA and gives HHS oversight over the privacy and security of medical records and the development of medical records interoperability. At the same time, the FTC has primary authority over consumer protection and identity theft issues. Recent regulatory activity by both HHS and FTC will require notification of consumers by health care providers if personal data held by the health care provider has been breached. In addition, the FTC is considering implementation of new identity theft prevention rules that would be applicable to health care providers. Neither the FTC nor HHS however has taken a lead role in the specific problem of medical identity theft. As a consequence, neither HHS nor the FTC's have addressed the structural issues an individual medical identity theft victim faces when trying to remedy the harm caused by an identity thief.

1. HIPAA and the HITECH Act

HIPAA was primarily intended to permit employees to keep their health insurance when they transferred jobs. (54) The statutory provisions relevant to the security and privacy of health records were inserted as administrative simplification provisions. (55) HIPAA's Administrative Simplification section directed the Secretary of Health and Human Services to establish security specifications for the electronic exchange of medical information. (56) The administrative simplification section also established penalties for the wrongful disclosure of "Individually Identifiable Health Information" (57) and directed HHS to make recommendations to congressional committees about individual rights to their health information and when disclosures should be allowed. (58) When Congress failed to act on HHS's recommendations, HHS was permitted to promulgate its own security and privacy rules under the administrative simplification section. (59) The Security Rule became effective in April 200360 and the Privacy Rule became effective in April 2001. (61) HHS oversees compliance with HIPAA's security and privacy requirements. (62)

Until 2009, regulations promulgated under HIPAA were limited to covered entities. Covered entities included health plans, third party administrators, other administrative service providers, and health care providers. (63) Health care providers were defined as "anyone who furnishes, bills, or is paid for healthcare in the normal course of business." (64) Thus hospitals, clinics, insurers, benefits providers all fall under the scope of HIPAA's regulations. The American Recovery and Reinvestment Act of 2009 (2009 Stimulus Act) expanded HIPAA's scope to include "business associates" of covered entities.

In enacting HIPAA, the prospect of medical identity theft was not considered by Congress. Rather, the majority of Congressional debate concerned whether HIPAA increased the affordability and availability of health insurance. (65) Debate over the regulation of theft and fraud was limited to provisions regarding traditional health care fraud and abuse, not medical identity theft. (66) The administrative simplification provisions, which gave HHS authority to promulgate regulations regarding individual access and amendment to health records, were only discussed in passing. (67)

Individually identifiable health information, which is defined as records regarding past or current medical or mental health treatment that can be linked up with and individual's identity, is the information subject to protection under HIPAA. (68) Since individually identifiable health information is both the target of medical identity theft and what is corrupted by a completed theft, HIPAA's rules governing the use and disclosure of Individually Identifiable Health Information provide some incidental protection from medical identity theft. (69) Given HIPAA's legislative history, however, it is not surprising that the applicability HIPAA's regulations to victims of medical identity theft is limited. The combination of HIPAA's regulation of medical records access and amendment with the privacy and security rules, can even in some cases make it more difficult for victims to fix damage done to their medical records.

In promulgating specific guidelines for the federal regulation of health information privacy, HHS created two sets of regulations-- the "Security Rule" (70) and the "Privacy Rule." (71) The Security Rule established transactional security requirements for health care providers as a matter of federal law in order to regulate the increased of electronic data storage and transmission in the health care sector. (72) These regulations created a federal floor for the technical security of health information. (73) Among its requirements, the Security rule specifies security and electronic signature standards for transactions that use electronic health records, (74) using a "reasonable and appropriate" standard of protection. (75) Since implementation of the provisions of the Security Rule likely prevents some types of hacking and data intrusion, compliant health care providers may incidentally prevent some types of medical identity theft by making it harder for identity thieves to gain access to the data. The Security Rule, however, does not prevent medical identity theft from occurring when a third party has already gained access to a victim's protected health information.

Whereas the Security Rule is focused on technical standards and procedures, the Privacy Rule is focused on regulating the disclosure of protected health information, although it is primarily concerned with commercial misuse of protected health information. (76) In addition to regulating who should have the ability to see an individual's protected health information, the Privacy Rule establishes a right for the patient to review medical records for accuracy, with exceptions. (77) In addition to the right to review,

HIPAA also grants patients a limited right to amend their medical records. (78) The access and amendment portions of HIPAA, although not created to specifically deal with medical identity theft, may provide some assistance to victims of medical identity theft, however neither the right of access nor the right to amend is absolute. For example, covered entity can deny a victim's request for review, although it must give the person requesting the review the right to have the denial reviewed by a health care professional. (79) Similarly, victims of medical identity theft have the right to amend their records as long as they are held in a designated record set, (80) but requests for amendment can be denied by the covered entity. (81)

Unfortunately, under the HIPAA regulations, a covered entity may deny an individual's request for amendment if the terms of the protected health information or record that is the subject of the request was not created by the covered entity, is not party of the designated record set, will not be available for inspection, or is accurate and complete. (82) Essentially, this means that providers are only responsible for responding to requests for amendment to records that they themselves generated. Although covered entities are required to forward requests for amendment to other entities, which would conceivably allow a victim to fix their records through dealing with a single provider, the other entities are not required to act on the forwarded request. (83) Further, HIPAA does not give victims the right to demand that their health care providers correct erroneous information created by third parties. (84) This applies even when the provider has used or will use incorrect medical records created by third parties to make medical decisions about the victim. (85)

A second problem arises due to the large number of potential health records that are generated by different entities as the result of a single patient encounter. Since covered entities are not responsible for the amendment of records created by third parties, a victim will need to track down each and every provider that may have generated incorrect medical records and petition each one for an amendment in order to correct their medical records. "Third parties" includes health insurers, so a victim's insurance company is not responsible for amending the erroneous information--the victim must track down the health care provider who submitted the claim. (86) This presumes that a victim is able to identify all of the providers that may have reported the erroneous information. (87)

Even if victims are able to track down all of their records and each health care provider acquiesces to a victim's request for an amendment, the erroneous information is not necessarily purged from the victim's medical records. Under HIPAA, when a healthcare entity is certain that the erroneous information had nothing to do with the victim, the entity can elect to separate erroneous information from the victim's medical record. (88) Essentially, a new record is created containing the health information pertaining to the thief. (89) This walling-off of incorrect information, however, is only available when the provider has not made any subsequent decisions regarding the victim on the basis of the erroneous information in the victim's medical records. (90) In cases where the erroneous information was subsequently used to make medical decisions regarding the victim, providers are limited to striking through or amending the information. (91) Given the amount of time that may lapse between the medical identity theft and its discovery by the victim, it seems highly likely that the incorrect medical information would be "relied on" in some way prior to a victim's request for medical records amendment.

Another, more theoretical, problem related to HIPAA's statutory privacy requirements may arise when a victim is able to prove that the erroneous health records do not actually belong to the victim. (92) Since, under HIPAA, the disclosure of another person's health records is not allowed, a provider could conceivably deny a victim's request to examine medical records generated by medical identity theft on the basis that they are not the victim's records. (93) One potential way to resolve this Catch-22 would be for the victim to obtain either a subpoena or a court order for the erroneous records directed to the healthcare provider. (94)

Although it recognizes a general right to have health information safeguarded appropriately by health care providers, HIPAA does little to specifically protect or assist victims of medical identity theft. This is not surprising since Congress did not consider medical identity theft was when it enacted HIPAA. Thus, resources for victims of medical identity theft provided by HIPAA, such as the right to review or amend some medical records, are incidental to HIPAA's main goals. HIPAA's failure to provide robust resources for medical identity theft victims is exacerbated by industry practices that result in the creation of multiple sets of records containing protected health information for a single health care encounter. Victims of medical identity theft may have difficulty tracking down these records, and, if they are able to do so, each individual provider must agree to amend the records--there is currently no requirement that records be amended simultaneously. Finally, a literal reading of HIPAA's regulations could lead some providers to altogether deny victims' requests to amend their records. Recent amendments to HIPAA, although they do not fix the access and amendment problems discussed above, may provide some additional assistance to victims of medical identity theft.

2. Data Breach Notification Requirements Under the HITECH Act

The Health Information Technology for Economic and Clinical Health Act (HITECH Act), enacted as part of the 2009 Stimulus Act, (95) inter alia, extends enforcement of some of HIPAA's security and privacy provisions to business associates, who had previously been excluded from the requirements for covered entities. (96) The HITECH Act also requires that the Secretary of HHS submit a report to Congress within a year of the HITECH Act's passage with recommendations regarding privacy and security requirements for PHR vendors that are not currently covered by HIPAA. (97)

Most importantly with regard to the problem of medical identity theft, the HITECH act requires HHS and the FTC to promulgate regulations regarding the notification of victims of data breaches of unsecured protected health information held by HIPAA-covered entities and their business associates, or by vendors of personal health records (PHRs), respectively. (98) These new notification requirements may be helpful to some victims of medical identity theft since it may put them on alert that something has gone wrong or may go wrong with their medical records. Whether notifying consumers after their data has been breached, however, may not do much to actually prevent or mitigate medical identity theft. (99) This section will examine when and to whom a breach of protected health information must be disclosed under the HITECH Act.

a. FTC Notifieation Requirements for PHR Providers

PHRs are a relatively recent innovation in health information technology. (100) The HITECH Act defines PHRs as an "electronic record of PHR identifiable health information that can be drawn from multiple sources and that is managed, shared, and controlled by or primarily for the individual." (101) Generally speaking, PHRs consist of a web-based interface hosted by a third party such as Microsoft (102) or Google (103) and maintained by the patient. Since PHR vendors host protected health information, PHR users face a risk of medical identity theft similar to that of any other health care user. Thus, the HITECH Act gives the FTC jurisdiction over consumer notification of data breaches involving PHRs until Congress acts on HHS' forthcoming report regarding PHR vendors. The FTC promulgated its Final Rule regarding data breach notification on August 25, 2009. (104) The FTC's notification rules do not apply to "HIPAA-covered entities, or to any other entity to the extent that it engages in activities as a business associate of a HIPAA-covered entity." (105)

Under the FTC's Rules, PHR providers that discover a breach of security of an unsecured PHR must notify each affected individual and the FTC. (106) Notification must be made either by mail or e-mail if possible, and local media outlets must be notified if 500 or more individuals in a given state are affected. (107) Violations of the FTC notice rule will be treated as unfair or deceptive trade practices. (108) For the subset of healthcare consumers that are using personal health records offered by PHR vendors, the FTC's requirements will decrease the risk of undetected medical identity theft. PHRs, however, are not the same thing as the medical records upon which a healthcare provider makes diagnostic and treatment decisions. (109) The burden for monitoring a data breach victim's other health records for alterations as a result of a PHR data breach, would remain on the consumer.

b. HHS Notification Requirements for HIPAA Covered Entities and Business Associates

The HITECH Act also directed HHS to develop rules for data breach notification by HIPAA-covered entities and their business associates. (110) HHS published its Interim Final Rule regarding Breach Notification for Unsecured Protected Health Information on August 24, 2009. (111) HHS developed its Interim Final Rule in close consultation with the FTC. (112) For purposes of this analysis, the HHS and FTC notification rules are substantially similar. HHS requires HIPAA-covered entities to report data breaches directly to victims, whereas business associates must notify covered entities of a breach. (113) As with the FTC regulations, the HHS notification rule does not provide any assistance with the monitoring or correction of medical records as a result of the data breach.

These regulations fail to address some practical problems. First, in order for breach notification to serve its intended purpose of putting a health care consumer on notice of potential problems with his or her medical records, the breach must be of a type subject to notification. This seems simplistic, but if the medical identity theft is committed by an individual who has convinced health care providers that they are the victim, there is no "breach" per se--the files were accessed by medical personnel in the course of providing care to someone whom the provider believed was a patient. Thus, the damage to a victim's medical records will be complete prior to any realization that the victim's protected health information has been inappropriately accessed. Further, even if a breach notification does reach a patient before harm has been done to the patients' medical records, and the patient chooses to act on the notification, there is nothing that a patient can do to prevent or block incorrect entries from being made into his or her files in the future. There are however, some recent regulatory initiatives that may benefit patients by requiring health care providers to engage in measures designed to prevent identity theft.

3. The FTC's "Red Flags Rules" for Health Care Providers

As part of its mission to prevent identity theft and to assist its victims, (114) the FTC recently promulgated a set of regulations known as the "Red Flags Rules." The rules are broadly applicable to financial institutions and "creditors," (115) which are defined as "any person who regularly extends, renews or continues credit...." (116) Under the Rules' enabling statute, creditors must establish and implement identity-theft prevention programs. (117) A memo issued by the FTC after the promulgation of the Red Flags Rules indicates that most health care providers are required to comply on the basis that they are creditors if they "accept deferred payments for goods or services ... [h]ealth care providers that accept insurance are considered creditors if the consumer ultimately is responsible for the medical fees," and "continuing relationships with consumers for the provision of medical services [constitute 'covered accounts']." (118) Thus, the FTC has jurisdiction to require most health care providers to implement procedures designed to prevent identity theft. The FTC will begin enforcing the Red Flags Rules on June 1, 2010. (119)

Under the Red Flags Rules, creditors are required to establish a written identity theft prevention program for covered accounts. (120) The program must include provisions to detect "Red Flags"--criteria that indicate the presence of identity theft (121)--and be tailored appropriately to the creditor. (122) By requiring health care providers to adequately identify patients, the Red Flags Rules may ultimately prevent at some of the instances of medical identity theft where the theft is accomplished by the impersonation of the victim at the point of service. The Rules do nothing to prevent medical identity theft accomplished by stealing and misusing patient data in health care providers' possession. Further, the Rules do not provide remedies, such as stronger access and amendment rights, to victims of medical identity theft. Ultimately, despite HIPAA's recognition of the importance of medical records privacy and the regulatory efforts of HHS and the FTC, federal statutes do not offer remedies to victims of medical identity theft. The next section will explore whether there are judicial remedies available to victims of medical identity theft.

B. Potential Judicial Remedies for Victims of Medical Identity Theft

Given how difficult it is for victims to amend their own medical records after a thief has altered them, litigation may be another option to give victims some financial recovery for the problems caused by medical identity theft. Theoretically, a robust set of judicial remedies would create a strong incentive for healthcare providers to do a better job of preventing identity theft from occurring in the first place. Since HIPAA does not create a private right of action, victims of medical identity theft are limited to state causes of action. (123) Since even closed proceedings require the semi-public airing of private matters few cases go to trial, and many areas of privacy law are still unsettled. Even high-profile victims of medical records breaches generally do not sue the parties responsible for the breach. (124) Further, theories of legal liability are complicated by the different ways in which medical identity theft can occur.

First of all, identifying the proper defendant may be difficult. The actual identity thief is likely to be judgment-proof. Even in instances where an identity thief can pay damages, injunctive relief in the form of an order to amend a victim's records would appear to be necessary to make the victim whole. This type of injunctive relief, however may be limited by privacy laws and by the same structural impediments faced by victims of medical identity theft. Thus, the health care provider that allowed the thief to utilize the victim's medical identity and thereby corrupt the victim's medical records may be a better target for two reasons--better financial resources, and the potential for injunctive relief in the form of an order to amend the victim's medical records.

1. Healthcare Provider Liability
A lawsuit against a healthcare provider would likely be premised on a theory of vicarious liability. The burden would be on the victim to prove both the healthcare provider's eligibility under either respondeat superior or vicarious liability and that the medical identity theft constituted a cognizable tort. (125) A respondeat superior action would likely lie in instances where a victim's medical identity was compromised due to the actions of a healthcare provider's employee. The main challenge for a victim of medical identity theft would be to show that the actions of the employee were within the scope of their employment. (126)

Where the individual responsible for the identity theft was not an employee of the health care provider, such as a physician hired as an independent contractor, it may not be possible to maintain a cause of action under respondeat superior. (127) A victim may, however, be able to bring suit against a health care provider on a theory of vicarious liability. (128) A victim will need to show that the health care provider held out the perpetrator of the identity theft as an agent of the hospital. In cases where the identity theft was the result of a theft by an agent of the health care provider who never met or interacted with the victim, vicarious liability may not be available.

Finally, the health care provider may be directly liable to the victim of medical identity theft on a theory of negligence for failure to protect a patient's medical information. In order to prevail, a victim will need to show that the health care provider had a duty to maintain its systems or to supervise its employees so as to protect patient confidentiality. (129) The duty breached by the health care provider may vary based on the facts. On the one hand, a health care provider who failed to protect patient information may be directly liable for negligence for either failing to create a system to protect patient confidentiality or for failing to ensure that patient files are in fact protected. (130) On the other hand, a health care provider that fails to adequately identify a patient, and thus allow an identity thief to obtain medical treatment at the victim's expense, may be directly liable on a theory of negligence, or medical malpractice on a theory of breach of the standard of care for failure to identify. (131)

2. Tort Theories of Health Care Provider Liability to Victims of Medical Identity Theft

In eases where a victim wants to bring an action against a health care provider or an individual employee for damages due to identity theft, the victim will have to prove the underlying tort. Breach of confidentiality and invasion of privacy would appear to be the most obvious theories of liability, however in some respects neither theory fully fits with medical identity theft. Breach of confidentiality would be most relevant in situations that involve a breach of the victim's confidential information by physicians or other licensed health care providers, (132) unless the local jurisdiction has recognized that the duty of confidentiality extends to all hospital staff. (133) It is not clear, however, if medical identity theft by a party, such as a hacker, not privy to the relationship between the patient and the physician constitutes a "disclosure" unless the victim can prove that victim's medical history was discussed with or disclosed to the thief. (134) In situations where a victim seeks redress for an individual identity thief's utilization of health care from a provider that does not have access to the victim's health records, disclosure may be even harder to prove.

A victim of medical identity theft may have more success under the broader doctrine of invasion of privacy. Since the tort may be committed by anyone, the victim would not have to prove that the breach occurred within the existence bounds of a physician-patient relationship. (135) There are four types of invasion of privacy. (136) Of the four types, intrusion on a medical identity theft victim's seclusion would likely be the most relevant. (137) A victim would likely have a claim for intrusion as long as the victim could show that the invasion of privacy was intentional. Another potential theory for a claim of invasion of privacy is publicity given to private life. (138) Identity theft victims may have difficulty proving that their private life was given publicity if all of the subsequent communication regarding the victim occurred within the bounds of the physician-patient relationship, even if the "patient" was actually a third party. Similarly, a claim for false light may lie if the victim can show that false information regarding the victim was publicized as the result of the identity theft. For example, publicity regarding a victim of medical identity theft who was visited by child protective services after the thief gave birth to a drug-addicted baby under the victim's identity may have a claim for false light. (139)

If a victim of identity theft is unable to prove that a cognizable tort was committed on the part of the health care provider, the victim may still have a cause of action under medical malpractice or on a theory of breach of contract. For a medical malpractice action to succeed, the victim must show that the disclosure or intrusion that occurred constituted a breach of the standard of care by the health care provider. (140) A victim may also be able to bring a case against a health care provider for breach of confidentiality if the victim can prove the existence of a contract governing disclosure of patient information. (141) Damages in a breach of contract case would likely be limited to standard contract damages, whereas a tort claim could result in punitive damages.

Finally, a victim of medical identity theft would have a cause of action against the identity thief, separate from any health care provider liability. Such an action would likely include the invasion of privacy torts discussed above. In addition, a victim may be able to make out a claim for misappropriation of name or likeness. (142) Finally, a claim for conversion may exist if the victim can show that the victim's records constitute personal property. (143) This may be difficult since medical records are generally held to be the property of the entity that generates the records.

Thus, in an action to recover damages for medical identity theft, a victim's potential causes of action will depend on under what circumstances the victim's medical records were accessed, who used the medical records, and to what extent information about the victim was shared with non-privileged third parties. No extant tort fully encompasses medical identity theft liability. Since it is so difficult to establish liability for medical identity theft, victims may not be able to recover damages or equitable relief for errors introduced into their medical records.

By failing to remedy the fundamental threat faced by victims of medical identity theft both statutory law and common law fail to grant victims adequate relief. (144) A new system is needed to prevent further harm to victims of medical identity theft, yet private incentives to improve the handling of medical records and claims billing are lacking. In the context of financial identity theft, however, Congress has dealt with a similar regulatory vacuum by creating a combination of public and private initiatives. The next section will explore remedial solutions available to victims of financial theft that allow victims to review and amend their financial records as a potential model for medical records access and amendment problems faced by victims of medical identity theft.

3. Resources for Victims of Financial Identity Theft: FACTA & the Credit Reporting System

Unlike the paltry resources available to victims of medical identity theft, the credit reporting system is a robust system for victims of financial identity theft. The credit reporting system serves two functions: it is the mechanism by which the consumer financial services industry assesses individual risk and, under federal legislation, is the means by which victims can remedy financial identity theft. In contrast to the myriad record-keeping and billing systems used in the health care sector that developed due to a lack of incentives for systemic uniformity, the credit reporting did not develop organically.

Rather, credit reporting is the result of lenders' need to have a reliable means of evaluating an individual's credit risk. (145) As a result, almost every adult that has a credit card, loan, or other credit-related financial product has a credit file with at least one of the three credit bureaus. (146) Lenders use the reports generated by the three national credit bureaus, TransUnion, Experian, and Equifax, (147) in order to determine whether an individual presents a good credit risk. (148) In addition, credit reports play an important role in mitigating identity theft by allowing an individual to see all credit transactions attributed to their identity, which can give consumers an early warning of problems with their accounts. (149)

The Fair Credit Reporting Act (FCRA), (150) and the Fair and Accurate Credit Transactions Act of 2003 (FACTA) (151) both regulate the behavior of the credit bureaus and in order to increase consumer protection in the financial sector. (152) Congress passed FACTA amid increasing concerns about identity theft. (153) FCRA requires the credit bureaus to employ more stringent data security. (154) The most-publicized aspect of FACTA, however, is that it gives consumers a right to a free annual credit report from each of the credit bureaus. (155) By creating this right, FACTA takes advantage of a privately-developed feature of the financial sector in order to further the goal of consumer protection.

Credit reports contain information about an individual's name, Social Security number, current and previous addresses, credit cards, (156) loans, and the names of any entities that have requested access to an individual's credit account. (157) Credit reports may also include adverse information such as past-due bills, including medical bills, public records such as bankruptcies, foreclosures, liens, and other judgments, and information from collection agencies. (158) Unpaid medical bills make up a substantial portion of collections actions. In a sample of 249,000 credit reports, researchers at the Federal Reserve found that fifty-two percent of collections actions in the sample came from unpaid medical bills. (159) Thus, in addition to damage to victims' medical records, there are financial consequences for victims of medical identity theft caused by unpaid bills generated by the thief in the victim's name. Even when the initial health care provider has agreed that the victim was not responsible for the thief's bills, collections agency practices wherein an unpaid bill is re-reported to the credit bureaus each time it is handed over to a new agency. For example, Lind Weaver's foot amputation bill (160) was submitted to the credit reporting agencies as a new bill each time a different collections agency tried to collect on it. (161)

The collections problem illustrates one of the ways in which the credit reporting system is far from perfect. Additionally, completeness and accuracy of credit reports is in dispute. (162) Over time, technology has improved the accuracy of credit reports. (163) Nevertheless, a 2004 study of 197 credit reports found that 25% contained errors serious enough to jeopardize the availability of credit. (164) The inaccuracy of credit reports may be attributable to several factors. First, credit reporting by credit card issuers, lenders, creditors, and collection agencies to the credit bureaus is entirely voluntary. (165) Even under FACTA's tighter reporting standards there are no mandatory standards for entities that provide credit data. (166) Mistakes on credit reports can also be the result of error on the part of the credit bureaus. (167) Additionally, incorrect information on credit reports may be attributable to fraud or identity theft. Finally, assuming that negative information on credit reports is accurate as of the time of its submission to the credit bureaus, it is generally not updated on a regular basis and may not reflect payments made by the consumer. (168)

The accuracy of a credit report is important because it is used to generate a consumer's credit score, (169) and thus determine one's eligibility for credit. Credit scores are calculated by applying statistical models to information in a credit report. (170) Credit scores are a way for card issuers to distinguish the credit risk of one individual from another. (171) The statistical models used are considered proprietary and their exact weighting of various factors in a credit report is not available to the public. (172) The factors in a credit report are grouped into payment history, amount of debt, length of credit history, and whether any new credit accounts have been opened recently. (173)

Of these four areas, repayment history and the presence of any bankruptcies, liens, foreclosures or other judgments are the most important. (174) Repayment history includes the timely payment of balances, late payments or failure to repay, and the amount of delinquencies. (175) Any past-due and unpaid medical bills would be included in an evaluation of an individual's payment history. Thus, an unpaid medical bill, even if not incurred by the person listed on the credit report, could have a serious impact on that person's eligibility for low interest rates and their ability to open new lines of credit.

As in medical identity theft, the time lag between when credit is extended, becomes outstanding, and is entered onto a credit report can make it difficult for consumers to remedy the problem once it reaches the credit report stage. (176) Further, the amount of time that can lapse between the crime and its discovery makes it difficult for the perpetrator to ever be caught. (177) Victims of financial identity theft, as compared to victims of medical identity theft, have several remedies available.

For charges incurred on credit cards, once the theft has been discovered but before an entry is made on their credit reports victims can initiate a chargeback dispute with their credit card provider. Most major credit card networks have systems that allow consumers to dispute charges made on their accounts. (178) This system, called a "chargeback," allows transactions to be reversed, with the consumer credited for the transaction. (179) Each credit card company has its own standards as to what constitutes a valid reason for a chargeback.

(180) After a request for a consumer initiates a chargeback, the card company must investigate the matter. (181) Identity theft is a common basis for a successful chargeback request. (182)

Second, for erroneous or fraudulent items on a credit report, victims can request that the credit reporting bureaus amend their credit reports. FCRA and FACTA both allow consumers to dispute errors on their credit reports. (183) Under FCRA, credit bureaus must investigate consumer complaints within thirty days of the consumer's request and at no charge to the consumer. (184) Most errors disputed by consumers are resolved within ten working days of notice to the credit bureau. (185) Both FCRA and FACTA place the burden on the consumer to dispute information in a credit report. (186) In order for access to credit reports to be an effective tool to fight against identity theft, a consumer must be sufficiently vigilant to routinely request credit reports, review them for any discrepancies, and then notify the appropriate credit bureau and request that the erroneous items be investigated. (187)

FRCA protects consumers by granting victims of financial identity the ability to dispute errors on their credit reports. Victims also benefit from being able to monitor their credit reports under FACTA's grant of access. The access and amendment allowed under FCRA and FACTA, enacted in part to protect consumers and combat identity theft, are in stark contrast to HIPAA's privacy protections, which were a reaction to potential commercial misuse, but not the issue of identity theft. Victims of financial identity theft also benefit from the ability to see all of their credit history in one place, with a statutory right to dispute entries they believe to be erroneous. In contrast, victims of medical identity theft must navigate the review of medical records kept in disparate locations and formats, with no guarantee of an ability to amend. FACTA's use of credit reports to provide financial identity theft victims some ability to control their core financial records provides a blueprint for consumer-directed medical records access and amendment. The next part will suggest ways that government and health care industry stakeholders can prevent medical identity theft and develop a system analogous to the credit reporting system in order to assist its victims.

V. CREATING REMEDIES FOR VICTIMS OF MEDICAL IDENTITY THEFT: A FEDERAL LEGISLATIVE PROPOSAL

Assuming that a victim of medical identity theft has become aware of damage done to their medical records, the current remedies available to victims leave something to be desired. The burden is entirely on the victim to navigate the healthcare system, track down all of the disparate record custodians, and convince them of the victim's right to amend their records. There are several potential ways in which the burden on victims may be eased. First, the healthcare industry can self-regulate and implement safeguards to prevent medical identity theft from occurring. These steps would not solve the remediation problem for victims, however. Although a system analogous to the credit reporting system would provide benefits to victims of medical identity theft, there is little economic incentive within the health care industry to change the way in which medical records are maintained or to institute centralized reporting. Thus, it seems unlikely that a centralized medical records system analogous to the credit reporting system would develop without government intervention. Therefore, this Part will explore some potential avenues of market self-regulation but then focus on legislative solutions to the remediation issue.

A. Current Market-Based Solutions Focus on Prevention, Not Remediation

Accreditation and technological innovation present the most likely means by which the private sector could ease the burdens on victims of medical identity theft. Already the competitive healthcare market has prompted some providers to institute technological and organizational innovations to combat identity theft. (188) Licensure and accreditation premised on the non-occurrence of medical identity theft is an additional way to encourage the private sector to adopt such safeguards. Similarly, ongoing government initiatives that push for the adoption of electronic, interoperable health records may eventually provide some benefit to victims of medical identity theft. (189) Prevention efforts do not remove the incentive to commit medical identity theft, and it is unlikely that any of the initiatives discussed in this section would be capable of preventing all instances of theft.

1. Accreditation and Licensure
One market-based measure is to make the prevention of medical identity theft a condition of licensure or accreditation. (190) The Joint Commission's (191) 2008 Patient Safety Goals listed proper identification with a focus on the prevention of medical identity theft as the highest priority safety goal. (192) However, the 2009 Goals recast the initiative into one of proper patient identification in order to eliminate wrong treatment caused by providing services to the wrong patient, rather than to eliminate medical identity theft. (193) Going forward, a stronger initiative would be to include occurrences

of medical identity theft as one of the Joint Commission's "never events." (194) Similarly, mandatory assistance for victims of medical identity theft could be required as a condition of state licensure or accreditation. Accreditation and licensure, while they would motivate healthcare providers to prevent medical identity theft from occurring, would not assist victims after the theft has already occurred.

2. Technological Innovations

There are two categories of technological improvements that could be implemented by individual healthcare providers. The first is point-of-service initiatives such as increased identification requirements, either as part of the Red Flags Rules or privately initiated. (195) These types of safeguards, however, do little to prevent theft and fraud committed by employees or hackers. The second category of technological improvements includes instituting changes to the healthcare provider's information technology infrastructure and limiting employee's access and scope of access to medical records. (196) As with licensure and accreditation, implementing technological safeguards may prevent some instances of medical identity theft, but will not assist those that are already victims. Further, unlike licensure and accreditation, implementation of improved healthcare information technology relies on private initiatives, and it is not clear how much of a competitive advantage can be gained by instituting procedures largely invisible to healthcare consumers.

3. Electronic Health Records

By improving access and interoperability, EHRs would appear to have the potential to ease some of the burden on victims of medical identity theft. Although an in-depth analysis of all of the potential problems and promise of electronic health records is beyond the scope of this paper, the claims made for EHRs as they relate to the problems faced by victims of medical identity theft can be evaluated. For example, one of the touted benefits of EHRs is the possibility of "an integrated, centralized database that can hold the patient's entire medical history ..." (197) Similarly, EHRs could be networked into a national health information network (NHIN) so as to allow physicians in disparate locations to coordinate patient care.

Benefits from streamlining access, however, are premised on the accuracy of the contents of the patient's medical record. (198) If a patient's records are corrupted by the insertion of erroneous information, improved physician access to incorrect information is of little benefit and could increase the level of harm caused by an identity thief. Interoperability also does not deal with issues regarding custodial access faced by victims. Answers to questions such as who is the correct entity to amend a medical record and what parties should be required to honor amendment requests are currently unclear. Further, setting aside technical issues of network security and vulnerability to attack, electronic health records could provide more points of access for individuals that seek to misuse protected health information, (199) rather than confining patient data to the locations in which it has been generated. (200) Thus, the implementation of electronic health records without something more may do little in the short term to combat the problem of medical identity theft. (201)

B. Legislative Solutions

Since there is little private market incentive to develop comprehensive solutions to medical identity theft, government intervention is necessary to protect victims. This section will explore are two possibilities for legislative reform. First, Congress could amend HIPAA to clarify its access and amendment provisions with respect to medical identity theft. Such a HIPAA amendment would assist victims, but would not solve access problems due to the way in which medical records are kept. A second, more comprehensive solution would be for Congress to create a new statutory system with regard to medical records that gives patients more control, similar to the credit reporting system. (202) This type of system would aggregate certain categories of medical data, permit individuals to view major events in their medical histories and set up a dispute resolution system for erroneous entries.

1. Amending HIPAA

Modification of HIPAA's privacy regulations beyond the data breach notification requirements under the HITECH Act are necessary to assist victims of medical identity theft. One option is to allow a private right of action against healthcare providers in cases of medical identity theft. (203) This change would allow victims to seek recovery, including amendment of all erroneous medical information, from the entities that permitted the identity theft to occur. By opening up healthcare providers to liability for breach of HIPAA, the incentive for prevention of medical identity theft would shift to healthcare providers. Such a change could open a flood of litigation. Further, allowing a private right of action does not necessarily remedy the access and amendment problems faced by victims, even if a victim prevails in litigation with a covered entity or business associate for damages from a HIPAA breach.

Strengthening victims' rights to amend records under HIPAA is another option to mitigate the harms caused by medical identity theft. Again, this modification should be narrowly tailored so that it is available to victims that are able to prove that medical identity theft has already occurred or is ongoing. Such a modification should allow a victim's to change all records, not just those held by the covered entity currently using the records. Thus, a modification to the regulations should include language that prevents covered entities from declining to disclose medical records when the victim claims that the treatment was not theirs. (204)

2. Creating a "Heath Care History Report"

A regulatory framework similar to FACTA is necessary to facilitate victim recovery after medical identity theft would be a more comprehensive option than creating a private right of action or expanding HIPAA's access and amendment provisions. (205) A similar system that focused on medical record could provide an individual with free access to an annual report that lists all medical services related to an individual's social security number for that year, as well as any outstanding bills, upon request by the consumer. (206) Such a system would also give healthcare consumer the right to initiate fraud alerts and holds, resulting in a notification when changes are made to their health care history report. Individuals would also be eligible for a report that lists all entities to which an individual's medical records were disclosed during a given year. (207) Finally, individuals would be allowed to dispute items within their health care history report. (208)

Unlike the financial industry, however, there is no pre-existing aggregation of medical claims data that could be used to provide victim access and dispute resolution. Instead, health care providers submit reimbursement claims to state and federal government programs and private payers and bill patients directly. Data would therefore have to be reported to a new entity. Thus, this proposal involves more structural complications than allowing consumer access to a privately-held industry rating tool, as was done under FACTA. Given the complexity and regional variability of the healthcare system, the creation of a health care history reporting system should be initiated by the federal government since it already has administrative expertise in consumer protection, identity theft, medical records security and privacy and health information technology. In addition, the federal government is best situated to provide uniformity of access to healthcare consumers.

Unfortunately, expertise in the areas relevant to medical identity theft is currently fragmented across several discrete administrative agencies and task forces. For example, there is a Presidential Task Force on Identity Theft created in 2006, (209) and the Federal Trade Commission (FTC) provides comprehensive resources for victims of financial identity theft. (210) Responsibility for medical identity theft falls in between the Department of Health and Human Services and the Offices of the Inspector General (OIG). (211) HHS, however, did not release guidance on the issue until its January 2009 report on medical identity theft. (212) Thus the implementation of a health care history reporting system would likely require the creation of a separate administrative body within either the FTC or HHS that would provide recommendations for victims of medical identity theft and also regulate the creation and operation of the health care history reporting system. (213)

Delegating authority to deal with the problem of medical identity theft does not dispose of the issue of who should be the stakeholders in a centralized medical records reporting system. In order for such a system to be comprehensive enough to be useful, the majority of healthcare providers would need to contribute data. The types of data that must be reported could be limited to medically significant clinical encounters (e.g. with a non-negotiated price above a certain threshold) or events that are clearly inconsistent with an individual's past claims experience. The burden of this reporting task would be considerably eased in an interoperable EHR environment. Thus, a reporting requirement could create an additional incentive for healthcare providers to adopt EHR.

Ultimately, however, there will be some administrative cost burden in creating and maintaining such a system and facilitating the resolution of disputes. Given the potential value created by a data set of this size, the cost could be shared between the government and third party payers by having the government administer the system and charge insurers for access to de-identified data. Alternatively, third party payers could be encouraged to administer the program through tax incentives and direct access to the data within the reporting system.

Under the proposed system the burden to monitor reports and dispute entries would be on consumers, but the burden to collect the records and amend them would be on the health care system. This sort of consumer-directed system provides the best balance between consumer needs and administrative cost since it will likely be utilized by consumers to whom the integrity of their medical records is important. Keeping some of the burden on the consumer is cost-effective since a patient "is most knowledgeable about his or her own health record and, therefore, is the first line of defense for protecting against medical identity theft and identifying a potential issue early, which may help to reduce the damage." (214) Of course, in order for healthcare consumers to engage in these activities, a certain level of consumer education will also be necessary. Patient education campaigns regarding the risks of medical identity theft and their ability to review and amend these records are a necessary part in the creation of a medical credit reporting system. (215)

VI. CONCLUSION

Medical identity theft has emerged as a new way for thieves to defraud the health care system by taking advantage of the complex and inefficient billing and claims processing procedures inherent in the system. Some thieves commit identity theft in order to obtain health care. Others do it to make money by charging for services never rendered. For victims, the damage to their finances and the integrity of their health records is the same and, there is currently no one place to go in order to fix it, in contrast to victims of financial identity theft. Current regulations, such as HIPAA, may actually exacerbate the problem by making it more difficult for victims to correct their medical records, and other regulations, such as data breach notification rules and the Red Flags Rules, do not address the problems that victims face when trying to track down and amend their records. Although Congress and the Executive branch have begun to recognize that action is needed, progress to date has been piecemeal. A comprehensive legislative approach that creates a separate administrative scheme to deal with medical records in a way analogous to the credit reporting system is needed to centralize the review and amendment of medical records. By creating a health history reporting system, Congress can combat the problem of medical identity theft and to prevent patients from becoming victims.

NOTES DELETED

Katherine M. Sullivan, J.D., Boston University School of Law, 2010; B.A., Georgetown University 2004. Thank you to the AJLM Editors and Kevin Outterson for their assistance with this note, and to my friends and family for their support.

Part VII

EXPLAINING WHITE COLLAR CRIME: THEORIES AND ACCOUNTS

17

Nobody Gets Hurt?

Moral Outrage Against Bribery

Elizabeth Spahn

Bribery is sometimes justified on the theory that it is a victimless crime, that everybody does it and no body gets hurt. This article examines the assumptions underlying those justifications. First, the article reviews recent macro-economic scholarship refuting the older thesis that bribery 'greases the wheels of commerce.' Modern economic research reveals that while bribery may facilitate an isolated transaction, when examined over a longer timeframe bribery provides market incentives to increase regulations. Bilateral monopolies of insiders (business and government), misnamed crony 'capitalism,' use their relationships to restrict market access and harass competitors, reducing actual market-based competition. 'Friendly' regulatory environments, reducing regulatory burdens for bribe-paying insiders, erode safety regulations and distract business from tending to safety and quality control, focusing business efforts instead on developing relationships with powerful officials. The longer timeframe reveals an eco-cycle of regulations, bribery and deteriorating safety/quality control.

As a business transaction from the micro-economic viewpoint, bribery is a high-risk business model The second section of this article provides specific examples of various risk-points in a bribe-transaction, including unreliability of corrupted partners and intermediaries, difficulties establishing fair prices for bribes, and very risky exit strategies. Where entire cultures tolerating bribery arise, modern scholarship reveals opportunistic penetration by transnational organized criminal syndicates.

Nobody gets hurt? Is Bribery a Victimless Crime? Elizabeth Spahn. Georgetown Journal of International Law Summer 2010 v41 i4 p861(45) (18784 words)

Examples of individual victims of crony relationships between government and business are provided in the third section of the article, including humans injured or killed by 'low quality control' or eroded safety standards including consumers of fake pharmaceuticals, toxic toothpaste, melamine poisoned pet food and lead in children's toys. Economic analysis of environmental regulations demonstrates an overall negative correlation between effective environmental enforcement and high levels of corruption.

Legitimate business efforts to remain clean even if others cheat, avoiding bribe-based relationships, are addressed in the concluding section of the article, along with some initial recommendations for strengthening practical, legitimate business strategies. Established profit systems, such as slavery/apartheid or dumping raw toxins, were altered once humans perceived the harms, the actual human costs of doing business under the older, discredited model.

TABLE OF CONTENTS

I. INTRODUCTION

Bribery is sometimes justified on the grounds that it greases the wheels of excessive government regulation, and that no real harm is done by it. It is not that bribery itself is actually a good thing, or even that bribery is morally justified. In this worldview it is not that bribery is right, but rather that bribery is necessary. Bribery is practical, bribery helps business, bribery is how the real world works. Everybody does it and nobody gets hurt.

This article examines the assumptions underlying a practical business worldview that tolerates bribery. Is anyone getting hurt by bribery? If so, who are they? What specific harms, other than moral outrage, do victims suffer? Is everybody really doing it?

Although the focus of this article is not on the moral aspects of bribery, moral outrage is a factor that practical business realists should consider. Condemnation of bribing public officials is a universal (1) value expressed in human cultures throughout various periods of history going back to the Code of Hammurabi's prohibition on bribing judges. (2) Moral outrage against bribery is not limited to European-derived Judeo-Christian cultures. "The Apostle of Allah (peace be upon him) cursed the one who bribes as well as one who takes bribe." (3) China, (4) Russia, (5) and India (6) all criminalize bribery of public officials. Many Nigerians are deeply troubled by bribery while still engaging in it themselves out of perceived necessity. (7)

Widely shared moral outrage, especially if based on religious doctrine, can become a "crusade" or "jihad." Indeed some opponents of bribery call for reform in those terms. (8) Widespread popular revulsion against perceived systemic corruption can destabilize even well-established powerful global institutions, as the world discovered in 1517. (9) For practical business people, crusades or jihads destabilize markets and generally undermine consumer confidence.

While acknowledging both moral dimensions and the dangers of public outrage in the bribery problem, this article approaches the topic from a different perspective. This article addresses the assumptions of pragmatic business realists and policy-makers in terms that are more likely to speak to them directly: money. The topic is also narrowed from "corruption" (10) generally to the more concrete legal prohibitions against international bribery found in U.S. law, the Foreign Corrupt Practices Act (FCPA). (11) Domestic laws of all Organisation for Economic Cooperation and Development (OECD) (12) member states, including the United States, now prohibit bribery of foreign officials by their corporations doing business abroad.

The article examines the issue of whether any real harm is being done by multi-national corporations (MNCs) bribing foreign government officials to do business abroad. The central question is whether anybody is getting hurt. Approaching this question deductively from three perspectives--macro-economics, business transactions (microeconomic) and consumer/environmental--the article concludes by briefly examining practical strategies for strengthening legitimate businesses' abilities to compete in a fair and rational competitive market.

II. GREASY WHEELS?

Bribes "grease the wheels" of excessive government regulation. This is the classic older formulation of why bribery is tolerated as a practical business necessity. In this view, bribery is sometimes actually a good thing in terms of economics because it makes cumbersome government bureaucracies work more efficiently. Market efficiency is the most significant value, and bribery is just the sadly necessary mechanism to avoid political bottlenecks.

This argument became fashionable (13) in the 1960s. (14) Often known as the 'contrarian' view, its primary architects' "first instinct was to applaud rather than condemn" bribery (15) on the grounds that it opened market access in heavily regulated closed bureaucratic economies.

Occasionally modern contrarians are found too. (16) The older contrarian view is largely discredited by more recent as well as vastly more extensive economic research, which demonstrates that using bribes replaces political inefficiencies with the inefficiencies caused by a lack of competition. (17) Accepting, arguendo, the argument that efficiency of markets is the single most important value, (18) modern economic research demonstrates in excruciatingly specific detail (with competing mathematical formulas and databases) that market efficiency is not only harmed by excessive government regulation, market efficiency is also harmed by lack Of competition.

A. Sand in the Wheels: Bribes Create Incentives to Increase Regulation

As Judge Posner observed, "Governments operate with reasonable efficiency to purposefully attain deliberately inefficient goals." (19) While ascribing purposeful intent to governments' inefficiencies might appear paranoid, when analyzing bribery, this observation is right on the money.

For non-economist lawyers, it may be helpful to understand bribery using an analogy. Think of the relationship between bribes and government regulation as an eco-cycle. Excessive government regulations cause practical business people to bribe government officials to avoid regulatory bottlenecks. The government official accepts the bribes and returns the favor by reducing the regulatory obstacles for the bribe-giver. It is analogous to throwing garbage out the car window or dumping it in the ocean. The problem is "gone, now that it cannot be seen it anymore. For those adopting the older contrarian view, the eco-cycle stops here. Bribes reduce regulation-- the garbage is gone--problem solved.

Modern economic analysis continues to examine what happens after a successful bribe-transaction. What does a rational, self-interest-maximizing (and now corrupt) government official who has just been bribed to reduce regulation do? He looks for economic opportunities to maximize his economic self-interest--that is, how to get more and bigger bribes. He knows that practical business people will pay good money to avoid regulations, so the obvious way to get more and bigger bribes is to create more and bigger regulations, and wherever possible to seek bigger, deeper business pockets.

This describes the first phase of the self-reinforcing eco-cycle of bribes and regulation. Regulations generate bribes; bribes generate more regulations.

The first piece of rebuttal evidence to the contrarian 'grease the wheels' and tolerate bribery view comes from extensive modern economic research which demonstrates that rather than avoiding excessive government regulation, bribes create market incentives for officials to increase regulation. (20) Rose-Ackerman, a leading analyst of the economic impact of bribery, examined both anti-bribery and bribery-tolerant economic studies. (21) The conclusion is that even routine corruption to avoid regulation is not tolerable because it "may give officials an incentive to create more delays and red tape and to favor the unscrupulous and the well-off." (22) Johann Graf Lambsdorff (23) is another leading modern economist rejecting the contrarian view that greasing the wheels through bribery reduces government regulation. He describes a number of specific case studies in various countries where bribery created incentives for additional regulation, for example the Pakistani gold trade, taxi licenses, and the Nigerian barite trade. (24) He also summarizes a considerable number of additional economic studies supporting the view that bribery increases regulation. (25) Tariffs, customs fees and trade barriers studies provide additional examples of the self-reinforcing cycle of bribery providing incentives to create additional new regulations. (26)

Lambsdorff explains, "There is therefore consensus nowadays that corruption does not 'grease the wheels,' as suggested in some older pieces of literature. For a recent empirical assessment, see Meon and Sekkat (2005). (27) Corruption does not help to overcome cumbersome regulation but acts as an inducement to public servants to create artificial bureaucratic bottlenecks. Corruption acts, therefore, as sand in the wheels." (28)

Toke Aidt's (29) careful analysis of the development of 'grease' versus 'sand' debates in economics scholarship describes the ostensible short term benefit of greasing to reduce specific regulations as the "fallacy of efficient corruption." (30) Noting that the "critical point is that corruption and inefficient regulation are two sides of the same coin" (31) speeding while simultaneously providing incentives for additional regulations, Aidt also highlights the economic waste involved in rent-seeking government-jobs. (32)

Even De Soto (33) himself, oft-cited by old contrarians to support the grease-the-wheels view, concludes that excessive bureaucratic regulation was largely motivated by the desire to generate corrupt revenues. (34) Modern contrarians Meon and Weill, while rejecting the sand in the wheels conclusions, also describe a policy allowing corruption to grow unchecked as "extreme" and "risky." (35) Even for modern contrarians, the key factor is the time frame. "[A] country that would let corruption run rampant may find itself stuck later on with an even worse global institutional framework, and thus end up in a bad governance/low efficiency trap." (36)

The key variable is the timeframe in which economic data is measured. (37) "[C]orruption, theft and rent-seeking often feed on rents generated through unsustainable use of natural resources or through under-investment in human and manufactured capital." (38) An isolated snapshot may find bribes temporarily increasing efficiency (assuming, arguendo, that narrowly defined efficiency without regard to quality and safety costs are the sole goal). When we view the entire eco-cycle of bribery and regulations, however, we see temporary or localized efficiency gains ("fallacy of efficient corruption" (39)) evolving into inefficient market-destroying monopolies.

B. Bribes Destroy "Rational" Markets

The second major rebuttal to the contrarian grease-the-wheels view is that when government decisions are based on the personal greed of individual bureaucrats, the public interest is subordinated to private individual gain of officials who abuse public power. Focusing on bribery as an abuse of the agent/principal relationship, Rose-Ackermann describes bribery as involving "pathOlogies in the agency/ principal relation.., at the heart of the corrupt transaction."

(40) Government officials (agents) breach their fiduciary duty to the public (principal) in favor of self-interest.

Instead of rational economic choices based on traditional market factors (e.g., price, service, and quality) with competition providing market discipline, bribe-based decisions involve personal gain of individual government officials as one, or perhaps even the major, factor. Personal self-interest (greed) of individual officials overrides judgments based on the best public interest value for the government spending.

Wasting taxpayer money is one obvious negative consequence of corruption. Government projects are selected based on bribe-getting opportunities for powerful officials, rather than what might benefit the country as a whole. The wrong competitors are chosen based on willingness to bribe rather than consideration of traditional rational market factors (e.g., price, service, quality). Quality control is undermined in favor of reducing regulatory costs for the bribe-giving business partner.

1. Wrong Project, Wrong Competitor, Low Quality Control

Often known as 'white elephant' projects, bribery provides incentives for officials to choose capital-intensive, technologically sophisticated and custom-built products and technologies. (41) Large, centralized, wasteful projects are selected because bribes are larger and easier to collect. (42) Officials need only to go to one, centralized big bribe-supplier instead of spending time and energy shaking down many small, local, decentralized bribe-suppliers. The economies of scale apply to bribe-getting as well as other economic transactions.

Bribery leads to the misallocation of government funds. Vital projects that are greatly needed and directly benefit citizens are ignored. Large-scale "vanity" or "white elephant" construction projects, natural resource extraction and military armaments purchases are three examples of preferred investment areas that are known to maximize bribe opportunities for corrupt government officials. Choosing to allocate government funds to these types of projects rather than competing areas such as education or basic healthcare delivery--which provide less centralized and smaller, less lucrative, less efficient opportunities for bribe-getting--is one major harm of bribery. (43)

Development economists have produced a plethora of individual national and systemic studies demonstrating the harms of over-investment in white elephant projects at the expense of basic economic development investments. (44) There is a strong correlation between perceived high levels of corruption and low economic growth. "High perceived corruption and low growth rates are associated, but the causation can run from corruption to low growth or from low growth to corruption or more likely, the causal arrow runs both ways, creating vicious or virtuous spirals. To complicate matters further, there are some cases of very corrupt countries that, nevertheless, have strong growth experiences." (45)

High levels of corruption and low growth are strongly associated, creating their own "iterative" cycle. (46) Corruption may not "cause" grinding global poverty in which billions of human beings are struggling to survive on less than one dollar a day in a linear sense. The economic data demonstrates that the relationship between corruption and poverty is not simple linear causation, but synchronistic. (47)

2. Regulations Harass Competitors and Restrict Market Entry

While it may be unfortunate that some countries are plagued with self-seeking corrupt officials who exploit their own countries for petty, personal, short-term gains, practical business people do not see how they could possibly be blamed for this problem. In fact, business people often see themselves as the victims of a corrupt system, not its cause; this is the heart of the problem. Business people, the bribe-payers, see themselves as double victims. First they are the target of shake-downs and extortion schemes by bribe-seeking foreign officials. Then they are the targets of very serious criminal prosecutions and civil sanctions at home in the U.S. or in other OECD member states. Business people are besieged by governments at both ends of many international transactions.

Of course business people view the problem in micro-economic terms. Their duty is to focus on individual transactions, maximizing short-term profits for their own shareholders. Yet some efficient business practices, dumping garbage in the ocean for example, are defined as illegal because of the perceived larger harms to society as a whole. Like our analogy to throwing garbage out of the car window or dumping it into the ocean, such business practices may be more profitable and easier with regard to individual business transactions. However, as a society we decided to create legal sanctions and cultural pressure to resist certain profitable and easy behaviors.

But, business people object, it is not the businesses dumping garbage in corrupt transactions. It is the bribe-seekers, the corrupt foreign officials, who create the harm. Business representatives are just responding to extortionate demands of foreign officials. Why punish the (business) victims?

The problem is that this view cuts off the analysis too soon without carefully examining the entire eco-cycle in a corrupted system. Looking at the entire cycle of bribes and regulations, it becomes clearer that, while some business people might be characterized as pure 'victims' of foreign extortion, others most certainly are active participants, colluding with their bribe-receiving foreign partners.

In fact, the relative power between bribe-seeking foreign officials and bribe-giving business interests may be very complex. "The extremes are kleptocracy [rule by thieves], (48) on the one hand, and state capture (49) by powerful private [business] interests, on the other. In some cases, concentrated power exists on both sides, and we have a bargaining situation similar to a bilateral monopoly [crony "capitalism"] (50) in the private market." (51)

Bribe-seeking foreign officials are not the only self-interest maximizers in this story. Business people also seek to maximize profits, and they are often innovative in their efforts. For a rational, profit-seeking (now corrupt) business person who has learned that bribes can be effective in reducing costly regulations, it is but a short step to the realization that bribes can also be used to raise costs and restrict market entry for one's competitors. (52) Raising costs and restricting market entry prevents competitors from cutting into the favored corporation's monopoly profits. Capturing the state--the regulatory, administrative and law enforcement officials of a government- by bribing higher-level officials is the mechanism used by the now-corrupt corporation.

"State capture occurs when, in contrast to mere bribe-making to secure access to a good or an exception to existing rules, interested parties exploit the malfeasance of officials to change the rules (laws, judicial rulings, or bureaucratic regulations). Rather than state officials and bureaucrats extorting business firms or ordinary individuals, powerful individuals or groups use material rewards or physical threats to reshape the state." (53)

Denver-based Newmont Mining's difficulties in Peru at the Yanacocha gold mine provides one specific example of a bilateral monopoly capturing the regulatory organs of a sovereign state through the use of bribes. The corporate goal is to restrict competition and alter judicial processes to obtain competitive advantages. In the initial stages of this saga, Newmont's officials believed that their French governmentowned partner (Bureau de Recherches Geologiques et Minieres) was bribing the notoriously corrupt Peruvian Fujumori regime to sell the French stake in the huge gold mine to an Australian company. Newmont then arranged to become "friends for life" with Fujimori's murderous right-hand man, Vladimiro Montesinos ("Rasputin, Darth Vadar, Torquemada and Cardinal Richelieu rolled into one"). Eventually, public release of tape recordings of these and other corrupt deals caused the Fujimori government to fall. The entire saga is found in the PBS/Frontline documentary The Curse of Inca Gold (2005), and in an article by Jane Perlez and Lowell Bergman, Tangled Strands in Fight Over Peru Gold Mine, New York Times, October 25, 2005. (54)

In this model, bribe-seekers and bribe-givers collude. The regulatory organs of a sovereign state are used as personal tools to establish and maintain personally profitable deals for insiders. The insiders include both select government officials and favored corporations--the "dynamic duo" of bribe-takers and bribe-givers. (55) Laws, regulations, and licensing procedures are used to harass competitors or restrict market entry; the market itself is no longer rational or free. In fact, there is no actual market at all. Government regulation is very high for outside competitors, while it is lowered via bribery relationships for insiders. The real harm here is lack of open market competition.

Economists characterize this dire situation as a 'bilateral' monopoly between the bribe-givers (favored businesses) and the bribe-takers (favored officials). (56) "'Grand corruption'--can be more deeply destructive of state function--bringing the state to the edge of outright failure and undermining the economy." (57)

The absence of competition destroys any possibility of an actual market, since competition is suppressed. Suppressing competition allows the monopoly of insiders to charge higher prices for lower quality goods and services while escaping taxes and fees. (58) Without a viable tax revenue base, the country is unable to provide basic services. (59) Successful bribe-givers are able to use their insider relationships with high-level government officials to reduce economic choices. (60)

Sometimes this situation is referred to under the misnomer "crony capitalism." Although there are most certainly "cronies," there is no "capitalism" in the sense of an actual market with competition. Economists refer to this as a "bilateral monopoly." Bilateral monopolies are actually the opposite of a notion of capitalism based upon open, competitive markets. What is actually occurring in a bilateral monopoly is business and government insider cronies colluding to loot the country. There is no actual market. This is not capitalism.

The third phase of the eco-cycle of bribery and regulation occurs when insider, favored bribe-givers have built successful relationships with insider government officials who can increase or decrease regulatory enforcement to help their bribe-supplier business friends. Waiving regulations for their well-connected bribe-suppliers, insider officials can raise regulatory barriers for pesky competitors. The rich get richer, elite government and business insiders profit, and any competitors are crushed or swallowed up. This is not market capitalism. In fact, it resembles a mafia-controlled state.

It would be helpful if U.S. and OECD member states' prosecutors could allocate scarce prosecutorial resources to target the most harmful forms of international bribery, where kleptocracy, state capture or bilateral monopolies have arisen. Enforcement efforts in the bribe-receiving nations often present insurmountable political difficulties, not only because of relatively less-developed local legal systems, but because these most egregious forms of corruption also involve the most powerful foreign officials, who are above the law inside their own jurisdictions. (61) Although U.S. and OECD member states do not assert jurisdiction over the foreign official bribe-takers, prosecution of the supply-side, Western, bribe-giving multinational corporations (MNC) would disrupt the cash flow supporting kleptocrats and their bilateral monopoly corporate cronies.

C. Shanghaied

China provides an interesting case study into the relationships between bribery, market restrictions and inefficiencies. While Western economists have engaged in extensive studies, debates and analyses of the problems of kleptocracy, captured states and bilateral monopolies in a variety of nations, they seem to avoid discussing China, except in passing and from a distance. (62) There are undoubtedly a number of valid reasons, including lack of access to good data and a shortage of economists writing in English (63) who also have a deep understanding of Chinese language, economics and political culture. Indeed, there appear to be only a few books (64) in English specifically discussing corruption in China, despite China's significance in the global economy, the large number of U.S. and OECD corporations doing business in China, and its well-known problems with systemic bribery. China is also puzzling because its

288

apparently very high growth rates (65) seem to undermine the thesis that high levels of corruption are associated with low growth. (66)

Professor Yasheng Huang, a political economist from MIT, has written extensively on this topic. His books, written in English, are very influential among younger Chinese reformers. (67) Professor Huang analyzes foreign direct investment (FDI) in China since the reform and opening-up (1980s). In his most recent book, Professor Huang engages in a massive analysis of raw data from the past three decades, much of it never before examined by Western economists, to analyze the rapid development of the People's Republic of China PRC's economy. (68)

Huang's data amply support the thesis advanced by modern Western economists that bribery provides an incentive for increasing government regulation and that bribery is used in practice by business interests to reduce competition through regulatory harassment and restrictions on market entry. Huang carefully examines a large number of specific Chinese regulations of the 1990s, which systematically disadvantaged and harassed domestic Chinese business enterprises (e.g., credit restrictions for domestic business, (69) suppression of informal finance, (70) and financial repression of domestic private enterprise (71).

Huang's thesis is that a "Shanghai Style" bilateral monopoly (crony "capitalism") distorted economic liberalization in favor of Foreign Direct Investors (FDI) and at the expense of indigenous Chinese entrepreneurs. (72) Top-level Chinese officials "wooed" multi-national foreign investors through the bestowal of tax breaks, (73) while at the same time disadvantaging domestic Chinese businesses through financial restrictions and regulatory harassment. At one point, for example, Shanghai department stores actually banned domestic products to make space for international brands. (74) More serious were the financial and tax regulations used to favor foreign investors and disfavor domestic businesses. (75)

Why would Chinese officials adopt regulations that favor foreign businesses while simultaneously enacting regulatory measures that shut off finance for disproportionately tax and increase regulation on their own domestic Chinese businesses?

Chinese policies favoring foreign investors over domestic business development are "often justified by the rationale that foreign capitalists bring financial resources and technology. This reasoning lacks both conceptual and empirical support ... China, for example, attracts a huge level of FDI in sectors that have very little technological content and in sectors where indigenous entrepreneurs are expected to possess superior know-how (e.g., herbal medicine)." (76) Regulatory favoritism toward foreign investors often resulted in fake or round-trip FDI, as indigenous entrepreneurs simply dressed up their products as 'foreign' to evade the regulatory restrictions. (77)

FDI was also wooed through the construction of industrial parks. Government interventions increased during the 1990s, favoring large, centralized, 'statist' projects. (78) Larger 'white elephant' projects, following the Pudong model, and the Maglev train in Shanghai, (79) involve massive land-grabs, which increased fifteen-fold over the past decade. (80)

"The most likely reason for the land grabs in the rural areas and forced evictions in the urban areas is corruption. Politically connected developers bribe government officials to acquire sweetheart deals on the one hand and to lean upon the coercive power of the state on the other- as the entrepreneur who gained the management rights to the new Xiuxhui [Silk] Market did--to enforce the eviction orders." (81)

These land grabs also produce vanity construction skyscrapers with astronomically high price tags. (82) "The financial costs of these skyscrapers, as stratospheric as these skyscrapers themselves, do not even begin to describe the full adverse effects ... The opportunity costs are massive ... [O]ne result is rising illiteracy- to the tune of 30 million people--between 2000 and 2005." (83) "It is well established that China today is among the most unequal societies in the world [comparing various Gini coefficients]." (84)

Large-scale white elephant projects, as predicted, provide more efficient and larger 'rent-seeking' opportunities for major bribes. Large-scale foreign direct investments provide access to significantly deeper pockets than domestic Chinese enterprises and also provide better bribe opportunities than investments in education or healthcare, both of which have declined significantly during the FDI gold rush in China.

"The Chinese state today--especially at the local level--is dangerously proximate to 'a grabbing hand,' a term coined by Frye and Shleifer (1997) to describe the Russian state of the 1990s. Exercise of power for pecuniary interest and corruption were hallmarks of Russia's distorted transition to oligarchic capitalism. In the Chinese context, the state literally grabs--for land." (85) "Protests in China increased at a stunning rate [reviewing various studies]," including some very large and violent ones. (86)

Bribery plays a central role in Huang's description of PRC growth in the 1990s. Corruption is certainly not new to China; the Great Wall was breached not by military force but because the Mongolians were able to bribe a Han Chinese general to open the gate. (87) The general consensus among Chinese economists, however, is that corruption intensified massively during the influx of vast FDI in the 1990s. (88)

Drawing from CUNY Queens Professor Yan Sun's very substantial analysis of primary source data, the public records of corruption prosecutions, including both the Communist Party disciplinary apparatus and the public prosecutors' records, (89) Huang compares the economic impacts of corruption prior to substantial FDI in the 1980s and during the FDI influx of the 1990s.

"Corruption in the 1980s can be described as individual cases of malfeasance; in the 1990s it has intensified to a systemic proportion." (90) Bribe sizes increased four times in nominal terms and 2.3 times in real terms during the MNC influx of FDI. (91) "The size of the Chinese bureaucracy has roughly doubled in the last two decades and there are powerful vested interests in the status quo. Corruption has intensified greatly in scope and scale." (92)

High growth rates and a 'friendly' regulatory environment for foreign investors have generated favorable press for China among Western business interests. Western expatriate businessmen are insulated from the petty annoyances of police roadblock shakedowns or paying off local gangs of thugs which are the hallmarks of corruption in many developing and transition societies. "[M]any foreign investors and observers would describe Shanghai as quite clean. They seem to know the trees of petit corruption but miss the forest of grand theft." (93) "Wu Jinglian, probably China's best-known economist, has forcefully argued that without genuine political reforms, China faces a real risk of falling into the trap of crony capitalism." (94)

Economic growth certainly did not cure China's corruption problems. Huang's evidence suggests, in fact, that growth attracted deeppocket foreign investors, who then greatly exacerbated pre-existing corruption problems. The bureaucracy doubled in size; the going rate for bribes rose 2.3 times in real terms while the Gini coefficient fell. Only a select few are benefiting from China's massive FDI-fueled growth.

From this perspective, our business people are not innocent bystanders, blameless victims of extortionate demands from greedy foreign officials. Western MNC business representatives are the deep-pocket partners in collusion with local officials, who exploit local economic opportunities (in China's case access to the much sought-after 1.3 billion person consumer and cheap labor market) while using their money to encourage local officials to harass and restrict competition.

This view of international bribery is not limited to China. (95) People living in other developing and transition nations have widely held views that see rich foreign businesses as the true culprit in the downward spiral of bribery and corrupt government. "Citizens [in poorer countries] do not view corruption in the way suggested by some economists. They do not think of it as a way for business to get around illegitimate and inefficient state rules and regulations. Instead they view it as a way for business to avoid legitimate laws and to benefit at the expense of ordinary people." (96) "[A] commonplace complaint of developing countries; they blame multinational firms for pushing corrupt inducements on reluctant local politicians." (97)

From this viewpoint of local people living inside corrupt regimes, corruption is not designed to get around burdensome rules in the way Western economists frame the problem. Poor countries face two basic problems--insufficient revenues from tax collection and a productive capital sector that is relatively small so that most people do not believe their personal well-being is tied to capital success. (98) This can lead to redistributive demands.

It is not merely the 'lost generations' [who grew up during the Cultural Revolution] inculcated with anti-capitalist fervor under Mao exhibiting moral confusion about market profits. (99) New generations of Chinese entrepreneurs are directly harmed in their ability to compete in a 'rational' 'market.' They are increasingly skeptical of the American version of capitalism, seeing 'free markets' and 'reducing trade barriers' as propaganda to justify bilateral monopolies favoring foreigners with deeper bribe-pockets. They have no experience with an actual free market operating with genuine competition based on price, quality, and service. The word "capitalism" has been appropriated in China, as elsewhere, as propaganda to legitimize bilateral insiders' crony monopolies. These monopolies are, in fact, the opposite of market capitalism.

"It is condescending for multinational companies to determine that the payments contribute to some vaguely beneficial redistribution of wealth and so are appropriate in spite of local legislation rendering them illegal ... We should not assume that developing countries welcome foreign intervention of this kind--

intervention that permits companies to buy the police protection they need and leaves local citizens underserved." (100)

A more objective view sees both parties to corrupt transactions, both bribe-seeking local officials and bribe-paying foreign businesses, as culpable. When examining bilateral monopolies and state capture it is best to keep in mind that in all cases it takes two to tango. Neither foreign officials nor multi-national businesses by themselves can accomplish this result. Professor Huang clearly understands the significant role of domestic Chinese officials in the corruption epidemic; indeed, the thrust of his work is focused on taming domestic Chinese FDI-driven corruption increases by increasing competition from domestic Chinese entrepreneurship.

But the view from abroad from less sophisticated observers who have not benefited much personally from the great leap forward into 'capitalism' is that foreign corporations have 'Shanghaied' their economies. Any criticism of local wealth inequalities can now be deflected by xenophobic nationalism--those foreign business devils caused grinding poverty by their corruption. Like our innocent business 'victims' who blame corruption on extortion by evil foreign officials, it is always easier to blame the foreigners when caught in the act.

This brings us to the fourth stage in the eco-cycle of bribery and regulations. In the first phase, bribes are used to reduce regulations. Next, bribe-givers use bribe-based relationships to harass and eliminate competition. In the third phase, bribe-taking officials maximize the scale of projects, centralizing the bribe-getting operations, and perfecting the bilateral monopoly. As the cronies squeeze and loot the country, local popular unrest rises threatening to destabilize the profitable cronies' base. As reform pressures mount, each of the cronies can point the finger at the other, the "foreigner" who "caused" the corruption. Xenophobic nationalism, with more than a touch of racial overtones on both sides, can now be used to deflect and stampede popular unrest, buying additional time for the cronies to continue their looting masquerading as global 'capitalism.'

Neither partner in grand corruption bribery is actually what one normally thinks of as a "victim." They are getting very, very rich. Real 'victims' are found buried alive inside that dry, bloodless, macroeconomic phrase "declining Gini coefficient." (101)

Thirty million additional illiterate people in China 2000-2005 provide one small example of the declining Gini coefficient. (102)

Pause for a moment to think about what it means to be illiterate in the modern age of technology information and global capitalism. Condemned by illiteracy to a lifetime of the lowest wage work, (103) it is really easy to cheat illiterate workers and farmers out of their pitiful wages. Nobody got hurt?

III. GREASY DEALS

Moving to the microeconomic perspective, the focus now shifts to analyzing available business strategies for each stage of the business transaction in a systemically corrupted environment. Analyzing each phase of the business transaction, the focus is on how bribery impacts the practical operation of a business.

How would a businessperson actually go about bribing a high-level foreign government official? Corrupt transactions are generally limited to insiders with established links to reduce risks of getting caught or double-dealing. Bribery is not an easy business; it requires criminal skills.

A systemically-corrupt market requires connections for a foreign business outsider to penetrate. Often the outsider business creates a joint venture, hires a local agent, a middleman, a sub-contractor or someone with close ties to the local kleptocrat. This strategy rests on using a middleman who provides good access plus plausible deniability insulating higher-level executives in case the middleman gets caught giving out bribes.

As a business strategy the local middleman approach is risky, as a number of successful prosecutions have demonstrated. (104) One American lawyer, Philippe S.E. Schreiber, has been sued for malpractice by his corporate client. The client was caught violating the FCPA after allegedly relying on the lawyer's advice to use a local foreign middleman and foreign banks when bribing abroad. (105) Another American lawyer, James H. Giffen, is now the criminal defendant in a major FCPA prosecution after allegedly setting up shell corporations and laundering bribe money for the President of Kazakhstan in major oil and gas deals. (106)

The focus in this article, however, is not on good corporate governance compliance programs, preventive legal advice, finding loopholes, or legal defense strategies. The focus is on whether anybody is actually hurt by bribery, and 'hurt' is defined in terms that speak to money-motivated business people.

Former in-house counsel for both the Northrop Grumman Corporation and MCI Communications, Alexandra Addison Wrage, is an international attorney and President of TRACE International, a nonprofit, anti-bribery business association with over 1,000 corporate members in 100 countries. (107) In her book, Bribery and Extortion, Wrage presents the thesis that bribery hurts business, not merely because of the risk of getting caught by prosecutors (which is admittedly small), but because bribery is too risky when viewed as a business transaction in itself. (108) (The academic economists agree.) (109)

A. Greasy Partners, Slippery Terms, and Messy Exits

Finding the right person to bribe is tricky. (110) One cannot advertise on Craigslist to find a bribe partner. Even if the business is being solicited for bribes (extorted?) by a foreign official or his intermediary, is it real? The foreign official may not actually have the authority to do the deal, lift the regulation or whatever advantage is allegedly being offered. (111) The foreign official may also decide to take the money and double-cross the business. (112) Or a higher-level official may see an opportunity and cut the bribe-taking official out after the bribe is already paid. What if it is an FBI sting? (113) Or worse, some foreign corruption reform campaign? (114)

Wrage describes how business people can be gradually seduced into bribery relationships by carefully orchestrated hints and requests for what appear, at least initially, to be harmless relationship-building gifts, advice and favors. (115) In one very poor Middle Eastern country, for example, the foreign business representative agreed to participate in a new, non-profit committee to explore economic development. Over time, bit by bit, the non-profit project escalated into a demand for a five-day, all-expenses paid shopping spree to Paris for the officials and their relatives. (116)

Using an intermediary is risky as well, since the intermediary may not really have the right contacts, or he might claim money is needed to bribe officials and simply pocket some or all of the money himself. (117) Keeping track of bribe money is difficult because bribe payments must be disguised as something else on the corporate records. Otherwise the business's own auditors, any acquiring merger partner's due diligence, the SEC, or the IRS might notice. (118) The business's own (now corrupt) employees may collude with the (corrupt) middleman to siphon off the alleged bribe money. (119) In fact, there may be no bribe payments at all; the "bribes" may actually be a cover story for embezzling employees or agents.

How much is a fair price for the bribe? (120) Normally there are no indexes or markets to set bribe prices. (121) Is the bribe-giver over-paying? The entertainment expenses, endless drinking, call girls, banquets, and gambling jaunts disguised as factory inspection trips to woo insatiable officials are major wastes of time and money.

Contracts to bribe are not legally enforceable. (122) Even if the business manages to find a reliably corrupt partner for a while, he may sell out if a higher bidder comes along. The official or intermediary can raise the price at any time with impunity. There is no end to the haggling. Once a businessman has a reputation for being willing to bribe, he is fair game for every ambitious official who hears about it. He has a reputation for being easy. The bribe price goes up. (123)

There are also significant transaction costs involved in bribery. These costs include setting up shell corporations and wiring the bribe money around to launder it. (124) Ensuring secrecy of Swiss and other "private" bank accounts abroad is no longer as easy or reliable as it used to be. (125)

In one tragically comic case, the courier delivering the bribe cash to the President of Azerbaijan was literally taken hostage by armed men and held until the American bribe-paying business partners agreed to increase the price by a third. (126) If there are large "sunk cost" investments abroad, the business becomes physically hostage to bribe seekers. If the business has trade secrets, patents, or copyrights, it must consider that intellectual property piracy is a major source of revenue for high-level officials abroad. (127)

Even if everything else is going well, the business can get caught in the crossfire (sometimes literally) of factional struggles for power in the foreign nation. (128) If businesses get caught on the wrong side of a factional struggle, the bribe investments are lost, and the business might be too. Of course one could pay off all the factions, but that strategy can become excessively expensive. Seeing opportunities, more factions will undoubtedly arise and splinter off in pursuit of their share.

Once a business is in the bribe relationship, each party is hostage to the other. Either partner can denounce the other if things go wrong. If the Western business is denounced, First World prosecutors will welcome the representatives home with open arms and handcuffs. But if the foreign official bribe-partner is very high level, it might not matter if his own people know he is taking bribes--

he is above the law as an autocrat with a large, armed clan running a sovereign state; the Western business people are the sole hostages. Extortion and blackmail are real possibilities here. (129) The company's stock may be adversely affected. (130)

Exit strategies are a problem. (131) The business bribes are the cash cow for the foreign official(s). How can the business exit this deal? There is no pre-nuptial agreement. Actually repatriating any profits--taking actual money out of the foreign country--is a significant problem. (132)

Just empty your pockets and walk away slowly with your hands in the air. Nobody will get hurt. (Except maybe in Russia (133) where Western business representatives are occasionally murdered; drive-by shootings are a possible exit strategy for unwanted partners. (134) Higher level Russians, KBG-trained, prefer poison. Easy to administer, harder to trace, and a slower, more painful death that also provides a significant deterrent effect.) (135) Or China, which has, and uses, the death penalty for bribery, though so far it has only executed Chinese nationals. (China recently sentenced four employees of Australian steel giant Rio Tinto, one of whom is an Australian citizen, to seven to fourteen years in prison for taking bribes and stealing commercial secrets.) (136)

Bribery is a very risk activity. American MNCs are, for the most part, amateurs when it comes to bribery as a business strategy.

B. Meet the Professionals: Transnational Criminal Organizations

If legitimate Western MNC businesses are amateurs dabbling in bribery-based business strategies, there are others for whom the skill set of illegal deal-making and, more importantly, illegal deal-enforcing is already highly developed. For pragmatic contrarians opting out of a legitimate business competition-based rational market and still justifying bribery as a viable business model, it should be noted that their actual business model competitors are Transnational Criminal Organizations (TCOs).

"Regardless of corruption's specific nature, it effectively 'blurs the line' between states and TCOs. Corruption offers criminal groups the means to penetrate markets with relatively low transaction costs and then to exploit those markets largely unregulated...." (137) Systemic bribery opens the gateways for organized crime.

Professor Kelly Greenhill's chilling analysis of "kleptocratic interdependence" self-reinforcing domestic and international relationships between organized criminal groups and government officials should cause any free-market believer to pause before continuing on the path of bribery-based business strategies. (138) Her chart of the top ten TCOs is enlightening. (139) The Albanian mafia, for example, is now colluding with the Turkish mafia, making it into the top ten. (140) Greenhill's research indicates that home-country bases for six of the top ten TCOs are highly functioning democracies; the other four are in hybrid regimes. (141)

While the home-bases for TCOs may be in more developed states, their prey is found inside regimes that have been weakened through systemic corruption. Human trafficking studies estimate that nearly 10% of the female population of Moldova were trafficked in the first decade after the Soviet Union's collapse. (142) Wildlife and animal parts, such as Siberian tiger skins, Amur leopards, and bear paws, are also trafficked. (143) Global networks of organized crime exploit corrupted regimes' weaknesses, using them for profitable drug (144) and illegal arms trades. (145)

The grisly trail of death and destruction left by Viktor Bout, "the world's most notorious illegal arms merchant, until he was arrested in Thailand in 2008," stretches from the FARC in Columbia to Afghanistan, Rwanda, South Africa, and Sierra Leone, built on his fleet of 60 Soviet-era transport aircraft and a staff of 300 pilots. (146) While the profits are deployed in many different ways, in some cases the profits are used to fund terrorist groups such as the FARC. (147) The risks of nuclear proliferation where systemic corruption has weakened both legal systems and personal inhibitions must also be considered.

There is a bit of good news. In Professor Matthew Bunn's expert analysis, nuclear proliferation is not widespread through TCOs at the moment despite some individual lapses. (148) The most serious case, that of Pakistan's A.Q. Khan's network of proliferation to Libya, Iran, North Korea, "and possibly others" was certainly fueled by Khan's vast personal greed-amassing significant individual wealth, despite his modest government salary. (149) Personally-corrupted deal-makers (150) and suppliers in the Khan network provided openings for foreign intelligence services to penetrate and eventually dismantle the Khan proliferation network.

The moral fabric of cultural norms against terrorism and loose nuclear materials, combined with still viable moral and cultural norms in favor of duty and patriotic pride remain sufficiently strong in Russia, in Professor Bunn's analysis, to probably forestall nuclear proliferation for personal gain. (151) One hopes Pakistan, North

Korea, and their Chinese (152) patrons can also achieve the apparently higher Russian levels of cultural norms on this very important issue. Those more familiar with India, Israel, Pakistan, or Iran should be invited to share their expertise on this crucial issue. While one does not wish to engage in reductio ad terrorem here, people might really get hurt if this is not correctly analyzed and addressed.

IV. TOXIC GREASE

Fortunately, these very dire scenarios are either speculative or happening to other people far away. None of it actually hurts wealthy residents of the West in any concrete, immediate way. In order to motivate people to change personally-profitable-bribe-based-business-as-usual by convincing them that bribery really does harm people and should not be tolerated, the hurt must be brought home, directly into their personal lives.

A. Facing Victims

Abstract arguments about harm to society as a whole are generally not effective in motivating people to change profitable, entrenched behaviors. "In the specific case of corruption it would seem useful (i) to present the concrete victims that suffer the final consequences and (ii) to show the causal links that tie a present act of corruption with its victims." (153) In order to trigger the neural-causal link between an action and the harm caused, visual perception of the human victim is generally needed. Faces are the most effective. (154)

Neurological research studies have shown that visual perceptions of another person's pain act as a stimulus for our own perception of pain. (155) "Under normal conditions, when our actions affect someone else, we generate inner disgust and discomfort, which leads us to abandon such acts. Some theories propose that the inadequate functioning of the [m]irror [n]eurons allows a person to hurt another without feeling remorse." (156) Immature neural development explains why young children have difficulty perceiving harmful consequences to themselves or others, living in the here and now moment. (157)

Perceiving the person being hurt as a real human may be culturally influenced by racism--refusing to recognize other races as equally and fully human. (158) In extreme cases the inability to perceive other people as human may be associated with autism, a condition in which the patient is completely focused on himself and his interests while overlooking the interests, feelings, and emotions of others. (159)

To persuade people that bribery actually harms real humans, the causal links between acts of bribery and either real harm to someone perceived as a fellow human or to ourselves must be demonstrated. Viewing the faces of human victims triggers the mirror neurons.

Fifty-one people died from contaminated toothpaste manufactured abroad. (160) Fake baby formula killed dozens of infants. (161) Lead and other toxins are found in children's toys manufactured abroad. (162) Dogs and cats died after consuming pet food poisoned with melamine. (163) Vast amounts of imported drywall used in residential home construction in America turn out to be so contaminated with toxins that the homes are literally uninhabitable. (164) Hundreds of children attending school died or were terribly injured, in Sichuan, China, and in Haiti, when shoddy construction resulted in their schools collapsing during earthquakes. There are so many specific examples of "low quality control" killing and injuring people that it could fairly be characterized as an avalanche of death due to corruption. Do human faces make the harm less abstract?

B. It is Not My Fault

The starting point of this article's analysis was the argument that bribery greases the wheels to reduce excessive and burdensome government regulation. Some of those regulations are legal or bureaucratic; for example, how many different licenses, permissions, stamps, and seals it takes to incorporate a new business. Some of those regulations, however, are safety-related quality control.

In a business culture where bribing regulators abroad is justified because they are corrupt foreigners and in a government culture where bribe-taking is culturally acceptable, the rules are not enforced for deep-pocketed foreign business partners. Safety rules suffer. Where the primary goal of both business and government is to personally make as much money as fast as possible, quality control suffers. Where business people spend their most significant efforts bribing government officials, they are not actually tending to quality control in their own business.

There is no rational market competition to provide market discipline on quality control, since market entry is limited to insiders who bribe lavishly and reliably. Government regulatory checks are ineffective if the bribe-giver has obtained high enough official

patrons who outrank the safety agency officials. There is no private
market legal check, such as products liability lawsuits, where the
judicial system is subordinated to political (bribe-taking) interests.
Independent consumer organizations testing product safety are
forbidden; even private individual consumer complaints warning
other consumers are censored or suppressed in the most authoritarian
censorship regimes such as Saudi Arabia or China. (165)

> U]nlike South Korea and Taiwan where the quality issues
> were a "teething" problem naturally characteristic of early
> industrializing economies, in China many of the quality
> problems were not due to lack of knowledge. Chinese firms
> knowingly and deliberately committed fraudulent business
> practices in order to skimp on costs. (166)

> The persistence of a business model centered on low costs
> rather than technology and upgrading and the lack of maturity
> in the corporate development of Chinese private firms are
> results of two matching problems in the Chinese economy.
> One is that political legitimacy, legal support, and financial
> resources are not matched with the most efficient firms in the
> economy--private-sector firms and entrepreneurial businesses
> that have an arm's length relationship with the government....

> Private entrepreneurs, instead of focusing on business and
> product development, spend their time cultivating
> particularistic ties with the government and currying political
> favors. Rather than investing in technology and product
> quality, this is the focus of their competitive strategy.
> Valuable time, talents, and efforts are lost to rent-seeking
> activities. (167)

The role of multi-national business, the supply-side of bribe-
givers, is central here. Recall that during the 1990s gold rush of
foreign direct investment by multi-nationals, the bureaucracy in
China doubled in size. (168) The going rate for the size of a bribe
increased four times in nominal terms during the same era. (169)
Escalating demand (more bureaucrats, bigger bribes) on the side of
the bribe-takers generates pressure to cut costs by any means possible
on the part of bribe-giving businesses, which are often also being
pressured by Wall Street and their own corporate executives whose
personal compensation packages depend on short-term profits. It is a
greasy fast-food syndrome of instant gratification of what they think
will be easy profits without actual competitive work (ignoring the

substantial risks of doing business with crooks), while in deep denial about facing human victims.

C. More Than "Inconvenient" Harm

If wealthy residents of Western nations get rich enough, maybe they could afford to personally avoid the avalanche of toxic products descending on clueless consumers of global products. Someone else's puppies and babies get killed. Rich, educated, very much First World Americans and Europeans can afford organic, locally-grown slow food and children's toys that are hand-carved in Vermont or Tyrol. Caveat emptor.

The impact of a self-reinforcing cycle of bribes, regulations and deteriorating quality control is not limited to consumer purchases however. Even the truly wealthy consume air and water. Systemic bribery has a negative impact on environmental regulation. (170)

Analysis of a cross-section of more than 100 countries leads to the conclusion that corruption negatively impacts pollution control. (171) Bribery reduces the effectiveness of environmental regulation. Although an adverse impact on emissions cannot be demonstrated, Welsch thinks that this may be due to lack of accurate reporting of data in corrupted systems. Significant results can be found for ambient pollution of air (urban sulfur dioxide and suspended particulate concentration) and for water pollution (dissolved oxygen demand and suspended solids). These results hold regardless of income. (172)

Faces of individual victims of environmental damage can be found in a variety of places. The effects of untreated mercury poisoning on humans, for example, have been documented by filmmaker Ernesto Cabellos in two films about the people affected by the Yanacocha Gold Mine mercury spill. (173) Newmont Mining Corporation of Denver, owner of the mine, and their "friend for life" kleptocrat (and Fujimori's notorious sidekick), Vladimiro Montesinos, can be seen doing business on the PBS Frontline-New York Times documentary The Curse of Inca Gold (2005), with actual audio tapes of the bribery negotiations. Newmont is trying to purchase a favorable decision from the Supreme Court of Peru by out-bribing the French. (174)

The problems are not confined to impoverished victims in faraway, poorly governed places with inadequate democracy and rule of law institutions. The U.S. government agency charged with regulating oil-drilling safety (175) was corrupted by multi-national oil and gas corporations with the usual tools of sexual bribery (orgies), lavish gifts, vacations, and in the U.S. case, cocaine. (176) Safety regulations for oil drilling were left largely to the industry's own voluntary self-regulation. (177) As it turned out, bland assurances about how safe oil drilling is today with modern technology to prevent major spills were not entirely accurate. (178)

If MNC oil corporations invested in blow-out valve safety research and testing spill-control technology instead of investing money and time in corrupting U.S. regulatory agency officials with cocaine and orgies, perhaps the overall economic result would have been more "efficient" on both macro and micro-economic levels. Short time flame efficiency (reducing business costs) may not be the only important value. It was certainly not the only economic cost.

Business leadership's attention to, and investment in, quality and safety control instead of bribery might have helped the eleven people who were killed when the Deepwater Horizon oil rig exploded. The damage to the people and environment of the Gulf of Mexico is potentially very significant.

That analogy between bribery and garbage turns out to be more than merely hypothetical. Like it or not, all who breathe air or drink water are in this together. Everybody gets hurt.

V. NOT EVERYBODY IS DOING IT: CARROTS AND STICKS

Everybody does it and nobody gets hurt? If the argument justifying bribery turns out to be wrong about the allegedly victimless nature of the crime, maybe that argument is also wrong about the claim that everybody does it. Is everybody giving and taking bribes? Is the idea of a rational free market, disciplined through competition, just cynical propaganda? Do only naive suckers try to play fair and compete by the rules?

There is good news here. Many very successful multi-national corporations are struggling mightily to prevent their own participation in the bribery cycle. Corporate compliance is a growth industry. Whether motivated from religious or ethical considerations, hard-headed recognition of excessive transactional risks of a bribery-based business plan, fear of public relations damage to the brand, negative impact on the stock price, or of personal prosecution and jail time for MNC executives, many successful multi-nationals are trying hard to compete rationally and avoid bribes.

Highly-regarded corporate leaders are stepping up, calling for a cleanup in business practices. To select just one example, General Electric's Senior Vice President-General Counsel from 1987 to 2004, Ben W. Heineman, Jr., provides concrete and practical analysis of the role of MNCs in combating global corruption. (179) Giving very specific advice about how to implement corporate compliance, with a realistic assessment of the countervailing pressures on MNCs, Heineman concludes:

> In the end, one might ask whether this broad multi-faceted role that I have suggested for MNCs in the long war against corruption is too idealistic or naive. I began this chapter by recognizing that there are powerful internal and external forces within the global corporation that promote corruption. But I also explained that an MNC that combines high performance with high integrity can realize benefits inside the company, in the marketplace, and in the global society by operationally fusing these foundational goals. Ultimately, developing nations that can achieve economic growth and build institutional infrastructures are of profound long-term benefit to MNCs because they provide a sound environment for sustainable economic activity. Just as it is in the corporation's enlightened self-interest to fuse high performance with high integrity, so too is it in the MNC's interest, in all the ways that I have suggested, to add its resources, expertise, and commitment to the building of social, economic, political, legal, and administrative institutions that are transparent, accountable, and durable and in which there is but an irreducible minimum amount of corruption.

> MNCs are not sufficient for economic growth and institution building in the developing world. But they may be necessary and are at least important--and at the very least should do no harm. If they act in their enlightened self-interest, they, in sum, have a significant role in shortening the long war against corruption. (180)

Obvious victims actually harmed by unfair bribery-based competition are compliant and legitimate private sector business competitors economically injured by bribe-payer business cheating. It is not easy to stay clean when others cheat. Those seeking to reduce corruption should consider offering additional tools to legitimate businesses that they might choose to deploy against unfair competition, or use for leverage in their efforts to compete rationally.

Strengthening legitimate business efforts could provide a natural constituency and significant ally in reform efforts.

Legitimate businesses cheated out of market share and profits by bribe-payers should have ready access to civil lawsuits for damages. This would provide an additional mechanism to level the playing field through private choices to sue (or not to sue) by legitimate business competitors. It would also provide an efficient private market incentive for those with the best access to information about greasy or toxic deals to self-regulate by offering damages as compensation for their lost profits and recover costs incurred in the efforts to self-regulate a given industry.

Private rights of action are developing in Europe. (181) Germany has already adopted a civil right of action for parties injured by briber payers. (182) Legitimate MNCs may wish to consult with German lawyers about obtaining jurisdiction there to obtain compensation for economic losses due to competitors' bribes.

Although there is currently no specific statutory private fight of action under the FCPA, in the U.S. various legal strategies including lawsuits by disappointed competitors (183) are having some limited success. (184) Civil RICO anti-racketeering laws, both federal and state, and state tort law on intentional interference with contractual relations have generated the best success at the moment, although shareholder derivative suits, ERISA fiduciary duty, and antitrust suits are also obvious legal avenues to challenge bribe-based competitors.

The advantages of private civil over public criminal litigation as an enforcement mechanism are substantial for the business community, particularly under Sarbanes-Oxley's rules about corporate insurance for litigation costs. It is possible that legitimate businesses will adhere to the no-snitch rule of street gangs. It is also possible that legitimate businesses will see an opportunity to compete within the law, recouping profits lost to unfair bribe-based competition. There is no expert plaintiffs' bar at the moment, to my knowledge. It remains to be seen whether business interests actually hurt by unfair bribe-based competition are able or willing to sue civilly.

Voluntary industry cooperation efforts are expanding. Transparency International founder Peter Eigen has launched a "Publish What You Pay" (185) voluntary transparency co-operative initiative with the extractive industries MNCs (oil, gas, minerals) and natural resource-rich nations. (186) TRACE International, a non-profit association of business organizations and law firms representing business, is making substantial efforts including an anonymous hotline for businesses to report extortion demands from specific officials abroad. (187)

For those who are not yet convinced that a new era of higher global business ethics has begun, it should be noted that U.S. prosecutors' batting average on FCPA prosecutions to date is 100%. Not one U.S. jury has allowed a person charged with international bribery to get off scot-free.

Some OECD member states are prosecuting their own with vigor. The French prosecuted their state oil company, Elf-Aquitane. (188) The Germans prosecuted Siemens. (189) For OECD member states still parochially protecting (190) their own major MNC bribers, note that a name and shame campaign by British investigative journalists (191) appears to have Successfully (192) disclosed the British government's cover up of the BAE-Saudi corrupt arms deals. (193)

The U.S. State Department should be encouraged to continue their ongoing diplomatic efforts to persuade fellow OECD member states to seriously discipline their own MNC bribe-givers. Assisting U.S. prosecutors in the enforcement of the FCPA on U.S.-listed corporations are the new money laundering reporting requirements (194) for lawyers, accountants, bankers, broker-dealers, real estate agents, casinos, yacht and jet sales, and jewelry suppliers. (195)

Leveling the international playing field for responsible MNCs is critical if internal corporate self-discipline is to succeed. It would also be very helpful if the State Department would assist in streamlining transnational discovery mechanisms for both civil and criminal cases (196) facilitating external checks that could enhance incentives for MNCs to clean up, or at least increase transaction costs and litigation risks for non-compliant unfair MNC competitors.

Leadership from the top matters. If the global business climate is to change direction on whether bribery is tolerated or not, real change must begin at the very top. Robert Rotberg analyzes several relatively successful corruption reform efforts abroad (Singapore, Hong Kong, Botswana and surprisingly, Rwanda) emphasizing the possibilities of transformative leadership from the top. (197) Lambsdorff, on the other hand, emphasizes grassroots bottom-up social movements and has some very interesting data on the successes and failures of specific anti-corruption reform strategies. (198)

It is very important for those of us entrusted with the education of future leaders, particularly in law, government and business, to discuss bribery clearly and frankly with our students. If educators permit students to go forth into the global business world without having "the talk" first, we leave them to learn about bribery from sleazy predators in back alleys claiming "everybody is doing it and nobody gets hurt." Law students and lawyers need to clearly understand that they will be disbarred and sent to jail if caught structuring bribery deals. (199)

There is no doubt that people can change deeply entrenched, profitable but destructive customs. But old habits are difficult to change. In modern times those same habits seem barbaric. Dumping toxins or patronizing racially segregated hotels and restaurants now seems unthinkable to civilized people. Yet Slavery and Jim Crow, like indiscriminate dumping, were very profitable business strategies lasting centuries, in part because many white people could not or would not perceive African people as fully human and of course because free or cheap labor is profitable. (200)

Humans are an adaptive and resilient social species. If we can agree on fundamental values, we can change course. Bribery is harmful, and not everybody does it. It is a choice, and that choice has real life consequences. Shutting off the supply side of bribe money provided by MNCs will not cure corruption all by itself. It will not end greed. But it will disrupt cash flow and business as usual for kleptocrats abroad and their cronies at home in the West.

Reform begins at home. Supply side, top down reform. If the U.S. and other wealthy OECD member states take responsibility for the behavior of our own MNCs, we can at least ensure that we are not exacerbating destructive corruption abroad.

NOTES DELETED

ELIZABETH SPAHN, Professor of Law, New England Law I Boston. I am very grateful to Sandra Lamar, Research Librarian at New England Law I Boston for producing the PowerPoint victims' photographs slide show. Thanks also go to my invaluable research assistants, Rochelle Meddoff and Andrew Sabino, to my colleague Kent Schenkel, and Rafael S. Mena. [c] 2010, Elizabeth Spahn.

Part VIII

POLICING AND REGULATING WHITE COLLAR CRIME

18

Microsoft and National White Collar Crime Center Make Digital Forensics Tool Available to U.S. Law Enforcement Agencies

Today at the Digital Crimes Consortium, Microsoft Corp. and the National White Collar Crime Center (NW3C) -- the nation's premier provider of economic and high-tech crime training to law enforcement agencies -- announced an agreement establishing NW3C as the first U.S.-based distributor of the Computer Online Forensic Evidence Extractor (COFEE). A Microsoft-developed program, COFEE uses digital forensic technologies to help investigators gather evidence of live computer activity at the scene of a crime, regardless of their technical expertise. This agreement will make COFEE available to law enforcement agencies at no charge so they can better combat the growing and increasingly complex ways that criminals use the Internet to commit crimes. This distribution agreement broadens availability for law enforcement agencies, building on Microsoft's April 2009 distribution agreement with INTERPOL, which is making the COFEE tool available to law enforcement in each of its 187 member countries (see also Microsoft Corp.).

"The COFEE distribution agreement will be of enormous benefit to U.S. law enforcement agencies dealing with technologically sophisticated cybercriminals," said Donald J.

Microsoft and National White Collar Crime Center Make Digital Forensics Tool Available to U.S. Law Enforcement Agencies. Copyright 2009 Microsoft News Center.

Brackman, director of NW3C. "NW3C is very pleased to partner with Microsoft in making this tool available and contributing to the fight against cybercrime."

A common challenge of cybercrime investigations is the need to conduct forensic analysis on a computer before it is powered down and restarted. Live evidence, such as some active system processes and network data, is volatile and may be lost while a computer is turning off. This evidence may contain information that could assist in the investigation and prosecution of a crime. With COFEE, a front-line officer doesn't have to be a computer expert to capture this volatile information before turning off the computer on the scene for later analysis. An officer with minimal computer experience can be tutored to use a pre-configured COFEE device in less than 10 minutes. This enables him or her to take advantage of common digital forensics tools the experts use to gather important volatile evidence while doing little more than simply inserting a USB device into the computer.

The agreement with NW3C, a nonprofit membership organization dedicated to supporting law enforcement agencies in the prevention, investigation and prosecution of economic and high-tech crime, is the latest example of Microsoft's ongoing commitment to building partnerships that help create a safer, more trusted Internet experience for everyone, not just Microsoft customers. The announcement comes as law enforcement, industry, academic and government cybercrime experts around the world meet in Redmond at the Digital Crimes Consortium. This consortium will provide a mechanism for information sharing, tools development and community building to help industry, government, academia and law enforcement agencies better address the complexity of the evolving threat landscape.

"Criminals are working in a new digital age, and it is essential that law enforcement agencies have the latest tools and technology to help them fight the cyberthreats facing the global community," said Tim Cranton, associate general counsel of Worldwide Internet Safety Enforcement Programs at Microsoft. "Microsoft is proud to be working with NW3C and INTERPOL to make COFEE more broadly available to law enforcement agencies and to host the Digital Crimes Consortium bringing industry, government, academic and law enforcement cybercrime experts from around the world together to build a long-term coordinated effort in the fight against digital crime. By working together, we can be most effective in making the Internet safer for everyone."

Working with INTERPOL, the Florida State University and University College Dublin, NW3C will also continue the research and development that will ensure that COFEE serves the needs of law enforcement agencies as technology evolves.

"Florida State University's E-Crime Investigative Technologies Laboratory has extensive expertise in software tools and systems to support law enforcement, and we were pleased to assist the National White Collar Crime Center in evaluating COFEE for its continued use and development," said computer science professor Sudhir Aggarwal, director of the ECIT Lab. "We look forward to future collaborations in the effort to win the fight against cybercrime."

"COFEE is a very valuable tool in the arsenal of law enforcement agencies to fight cybercrime," said Professor Joe Carthy of University College Dublin's (UCD) Centre for Cyber Crime Investigations, which is partnering with Microsoft and INTERPOL to develop training programs to enable law enforcement officers to use COFEE. "It will help to establish a recognized international standard in digital forensics and cybercrime investigations. It will also assist law enforcement agencies to develop internal the expertise which they require in dealing with cybercrime investigations."

19

Self-Detection

So Key, So Difficult

Laura A. Brevetti

When it comes to white-collar crime, popular opinion today is to view American corporations solely as perpetrators. However, this public ire ignores the documented reality that corporations and institutions are just as likely to be the victims of internal fraud and financial crimes, suffering direct losses in the hundreds of billions of dollars.1

Rather than act as sitting ducks hoping to be unaffected, corporations and institutions must remain vigilant in their efforts to detect fraud and other criminal violations and respond immediately upon detection to mitigate the harm. This article will examine the importance of detection and why it is such a difficult task, as well as offer suggestions for best practices to go about detecting white collar crime.

THE IMPORTANCE OF EARLY DISCOVERY

The types of white-collar crime confronted by corporations range widely from complex financial and corruption schemes, including fraudulent financial statements, investment schemes and bribery, to the more common embezzlements and employee expense fraud. What is certain is that whenever a crime has been committed within or through the corporation, revenues decline and shareholders' value is lost, confidence in the business is eroded and the reputations of the board members and officers, even those not involved in any way with the wrongdoing, are damaged.

Self-detection: so key, so difficult. white-collar crime Laura A. Brevetti. New York Law Journal July 13, 2009

314

Even small, closely held companies are not immune to fraud by insiders or third parties. Nor should owners and managers remain complacent because "trusted" employees are in charge of the company's assets. The negative financial impact from employee fraud and embezzlement is often more devastating on the small business, since the resulting losses eat into already-thin profit margins and corporate goodwill is more closely associated with the integrity of individual employees.

Setting aside the need to mitigate financial and reputational losses, a corporation itself may also face the threat of prosecution, even though it has suffered its own financial losses through the illegal conduct of one rogue employee or small group of employees viewed as improperly supervised. As long ago as 1940, then-Attorney General and later-U.S. Supreme Court Justice Robert H. Jackson chillingly observed that the Department of Justice (DOJ) and its 93 U.S. Attorneys have "more control over life, liberty, and reputation than any other person in America."2 That assessment of prosecutorial power is surely still true today.

According to a 2007 study, there were nearly 4,500 separate criminal offenses enumerated within the thousands of pages of the U.S. Code.3 In addition to those criminal statutes, it is estimated that the number of regulations in the Code of Federal Regulations, many of which carry the "tag-line" that violations may be punished criminally, reaches a staggering number.4

Given the choice, it is often more likely for the government to view corporate conduct as criminal and opt for prosecution of the corporation and its executives, even where civil administrative and enforcement alternatives are available. In 2007, five years after it was established contemporaneously with the enactment of Sarbanes-Oxley in July 2002, the DOJ's Corporate Fraud Task Force reported 1,236 corporate fraud convictions, including 214 CEOs and presidents; 53 CFOs, 23 corporate counsels or attorneys, and 129 vice presidents,5 which means the DOJ initiated exponentially more investigations, inquiries and prosecutions than the convictions it reported.

Regrettably, in times of depressed economic conditions, there is the likelihood of an increase in instances of employee fraud and illegal methods to increase revenues. Thus, now more than ever, a well-conceived program of risk assessment and self-detection is critical to the financial health and survival of any business, large or small. Further, self-detection may be the first step to saving a corporation from the brunt of that awesome prosecutorial power spoken of by Justice Jackson 70 years ago.

WHY DETECTION IS DIFFICULT

Fraudulent and corrupt conduct is indeed difficult to detect. Surveys of corporate insiders reflect estimates that as little as 10 percent to 25 percent of fraudulent acts committed within a company are ever detected.6 The factors complicating detection are varied and depend in some measure upon the type of business in question.

In the financial and credit marketplace, the sheer complexity of the alleged schemes is frequently to be blamed for their longevity before detection. Many recently reported fraudulent schemes, especially those resulting in staggering losses, relied on different actors (all complicit to some degree), who were financially sophisticated and inter-related in commerce so as to facilitate and obscure complex, exotic financial transactions that very few would have been able to unravel.7

Yet, the public and private reaction to instances of fraud and outright theft of billions of dollars is usually, "Why wasn't this caught sooner?" Government regulatory bodies no less sophisticated than the Securities and Exchange Commission have also been confronted by this very question.8

Large or small businesses can fall victim to less sophisticated criminal conduct. Usually, in those instances, the crime was committed by a valued employee, since owners and managers tend to give trusted employees the closest access to information and assets, the key ingredient for any successfully designed fraud. And despite the prevalence of such crimes, many companies do not have checks and balances or any semblance of an effective risk management program.

Instead, corporations appear to rely solely on accounting and auditing programs to uncover employee or third-party schemes, which, many times, are designed by trusted insiders to conceal and evade detection. Significant percentages of company budgets are expended on audit and accounting services in the hope that the review will unmask any fraud or waste. However, there are inherent deficiencies in typical audit procedures that render complete reliance on them misplaced.

It has not been unusual, following recent scandals, for a company's auditors to appear as dumbfounded as the public to the news that a client has suffered a major fraud. Embezzlements illustrate the difficulty of detection in audits.

It is standard practice for corporations to establish and rely on set procedures for the approval of invoices. Auditors, familiar with the corporation's established procedure, conduct their audits by "spot checks" of those practices and look for anomalies or "red flags" (for example, invoice amounts that exceed the approval level of the employee). A flaw in that audit procedure is that embezzlement schemes, whether large or small, are frequently conceived by insiders familiar with standard corporate practices and designed specifically to mimic legitimate invoices or expenditures.

Without specific instructions of what to look for, auditors would find nothing to report, even if chance led their random samples to include fraudulent invoices. Bogus, but technically compliant, "consulting" invoices used to funnel corporate money to third parties to make bribes or to pay kickbacks to insiders, are classic examples of the flaws of this audit technique.9

Even when a "red flag" does arise, the intent of the individual or individuals who are responsible may not be readily discernible: Was it a crime or a mistake? Also, for many companies, the internal approval or even audit exercises are rote, box-checking activities that never change. Risk managers need to be more nimble and creative in designing internal procedures and oversight. Review should be frequent and change instituted more easily so that the insider with fraudulent intent does not know what to anticipate in terms of oversight.

BEST PRACTICES

It is well accepted that the most common and cost effective way schemes are revealed is through a tip from an employee, customer or vendor. Corporations must encourage, not ignore, this reality.

Further, the corporation must dispel a corporate culture of silence and instead actively promote an ethic of zero tolerance for the commission of any (even petty) fraud. A corporation must institutionalize the avenues for complaints of, or information relating to, suspicions of fraud.

For example, it is not expensive to establish and promote the use of an "800" number for reporting. Above all, it must be made known to the employees, vendors and customers that the company wants to know about fraud and other potential criminal violations, will protect those who come forward with that information and will seriously investigate all leads.10

At some point there will exist a need to roll up one's sleeve to conduct internal investigations. More often than not, such investigations are commenced based upon reasonably believable allegations or information of criminal wrongdoing, misconduct or ethical violations committed by employees or company practice.

As mentioned previously, if encouraged, it is not unusual for these allegations to be brought to management by whistleblowers. On fewer occasions, they may arise from internal or external audits.

The benefits and significant risks to conducting an internal investigation must be clearly articulated and considered before it begins. Government authorities encourage self-detection and disclosure. The DOJ recently re-iterated as a matter of policy that a corporation's timely and voluntary disclosure of wrongdoing and its willingness to cooperate in the investigation of its agents is a factor that will determine whether the corporation will be prosecuted, a benefit not to be lightly dismissed.11 Other enforcement agencies have similar voluntary and, even, mandatory policies regarding timely disclosure.

However, disclosure is no absolute shield to prosecution or heavy penalty. Companies must also be alert to the "boomerang effect"; internal investigations can also serve as blueprints for prosecutors to come back after the company, particularly if the government determines that the business has failed to reveal all "relevant facts" or is just going "through the motions" of appearing to be helpful.

On balance, while professionals may debate whether or not the value of disclosure can be overstated in light of past difficult experiences with a particular prosecutor or enforcement agency, it is this author's opinion that the value of detecting corporate fraud and criminal behavior, whether committed by individuals within the company or from without, cannot be overstated.

Internal corporate investigations are often conducted by a company in-house, utilizing its own staff to perform the investigation, usually under the guidance of in-house counsel. In-house staff is most familiar with the company's procedures (no need to "re-invent the wheel") and it keeps costs down.

However, in-house inquiries will rarely uncover misconduct by corporate officers, board members or senior management. Thus, the retention of independent outside counsel is recommended.12 In addition, the gravitas of the investigation's findings will be immeasurably enhanced if it was conducted with objectivity by an experienced, independent, outside counsel and staff.

The famed Yogi Berra once observed: "If we don't know where we're headed, we're liable to end up someplace else." While investigations can take the participants to different areas than originally conceived, it is not in the company's interest to initiate an investigation with an open-ended plan. The team should be prepared to deal in all respects with the two most significant sources of information: documents and interviews.

With regard to documents, suffice it to say that attorneys must make sure internal documents are preserved and made available, and when gathered are examined and appropriately indexed for content and reference. Electronic information is an area best left to a designated team member with expertise in methods of retrieval and storage. There is no substitute for the team leader to personally review key documents.

Interviews are the life blood of any internal investigation. Careful consideration should be given to the list of potential witnesses, the order of interview, and the level of experience of the interviewer. More than one attorney should be present at the interviews and the better practice is for all interviews to begin with what is known as the "Upjohn warnings."13

What should be done with the information gathered, particularly if it has detected criminal violations, is a singularly important question. It may lead to disclosure to the government or to the public or both. It is important to remember that controlling the timing of disclosure, particularly for high-profile matters, is a critical advantage, but one that is most elusive. One should bear in mind the old saw that nothing is secret if known by another.

Consideration of preserving the corporation's attorney-client and work product privileges is critical. The corporation must be alert to prevent any lapse from occurring during the investigation or in its presentation to the government, if it wishes to guard the integrity of the privilege from waiver claims in potential derivative or third-party lawsuits.

Current DOJ policy prohibits its prosecutors from even requesting that the corporation waive the privilege and waiver of the privilege is not a "credit" factor to be considered by the prosecutor.14 However, as a practical matter, a business may nevertheless decide later voluntarily to waive the privileges to enhance the effectiveness of counsel's presentation to the government on its behalf.

People who are found to have been involved with a corporate fraud must be dealt with, with commensurate measures, including discipline and separation, even if the findings need not be referred to the authorities. Companies should also consider the deterrent effect of letting employees know that the matter was dealt with thoroughly, professionally, swiftly and with certainty of result. Remedial action, besides changing the procedures that led to the violations, might also include using the investigation to illustrate to employees, shareholders and the public that the corporation values transparency and will act on information of fraud or misconduct.

CONCLUSION

Businesses that fail to recognize the ever-present risk of becoming victims, as well as unwitting violators, of white-collar crime are certainly foolish, and more probably doomed.

Prevention is certainly an important part of a company's bulwark against fraud. However, more likely than not, at some point, fraud will occur, and when it does, swift detection is key. The pathway to the detection of criminal conduct within the corporation is made infinitely easier if the organization promotes transparency in its governance and integrity in its management and operations. The better practice is to utilize professionals to conduct internal investigations and guide the company through the maze of regulatory and enforcement proceedings.

ENDNOTES DELETED

Laura A. Brevetti, a former federal and state prosecutor in New York, is a partner in the New York office of K&L Gates, in the areas of white-collar criminal defense, government regulatory and enforcement proceedings, and internal investigations. Alyssa Cohen, an associate of the firm, assisted in the preparation of this article.

20

Whistleblowing and White Collar Crime: Why Ireland Needs Legislative Change

Ireland Could Learn Useful Lessons from the Protections Afforded to Whistleblowers in Other Jurisdictions

Leo Fleming

The issue of whistleblowing has been getting column inches in recent times. In May 2010 the Minister for Justice and Law Reform, Dermot Ahern, announced that he would shortly be bringing the Prevention of Corruption (Amendment) Bill before the Dail Committee, with a view to securing its early enactment. Part of that Bill, once enacted, provides 'blanket whistle-blower protection' to employees including those in the public sector. Currently, Ireland does not have general whistleblowing legislation, although there is legislative provision for whistle-blowers protection in certain sectors.

There are two key obstacles to the successful prosecution in Ireland of white collar crime:

Whistleblowing and white collar crime why Ireland needs legislative change: Ireland could learn useful lessons from the protections afforded to whistleblowers in other jurisdictions. Whistleblowing Leo Fleming. Accountancy Ireland Dec 2010 v42 i6 p36(2).

- finding a jury to handle complicated financial crime cases; and

- the absence of whistleblowers to offer evidence in court of the alleged crime.

The promise of further legislation should help to address the latter.

There has been mixed support for whistleblowing legislation in Ireland and this must be due to cultural and historical reasons. In its 2008 annual report the Office of the Director of Corporate Enforcement (ODCE), Ireland's company law regulator, noted that it had presented a 'modest legislative proposal' on whistleblowing in Irish company law to the Company Law Review Group (CLRG). However, the ODCE report also noted that "the proposal did not attract CLRG support" and "the CLRG in its own report to the Department of Enterprise, Trade and Employment recommended that no company law specific to whistleblowing provisions should be included in company legislation". The ODCE says it understands that the CLRG recommendation has been accepted by the Department.

STATE BODIES

One area where there have been some changes in the requirements recently is that for state bodies. The 2009 Code of Practice for the Governance of State Bodies requires boards to put in place procedures whereby employees in state bodies may, in confidence, raise concerns about possible irregularities in financial reporting and other matters. This is, no doubt, the embodiment of whistleblowing provisions in the way that state bodies shall henceforth organise this aspect of their affairs. Indeed, many of the state bodies have developed their own whistleblowing policies in the last year in response to the Code's requirements.

BLUEPRINT POLICY

In addressing the issue of protection for whistleblowers, Ireland can learn from good practices developed elsewhere. The Committee on Standards in Public Life in the UK has highlighted the role that whistleblowing plays "both as an instrument of good governance and a manifestation of an open culture". The Committee's recommendations have been adopted by many regulatory bodies. The principal recommendations made by the Committee in relation to an organisation's whistleblowing policy are that the following points should be made clear:

- The organisation takes malpractice seriously-- distinguishing whistleblowing concerns from grievances;

- The whistleblowing policy should provide examples of the type of concerns to be raised;

- Staff have the option to raise concerns outside of line management;

- Staff are enabled to access confidential advice from an independent body;

- The organisation will, when requested, respect the confidentiality of the member of staff raising the concern;

- When, and how, concerns may properly be raised outside the organisation;

- It shall be a disciplinary matter to victimise a whistleblower who acts in 'good faith' and for someone to maliciously make a false allegation;

- Staff are made aware at their orientation into the organisation and periodically thereafter of the whistleblowing avenues in operation.

These recommendations provide a very useful framework for a whistle-blowing policy. One can envisage using hotlines and web technology for the submission of concerns, anonymous or otherwise. In any event, at least two people in the organisation and the audit committee should be privy to the information submitted and concerns raised should be dealt with promptly.

PITFALLS

The potential pitfalls for the whistle-blower have been dearly shown in other jurisdictions. Reflect on what happened to Bradley Birkenfeld who tipped off the US Internal Revenue Service and the US Department of Justice in late 2007 about potential tax issues involving 19,000 people when he worked at Union Bank of Switzerland (UBS) in Geneva. His disclosures resulted in what many commentators say is the largest tax fraud case of its kind and may make it more difficult for the tax haven industry to operate in the years ahead. As a result of Birkenfeld's disclosures, UBS paid a US$780m fine to the US for facilitating undeclared offshore accounts that held some US$20bn for US citizens or residents. The bank had little choice other than to pay up as it risked the revocation of its banking licence in the US. But in a bizarre turn of events Birkenfeld was given a 40-month jail sentence at the US government's pleasure for aiding and abetting one individual to evade US tax while he was a UBS employee.

The unfolding events in the type of situation described above may contain unexpected outcomes for those who report concerns about misconduct, either within or external to their organisation. The case also illustrates that whistleblowing cannot be undertaken lightly. If one does not have guaranteed immunity from prosecution or an explicit assurance of non-victimisation, why be a hero?

The Birkenhead example underlines the importance of having effective legislation in place that offers unambiguous protection to the whistleblower acting in good faith. And just as organisations can learn from experiences in other jurisdictions, so too can Irish policymakers as they bring in further legislation on whistleblowing. In the broader commercial environment, any legislation in this area will need to meet a standard of good practice and be on a par with what operates in other comparable jurisdictions.

EFFECTIVE PROTECTION

In Canada, Australia, the US and the UK there has been broad legislative protection for whistleblowers for at least the last decade. The UK Public Interest Disclosure Act 1998 provides protection for individuals who make qualifying disclosures. One of the accepted outcomes of this type of legislative protection is that the act of whistleblowing is, to some extent, destigmatised. Individuals feel less threatened in reporting malpractices or wrongdoing than they might have prior to the legislative enactment.

In the US there is significant focus in the whistleblower model on driving efficiencies and effectiveness in agencies. The US model also offers to pay a whistleblower up to 30% of the identified savings arising from a protected disclosure--provided that it meets certain criteria. In some situations this has led to substantial settlements for whistleblowers.

CONCLUSION

It is fair to say that Ireland does not meet the type of standards and protection for whistleblowers that other countries have set for themselves. We lag behind in terms of broad legislative protection for whistleblowers and especially the type of legislative protection for individuals that is required in commercial organisations and the public sector. But it is hoped that the proposed legislation--whenever it is enacted--will go some way to addressing these concerns and will follow the lead set by other countries. Ireland's legislative deficit in this area should not be allowed to continue in view of the many crises and governance failings suffered in the public and private sectors in recent times.

Leo Fleming, FCA is a Director in the Enterprise Risk Services Division of Deloitte Ireland. He was Chairman of the Institute of Internal Auditors in Ireland from 2002 to 2005. Email:. lfleming@deloitte.ie.

21

Feds Ready to Tackle Cybercrime

New Law Gives U.S. Another Weapon

Richard Acello

As the threat of cybercrime continues to mount, the U.S. Department of Justice says it's ready to make more of a federal case out of the issue.

A December survey by the Ponemon Institute, which researches and educates about data security issues, showed that nearly half of IT security professionals and about a quarter of IT operations experts saw cyberthieves as their biggest concern as far as data loss and whether it affects their employers or the employers' customers.

The survey also found a whopping 92 percent of responding organizations had suffered some form of cyberattack. Consumer complaints are also rising. The Federal Trade Commission has collected data for all 50 states on consumer complaints related to Internet fraud. These include complaints submitted not only to the FTC, but also to the Justice Department, Better Business Bureau, National Consumers League and 13 state attorneys general.

For 2007, the FTC reported 221,226 Internet-related fraud complaints, up almost 16,000 from 2006 and more than 24,000 above the 2005 total. And those numbers may understate the problem since consumers are often unaware of the presence of "malware" on their computers.

Feds ready to tackle cybercrime: new law gives U.S. another weapon. Richard Acello. ABA Journal Feb 2009 v95 i2 p37(1)

But federal prosecutors say new legislation will allow them to better pursue cybercriminals and compensate victims.

The Identity Theft Enforcement and Restitution Act of 2008 targets identity theft, phishing and spam. ITERA also eliminates a requirement that victims show $5,000 in damages before prosecution for hacking or other cybercrimes can proceed.

"ITERA makes significant improvements in the law but doesn't necessarily create whole new categories of criminality," says John Lynch, a deputy chief in the computer crime and intellectual property division of the Justice Department.

[Graphic omitted] "One significant change to the statute targets 'botnets,' which are networks of infected computers used for sending spam, conducting identity theft schemes and phishing," Lynch says. "In these cases, often the victims don't know their computer is infected or damaged.

"Instead of prosecutors having to prove 100 victims who suffered $50 each worth of damage to their computers to meet the statute's $5,000 monetary threshold, the statute allows us to demonstrate that there were at least 10 damaged computers in a botnet."

ITERA also makes it easier for the federal government to take jurisdiction.

"In the prior law, ... one of the elements of proof was there had to be some interstate communication," says Lynch. "But sometimes an attack would happen--for instance, against a hospital by somebody in the parking lot using the hospital's wireless network. The federal government might want to prosecute such a case because it had better resources, but could not because there was no interstate communication. The new bill removes that requirement."

Lynch says the DOJ has the personnel to staff ITERA.

"The Department of Justice can call on more than 200 assistant U.S. attorneys trained to work on computer crime and intellectual property cases," Lynch says.

ITERA also expands the definition of cyberextortion. "The old statute had only covered one type of extortion, which was a threat to cause damage--for example, 'If you don't pay me $100,000, I will harm your system,' " Lynch explains. "We saw extortion that went beyond that to the potential resale and intrusion into personal data, so that extortion could be 'I hacked your system. Unless you pay me X dollars, I will make your data public.' The statute now covers this type of extortion."

Part IX

PROSECUTING, DEFENDING, AND ADJUDICATING WHITE COLLAR CRIME

22

White Collar Crime's Gray Area

The Anomaly of Criminalizing Conduct Not Civilly Actionable

Wendy Gerwick Couture

Substantive and procedural differences between criminal and civil treatment of conduct sounding in securities fraud combine to cause the following anomaly: certain false statements to investors may be actionable criminally--subjecting individual defendants to imprisonment--but not civilly--leaving victims without remedy. The imposition of criminal punishment for conduct that does not invoke civil liability risks disrupting the current scheme of securities regulation, at the expense of considerations deemed important by Congress and the courts. Moreover, the extension of criminal liability beyond the scope of civil liability debunks the assumption, which underlies the current scholarship on the civil-criminal divide, that criminal liability is a subset of civil liability in circumstances where the relevant conduct injures identifiable individuals. This article demonstrates that criminal liability is more expansive than civil liability in the context of securities fraud, analyzes the impact of this anomaly on the current scheme of securities regulation, and considers whether the rationales underlying the leading theories of the civil-criminal divide explain this unique liability configuration. This article concludes that, although this configuration has destabilizing effects, it is arguably consistent with many of the theories underlying the civil-criminal divide. Therefore, this article proposes a two-step solution to further the rationales of the civil-

---

White collar crime's gray area: the anomaly of criminalizing conduct not civilly actionable. Wendy Gerwick Couture. Albany Law Review Wntr 2009 v72 i1 p1(55).

criminal divide while preserving the delicate balance of the current scheme of securities regulation.

I. INTRODUCTION

Substantive and procedural differences between criminal and civil treatment of conduct sounding in securities fraud combine to cause the following anomaly: certain false statements to investors may be actionable criminally--subjecting individual defendants to imprisonment--but not civilly--leaving victims without remedy. This article examines five of these differences, demonstrates how they combine to cause this anomalous civil and criminal treatment of conduct sounding in securities fraud, analyzes the impact of this anomaly on the current scheme of securities regulation, and considers whether the rationales underlying the leading theories of the civil-criminal divide explain the anomaly.

Part II of this article demonstrates that discrepancies between criminal and civil liability for securities fraud result in the criminalization of conduct not civilly actionable. First, the elements of the federal crime are often broader than the elements of the civil cause of action. In federal criminal prosecutions for conduct sounding in securities fraud, a lower materiality standard often applies than in civil cases, forward-looking statements are not protected by the "safe harbor" that is often invoked in civil cases, and liability is not confined to primary violators as in private civil actions. Moreover, at the state level, broad blue-sky laws and federal preemption of state civil securities class actions combine to criminalize conduct that is not civilly actionable. Finally, courts do not subject criminal indictments to the same level of pretrial scrutiny as civil complaints, and motions to dismiss are less favored in criminal cases than in civil cases.

Part III of this article shows that the imposition of criminal punishment for conduct not civilly actionable risks disrupting the current scheme of securities regulation, at the expense of considerations deemed important by Congress and the courts. The lower materiality standard and the unavailability of the safe harbor in criminal cases may chill corporate disclosure and may affect what information reasonable investors rely upon when making investment decisions. In addition, the potential of criminal aiding and abetting liability may discourage secondary actors from advising less established companies. Further, the broader criminal statutes may shift enforcement responsibility away from the Securities and Exchange Commission ("SEC") to the Department of Justice and to the states. Moreover, the criminalization of wide swathes of corporate conduct affords prosecutors broad discretion to decide whom to prosecute, invoking concerns about selective prosecution and separation of powers, and affords the SEC remarkable leverage in negotiating civil settlements. Finally, the narrow scope of private civil liability leaves injured investors without remedy.

Part IV of this article examines whether any of the dominant theories about the civil-criminal divide explains the anomalous relationship between civil and criminal liability in the context of securities fraud. The extension of criminal liability beyond the scope of civil liability debunks the assumption underlying the current scholarship on the civil-criminal divide that criminal liability is a subset of civil liability, but an examination of the rationales behind the leading theories of the civil-criminal divide lends some support for this unique configuration of liability in the context of securities fraud.

Finally, Part V of this article proposes a two-step solution. First, in light of the wide-ranging consequences of imposing criminal liability for conduct that does not incur civil securities fraud liability, Congress should reign in the scope of criminal liability to the current reach of private civil liability for conduct sounding in securities fraud. Second, because the more expansive reach of criminal liability is arguably consistent with many of the theories underlying the civil-criminal divide, Congress should consider carefully whether to expand the reach of criminal liability--while recognizing and compensating for the impacts of that expansion on the carefully balanced scheme of securities regulation.

II. CONDUCT THAT IS NOT ACTIONABLE AS CIVIL SECURITIES FRAUD MAY BE CRIMINALLY PROSECUTED.

Five major differences between criminal and civil treatment of conduct sounding in securities fraud create an anomaly in which conduct not actionable as securities fraud may nonetheless be criminally prosecuted. First, prosecutors may use the criminal wire and mail fraud statutes, which have no civil equivalent, to prosecute conduct that does not violate the securities fraud statute ("the wire/mail fraud run-around"). Second, an individual defendant may be held criminally, but not civilly, liable for allegedly false forward-looking statements accompanied by meaningful cautionary language. Third, an individual defendant may be criminally prosecuted for aiding and abetting securities fraud, but an investor injured by the defendant's conduct is barred from asserting a private right of action. Fourth, some state blue-sky laws impose criminal liability for conduct that is not civilly actionable as securities fraud. Fifth, courts do not subject criminal indictments for securities fraud to the same degree of pretrial scrutiny as civil securities fraud complaints, leaving more issues to the jury. As shown below, these differences allow conduct that is not actionable as civil securities fraud to nonetheless be criminally prosecuted.

A. Differing Materiality Standards for Wire and Mail Fraud and for Securities Fraud Create the "Wire/Mail Fraud Run-Around."

Conduct cognizable as securities fraud is often within the scope of the wire and mail fraud statutes. Securities fraud liability, both civil and criminal, is premised on (1) a false or misleading statement or omission (2) that is material and (3) made with scienter. (1) Wire and mail fraud require the following elements: (1) "existence of a scheme to defraud"; (2) "using or causing the use of the mail [or wires] to execute the scheme"; and (3) "specific intent to defraud." (2) Virtually every statement that could form the basis of a securities fraud claim (e.g., a statement in an analyst call, in a webcast, in a press release, or in a Securities and Exchange Commission filing) is disseminated via the wires or mail, thus satisfying the jurisdictional requirement for mail or wire fraud. (3) For example, prosecutors have charged defendants with wire fraud for allegedly making false statements in forms filed electronically with the SEC, (4) in press releases distributed via the wires, (5) and in analyst and investor conference calls. In other words, if a prosecutor determines that an individual defendant made an allegedly false statement to investors, the prosecutor may often choose whether to charge securities fraud, wire fraud, mail fraud, or some combination thereof.

If the same statements were actionable as securities fraud, wire fraud, and mail fraud, a prosecutor's decision to prosecute the conduct as wire or mail fraud would have little practical consequence, other than perhaps an increased incentive for the defendant to accept a plea deal. Since each use of the mail or wires can be separately charged, prosecutors have tremendous leverage in convincing defendants to plead guilty to just one count of mail or wire fraud--rather than face trial on numerous counts. (7)

The same statements are not, however, actionable as securities fraud and as wire or mail fraud. The materiality standard for wire and mail fraud is lower than for securities fraud, opening the door of criminal prosecution to more statements. (8)

1. The Materiality Standard for Wire and Mail Fraud Is Lower than for Securities Fraud.

Materiality is an essential element of securities fraud and of wire and mail fraud, but materiality is defined differently in the two contexts. The materiality bar to securities fraud liability is higher than the materiality bar to wire and mail fraud liability.

In the securities fraud context, materiality is an objective standard. (9) A statement is material if "'there is a substantial likelihood that a reasonable shareholder would consider it important in deciding how to vote.'" (10) In other words, "[i]t is not enough that a statement is false or incomplete, if the misrepresented fact is otherwise insignificant." (11) This standard depends on "the significance of an omitted or misrepresented fact to a reasonable investor." (12) When applying this objective materiality standard, courts routinely dismiss securities fraud claims based on vague forward-looking statements and vague characterizations of present fact. (13) For example, courts have held that the following statements are immaterial as a matter of law:

"Advanta's credit quality continues to be among the best in the industry." (14)

"Our emphasis on gold cards--and targeting of high quality customer prospects with great potential for profitability--sets us apart from other credit card issuers." (15)

"Our superior cost structure for delivering and servicing financial products allows us to achieve outstanding returns with highly competitive pricing and flexibility." (16)

"We believe that Food Lion's Extra Low Prices and its clean and conveniently located stores are especially well suited to the demands of our customers." (17)

The company "was 'optimistic' about its earnings and 'expected' Marlboro to perform well." (18)

The immateriality of allegedly fraudulent statements is one of the most heavily litigated--and most frequently successful--issues in securities fraud litigation. (19) In a recent study, David A. Hoffman analyzed 472 securities fraud opinions and found that 385 of them addressed materiality. (20) Of those addressing materiality, forty-four percent dismissed at least one claim as immaterial as a matter of law. (21)

In the wire and mail fraud context, on the other hand, materiality is a subjective standard. In the landmark Supreme Court case imposing a materiality requirement in wire and mail fraud cases, Neder v. United States, the Court cited with approval two definitions of materiality. (22) The first definition, previously articulated in United States v. Gaudin (23) and subsequently adopted by most courts for use in wire and mail fraud cases, (24) states: "[A] false statement is material if it has 'a natural tendency to influence, or [is] capable of influencing, the decision of the decisionmaking body to which it was addressed.'" (25) The second definition is derived from the Restatement (Second) of Torts, which instructs that

> a matter is material if: '(a) a reasonable man would attach importance to its existence or nonexistence in determining his choice of action in the transaction in question;' or '(b) the maker of the representation knows or has reason to know that its recipient regards or is likely to regard the matter as important in determining his choice of action, although a reasonable man would not so regard it.' (26)

Both definitions of materiality cited in Neder include within their reach statements that an objectively reasonable person would not regard as important. The Gaudin definition includes statements that, although not having a "natural tendency to influence," are nonetheless "capable of influencing" the decision. Similarly, part (b) of the Restatement definition explicitly extends to statements that a reasonable person would not regard as important in determining his choice of action. Consistent with these definitions, the Ninth Circuit has rejected the argument that an objective materiality standard should be applied in wire and mail fraud cases. (27) In addition, the Eleventh Circuit has noted that the materiality threshold for wire and mail fraud is akin to a "minimal relevance" standard. (28)

The subjective materiality standard used in wire and mail fraud cases is also consistent with the companion doctrine, adopted by a majority of the circuits, that a victim's gullibility is irrelevant to liability for wire or mail fraud. (29) A few circuits have, without connecting their pronouncements to the materiality standard, stated that a fraudulent scheme must be credible enough to influence a reasonable person in order to be actionable as wire or mail fraud. (30) The trend, however, is away from this minority rule and toward using the credibility of the scheme merely as an indicator of whether the defendant possessed the requisite intent to defraud. (31)

2. Prosecutors Are Using the Wire/Mail Fraud Run-Around.

Prosecutors may evade the objective materiality standard required under securities fraud jurisprudence by charging wire or mail fraud rather than securities fraud. The data shows that prosecutors are indeed as eager to charge conduct sounding in securities fraud as wire or mail fraud.

The criminal cases chosen by the Department of Justice's ("DOJ") Corporate Fraud Task Force as "Significant Criminal Cases and Charging Documents" provide a telling snapshot of how prosecutors are using the wire and mail fraud statutes. Of the seventy-nine cases sounding in securities fraud on this list, prosecutors charged wire or mail fraud in forty-nine cases, or sixty-two percent. (32) Moreover, in forty-nine percent of the cases charging mail or wire fraud for conduct sounding in securities fraud, prosecutors did not even charge securities fraud. (33)

Prosecutors' heavy reliance on wire and mail fraud is further evidenced by the overall charging statistics. According to the data compiled by the Federal Justice Statistics Resource Center for the years 1999 through 2006, the number of defendants charged with securities fraud is dwarfed by the number charged with mail or wire fraud. On average during this time period, 119 defendants were charged with securities fraud each year. (34) During this same period, an average of 720 defendants were charged with mail fraud per year, and an average of 404 defendants were charged with wire fraud per year. (35) In other words, on average, almost ten times as many defendants were charged with mail or wire fraud as with securities fraud. Even taking into account that many wire and mail fraud cases do not sound in securities fraud, the disparity is staggering.

Prosecutors' predilection for using the wire and mail fraud statutes to prosecute white collar crime has not gone unnoticed. Congress recognized, and approved of, the use of mail and wire fraud to prosecute corporate executives' wrongdoing when it passed the White Collar Crime Penalty Enhancement Act of 2002 (the "WCCPA") as part of the Sarbanes-Oxley Act. The WCCPA increased the maximum sentences for mail and wire fraud from five years to twenty years. (36) By including these enhancements in the Sarbanes-Oxley Act, which was intended to address corporate fraud, (37) Congress implicitly approved the use of the mail and wire fraud statutes to prosecute corporate executives. Moreover, on the Senate floor, Senators Trent Lott, (38) Joe Biden, (39) and Orrin Hatch (40) explicitly voiced their approval of this use of the mail and wire fraud statutes. In addition, numerous commentators have recognized that prosecutors rely heavily on wire and mail fraud to prosecute white collar crime. (41) In fact, the DOJ has explicitly encouraged its prosecutors to consider the mail and wire fraud statutes as "important tools" to address fraud within the scope of other criminal statutes. (42)

3. The Wire/Mail Fraud Run-Around Results in the Criminalization of Conduct That Is Not Civilly Actionable.

The wire/mail fraud run-around permits defendants to be held criminally liable for conduct that does not violate the securities fraud statutes. Unlike the securities fraud statutes, the wire and mail fraud statutes do not have companion civil causes of action. (43) As a consequence, civil plaintiffs may not use the wire/mail fraud run-around, resulting in the criminalization of conduct not civilly actionable.

This anomaly has gone unremarked. Although courts have rejected the argument that a more general criminal statute, like the mail and wire fraud statutes, should not be used to prosecute conduct that is more narrowly addressed in another criminal statute, (44) courts have not specifically addressed whether it is appropriate to use a general criminal statute to criminalize conduct that is not even civilly actionable. Moreover, those decrying the expansive interpretation of the mail and wire fraud statutes have not objected that it criminalizes conduct that is not even civilly actionable. (45) Even the Supreme Court appears to have overlooked this bizarre ramification of the breadth of the wire and mail fraud statutes. In United States v. O'Hagan, the majority mused that "practical consequences for individual defendants might not be large" if misappropriation conduct were classified as mail fraud but not securities fraud. (46) This rumination failed to recognize the impact on individual defendants' exposure to civil liability. If the conduct were classified as securities fraud, the defendants would be subject to civil liability for insider trading to contemporaneous traders. (47) If the conduct in O'Hagan was classified as mail fraud but not securities fraud, no private right of action would exist. (48)

B. A "Safe Harbor" Shields Forward-Looking Statements from Civil, but Not Criminal, Liability.

A second substantive reason for the anomalous civil and criminal treatment of conduct sounding in securities fraud is the Private Securities Litigation Reform Act's ("PSLRA") "safe harbor" for forward-looking statements. The safe harbor shields an individual defendant from civil liability based on a false forward-looking statement if one of two disjunctive prongs is satisfied: (1) the statement is "identified as a forward-looking statement, and is accompanied by meaningful cautionary statements identifying important factors that could cause actual results to differ materially from those in the forward-looking statement"; or (2) "the plaintiff fails to prove that the forward-looking statement was made with actual knowledge by that person that the statement ... was false or misleading." (49) For example, if one of the prongs is met, the safe harbor protects "earnings estimates," (50) predictions that restructuring efforts "will lead to improved profitability," (51) and expectations that initiatives will "restore" positive cash flow. (52)

Under the plain language of the statute, a defendant is protected from civil liability if a forward-looking statement is accompanied by meaningful cautionary language--regardless of whether the defendant has actual knowledge that the forward-looking statement is false. This interpretation, although dramatic, is supported by the legislative history of the PSLRA, (53) the cases interpreting the safe harbor, (54) and the commentators. (55)

Not surprisingly, virtually every analyst call and SEC filing is accompanied by cautionary language, (56) and the safe harbor is frequently invoked by defendants to shield themselves from civil liability. For instance, out of a set of 248 civil securities fraud opinions issued by federal district courts in 2006 and 2007, the safe harbor was analyzed at least sixty-seven times. (57) In other words, the court addressed the safe harbor in twenty-seven percent of the opinions. Moreover, the safe harbor is so effective at protecting forward-looking statements that the number of securities class actions alleging false predictions has continued to decline. (58)

The safe harbor does not protect a defendant from criminal liability, however. By its terms, it applies only to "any private action arising under this chapter." (59) As a result, a defendant who makes a false forward-looking statement accompanied by meaningful cautionary language is shielded from civil liability but may be criminally prosecuted. For example, corporate executives have been indicted for making the following allegedly false predictions:

> WorldCom is certainly not immune to the effects of the economy. We are being impacted like everyone else. But, with the visibility we have in our significant growth engines, we continue to have confidence in our ability to achieve our [twelve] to fifteen percent] 2001 growth target on the WorldCom tracker. And I guess the thing that always frustrates me when I hear people talk about visibility as it's kind of like landing a plane--how much visibility do you really have? And so I thought I would just compare it to a

weather forecast and say that if we look out for the remainder of 2001, we do not see any storms on the horizon at this time. (60)

"[W]e may well have that asset and operate that asset for quite some time. It's not a bad asset, it's a good asset, just like a lot of the other assets in this portfolio." (61)

In the context of civil securities litigation, these defendants would have had a strong argument that their predictions were protected by the safe harbor, but that argument was not available in their criminal cases.

C. Aiders and Abettors of Securities Fraud Are Subject to Criminal Liability but Not Private Civil Liability.

Supreme Court precedent and congressional statutes interact to cause the following result: aiding and abetting securities fraud is criminally actionable and enforceable by the SEC, but private plaintiffs may not recover damages from anyone but primary violators of the securities laws.

In 1994, overruling "decades of lower court precedent that nearly universally recognized the propriety of ... secondary liability," (62) the Supreme Court in Central Bank of Denver v. First Interstate Bank of Denver held that a private civil plaintiff may not assert a cause of action for aiding and abetting under [section] 10(b) of the Securities Exchange Act. (63) The Court reasoned that the text of the statute does not mention "aiding" or "abetting"; and the Court inferred that, since Congress did not attach aiding and abetting liability to any of the express causes of action in the securities acts, it would have been unlikely to attach aiding and abetting liability to [section] 10(b) if it had been an express, rather than an implied, cause of action. (64) The Court's reasoning was widely interpreted as applying equally to abolish SEC enforcement actions against aiders and abettors. (65) The general United States Code provision imposing criminal liability for aiding or abetting an offense against the United States, however, preserved criminal liability for aiding and abetting securities fraud. (66)

In 1995, after debating whether to overrule or ratify Central Bank, Congress chose to forge a middle road. Congress declined to amend the Securities Exchange Act to provide for private aiding and abetting liability, reasoning that it would be "contrary to [the bill's] goal of reducing meritless securities litigation." (67) Congress did, however, explicitly recognize the SEC's right to premise enforcement actions on aiding and abetting conduct. (68)

Finally, in 2002, in response to public outcry over recent corporate scandals, Congress commissioned the SEC to conduct a study to determine the number of securities professionals who, during the period from 1998 to 2001, were found to have "aided and abetted a violation of the Federal securities laws." (69) The commissioning of this study implied that, depending on the results, Congress might extend private civil liability to aiders and abettors. (70) The study, published in 2003, reported enforcement actions against 1,713 securities professionals during the time period. (71) Out of these 1,713 securities professionals, only 297 were found to have aided and abetted a violation of the securities laws and, of those, only thirteen were not also found to have committed a primary violation. (72) The results of the study cut two ways. On the one hand, the paucity of aiding and abetting violations suggested that aiding and abetting behavior was not widespread, obviating the need to expand private civil liability. On the other hand, the results suggested that the SEC might not be aggressively pursuing mere aiders and abettors and that the expansion of private civil liability to aiding and abetting conduct would fill that gap. (73) In addition, notably, the study did not address the number of securities professionals criminally convicted of aiding and abetting securities fraud. Congress has not acted in response to the SEC's report, and private aiding and abetting actions remain unavailable under the federal securities acts.

D. Criminal Liability Under State Law Is Sometimes Broader than Civil Liability Under Federal or State Law.

State criminal offenses are sometimes broader in scope than the civil causes of action that are available to private plaintiffs. Two factors contribute to this effect. First, state securities acts occasionally impose broad criminal liability without creating a companion private right of action--subjecting a white collar defendant to the prospect of criminal sanction but not affording injured investors a remedy. Second, even if a state securities act affords plaintiffs a private right of action, the broad preemption imposed by the Securities Litigation Uniform Standards Act often renders the private cause of action illusory.

1. A Few State Securities Acts Impose Broad Criminal Liability Without Creating a Private Right of Action.

New York's securities act, the Martin Act, (74) is a prime example of a state securities act that criminalizes conduct that is not civilly actionable. The Martin Act imposes criminal liability for conduct that would not be civilly or criminally actionable under the federal securities acts, but the Martin Act does not afford injured investors a private right of action. (75)

First, under the Martin Act, an individual defendant is guilty of a misdemeanor, "punishable by a fine of not more than five hundred dollars, or imprisonment for not more than one year or both," (76) for making a false statement if he or she "(i) knew the truth; or (ii) with reasonable effort could have known the truth; or (iii) made no reasonable effort to ascertain the truth; or (iv) did not ha knowledge concerning the representation or statement made.... (77) In other words, the Martin Act essentially eliminates the scienter requirement, (78) which is an element of both civil and criminal liability under the federal securities laws. Civil securities fraud requires a showing of at least recklessness, (79) and criminal federal securities fraud requires a showing of willfulness. (80) One commentator has noted that the Martin Act "seems to create strict liability for uttering a false statement." (81) As a result, a defendant who negligently makes a false statement could be held criminally liable under the Martin Act, despite the fact that the same conduct neither implicates federal criminal liability nor affords a civil remedy. (82)

Second, the Martin Act's definition of "security" (83) is potentially more expansive than the definition of "security" under the federal securities acts, (84) including more conduct within its reach than within the scope of the federal securities laws. For example, in 1996, John Moscow, then of the Manhattan District Attorney's Office, issued the following warning to attorneys:

> If any of you participate in the syndication of loans, you are involved in the negotiation, purchase and sale of securities in New York.... If any of you participate in transactions involving mineral leases, those are securities. Likewise, bunch of other things that you might not think of are covered as securities. (85)

Finally, consistent with its broad purpose of "prevent[ing] all kinds of fraud in connection with the sale of securities and commodities and to defeat all unsubstantial and visionary schemes in relation thereto whereby the public is fraudulently exploited," (86) the Martin Act is generally interpreted more loosely than its federal counterpart. (87) The terms of the Act are given a wide meaning, so as to include all acts which do by their tendency to deceive or mislead the purchasing public come within the purpose of the law. (88) As a result, it is possible to be convicted for conduct under the Martin Act that is neither civilly nor criminally actionable under the federal securities laws. For example, in a recent case, a defendant convicted of a Martin Act violation for failing to make certain disclosures in SEC filings argued on appeal that one of the disclosures was not required under federal law and could not, therefore, form the basis of state criminal liability. (89) The appellate court rejected this argument as unavailing because federal law does not preempt state law in this context. (90)

New York's criminalization of conduct not civilly actionable has a sweeping impact because of the Martin Act's broad reach. The criminal provisions apply to all false statements "engaged in to induce or promote the issuance, distribution, exchange, sale, negotiation or purchase within or from this state of any securities or commodities." (91) This territorial reach is arguably satisfied in virtually every case involving a publicly traded security because the New York Stock Exchange is located in New York, the National Association of Securities Dealers Automated Quotation System ("NASDAQ") is headquartered in New York, (92) and business transactions are routinely negotiated and financed in New York. (93) New York's state prosecutors have certainly interpreted the territorial reach of the Martin Act's criminal provisions broadly. For example, Mr. Moscow gave the following example of the breadth of the Martin Act's criminal provisions: "There was one Japanese swindler who committed a fraud from Miami on some people in Denver who is being prosecuted in New York because the stock was offered for sale here. His fraud affected the market price, and he is covered by the statute." (94)

2. State Securities Acts May Purport to Impose Broad Criminal and Civil Liability, but the Civil Liability Is Preempted.

Many state securities acts purport to expand the scope of criminal and civil liability beyond the scope of civil liability under the federal securities acts. For example, most state securities acts extend civil and criminal liability to aiders and abettors rather than merely to primary violators. (95) Further, state securities acts usually do not include safe harbors for forward-looking statements. (96)

These broad state civil liability provisions are preempted, however, when asserted in most class actions. (97) In general, the Securities Litigation Uniform Standards Act ("SLUSA") authorizes the removal and dismissal of state law class actions (98) alleging fraud in connection with the purchase or sale of securities that are traded nationally and listed on a regulated national exchange. (99) As a result, the expansive civil liability available under state securities law is often rendered illusory. (100)

SLUSA does not, however, preempt criminal prosecutions. After the civil liability provisions of state securities acts are preempted by SLUSA, the broad criminal liability provisions remain. As a consequence, state securities acts that impose liability beyond the scope of civil liability under the federal securities acts effectively criminalize conduct that is not civilly actionable.

E. Criminal Indictments Are Less Likely to Be Dismissed Pretrial than Civil Complaints.

In addition to substantive differences between criminal and civil enforcement of securities fraud, procedural differences contribute to the anomalous result that a defendant may be held criminally liable despite the fact that a civil lawsuit based on the same allegations would not survive dismissal. First, the pleading standards are far stricter for civil securities fraud complaints than for criminal securities fraud indictments. Second, motions to dismiss are more favored in civil securities fraud cases than in criminal cases. As a result, far more civil securities fraud cases are dismissed pretrial than criminal cases.

1. The PSLRA's Pleading Standards Are Stricter than the Pleading Standards for Criminal Indictments.

In 1995, Congress, with the goal of curtailing abusive strike suits, imposed strict pleading standards for private securities litigation. (101) In order to survive dismissal for failure to satisfy these pleading standards, a complaint must "specify each statement alleged to have been misleading, the reason or reasons why the statement is misleading, and, if an allegation regarding the statement or omission is made on information and belief, the complaint shall state with particularity all facts on which that belief is formed." (102) Moreover, the complaint must "state with particularity facts giving rise to a strong inference that the defendant acted with the required state of mind." (103) These stringent pleading standards, which must be satisfied before a plaintiff has performed any discovery, (104) nip in the bud many civil securities fraud cases. (105)

Unlike a civil securities fraud complaint, a criminal indictment need not allege fraud with particularity. An indictment need only be "a plain, concise, and definite written statement of the essential facts constituting the offense charged." (106) In other words, an indictment is sufficient as long as it "'(1) contains the elements of the offense intended to be charged, (2) sufficiently apprises the defendant of what he must be prepared to meet, and (3) allows the defendant to show with accuracy to what extent he may plead a former acquittal or conviction in the event of a subsequent prosecution.'" (107)

As a result of these different pleading standards, a complaint and an indictment containing identical securities fraud allegations could be treated quite differently. Theoretically, the civil complaint could be dismissed under the PSLRA, while the criminal indictment could survive dismissal.

2. Pretrial Motions to Dismiss Are More Favored in Civil Securities Fraud Cases than in Criminal Cases.

The motion to dismiss is an essential step in a civil securities fraud lawsuit. The Federal Rules of Civil Procedure explicitly recognize the availability of a motion to dismiss for "failure to state a claim upon which relief can be granted," (108) and the PSLRA instructs that a court "shall, on the motion of any defendant, dismiss the complaint" if the pleading requirements are not met. (109) In fact, commentators have characterized the motion to dismiss stage as "the primary battleground in the securities class action area." (110)

A motion to dismiss a criminal indictment is less favored. The Federal Rules of Criminal Procedure do not explicitly recognize the right to file a motion to dismiss an indictment, but Rule 12(b)(2) does allow a party to "raise by pretrial motion any defense, objection, or request that the court can determine without a trial of the general issue." (111) Among other issues that can be determined without a trial, (112) the failure of an indictment to allege conduct within the scope of a criminal statute is properly raised with a Rule 12(b)(2) motion. (113) As a practical matter, however, motions to dismiss criminal indictments are rarely asserted. In fact, the "system overview" prepared by the DOJ, which charts the progress of a criminal case from arrest through eventual release from prison, does not even recognize a motion to dismiss stage of the proceedings. (114)

3. More Civil Securities Fraud Cases Are Dismissed Pretrial than Criminal Securities Fraud Cases.

As a result of these two procedural differences--the pleading standard and the prevalence of motions to dismiss--far more civil securities fraud cases are dismissed pretrial than criminal securities fraud cases.

A large percentage of motions to dismiss civil securities fraud complaints are granted. (115) According to a report published by Cornerstone Research, for each year from 2001 through 2005, an average of thirty-eight percent of the securities class actions filed each year were dismissed. (116) This average excludes cases that were resolved through settlement and dismissed by agreement. (117) The percentage increases if partial dismissals are taken into account. According to one survey, seventy-nine percent of motions to dismiss securities fraud class actions were granted at least in part. (118)

In contrast, few criminal securities fraud cases are dismissed pretrial. According to data compiled by the Federal Justice Statistics Resource Center for the years 2001 through 2006, on average only 8.36% of criminal securities fraud cases were terminated each year by "dismissal or nolle prosequi." (119) This statistic does not differentiate between those cases dismissed on the prosecutor's motion and those dismissed on the defendant's motion. Even assuming that all of these dismissals were on the basis of defendants' motions to dismiss, the percentage of securities fraud dismissals in criminal cases is dwarfed by the number in civil cases.

The disparity in dismissal figures does not compel the conclusion that the same allegations are more likely to proceed to trial in a criminal case than in a civil case. Arguably, prosecutors in the exercise of their discretion are less likely to pursue unmeritorious claims than civil plaintiffs in a strike suit. Nonetheless, these procedural differences, at the very least, intensify the substantive differences addressed above, exacerbating the anomalous result in which a defendant can be held criminally but not civilly liable for the same conduct.

F. The Higher Mental State Generally Required for Criminal Liability Does Not Cure the Anomaly.

The mental state required to establish criminal liability under federal law is ostensibly higher than the mental state required to establish civil liability. This difference, however, is unlikely to close the gap between civil and criminal liability for conduct sounding in securities fraud because essentially the same evidence is sufficient in both contexts.

Civil securities fraud requires a showing of scienter, which is ordinarily defined as "recklessness." (120) A reckless statement is one "'involving not merely simple, or even inexcusable negligence, but an extreme departure from the standards of ordinary care, and which presents a danger of misleading buyers or sellers that is either known to the defendant or is so obvious that the actor must have been aware of it.'" (121) A few circuits require "'severe recklessness'" (122) or a "'high degree of recklessness.'" (123) If the allegedly false statement is forward-looking, the scienter requirement is raised to "actual knowledge." (124)

Criminal securities fraud, on the other hand, requires a showing of "willfulness." (125) Willfulness requires "intentionally undertaking an act that one knows to be wrongful." (126) Mail and wire fraud, similarly, require proof of the "specific intent to defraud." (127) The specific intent to defraud has been defined as "'willful participation in a scheme with knowledge of its fraudulent nature and with intent that these illicit objectives be achieved,'" (128) as "conscious knowing intent to defraud," (129) and as "reckless indifference." (130)

Although the criminal mental states are more stringent than civil scienter, this difference is diminished by the practicality of how a defendant's mental state is proven at trial. Direct evidence of a defendant's mental state is unusual; ordinarily, a person's mental state must be inferred from indirect evidence. (131) Prosecutors, therefore, use circumstantial evidence to prove that a defendant possessed the requisite criminal mental state. (132) A defendant's mens rea "may be inferred from the defendant's statements and conduct," (133) "evidence of actual or contemplated harm," (134) "a defendant's reckless indifference to the truth of a representation," (135) "misrepresentations made by the defendants, and the scheme itself." (136) It is unlikely, therefore, that a cognizable difference exists between the proof needed to prove criminal intent and the proof needed to satisfy civil scienter. (137) Moreover, in light of the PSLRA's heightened pleading standards for scienter, which require a civil plaintiff to "state with particularity facts giving rise to a strong inference that the defendant acted with the required state of mind," (138) it is arguable that the scienter bar in civil cases is actually higher than the mens rea bar in criminal cases.

Indeed, defendants charged with criminal securities fraud have found the purportedly higher criminal mental state to be of little comfort. Juries are comfortable convicting defendants of fraud based on circumstantial evidence that directly conflicts with the defendants' testimony on the witness stand. For example, despite denying "playing any role in the $11 billion accounting fraud at the telecommunications company," WorldCom CEO Bernard Ebbers was convicted of fraud. (139) Likewise, despite testifying that

> [t]he last thing I would do is step back in as CEO and pick up leadership of a conspiracy, having lived my whole life in such a way to make sure that I was doing at least what I thought, according to my moral code of conduct and according to my religious faith, was right or wrong, (140)

Enron CEO Kenneth Lay was convicted of securities and wire fraud. (141)

III. DIFFERING CIVIL AND CRIMINAL TREATMENT OF CONDUCT SOUNDING IN SECURITIES FRAUD MAY AFFECT THE CURRENT SCHEME OF SECURITIES REGULATION.

The current scheme of securities regulation reflects a delicate balance among numerous considerations. The imposition of criminal punishment for conduct that does not invoke civil liability risks disrupting this balance, potentially at the expense of considerations deemed important by Congress and the courts.

A. The Wire/Mail Fraud Run-Around May Disrupt the Balance Between Honest Markets and Optimal Levels of Disclosure.

When adopting the objective materiality standard for securities fraud, the Supreme Court balanced several competing considerations. On the one hand, the Supreme Court recognized the fundamental importance of fair and honest markets. (142) The Supreme Court identified "honest publicity" as an essential tool to prevent manipulation and dishonest market practices. (143) This consideration weighed in favor of a low standard of materiality--both to lower the bar for required disclosures and to limit the number of affirmative false statements. On the other hand, the Supreme Court recognized the dangers of setting the materiality standard too low. When applied to omissions by a company, "a minimal standard might bring an overabundance of information within its reach, and lead management 'simply to bury the shareholders in an avalanche of trivial information--a result that is hardly conducive to informed decisionmaking.'" (144) The Supreme Court adopted an objective materiality standard designed to achieve a delicate balance between these competing concerns to protect the integrity of the markets and to encourage the appropriate level of disclosure. (145)

The importance of the balance achieved by the materiality standard has been widely acknowledged. In fact, the necessity of preserving the materiality balance spurred Congress to amend the Racketeer Influenced and Corrupt Organizations Act ("RICO"). Prior to the passage of the PSLRA, plaintiffs could premise civil RICO claims sounding in securities fraud on violations of the mail and wire fraud statutes--thus avoiding the more stringent requirements of a securities fraud claim. (146) This run-around was widely criticized. For example, Justice Thurgood Marshall recognized that the use of civil RICO to pursue claims sounding in securities fraud "virtually eliminates decades of legislative and judicial development of private civil remedies under the federal securities laws." (147) Justice Marshall identified materiality as one of the crucial issues that RICO allowed plaintiffs to bypass. (148) The PSLRA closed this door by prohibiting civil RICO claims from being premised on claims that sound in securities fraud. (149) Although the same argument ostensibly applies in the criminal context, Congress left the wire/mail fraud run-around open to prosecutors.

The lower materiality standard available via the wire/mail fraud run-around risks disrupting the delicate balance achieved with the objective materiality standard. (150) The goal of encouraging fair and honest markets is furthered at the expense of the goal of achieving the appropriate amount of disclosure. The lower materiality standard compels disclosure of objectively unimportant details of a corporate event, flooding the market with too much information. By the same token, the lower materiality standard inhibits corporate executives from making voluntary statements to analysts and investors, for fear that their offhand remarks could form the basis of a wire fraud indictment. (151) The chilling effect of the lower materiality standard is compounded by the overdeterrence effect of criminal liability, which discourages even borderline behavior. (152)

In other words, the wire/mail fraud run-around risks changing the entire scheme of corporate disclosure. (153) Already, attorneys caution their corporate clients that "[s]lips of the [t]ongue and [p]en [a]re [d]angerous." (154) In light of the wire/mail fraud run-around, corporate counsel should warn their clients that off-the-cuff remarks risk imprisonment. The current editions of the National Investor Relations Institute's Standards of Practice for Investor Relations (155) and the Practicing Law Institute's Policy Statement Concerning Disclosure of Material Information continue to define materiality as an objective standard, (156) but these corporate handbooks should be amended to reflect the subjective materiality standard compelled by the wire/mail fraud run-around.

B. The Wire/Mail Fraud Run-Around May Affect What Information Investors Rely Upon When Making Investment Decisions.

A key assumption underlying the securities fraud materiality standard is that stock purchasers expect a company's representatives to make puffing statements and thus lend them no credence. (157) In other words, it is assumed that "reasonable" investors disregard some statements by corporate officers. Of course, this assumption is self-perpetuating. Presumably, one of the reasons that reasonable investors discount puffing statements is their understanding that these types of statements cannot support a securities fraud claim.

The use of a subjective materiality standard to prosecute corporate officers for wire or mail fraud may encourage investors to lend credence to vague statements of corporate optimism, undercutting the assumption that investors disregard puffery. Recognizing that corporate officers can face imprisonment for a false statement of corporate optimism, investors may begin to take every statement--even a puffing one--at face value. In effect, the prosecution of corporate officers for puffery could create a class of investors who make investment decisions on the basis of vague statements of corporate optimism rather than on statements of fact.

In addition to increasing market volatility, this new class of "gullible" investors could transform the meaning of materiality in the securities fraud context. Arguably, these investors--by taking into account the criminal disincentive facing corporate officers who make false statements of optimism--would be making an objectively reasonable decision to rely on corporate puffery. If courts were to accept this argument, even a vague statement of optimism by a corporate officer could form the basis for civil securities liability. In other words, the objective materiality standard would become coextensive with the subjective standard. As a result, the delicate balance achieved by the objective materiality definition would be disrupted, chilling voluntary disclosure and encouraging the flooding of the market with trivial information.

One commentator has suggested, however, that retail investors (as opposed to institutional investors) already rely on puffery when making investment decisions, that these retail investors are being driven out of the markets because of the disfavored treatment that they receive under the civil securities laws, and that this is adversely affecting market liquidity. (158) Under this analysis, lowering the securities fraud materiality standard to include puffery would achieve the positive effects of encouraging retail investment and improving market liquidity.

C. The Criminalization of Conduct Not Civilly Actionable May Transfer Enforcement Responsibility Away from the Securities and Exchange Commission.

"The SEC is vested with primary responsibility for enforcing the [Securities Exchange] Act and protecting the public interest." (159) In this role, the SEC's mission "is to protect investors, maintain fair, orderly, and efficient markets, and facilitate capital formation." (160) As such, the SEC has developed unique expertise in the securities field. (161) The anomaly of criminalizing conduct not civilly actionable may, however, jeopardize the SEC's primacy. The wire/mail fraud run-around may transfer enforcement responsibility away from the SEC to the DOJ, and expansive state securities statutes may transfer enforcement responsibility away from the SEC to the individual states.

First, the wire/mail fraud run-around, which is only available in criminal cases, is out of the SEC's reach. The SEC institutes civil securities fraud enforcement proceedings, while the DOJ institutes criminal prosecutions. The SEC may "in its discretion" refer a matter to the DOJ for prosecution, (162) but the DOJ has independent discretion to prosecute without SEC referral or to refrain from prosecution despite SEC referral. (163) As a consequence, the availability of the wire/mail fraud run-around shifts enforcement responsibility from the SEC to the DOJ. The Supreme Court recognized this enforcement policy consideration in United States v. O'Hagan. (164) The Court considered whether criminal liability under section 10(b) of the Securities Exchange Act could be based on the misappropriation theory of insider trading. (165) The Eighth Circuit Court of Appeals, refusing to recognize the misappropriation theory, had reversed both the securities fraud counts and the accompanying mail fraud counts because "the indictment was structured in such a manner as to premise the fraud for the mail fraud charges on the acts allegedly constituting the securities fraud." (166) On appeal, the Supreme Court upheld the misappropriation theory, thus mooting the issue of whether reversal of the securities fraud conviction necessitated reversal of the mail fraud conviction. (167) The majority nonetheless briefly discussed the enforcement considerations implicated by this issue: "[i]f misappropriation theory cases could proceed only under the federal mail and wire fraud statutes, ... 'proportionally more persons accused of insider trading [might] be pursued by a U.S. Attorney, and proportionally fewer by the SEC." (168) Justice Clarence Thomas, in dissent, rejected the misappropriation theory of securities fraud, but stated that the conduct could nonetheless be prosecuted as mail fraud. (169) Justice Thomas disregarded the enforcement considerations raised by the majority as "no business of this Court." (170)

Second, the breadth of civil and criminal enforcement under the state securities statutes--often exceeding the scope of the federal securities laws--may shift enforcement responsibility away from the SEC to the individual states. For example, the Attorney General of New York, exploiting the breadth of the Martin Act, achieved a landmark settlement with Merrill Lynch to prevent analyst conflicts of interest. (171) Theoretically, every state attorney general, if afforded the statutory tools, could force a company to enter into a separate settlement agreement, with the result that the companies would be required to comply with fifty different standards. (172) This effect, the so-called "Balkanization" of securities regulation, (173) has been widely decried as usurping the power of the SEC, (174) preventing uniformity, (175) and undermining market efficiency. (176)

As a practical matter, however, commentators have noted that state enforcement agencies are generally working together with the SEC and with each other to achieve consistency and prevent duplication of efforts. (177) In addition, the tremendous resources required to investigate and prosecute a large-scale securities fraud case are often beyond the reach of individual states, and these cases therefore default to the federal government. For example, during the course of its investigation, the Enron Task Force examined "more than four terabytes of data--equal to about [twenty] percent of all the information stored in the Library of Congress." (178)

D. The Inapplicability of the Safe Harbor to Criminal Liability May Discourage Forward-Looking Statements.

Congress intended for the PSLRA's safe harbor for forward-looking statements to encourage corporate executives to make predictions. Congress recognized: "Fear that inaccurate projections will trigger the filing of a securities fraud lawsuit has muzzled corporate management." (179) The safe harbor was meant to allay this fear. (180) Of course, unacknowledged by Congress is that fear of criminal liability is likely to muzzle corporate management even more effectively than the threat of a civil lawsuit. For this reason, the indictment of corporate executives for inaccurate projections is likely to counteract the calming effect of the safe harbor.

E. The Potential Exposure to Criminal Aiding and Abetting Liability May Discourage Professionals from Advising New Companies.

In Central Bank, the Supreme Court recognized that uncertainty about the scope of aiding and abetting liability could have ripple effects in the economy. (181) The Court warned that less established companies might have trouble finding professionals willing to tender their services and that the price of professional services--taking into account the professional's risk of potential aiding and abetting liability if the company were to fail--might render them out of reach. (182) The Court recently reiterated these concerns with private aiding and abetting liability. (183)

These same concerns are implicated--perhaps even intensified--by the potential of criminal aiding and abetting liability. Securities professionals may fear that, if a company to whom they have provided services were to fail, they would be at risk of criminal liability. This apprehension may deter professionals from providing services to emerging companies or may compel them to charge prohibitively high prices, both with the effect of stifling the economy. In addition, secondary actors may feel compelled, beyond their ordinary duties, to "monitor public statements made by others, thus straining the economy." (184)

F. The Breadth of Conduct Within the Scope of the Criminal Laws May Afford Prosecutors Undue Discretion.

The criminalization of conduct outside the scope of the civil securities laws, such as the making of false statements that are either objectively immaterial or forward-looking, affords prosecutors broad discretion to decide whether to prosecute a corporate executive. Every corporate executive who makes an optimistic statement or rosy prediction is potentially subject to prosecution if the company's stock later takes a downward turn. The virtual unavailability of pretrial motion practice to weed out unmeritorious claims strengthens the prosecutor's power to prosecute borderline conduct. This broad prosecutorial discretion has several ramifications.

First, the strategy of overcriminalizing conduct and allowing prosecutors to choose who is "deserving" of prosecution is an uninspiring rationale for criminal liability. (185) When two actors in the same position are treated differently--one vilified as a criminal and the other permitted to remain in society--it undermines society's justification for imprisonment. (186)

Second, the separation of powers doctrine is implicated when Congress enacts such broad statutes that it essentially abdicates its legislative role, allowing prosecutors and the courts to decide what conduct to criminalize. The separation of powers limits judicial review of prosecutors' discretion. (187) By the same token, however, the separation of powers also limits prosecutors' ability to usurp the legislature. When Congress overcriminalizes, prosecutors appropriate Congress's law-making functions. The executive branch decides which conduct to prosecute and which to ignore--without any of the public hearings, vigorous debate, or democratic process of the legislative branch. (188) For example, likely because of the breadth of the mail and wire fraud statutes, the DOJ has an official prosecution policy to avoid prosecuting schemes that "consist[] of some isolated transactions between individuals, involving minor loss to the victims" and to focus on "any scheme which in its nature is directed to defrauding a class of persons, or the general public, with a substantial pattern of conduct." (189) To the extent that courts are asked to decide whether conduct is within the scope of a broad, vague statute, the judicial branch--also without the hallmarks of the legislative process--performs legislative functions. (190)

Finally, this broad discretion allows prosecutors to make prosecution decisions based on improper factors such as "race, class, or ethnicity." (191) Moreover, especially relevant in the white collar crime context, broad prosecutorial discretion allows the executive branch to prosecute defendants in response to political pressure and public outcry. For example, during the Congressional hearings on the Enron collapse and bankruptcy, the company's top executives were called, variously, "the most accomplished confidence man since Charles Ponzi," (192) "a carnival barker," (193) and an "economic terrorist[]." (194) In this atmosphere, the Enron Task Force faced "pressure to deliver" (195) and eventually succeeded in indicting thirty-four defendants. (196)

G. The Criminalization of Conduct Not Civilly Actionable Affords the SEC Remarkable Leverage in Negotiating Civil Settlements.

SEC enforcement actions forge a middle ground between the breadth of criminal liability and the narrowness of private civil liability. As in a criminal case, the safe harbor for forward-looking statement is unavailable in SEC enforcement proceedings, the SEC may pursue aider and abettors in addition to primary violators, and the stringent pleading requirements of the PSLRA do not apply. (197) As in a private civil action, however, the wire/mail fraud run-around is unavailable to the SEC because the SEC institutes only civil proceedings, and defendants can draw on the civil tradition of filing motions to dismiss. (198) In sum, the gap between criminal liability and SEC enforcement liability is smaller than the gap between criminal liability and private civil liability, but the gap nonetheless exists.

The breadth of potential criminal liability increases the pressure on a defendant under SEC investigation to reach a settlement with the SEC, even if the defendant has strong defenses to liability. The SEC is explicitly authorized to refer matters to the DOJ for prosecution (199) and to transmit evidence that it has gathered to the DOJ. (200) As a result, the SEC and the DOJ routinely work together on investigations, (201) and the prospect of criminal indictment is often used as leverage to convince a defendant to agree to a settlement. (202) This "good cop/bad cop" tactic is extremely effective in achieving cooperation from the defendant. The threat, implicit or explicit, of criminal indictment, coupled with the reality that it is in many ways easier to criminally convict a defendant than to hold him civilly liable in an enforcement action, can render settlement with the SEC irresistible, even in cases where the SEC is overreaching.

H. The Narrow Scope of Private Civil Liability Leaves Injured Investors Uncompensated.

As a consequence of the narrow scope of private civil liability, investors who are injured by criminally actionable conduct are often uncompensated. For example, the following investors are generally without civil remedy: (1) investors who make investment decisions based on false, but objectively immaterial, statements; (203) (2) investors who make investment decisions based on false forward-looking statements that are accompanied by meaningful cautionary language; (204) (3) investors defrauded by insolvent primary violators; (205) and (4) defrauded investors who are unable to plead their case with the requisite specificity without the benefit of discovery. (206)

The possibility that the SEC might distribute to injured investors disgorgement and penalties that it has collected, although not "toothless," (207) is of little comfort to injured investors. The receipt of any compensation depends on numerous factors, including--most importantly--whether the SEC decides to pursue an enforcement action. (208)

The compensation of injured investors is not, however, a central goal of the securities acts, and the absence of compensation for certain investors does not necessarily impede the purposes of the securities acts. The securities acts were enacted to "insure the maintenance of fair and honest markets" (209) and "to protect investors." (210) In order to accomplish these goals, the acts promote "full disclosure of information thought necessary to informed investment decisions." (211) Full disclosure is mandated by the acts, and the enforcement mechanisms ensure compliance with the acts' mandates.

Consistent with these goals, the implied private right of action for securities fraud is primarily useful as a tool for deterrence. Together with the acts' other enforcement mechanisms, it ensures compliance with the acts' mandates. The private right of action has a side benefit of compensating investors, but that is not its central purpose. For example, Senators Paul Sarbanes, Barbara Boxer, and Richard Bryan, who strongly support the extension of private civil liability to aiders and abettors, crafted their argument in terms of its deterrence value, not its potential for compensating investors: "[T]he deterrent effect of the securities laws would be strengthened if aiding and abetting liability were restored in private actions as well." (212) Similarly, when recently reiterating that private civil liability extends only to primary violators, the Supreme Court emphasized the strong deterrent effect of SEC enforcement and criminal liability. (213)

Therefore, as recognized by the Supreme Court in Central Bank, it would not necessarily follow from an expansion of private civil liability to compensate additional injured investors that "the objectives of the statute [would be] better served." (214) If the potential of criminal liability and SEC enforcement were sufficient to ensure compliance with the acts' mandates, (215) the expansion of the private right of action would not necessarily advance the statutes' objectives and, in fact, might hinder those objectives by stifling "efficiency, competition, and capital formation." (216)

IV. THEORIES ABOUT THE CIVIL-CRIMINAL DIVIDE EXPLAIN SOME COMPONENTS OF THE DIFFERING CIVIL AND CRIMINAL TREATMENT OF CONDUCT SOUNDING IN SECURITIES FRAUD.

In addition to disrupting the current scheme of securities regulation, the anomaly of criminalizing conduct that sounds in securities fraud but is not civilly actionable undercuts an assumption underlying current scholarship on the civil-criminal divide. The two leading theories about the civil-criminal divide--one based on an economic analysis of the law and the other based on moral considerations-- assume that criminal liability is a subset of civil liability in circumstances in which the relevant conduct has identifiable individual victims. Applying the reasoning underlying these theories to conduct sounding in securities fraud, however, explains some aspects of the differing civil and criminal treatment of this unique conduct.

A. The Current Scholarship on the Civil-Criminal Divide Assumes That Civil Liability Is More Expansive than Criminal Liability.

As recognized by scholars on the civil-criminal divide, including Kenneth G. Dau-Schmidt, (217) Richard A. Posner, (218) Steven Shavell, (219) John Coffee, (220) Stephen Marks, (221) and Paul H. Robinson, (222) criminal liability is ordinarily a subset of civil liability in instances where the relevant conduct injures identifiable individuals. Some civilly actionable conduct is so wrongful that it is also a crime. If criminal conduct involves amens rea and an identifiable victim, the conduct is usually also civilly actionable. This relationship between civil and criminal liability is supported by the general rationale that criminal sanctions are more severe than civil liability. In other words, "conviction for crime is a distinctive and serious matter--a something, and not a nothing." (223) For this reason, criminal liability is more limited in scope than civil liability, and criminal defendants are afforded more procedural safeguards than civil defendants. (224)

The possibility that criminal liability could be more expansive than civil liability has been virtually ignored by the scholars, although Gerald E. Lynch has, in passing, noted this anomaly in the context of RICO:

> There is a distinct oddity here, from the standpoint of traditional distinctions between criminal and civil law:

Historically, we have expected the criminal law to be narrower and more precise than the law of civil wrongs, but in interpreting RICO, the courts have been distinctly more comfortable with broad interpretations in criminal cases, and correspondingly more hostile to civil applications. (225)

This "distinct oddity" in the context of conduct sounding in securities fraud suggests two initial conclusions about its causes and effects.

First, the differing civil and criminal treatment arguably balances two competing congressional concerns: appeasement of the public and protection of big business. Criminal prosecution of corporate executives for fraud permits injured shareholders to feel vindicated. (226) At the same time, the unavailability of civil remedies for this same conduct shields corporations from monetary losses. (227)

Second, the anomalous civil and criminal treatment of conduct sounding in securities fraud suggests that corporate defendants are being overpunished and overdeterred or that civil securities plaintiffs are being under-compensated. As a companion to the general assumption that criminal law is a subset of civil law, scholars typically agree that the criminal law punishes and deters and that the civil law compensates. (228) Ordinarily, therefore, if a person's conduct is worthy of punishment and deterrence, the harm caused by the conduct is civilly compensable. This relationship between punishment/deterrence and compensation is skewed in the securities context.

An examination of the reasoning underlying the leading theories of the civil-criminal divide, however, demonstrates that the causes and effects of the current scheme may be more nuanced than these two initial conclusions suggest. In fact, the anomalous civil and criminal treatment of conduct sounding in securities fraud is arguably consistent with some of the reasoning underlying the theories about the civil-criminal divide.

B. The Leading Theories About the Civil-Criminal Divide Shed Light on the Anomalous Civil and Criminal Treatment of Conduct Sounding in Securities Fraud.

The scholarship on the civil-criminal divide falls into two general camps: those that use economics to explain the civil-criminal divide and those that explain the divide with moral principles. (229)

Undoubtedly, there is some overlap between the two camps. For example, Professor Posner has noted that "on balance it would seem that adherence to generally accepted moral principles increases the wealth of society more than it reduces it," (230) and Alvin K. Klevorick has argued that an economic view of society presupposes a transaction structure formed by values. (231) This overlap does not, however, prevent the two theories from being useful analytic tools. Although the theories contain both normative and descriptive components, (232) for purposes of this article, the theories will be treated as descriptive. In other words, this article will examine whether either theory can explain the anomaly--not whether the anomaly is appropriate in light of either theory.

1. Economic Analysis of the Law Explains Some Components of the Differing Civil and Criminal Treatment of Conduct Sounding in Securities Fraud.

Economic analysis of the law purports to (1) identify what conduct is limited through the civil and criminal laws, and (2) explain when criminal liability is used, rather than civil liability, to limit that conduct. Applied in the context of securities fraud, economic analysis articulates why false statements to investors are limited by civil and criminal laws and may explain why criminal liability is broader than civil liability.

a. Economic Analysis Explains Why False Statements to Investors Are Limited.

Economic analysis of the law recognizes that the civil and criminal laws are used to achieve an optimal level of certain types of undesirable behavior. There are two general economic explanations of what behavior should be limited, both of which arguably apply to false statements to investors.

First, some proponents of an economic analysis of the law recognize that harm-causing behavior should be limited. (233) If conduct causes harm, the civil and criminal laws are used to limit that conduct to its optimal level, as determined through further economic analysis. Under this view, false statements to investors are limited because they cause harm to investors.

Other proponents of an economic analysis of the law characterize the conduct to be limited as the "bypassing of market transactions." (234) In other words, if an actor coerces a transfer, rather than engaging in a voluntary market exchange, the actor's behavior should be limited to its optimal level by the civil and criminal laws. As explained by Professor Posner, the victim of the coercive transfer need not be the person with whom the market transaction would have occurred:

> The role of the criminal law in discouraging market bypassing is obscured by the fact that the market transaction that the criminal bypasses is usually not a transaction with his victim. If someone steals my car, normally it is not because he wants that car and would have bought it from me if the criminal law had deterred him from stealing it. He steals to get money to use in buying goods and services from other people. The market transaction that he bypasses is the exchange of his labor for money in a lawful occupation. But it is still market bypassing. (235)

False statements to investors are arguably a market bypass. Individual perpetrators of securities fraud are generally motivated by job security and compensation. (236) Rather than achieving these goals through a market transaction--namely, by achieving favorable results--the perpetrators bypass the market and make false statements. It is irrelevant that the victims of the market bypass--the investors--are not those with whom the market transaction would have occurred. Under this view, false statements to investors are limited because they bypass the markets.

b. Economic Analysis Arguably Explains the Anomalous Civil and Criminal Treatment of Conduct Sounding in Securities Fraud.

Once the conduct to be limited is identified--either because it is harm-causing or market-bypassing--an economic analysis of the law determines how to limit the conduct to its optimal level, taking into account the costs and benefits to the actor and to society. Civil liability and criminal punishment are tools on a continuum to achieve this optimal level.

Proponents of an economic analysis of the law agree that criminal liability imposes a higher social cost than civil liability. (237) Unlike imprisonment--which imposes a hefty cost on the offender but does not compensate the victim--a transfer of money produces a gain to the victim equal to the cost to the offender. (238) Moreover, society's cost of imprisoning a person is far higher than the social cost of a transfer of money from the offender to the victim. (239) Gary S. Becker expressed the combination of these factors with the following formula for the total social cost of punishment: $f'=bf$ (where $f'=$social cost of punishment; $f=$cost to offender of punishment; and $b=$coefficient that transforms f unto f'. (240) Becker concluded that b equals approximately zero for fines (and, by extension, for civil liability), while b is greater than one for imprisonment. (241)

Under an economic analysis of the law, therefore, criminal liability is only optimal when the damages necessary to limit the offender's conduct to an optimal level are higher than the actor could pay. (242) In order to act as a deterrent, the amount of damages, when multiplied by the probability of liability, must be higher than the probability of success multiplied by the expected gain. (243) In addition, the amount of monetary liability must be within the defendant's ability to pay. (244) Once the ceiling of the actor's ability to pay is surpassed, additional monetary liability does not increase the level of deterrence and criminalization is necessary. (245)

In the context of securities fraud, criminalization is arguably necessary to achieve an optimal level of conduct. At first glance, the imposition of criminal liability might appear to be unnecessary because white collar defendants often possess the ability to pay large sums of money. (246) The practical reality, however, is that individual defendants seldom pay the damages imposed by civil securities fraud liability. Rather, these costs fall largely on the corporation and its insurer. (247) The expenses incurred by the corporation are ultimately borne by its shareholders. (248) As a result, the probability that an individual defendant would be required to pay monetary damages for his conduct is so low that the amount of potential damages required to achieve the optimal level of deterrence is often beyond even the wealthiest defendant's reach. The imposition of criminal liability for securities fraud is therefore arguably explained by an economic analysis of the law.

In addition, an economic analysis of the law may explain why, in the context of securities fraud, civil liability is more limited than criminal liability. An assumption underlying an economic analysis of the law, as detailed above, is that criminal liability imposes a higher social cost than civil liability. (249) Under this assumption, it is logical that criminal liability would be imposed for a smaller swathe of conduct than civil liability. This assumption arguably does not hold true, however, in the unique context of securities fraud. Securities fraud lawsuits are unlike other civil lawsuits because the total social cost of civil liability far exceeds the actual dollar amount of the damages imposed.

The filing of a securities fraud lawsuit causes a steep drop in the value of the sued company's shares, in excess of the dip caused by the disclosure of the "truth" to the marketplace and the eventual transfer of wealth from the defendants to the victims. (251) In other words, the mere filing of the lawsuit causes equity to disappear; it is not a "zero-sum game." (251) This excessive loss of shareholder equity is attributable to financial distress costs (such as reduced access to credit) and a diminished ability to conduct business. (252)

In addition, the filing of a securities fraud lawsuit against one company has spillover effects on the securities markets and the overall economy. Securities fraud class actions decrease stock prices overall, (253) increase the costs of raising capital, (254) and chill corporate disclosure. (255) Overall lower stock prices, in turn, negatively affect capital investment, job creation, and business expansion. (256) In addition, the threat of expansive civil liability may deter overseas companies from doing business in the United States and "shift[] securities offerings away from domestic capital markets." (257)

Finally, civil securities fraud class actions, with their voluminous pleadings and complicated motions to dismiss, consume considerable judicial resources, for which society foots the bill. (258) In fact, Professor Coffee has raised the question of "whether society is receiving an adequate return on its investment." (259)

In light of the spillover costs of a civil securities fraud lawsuit, above and beyond the mere transfer of a sum of money from the defendant to the victims, the total social cost of civil liability may be greater than the total social cost of criminal liability. Applying this proposition to Professor Becker's formula discussed above, in which b is the coefficient that transforms the cost of punishment to the offender into the social cost of punishment, b is arguably greater for civil liability than for criminal liability in securities cases. (260) In the unique context of securities fraud, therefore, it is arguably consistent with an economic analysis of the law for some conduct to be criminally, but not civilly, actionable.

2. Moral Analysis Explains Some Components of the Anomalous Civil and Criminal Treatment of Conduct Sounding in Securities Fraud.

Moral theories of the civil-criminal divide purport to (1) identify what conduct is classified as criminal and (2) articulate what goals are furthered through the imposition of criminal punishment. Applied in the context of securities fraud, moral analysis explains why false statements to investors are limited by criminal laws and highlights which goals are furthered, and which are hampered, by the anomalous civil and criminal treatment of conduct sounding in securities fraud.

a. Moral Analysis Explains Why False Statements to Investors Are Limited by the Criminal Laws.

Under a moral theory of the civil-criminal divide, a crime is different from a tort because it incurs "a formal and solemn pronouncement of the moral condemnation of the community." (261) As a result, only conduct that is morally repugnant should be classified as a crime. (262) In other words, a crime is conduct for which society values no social utility, while a tort is conduct for which the actor's utility is acknowledged by society. (263) Although this formulation uses the economic term "utility," it relies on "other disciplines, including sociology, psychology, political science, philosophy, theology, criminology, and jurisprudence" to determine what activities have no societal value and should thus be designated as crimes. (264)

Making false statements to investors arguably implicates moral concerns to such a degree that it is worthy of criminal punishment under a moral analysis of the law. Prohibitions on lying come from sources as varied as the Ten Commandments (265) and Immanuel Kant. (266) Kant states, "To be truthful (honest) in all declarations is, therefore, a sacred and unconditionally commanding law of reason that admits of no expediency whatsoever." (267)

b. Moral Analysis May Explain the Anomalous Civil and Criminal Treatment of Conduct Sounding in Securities Fraud.

Some theorists argue that criminal liability is reserved for a subset of conduct--that which is truly morally repugnant--because the imposition of criminal penalties is more costly to society than the imposition of civil liability. (268) Arguably, if civil liability were more costly to society than criminal liability, these theorists would support the imposition of civil liability on a subset of immoral conduct, leaving criminal liability for a wider swathe of conduct. As discussed above, (269) in the unique context of securities fraud, civil lawsuits may impose a higher social cost than criminal liability because of the various spillover effects--including lower stock prices, higher costs of raising capital, chilled corporate disclosure, and consumption of judicial resources. This reasoning may explain the breadth of criminal liability compared to the narrowness of civil liability for conduct sounding in securities fraud.

c. Moral Analysis Explains What Goals Are Furthered by the Differing Civil and Criminal Treatment of Conduct Sounding in Securities Fraud.

Several theories explain the imposition of liability for morally repugnant conduct: corrective justice, retributive justice, and compensatory justice. Traditionally, scholars discussed the goals of liability separately in the contexts of tort and crime, but, as noted by

364

Gary T. Schwartz, parallel theories developed in each context, permitting a merged analysis of the goals of tort and criminal liability. (270) These theories support some components of the anomalous civil and criminal treatment of conduct sounding in securities fraud.

Under a corrective justice theory, liability should have three components: (1) imposition of liability for immoral behavior; (271) (2) compensation of victims; and (3) financing of the compensation by the responsible party. (272) Under the current scheme of civil and criminal liability, only one of these elements is satisfied when an actor lies to investors about objectively immaterial matters, makes false forward-looking statements to investors, or aids and abets a perpetrator of securities fraud. This conduct is punished criminally, thus satisfying the first component, but is not civilly actionable, thus failing to satisfy the second and third components. The anomalous treatment of conduct sounding in securities fraud is not consistent with a corrective theory of justice.

Retributive justice focuses on punishing a blameworthy individual for immoral behavior, rather than on compensating the victims. (273) The imposition of criminal but not civil liability on corporate executives for making false statements to investors or for aiding and abetting securities fraud is consistent with the retributive theory of justice because the executives are punished. The failure of the victims to be compensated is irrelevant under this theory.

Finally, compensatory justice focuses--not on punishing the defendant--but on compensating the victims. (274) Under this theory, it is not necessary that the morally responsible actor compensate the victims, so long as the victims are compensated by someone. In the context of securities fraud, this theory does not explain why certain immoral conduct would be punished criminally but not civilly. When the conduct is punished only criminally, the victims are not compensated.

V. CONCLUSION

In conclusion, substantive and procedural differences between criminal and civil treatment of conduct sounding in securities fraud cause criminal liability to exceed the scope of private civil liability. The potential repercussions of this anomaly are far-reaching, including chilling corporate disclosure, creating a class of reasonable investors who make investment decisions on the basis of vague statements of corporate optimism, transferring enforcement responsibility away from the SEC to the DOJ and the individual states, discouraging professionals from advising emerging companies, affording prosecutors undue discretion in deciding what conduct to prosecute, coercing defendants into agreeing to unfavorable settlements with the SEC, and leaving injured investors without compensation.

The rationales underlying the theories about the civil-criminal divide explain some components of the anomalous criminal and civil treatment of conduct sounding in securities fraud. Under an economic analysis of the law, the immense social cost imposed by civil liability--arguably exceeding the social cost imposed by criminal liability--may explain why civil liability is more limited than criminal liability in this unique context. Under a moral view of the civil-criminal divide, the imposition of criminal liability, even without companion civil liability, satisfies the goal Shared by corrective and retributive justice theories of holding the morally responsible actor liable. The absence of civil liability for some conduct that violates moral lines, however, is contrary to the goal shared by corrective and compensatory justice theories of compensating the victims.

Therefore, this article proposes a two-step solution. First, in light of the far-reaching effects of the anomalous civil and criminal treatment of conduct sounding in securities fraud and the failure of the theories about the civil-criminal divide to explain the anomaly fully, Congress should reign in the scope of criminal liability to the current reach of civil liability by curtailing the use of the wire/mail fraud run-around, expanding the safe harbor for forward-looking statements to criminal actions, imposing stricter pleading standards for criminal indictments, and preempting broad state criminal laws.

Second, because the more expansive reach of criminal liability than civil liability is arguably consistent with many of the theories underlying the civil-criminal divide, Congress should consider carefully whether to expand the reach of criminal liability--while recognizing and compensating for the impacts of that expansion on the current scheme of securities regulation. For example, if Congress makes the deliberate decision to lower the materiality standard for criminal securities fraud, Congress should compensate for the chilling effect on voluntary disclosure by making more disclosures mandatory. Only by proceeding in a deliberate fashion can Congress simultaneously further the rationales underlying the civil-criminal divide and prevent the distortion of the carefully balanced scheme of securities regulation.

Wendy Gerwick Couture, Visiting Associate Professor at the University of Idaho College of Law (2008-2009); Associate at Carrington, Coleman, Sloman & Blumenthal LLP (2004-2007); Law Clerk to the Honorable Barbara M.G. Lynn (2003-2004); J.D., summa cum laude and Order of the Coif, Southern Methodist University Dedman School of Law (2003); B.A., summa cum laude and Phi Beta Kappa, Duke University (1998). The author would like to thank Professor Marc I. Steinberg for his insightful comments on an earlier draft of this article.

NOTES DELETED

23

Get the Down and Dirty on Practicing White-Collar Crime Law

Kimberly H. Smith

When American criminologist Edwin Sutherland coined the term "white-collar crime," Bernie Madoff was in diapers. At that time, in 1939, white-collar criminals comprised less than two percent of the people committed to prisons in a year. Sutherland idealized that white-collar crime was more prevalent than it seemed, yet was less visible and underreported.

Since that time, FBI reports have shown exponential growth in white-collar crime. National Fraud Center (NFC) statistics show a rise in the last 30 years in the cost of economic crimes alone, which rose from $5 billion in 1970 to about $100 billion in 1990. In its 2000 white paper, The Growing Global Threat of Economic and Cyber Crime, the NFC reports: "As the Internet and technological advances continue to reshape the way we do business in government and industry, and competition and economic pressures create quicker and more efficient ways to do business, the reality of increased economic crime having a serious impact on the economy grows geometrically."

[Graphic omitted] It is partially this focus on white-collar crime that has brought more awareness and stiffer penalties to crimes in this area. When Madoff was sentenced to 150 years, he epitomized Sutherland's depiction of a white-collar criminal--"a person of respectability and high social status," who commits a crime in the course of his occupation. Most white-collar crimes involve money, and after bilking his clients out of millions, Madoff is considered the most notorious white-collar criminal in history.

Typically fraudulent in nature, white-collar crimes include antitrust fraud, black market operations, forgery, identity fraud, loan sharking, obstruction of justice, perjury, and racketeering (to name only a few).

Judge Donald Shaver of the Stanislaus Superior Court of Modesto, California, says, "to that we may now add mortgage and real estate fraud and telemarketing fraud." As cochair of the International Criminal Law Committee of the ABA Section of International Law, Shaver adds, "The recent damage to the economy, worse than any time since the Great Depression, resulting from the mortgage fraud epidemic is incalculable."

"If you think you would be a good detective, you might make a good white-collar lawyer," says Tom Gilson, partner in the Phoenix, Arizona, firm Lewis and Roca and cochair of the Criminal Litigation Committee of the ABA Section of Litigation. Gilson explains that white-collar lawyers ask a lot of questions. Fact-finding missions are necessary to both bring charges and to defend charges. Gilson finds, "Good white-collar lawyers are inquisitive, tenacious, flexible, and creative. They must be prepared to deal with the highest of stakes, as their clients may face the loss of their liberty."

"What differentiates white-collar criminal litigation from other aspects of corporate litigation practice is that the stakes are much higher because they are deeply personal," says Tom Viles, vice chair of the International Criminal Law Committee with Shaver. Viles, who practices criminal defense as a partner at the Washington, D.C., firm Berliner, Corcoran & Rowe, explains, "Outcomes in white-collar cases cannot be measured in purely economic terms---as in all criminal cases, reputation, liberty, and the future happiness of entire families hang in the balance. For most people I know, these are the most important things worth fighting for in life. Accordingly, in most criminal cases, they're the most valuable things that a client expects a criminal lawyer to fight for."

Long-time lawyers will tell you how dramatically the focus of white-collar crime has changed in recent years. "The white-collar defense practice arose from the criminalization of what formerly were civil and regulatory matters," says David Gourevitch, chair of the White-Collar Crime Committee of the ABA Business Law Section. "Now, the government tends to prosecute a broad range of infractions of federal and state rules."

"Things that are prosecuted now would have been prosecuted differently 20 years ago," says Janet Levine, immediate past chair of the White Collar Crime Committee of the ABA Criminal Justice Section. "Some guy stealing your credit card is not what we do any more."

"Where it was once more common that the victim of a white-collar crime was a business or an individual, it is now more common that the victims are 'the shareholders' or 'society in general,' and the crime has repercussions across the entire economy," explains Shaver. "It is much more common now to prosecute corporate executives rather than individual con men. Federal sentencing guidelines have been ratcheted up, and sentences have become stiffer."

Not one lawyer interviewed said the practice of white-collar crime law is dull. Happy to come to work on a Sunday morning, Levine, from her Crowell & Moring office overlooking Los Angeles, says that every day brings something new and finds it interesting that cases are often impacted by what is happening in the news. "If you have mortgage issues, there's also mortgage fraud, stock issues, stock fraud."

There are many specialties of practice within the white-collar arena, such as securities, environmental, and health care. Having worked at the Securities and Exchange Commission (SEC) Division of Enforcement and the Manhattan DA's office prior to opening his own law office in New York City, Gourevitch finds most of his practice in the securities area. Most, but not all, white-collar defense lawyers he knows did a stint in government or with a public defender's office.

"The environment can be as varied as the crimes themselves are," says Judge Shaver, explaining that the opportunities to practice in this arena are virtually unlimited. "While most law firms advising corporations or individuals being investigated or prosecuted tend to be larger firms, some of the best lawyers in this area are solo or at smaller firms."

Most major white-collar crimes are handled at the federal level. "Both the SEC and the DOJ [Department of Justice] have expanded criminal prosecutions in this area, including international prosecutions for FCPA [Foreign Corrupt Practices Act] violations," says Shaver, but adds, "You shouldn't downplay the opportunities at the state level either. Many district attorneys' and state's attorneys' offices have received special grants to prosecute real estate and mortgage fraud cases and have special white-collar crime units as well."

Opportunities exist in this area for those interested in civil suits as well. Shaver says that not all white-collar crimes are prosecuted criminally, as I evidenced by the increased "number of civil suits related to investor or shareholder fraud ... since 2000." He adds, "This is a rapidly changing area of the law, and now is the perfect time to get involved at the critical initial stages."

To that end, he and others recommend involvement in the ABA sections and committees that specialize in white-collar crime law. You will receive publications with the latest developments of interest, learn about CLE programs, and have access to members-only areas of their websites, many of which have information specifically for law students and new lawyers. Attending ABA and other bar association events is a great way to meet and talk to leaders in this practice area, both prosecution and defense.

Kimberly H. Smith is a communications specialist and legal writer based in Cape Coral, Florida.

24

White-Collar Crime

Expert Testimony in Criminal Cases

Elkan Abramowitz and Barry A. Bohrer

White-collar cases frequently involve highly sophisticated financial transactions, voluminous documents, and the potential for significant sentences should the defendant be convicted. In order to assist the jury in wading through this information, both the defense and the government may seek the admission of expert testimony to assist the trier of fact to understand the evidence. Expert testimony can have a significant impact on the outcome of a criminal case.

Recent cases raise two separate issues with respect to expert testimony in criminal cases:

- First, the federal courts of appeals have recognized a defendant's right to present expert testimony in order to explain the defense to the jury.

- Second, two U.S. Court of Appeals for the Second Circuit cases have examined the government's sometimes questionable use of law enforcement officials as expert witnesses.

These cases demonstrate that the manner in which these expert witnesses testify and the substance of their testimony can seriously prejudice a defendant.

White-Collar Crime. New York Law Journal Nov 4, 2008.

A DEFENDANT'S RIGHT

The defendant's right to present expert testimony was addressed by the Tenth Circuit in **United States v. Nacchio**.[1] Joseph Nacchio, former chief executive of Qwest Communications, was convicted in the U.S. District Court for the District of Colorado of 19 counts of insider trading and sentenced to six years in prison, fines totaling $19 million, and ordered to forfeit over $52 million. In March 2008, a panel of the Tenth Circuit voted 2-1 to reverse the conviction, finding that the district court judge improperly excluded the testimony of Mr. Nacchio's expert witness.

The government alleged that Mr. Nacchio engaged in insider trading by selling Qwest stock while in possession of material nonpublic information. Specifically, the government asserted that Mr. Nacchio knew that Qwest was relying heavily on nonrecurring sources of revenue to meet its first- and second-quarter numbers and that the company had not shifted to recurring revenue streams as required to meet its year-end numbers. In defense, Mr. Nacchio disclosed his intention to call an expert who would analyze Mr. Nacchio's trading patterns and testify that his sales were not consistent with insider trading and that Qwest's stock price was not significantly affected when the allegedly material information was released.

The government objected to the admission of the expert evidence, arguing that the defense had failed to comply with the notice requirements of **Federal Rule of Criminal Procedure 16**, which governs disclosure obligations of both the government and defense. With respect to expert witnesses, the rule requires the defendant, "at the government's request, [to] give to the government a written summary of any testimony that the defendant intends to use [] as evidence at trial."[2] A defendant is only required to provide this information if the defendant had requested the same of the government and the government complied.

The district court concurred with the government that the defendant had failed to satisfy the requirements of Rule 16, finding that Mr. Nacchio had "offer[ed] no bases or reasons whatsoever for [the expert's] opinions contained in the summary" disclosure. Mr. Nacchio was instructed to file a revised disclosure, which he did. The subsequent disclosure included a "Summary of Opinions and Bases for Opinions" explaining the expert's intended testimony. Once again, the government objected, filing motion papers arguing that the Rule 16 disclosure was still inadequate. The government further reasoned that even if Mr. Nacchio had complied with Rule 16, the court should find that the defense had not established the admissibility of the evidence under **Daubert v. Merrell Dow Pharmaceuticals**, the Supreme Court decision relating to the admissibility of expert testimony.[3]

When Mr. Nacchio's defense team called their expert to the stand the following day, the court dismissed the jury and, without hearing argument from either party, ruled that the expert's testimony was inadmissible. Explaining his rationale, the district judge found the defendant's Rule 16 submission to contain significant deficiencies under *Daubert* and **Kumho Tire**. In addition, the court found that the expert disclosure failed to set forth any methodology. Finally, the court concluded that the testimony would not be helpful to the jury, as required under **Federal Rule of Evidence 403** or **702**, "because expert economic analysis would 'invit[e] the jurors to abandon their own common sense and common experience and succumb to this expert's credentials.'"[4]

TENTH CIRCUIT'S HOLDING

The Tenth Circuit panel disagreed. First, the Court of Appeals examined the disclosure requirements of Rule 16, finding that it did not include an extensive discussion of the expert's methodology. Rather, the court noted that the purpose of the rule was to give opposing counsel notice, allowing them "more complete pretrial preparation." The court strongly stated that the rule was not designed, however, to allow a district court to move immediately to a *Daubert* determination without briefs, a hearing, or other appropriate means of testing the proposed expert's methodology.

Observing that Mr. Nacchio's Rule 16 disclosure contained his expert's opinions, the bases of and reasons for those opinions, and a recitation of the witness' qualifications, the court found that the defense had adequately met its disclosure requirements under the rules. Speculating on the basis for the district court's ruling, the court noted that the district court judge may have confused the more stringent expert witness disclosure requirements under the Civil Rules of Procedure[5] with those required under Criminal Rule of Procedure 16.

The Court of Appeals then turned to the government's argument that even if the defendant had complied with Rule 16, the district court properly excluded the testimony under *Daubert* and F.R.E. 702. As an initial matter, the court found that the district court failed to make any genuine determination under *Daubert*, ruling instead on the Rule 16 disclosures. Further, the court found that such a ruling would have been an abuse of discretion, as the record was "devoid of any factual basis on which a *Daubert* ruling could be made." "The district court could not make an informed *Daubert* determination without hearing [] testimony or receiving submissions on the issue."[6]

Finally, the Court of Appeals concluded that the district court was erroneous in finding that the expert testimony would not have been helpful to the jury or was more prejudicial than probative. "This misunderstands the nature of economic expertise. An economic expert is permitted not only to tell the jury that an economic concept 'is an issue' but to analyze the concept and offer informed opinions. In other words, expert testimony may 'assist the trier of fact to understand the facts already in the record, even if all it does is put those facts in context.'"[7]

In reversing Mr. Nacchio's conviction, the Court of Appeals noted that the right of a defendant to call witnesses was a fundamental element of due process and crucial for defending the charges against him. In this case, the court found that the exclusion of Mr. Nacchio's expert's testimony was prejudicial and may have changed the jury's mind. Because the record did not otherwise contain "overwhelming evidence of guilt," the exclusion was not harmless and the conviction was reversed.

There is a post-script to the Tenth Circuit's decision, however. On July 30, 2008, the Tenth Circuit granted the government's petition for a rehearing en banc.

KEY QUESTIONS

As framed by the court, the questions to be addressed are: (1) whether the defendant was "sufficiently on notice that he was required either to present evidence in support of the expert's methodology or request an evidentiary hearing in advance of presenting the expert's testimony"; (2) whether the defendant had "an adequate opportunity to present such evidence or request an evidentiary hearing in advance of presenting the expert's testimony"; (3) whether the defendant had the burden of requesting such a hearing; and (4) whether the district court abused its discretion in disallowing the evidence and, if so, whether the appropriate remedy is a new trial or remand for an evidentiary hearing.[8] The case was argued on Sept. 25, and is awaiting decision.

The Second Circuit also has addressed the importance and admissibility of expert testimony on a criminal defendant's behalf. Most recently, in **United States v. Joseph**,[9] the court reviewed a district court's decision excluding expert testimony. The defendant was convicted in the Southern District of New York for traveling in interstate commerce for purpose of engaging in illicit sexual conduct with a minor. At trial, the defendant sought to call an expert to testify about the culture of role-playing in the context of sexually explicit conversations on the Internet. The district court rejected the admissibility of this testimony.

Although the Court of Appeals vacated the defendant's conviction and remanded specifically because of the trial court's erroneous jury instructions, the court noted that the issue of the admissibility of the expert testimony was likely to recur at retrial and "urge[d] the District Court to give a more thorough consideration to the defendant's claim to present [the expert's] testimony."

First, the court said that the social science expert's opinions were likely to help the jury understand the evidence. "Although some jurors may have familiarity with Internet messaging, it is unlikely that the average juror is familiar with the role-playing activity that Dr. Herriot was prepared to explain in the specific context of sexually oriented conversation in cyberspace."[10]

In addition, the court stated that the expert's testimony would be relevant, dismissing the dissent's argument that the defendant's testimony adequately addressed the role-playing explanation for the defendant's conduct. "[W]hen the Government implores a jury to find the defendant and his explanation not credible, we think the presentation of that explanation from a qualified expert would be significant, especially where the explanation is not one with which jurors are likely to have familiarity."[11]

GOVERNMENT'S EXPERTS

Although the admission of expert testimony in support of a defense theory is invaluable to white-collar defendants, the improper use of expert testimony by the government can be devastating, possibly amounting to a constitutional violation. Last month, the Second Circuit vacated the convictions of two gang members after finding that the admission of testimony from the government's law enforcement expert witness violated the Federal Rules of Evidence and the Sixth Amendment Confrontation Clause.

In ***United States v. Mejia***,[12] the government indicted a group of gang members, charging them with various racketeering activity for activities associated with two drive-by shootings. At trial, the government called Hector Alicea, an officer with the New York Sate police to serve as an expert witness on the gang's "structure and the derivation, background and migration of the [] organization, its history and conflicts, as well as its hierarchy, cliques, methods and activities, modes of communication and slang."

During voir dire examination and cross-examination, defense counsel elicited testimony from Mr. Alicea that revealed that a significant portion of his testimony and knowledge was based on information learned during custodial interrogations with various gang members. Defense counsel objected to the admission of Mr. Alicea's testimony, arguing that it was "impermissible hearsay." The trial court disagreed, allowing Mr. Alicea to testify. The defendants appealed.

Before reaching the substance of the defendants' arguments, the Court of Appeals chronicled the emergence of the law enforcement officer expert as a "skilled witness" in the 1980s, noting that it frequently had upheld the admission of that type of expert testimony because it aided the jury in its understanding of the evidence, such as the nature and structure of organized crime organizations. Law enforcement officers in these cases were able to testify about "much that was outside the expectable realm of knowledge of the average juror," such as the "operation, symbols, jargon, and internal structure of criminal organizations."[13]

The court noted, however, that the use of this type of expertise should be limited, stating that "[a]n increasingly thinning line separates the legitimate use of an officer expert to translate esoteric terminology or explicate an organization's hierarchical structure from the illegitimate and impermissible substitution of expert opinion for factual evidence." The court observed that the improper use of expert testimony in this way replaced a jury's factfinding function.[14]

The court concluded that this line had been crossed with respect to Mr. Alicea's testimony. First, the court found that much of Mr. Alicea's testimony concerned matters outside the scope of his expertise in violation of Federal Rule of Evidence 702. Specifically, the court said that the witness' testimony about the number of firearms seized from the gang, how many gang members had been arrested for dealing narcotics, and the number of murders committed by gang members during a given period of time was material "well within the grasp of the average juror" through the admission of separate fact evidence by the government. The court noted that the government could not use expert testimony as a substitute for factual evidence in the first instance, using as an example proof of a pattern of racketeering activity involving murder. "[T]hat an individual was murdered remains a *fact* that must be proven by competent *evidence*."

The court further concluded that Mr. Alicea's testimony was inadmissible hearsay, admitted in violation of Federal Rule of Evidence 703 and the Confrontation Clause of the Sixth Amendment. Although experts are permitted to rely on hearsay to form their opinion, they can not relay that hearsay directly to the jury, allowing the government to circumvent the hearsay rules. Because the hearsay statements relied upon by Mr. Alicea were made in the course of custodial interrogations of other gang members, they are deemed testimonial under *Crawford v. Washington.*

When faced with the intersection of the *Crawford* rule [prohibiting the introduction of out-of-court testimonial statements made by an absent witness unless that witness is unavailable and the defendant had a prior opportunity for cross-examination,] and officer experts, we have determined that an officer expert's testimony violates *Crawford* "if [the expert] communicated out-of-court testimonial statements of cooperating witnesses and confidential informants directly to the jury in the guise of an expert opinion."[15]

With respect to Mr. Alicea's testimony, the court concluded that he was simply summarizing the investigation that was not otherwise a part of the record and presenting it to the jury as an expert opinion. Furthermore, because of the officer's status as an expert, his factual testimony was likely to have "unmerited credibility" before the jury. Because these errors were not harmless, the court vacated the convictions and remanded the case.

The government's use of law enforcement expert witnesses to present summary factual information to the jury is not the only way in which expert testimony can be improperly presented. In *United States v. Scop*, the Second Circuit examined whether the testimony of the government's expert witness improperly included legal conclusions.[16] The defendants were convicted in the Southern District of New York of perjury, mail fraud, securities fraud, and conspiracy. At trial, an SEC investigator testified as an expert witness in the securities trading practices. Over defense objections, the witness was allowed to testify as to his opinion of whether the defendants had engaged in a scheme to defraud investors. On appeal, the defendants argued that the opinion testimony improperly embodied legal conclusions and was improperly allowed.

The Court of Appeals agreed, finding that the witness' repeated statements embodying legal conclusions exceeded the permissible scope of opinion testimony under the Federal Rules of Evidence. "Had [the witness] merely testified that controlled buying and selling of the kind alleged here can create artificial price levels to lure outside investors, no sustainable objection could have been made. Instead, however, [the witness] made no attempt to couch the opinion testimony at issue in even conclusory factual statements but drew directly upon the language of the statute and accompanying regulations concerning 'manipulation' and 'fraud.'" Finding that the opinions were highly prejudicial and invaded the court's province in instructing the jury as to the applicable law, the court concluded they could not have been helpful to the jury in carrying out its legitimate function. Accordingly, the convictions related to this testimony were reversed.[17]

CONCLUSION

White-collar defendants can benefit greatly from the use of expert witnesses to explain the evidence and their theory of the case. Counsel should advocate for the presentation of this evidence as integral to a defendant's right to present a defense. In addition, defense counsel should carefully monitor the government's use of expert testimony to ensure that neither summary factual information nor legal conclusions are improperly offered to the jury.

Elkan Abramowitz *is a member of Morvillo, Abramowitz, Grand, Iason, Anello & Bohrer. He is a former chief of the criminal division in the U.S. Attorney's Office for the Southern District of New York.* **Barry A. Bohrer** *is also a member of Morvillo, Abramowitz and was formerly chief appellate attorney and chief of the major crimes unit in the U.S. Attorney's Office for the Southern District of New York.* **Gretchan R. Ohlig,** *an attorney, assisted in the preparation of this article.*

ENDNOTES DELETED

Part X

CONSEQUENCES FOR WHITE COLLAR CRIME CRIMINALS

25

Go Directly to Jail

White Collar Sentencing After the Sarbanes-Oxley Act

We begin with the principle that the certainty of real and significant punishment best serves the purposes of deterring white collar criminals. ... [I]f it is unmistakable that the automatic consequence for one committing a significant white collar offense is prison, then many will be deterred.

--James B. Comey, Jr., United States Attorney for the Southern District of New York, explaining the rationale behind the White-Collar Crime Penalty Enhancement Act of 2002. (1)

In 2002, reacting to the devastating collapse of Enron and other major American corporations, (2) Congress enacted the Sarbanes-Oxley Act (3) ("Sarbanes-Oxley" or "the Act"). Passed hastily by a shaken legislature, the Act included a multitude of reforms aimed at preventing another meltdown. (4) One particular area of reform was white collar criminal sentencing: included in the Act was the White-Collar Crime Penalty Enhancement Act of 2002 (5) (WCCPA), which sharply increased penalties for various forms of fraud. Unfortunately, both the Act and the WCCPA have proven overly rushed and insufficiently prescient to deal with the changing face of business crimes in America. (6) This Note argues that a major reason for this result is that judges have reacted to the harsher WCCPA sentences by increasingly departing from the Federal Sentencing Guidelines. For this reason, WCCPA-enhanced sentences have become at least as disparate and unreliable as white collar sentences were in the past. Instead of deterring crime, the WCCPA has made criminal punishment less of a fear for those who would commit fraud. In order to remedy the damage caused by the last seven years of unpredictable sentences, either Congress or the United States Sentencing Commission must take steps to stabilize and rationalize the white collar sentencing system. This Note proposes that the best way to achieve this goal would be to tie Guidelines sentencing levels to actual loss, (7) rather than intended loss, which would better mirror the social impact and perceived moral culpability of white collar crimes. Only with a sentencing scheme that encourages judges to sentence systematically and consistently can the deterrence desired by the drafters of the WCCPA be accomplished.

This argument requires two brief qualifications. First, for the purposes of this Note the term "white collar crime" will be limited to the crimes covered by name in the WCCPA: false and incomplete SEC filings, (8) and mail and wire fraud. (9) Second, this Note assumes that individuals who contemplate broad-scale white collar crimes are sophisticated actors, familiar with the law and current events. As such, they know the available punishments and recent comparable sentences for their contemplated crimes, and they incorporate those potential downsides into their decisionmaking process. (10)

This Note proceeds in three Parts. Part I lays out a basic flaw in modern white collar criminal sentencing, discussing how the current sentencing scheme neither deters crime nor requires a just level of punishment, and is thus an ineffective and perhaps retrograde method of achieving societal goals. Part II proposes two possible reasons that this problem has arisen: First, from an institutional perspective, judges may perceive white collar crime as less dangerous and prone to recidivism than other crimes. Second, from a personal perspective, judges may be hesitant to impose upon a white collar criminal the same sentence they impose upon the murderers, rapists, and armed robbers they regularly see before them. Part III proposes several solutions to these problems, including alteration of the loss calculation mechanism.

I. THE PROBLEM

With the passage of the Sarbanes-Oxley Act and the WCCPA, Congress sharply raised penalties for many white collar criminal activities. (11) In so doing, Congress attempted to deal with a growing rash of major business crimes. (12) However, judges seem to be unwilling to consistently impose the higher sentences required by the WCCPA (13)--departures (14) from the Guidelines have increased since the WCCPA was passed. (15) This is a dangerous trend, not only because the deterrent effect of the higher penalties is lessened if they are so rarely imposed, (16) but also because it leads to problematic inter- and intra-jurisdictional sentencing disparities. Finally, even as the new system underdeters massive fraud, it simultaneously overdeters the much more common minor white collar crimes, such as low-value check forgery or minor Form 10-K undervaluation.

Before 2001, when the reforms that influenced the WCCPA began, white collar sentencing was flexible at best. The creation of the Federal Sentencing Guidelines in 1984 had been intended to standardize sentencing, (17) but even as of 2001 many white collar offenders faced no prison time at all. (18) The first version of the corporate reform bill that would become Sarbanes-Oxley, originated by the White House in early 2002, merely proposed to make disqualification from future fiduciary service mandatory in white collar sentencing. (19) Even this seemingly minor requirement, however, was a large step past the lenient sentences that previously characterized white collar sentencing.

Sarbanes-Oxley, in its final form, went much further. It quadrupled the maximum sentences available for mail and wire fraud (the most common forms of fraud) and criminalized certain actions that had previously been regulated by agencies. (20) Where previously such frauds had merited a maximum sentence of five years, after the WCCPA an identical crime could bring up to twenty years in prison. Or it could bring none at all--there was no floor set. The bill had a similar effect on securities and bank fraud sentencing. However, neither the Act nor the Commission took any steps toward actually standardizing punishment for white collar offenses--instead, they dramatically increased the range of sentencing without providing much guidance as to how to use that range to effectively punish and deter crime. (21) Within the range of permissible sentences, judges' discretion is almost absolute, (22) making the prediction of individual sentences a difficult, if not impossible, task. (23) This broad range with little guidance renders the legitimacy of the sentencing system suspect.

A. The WCCPA-Enhanced Penalties Are Not Effective Deterrents

1. The Theory Behind the Current System Does Not Ensure Deterrence.

The current system of sentencing has led to a growing number of departures from the Guidelines. (24) The high rate of departures naturally means that sentences are not consistent. An individual who contemplates committing a crime has no way of predicting whether he will face ten, twenty, or more years in prison, or receive merely a slap on the wrist for his actions. (25) Indeed, this broad range is one of the worst problems with the WCCPA: rather than acting upon the base Guidelines (26) and average sentences for white collar crime, (27) the bill simply increased the maximum sentence, thereby expanding the range within which judges may sentence. (28) An expanded range, without a rubric for sentencing within that range, invites unfair disparity between sentences for similarly situated offenders.

Deterrence works best when punishment is swift and certain. (29) White collar sentencing in the years since Sarbanes-Oxley, however, has been anything but. Given the broad range of potential sentences provided by the WCCPA, within which judges now have essentially complete discretion, (30) the sentence can range from mere months in prison to decades. (31) Moreover, unlike the average aspiring criminal actor, white collar offenders usually know that they will have access to a lenient plea bargaining system. They are also often well aware of instances in which a court has departed downward from a Guidelines sentence that "shock[ed] the conscience of th[e] [c]ourt." (32)

There is, of course, the alternative argument that deterrence is at its height when potential punishments are severe but unpredictable. (33) Such punishments may be imposed relatively randomly against some perpetrators but not others, and would theoretically provide a greater deterrent effect than a predictable but lower sentence--the probability of sentencing might be lower, but the risk would be much higher. An adherent to this view would see the Sarbanes-Oxley system, with all its disparities and broad-ranging discretion, as a step in the right direction, though one that perhaps does not go far enough. (34) However, that argument ignores the perceived justice aspect of deterrence: arguably the best deterrent (both the most effective and the most just) is one that has perceived legitimacy among both the regulated parties and the communities within which the parties live. Where those affected by a law perceive it as unjust, disobedience is more likely. (35) Conversely, when a law is perceived as fair and just, it is more likely that individuals will follow it. (36) A fairer law is more likely to have the support of the community, leading to social stigmatization of lawbreakers. In the white collar context, a more legitimate law is likely to be more vigorously pursued by prosecutors and more consistently and harshly applied by sentencing judges, leading to even further deterrence. (37)

Moreover, the idea that uncertainty increases deterrence is, though reasonable, countered by the mindset--especially prevalent among white collar criminals--by which defendants "overoptimistically" anticipate "abnormally low sentences" in their own cases. (38) Importantly, this phenomenon would have an even greater effect on sophisticated parties, such as prospective large-scale white collar offenders, who know how to use each available loophole and sentence-reducing argument. When the range of possible sentences for the same action is vast, this problem is magnified even further: potential offenders fall prey to the optimism fallacy and assume that they will receive a sentence in the lower part of the range. The WCCPA was intended to alleviate precisely this fallacy and strengthen the predictability of sentencing; (39) the evidence, however, suggests that it has not lived up to its intentions.

2. The Evidence Indicates that Actual Deterrence Is Not Occurring.

Recent events in the banking and finance world make it painfully obvious that frauds on or past the scale of the Enron scandal are still occurring, despite the higher sentencing ranges. It seems that every few months another potential fraud is discovered: AIG, (40) ImClone, (41) HealthSouth, (42) Bernard L. Madoff Investment Securities, (43) and many other corporations, small and large, have fallen prey to scandal in the years since Sarbanes-Oxley was enacted.

Additionally, the number of white collar criminal convictions has not fallen since the WCCPA was passed; on the contrary, 2B1.1-crime sentencings have increased. In fiscal year 2002, prior to the introduction of the Sarbanes-Oxley amendments, there were 6154 2B1.1 sentencings. (44) In fiscal year 2007, there were 8777. (45) These numbers suggest that, whatever the increased sentences are doing, they are not deterring the kind of criminal activity that the WCCPA was enacted to prevent. (46)

B. The WCCPA Regime Allows and Encourages Unjust Outcomes

1. The Broad Range of Possible Sentences Is Inherently Unjust and Encourages Unfair Disparities.

In addition to the deterrence problem, the mere existence of such a broad range of punishment options permits sentences to rest on impermissible factors, and is thus in and of itself an injustice. Recent sentencing jurisprudence has increased judicial discretion to an extent that was clearly not intended by the framers of the WCCPA. When the WCCPA was enacted, it made changes to the mandatory Federal Sentencing Guidelines. After United States v. Booker, (47) though, judges are not limited to the stiff sentences imposed by the WCCPA, but instead can choose sentences ranging from nominal to severe. Although judges must still begin the sentencing process by calculating the Guidelines level, (48) no further interaction with the Guidelines numbers is required. (49) The effects of Gall v. United States (50) and Rita v. United States (51) on this issue are difficult to determine just yet, as the decisions are still quite new; however, the two cases certainly will encourage the further expansion of judicial discretion.

Although judges often still sentence within the Guidelines range, (52) the Guidelines are no longer mandatory, and many judges depart from them at some time or another--meaning that the full range of Guidelines and non-Guidelines sentences are available to a judge otherwise unconstrained by statutory limitations. The Guidelines were originally intended to standardize sentencing and reduce disparities, in turn decreasing reliance on individualized factors such as financial position. A system that both permits and encourages departures from the standard allows judges to sentence based upon factors that were explicitly excluded as irrelevant, prejudicial, or unjust by the Commission's massive study of national sentencing practices. (53) More pragmatically, the broader the range of punishments, the broader the discretion, and the more opportunity there is for injustice to slip into the sentencing process. The availability of such an enormous sentencing range, coupled with the removal of almost every restraint on judicial discretion to an extent not seen in many other sentencing schemes, (54) virtually ensures that the legitimacy of sentencing will be called into question.

2. The WCCPA Unfairly Overdeters Small-Scale White Collar Criminals and Permits Unjust Outcomes.

The increased penalties from the Sarbanes-Oxley Act not only underdeter major fraudsters, but they inevitably also overdeter those individuals who commit small-scale crimes covered by the WCCPA. As has been discussed, the WCCPA penalties were rushed onto the books immediately after the discovery of several major white collar crimes affecting many people and billions of dollars. However, the WCCPA has a far broader effect--one that was perhaps not even considered by Congress when passing the legislation. Jeff Skilling and Bernie Ebbers were not the only people committing wire, mail, and securities fraud: individuals with far fewer resources commit correspondingly smaller crimes every day. (55)

Prior to Enron and the WCCPA, Congress apparently thought that five years in prison was an appropriate maximum sentence for mail fraud. Given the context of the legislation, the drastic increase in sentences was seemingly not primarily intended to deter the minor criminals who make up the vast majority of white collar fraud offenders. (56) Nevertheless, because of the actions of a few high-profile criminals, those individuals are punished on the same scale as the Enron offenders. The nature of the typical mail fraud case is no different than it was when Sarbanes-Oxley was written--the only thing that has changed is the penalty. The numbers illustrate this point neatly: In fiscal year 2008 there were 7713 sentencings for criminal fraud under 2B1.1. (57) Of those, likely few made the national news at all, let alone became a headline. The remainder, primarily minor frauds, simply do not induce the social stigma and fear that is created by the massive frauds that catalyzed Sarbanes-Oxley. It seems inherently unfair to drastically increase the punishment for a crime merely because some individuals have used the particular crime to perpetrate vast frauds. (58)

One of the legacies of the rushed passage of the Act is the overbreadth of the statute itself. Not only does the Act capture corporate frauds both large and small, but it also extends to such frauds as telemarketer scams, e-mail spam, and incomplete personal bankruptcy filings. These types of crimes have long been sentenced under the fraud guideline, and are indeed forms of wire and mail fraud--but they are nothing like the types of corporate crimes to which Congress was responding when it passed the WCCPA. Whether these crimes deserve increased punishment when considered in a vacuum is not the question at issue: they were caught up in Congress's push to penalize corporate fraud, making their thoughtless enhancement seem unjust.

Moreover, many of these lower-value fraudsters are unlikely to be aware of the increased penalties they face for their actions. Big firm CEOs have lawyers and boards of directors to inform them of the dangers they face should they stray from Sarbanes-Oxley's strictures (and to illuminate for them the many ways in which they can avoid stiff penalties). Minor white collar criminals, in contrast, likely neither know the possible penalties nor have access to the type of legal counsel that produced such good results for the HealthSouth defendants. (59) Fairness and deterrence seem to require individuals subject to sentencing to be aware of both the wrongness of their actions and the relative severity of sentences they might face; (60) it seems wrong to impute this knowledge to the more minor fraudsters. If the penalties were enhanced in order to deter mega-frauds, a correspondingly increased level of knowledge should be required of the penalties' recipients.

Looking at the above problem from a different angle, one must remember that reducing disparities among individuals who have committed the same quantum of harmful activity was a primary goal of the Guidelines. (61) However, the effects of the WCCPA have undermined this goal for white collar criminals. Not only do ordinary fraudsters bear the brunt of society's anger toward the infrequent-but-public Enron-level crimes, but even major criminals receive disparate sentences for substantially similar crimes. (62) Indeed, there is a perverse incentive to the Guidelines structure as it stands currently. The individuals who are the most morally culpable for a fraud will often also be the most knowledgeable parties, and thereby most useful to prosecutors seeking to "flip" a member of a conspiracy in order to procure testimony against the other members. For this reason, the individuals who most deserve punishment for a fraud are the ones who are most likely to escape it. (63) The current system rewards those criminals who planned most effectively to avoid the consequences of their actions, and who had the most access to legal help in those plans, while punishing the least sophisticated actors at the top of the scale.

II. WHY IS THIS HAPPENING?

In order to begin solving the problems posed in Part I, the reasons behind the disparities must be discerned and understood. Part I has already discussed the theoretical reasons for the failure of deterrence and the increase in injustice; Part II elaborates upon the practical role of the judge in implementing the highly variable sentencing ranges. The nearly unlimited discretion given to judges would be less of a problem if judges engaged in self-limiting; however, there is every reason to believe that they do nothing of the sort. Instead, they shy away from the harsh sentences required by the Guidelines--both for small-scale crimes and for multi-billion dollar frauds. (64) However, they do not do so in any systematic manner. Where one judge might depart from a life sentence to a fifteen year term, another might go to thirty years, and still another to probation. Thus, any inquiry into the legitimacy of the white collar sentencing guidelines must begin with the judges themselves, asking two fundamental questions: why do judges fail to sentence at the level provided by the Guidelines, and what does that failure tell us about the flaws in the WCCPA?

This Note argues that judges are reluctant to impose the types of sentences called for by the Sarbanes-Oxley Act for two reasons: First, on an institutional level, they may believe that the punishment does not fit the crime and that the sentences as applied are simply too high. Second, on a more personal level, they may be reluctant to impose upon individuals convicted of business crimes the same types of sentences that they impose upon murderers, felons-in-possession, and the like. Unfortunately, obtaining data about judicial attitudes toward white collar sentencing can be difficult--although 18 U.S.C. [section] 3553, the sentencing statute, requires judges to articulate a reason for their sentences, (65) it is fairly unusual for that articulation to come in written form. Instead, the majority of judges simply discuss their reasoning in open court, producing no paper opinion memorializing those reasons. (66) It is rare for a judge to put into writing his objections to specific sentences--indeed, sometimes a judge might not even realize that he harbors objections that are subconsciously incorporated into a departure. Nevertheless, a judicial skepticism toward the high sentences in the WCCPA seems clear from the evidence discussed so far.

In part, this disparity is the fault of the current confusion in federal sentencing. As was discussed in Part I, given the recent decisions in Rita and Gall, and dating back to Booker, judges have little guidance as to how, and to what extent, they are to incorporate the Guidelines into their own sentencing plans. Departures in many areas of white collar criminality have increased, (67) despite Booker's instruction to judges to begin with the Guidelines. Thus, it seems clear that judges, though given general instructions by [section] 3553, have been left without a definite rubric by which to narrow and standardize their sentencing options--a very dangerous position when sentencing ranges are as broad as they are in white collar cases. (68)

A. Judges May Perceive White Collar Crime As Less Harmful than Other Forms of Crime, and Sentence Accordingly

Judges who sentence white collar offenders are faced with a difficult problem: in many cases the harsh recommended punishment does not seem to accomplish the purpose for which the additional severity of the WCCPA was intended. Judges sentencing white collar offenders have a docket filled to bursting with other crimes--drug distribution, rape, murder, and more. In context, relatively "victimless" business crimes (69) look less problematic. Recidivism may also factor into the calculation: a judge who has spent her day handing down stiff sentences to people whose crimes are likely to be repeated (70) may well be reluctant to impose a similar sentence upon an individual with no prior criminal record (71) who will almost certainly not have the opportunity to commit such a crime again. (72) From a purposive view, a judge may not see much difference between sentencing a white collar offender to ten years or to twenty--both accomplish

Sarbanes-Oxley's goal of imposing prison time on financial crimes, and both seem initially quite harsh. (73) Because of the vast range of possible sentences available for white collar offenses, and the complete freedom granted by Booker, the judge does not need to overcome her gut reaction--she can, and will, depart (sometimes quite drastically) from the Guidelines sentencing structure. (74)

Judges likely perceive only minimal marginal utility in the extended sentence statutorily imposed upon the crime. There is an argument to be made that the bare fact of a prison sentence, be it five months or five years, is a sufficient of a deterrent to make an impact on the mind of a potential fraudster, and that enhanced sentences are simply not useful at the margins for increasing deterrence. Proponents of this position reason that when a potential sentence goes from ten to twenty years, the marginal deterrent value of those additional ten years diminishes, causing each additional year to be more fruitless in the overall goals of the sentencing scheme than the last. (75) This argument can be reworded as follows: as the marginal utility of each year decreases, the perceived marginal unfairness of each added year increases. Such an insight is a useful way of framing judges' reactions to the stiff sentences imposed by the WCCPA. Moreover, whereas the judge is used to sentencing individuals who, were they let out of prison, could easily be back before the bench within the year, the judge is well aware that a white collar offender is unlikely to be in a position from which he can commit further frauds--the individual offender need not be kept imprisoned in order to protect society. (76) When a judge sees many additional years of punishment with little deterrent payoff, those additional years can, as they did for Judge Glasser, shock the conscience of the court.

An interesting exception to the general rule that judges will sentence significantly below the Guidelines is in high-profile cases. A quick glance at some high sentences in white collar crime gives a strong sense of familiarity: Bernie Ebbers, twenty-five years; Jeff Skilling, twenty-four years; Timothy Rigas, twenty years; Chalana McFarland, thirty years. (77) Many of these individuals are still household names even years after sentencing. More importantly, their sentences are broadly known. Such severity for high-profile cases might be seen as evidence that the WCCPA is actually working--after all, it was enacted to prevent these major frauds, and surely these large and heavily publicized sentences were perfect for that purpose. Moreover, in these cases, there is no question that the punishment fits the crime--judges need not concern themselves with the ethical debate that is entailed by a criminalized regulatory case. Of course, the "success" angle is proven suspect by the continuing, regular discovery of additional massive white collar frauds. The justice of raising the punishment of all in order to provide an example to the few is questionable at best.

B. Judges Typically Undervalue the Moral and Social Harms Caused by White Collar Offenders

Judges might be sentencing lower not only because they find white collar crime to be less harmful, but also because they find the individuals who commit such crimes to be less worthy of moral condemnation than other criminals. There has been no physical harm, no bereaved family--in all but the worst frauds, the witnesses are pieces of paper. (78) For these reasons, judges (and society as a whole) seem to systematically undervalue the social and moral harms caused by white collar criminals relative to other criminal actors. The social damage and moral stigma of failing to sign an SEC filing, for example, initially seem minimal. Unlike punishments for most actions associated with minimal visible social damage, however, prison sentences as derived from the WCCPA can now stretch into decades. (79) Thus, one major factor in judges' decisions to depart may be that they simply cannot justify long sentences for individuals whose actions seem barely criminal.

Making judges' perception of white collar crime more problematic, such "criminal activities" after Sarbanes-Oxley can look very different from the classical definition of white collar crime: modern white collar crime includes many acts that, before the Act, would have been regulatory offenses. (80) Whereas before Sarbanes-Oxley white collar criminal liability required some sort of action that was clearly fraudulent--check fraud, for example--after the Act passed, the definition of fraud was expanded to include omission of material information, failure to sign an SEC disclosure, and other activities that in previous years would have carried no more than a civil penalty. Because the norms of moral condemnation vary tremendously between civil and criminal violations, making a civil violation criminal merely by changing its location in the statute books runs the risk of losing legitimacy and thus decreasing enforcement. (81)

When a crime is particularly well known, it is often (though not always) the case that the criminal has also inflicted a high degree of social harm. (82) However, the public may often perceive white collar crime as causing a similar level of social harm as, for example, a drug offense, (83) which has, in reality, far less of an impact than the well-known white collar offense. Because this undervaluing affects judges as well as ordinary citizens, one can extrapolate its effects upon white collar sentencing--and indeed, the visible differences between high-profile cases and small-scale individual criminal sentences seem to indicate that this phenomenon is quite active in the judicial mindset. The treatment of highly public cases (84) turns out to be the exception that proves the rule: What these cases have in common is that each was a major news story during its heyday, and each had a major impact on its victims' social and financial situations. Though the crimes were white collar and thus hurt people's pocketbooks, not their persons, they shocked the communities in which they occurred. Members of the community, including judges, were aware of the terrible harms perpetrated by the white collar criminals, and were willing to impose stiff penalties. On this view, the high sentences do not represent the success of the WCCPA, but a general public (and judicial) imposition of sanctions based upon perceived harm.

III. SOLUTIONS

If the problem with modern white collar penalties is that judges reject them as unreasonable, the best way to standardize punishment would be to increase the perceived reasonableness of recommended sentences. The Guidelines, despite the fact that they are no longer mandatory after Booker, are still the required starting point for all federal sentences. (85) This is primarily because the Guidelines, for all their flaws, are (at least theoretically) meant to represent the considered judgment of highly informed individuals as to the "reasonable" level of punishment for various crimes. Whether or not judges actually take into account the Guidelines' strictures, it is certain that sentencing courts are familiar with the Guidelines and consider their recommended range for a given crime. Accordingly, in order to standardize white collar sentencing and thereby create a legitimate, deterring system, one could begin by making the Guidelines more accurately reflect what judges find to be a reasonable level of punishment.

In the process of creating the Guidelines, the Sentencing Commission pored over thousands of records from various crimes. (86) By looking at those materials, the Commission extracted what it believed were the most standardized, reasonable, and fair sentencing ranges for each crime, and instituted those ranges as the end of the Guidelines calculation. Although the original intent of the Guidelines was to be a mere restatement of reasonable sentencing practices as they already existed, Sarbanes-Oxley has removed white collar Guidelines sentencing from that realm. If the Guidelines were amended to produce more reasonable-looking sentences upon first calculation--in other words, if judges were anchored to a more reasonable punishment level from the beginning of their sentencing process--judges would have less need to deviate from those sentences. Punishment would become more equal and more predictable, meaning that both fairness and deterrence would increase.

There are several options for revising the current system, plausible and implausible, simple or difficult to implement. The easiest would of course be either to simply cut each Guidelines level by a given multiplier (keeping the various levels proportional to each other), or to revert to the pre-WCCPA levels. (87) However, the reasons for the departures, the too broad range of punishments and the disparities between similarly situated individuals, would not be remedied by such changes. One somewhat better option would be to change the way in which loss figures or the Guidelines sentences themselves (88) are calculated; such a change could reduce the ease with which an individual's Guidelines range can reach life in prison. The remainder of this Note proposes a revision of the Federal Sentencing Guidelines along the lines of the latter option and responds to some of the more important counterarguments to the proposed revision.

A. Basing Loss Calculation on Actual Loss and Actual Culpability

In order to avoid "shocking the conscience" of the courts, Congress should consider changing the reason that the Guidelines for white collar offenders are so high: the loss calculation metric. Recognizing that sentences tend to deviate from the given starting point, this Note proposes to reduce that deviation by making the starting point more attractive. If judges are given a starting point that does not immediately give them pause, they may be more likely to build their sentences more closely around that starting point--even though those starting points would be no more mandatory than they are now. (89) Judges would have less need to depart substantially, as they currently do in a significant minority of cases, (90) since the probable sentence would be lower to begin with. On the other hand, when necessary, they would have the authority to depart upwardly. Disparities would still happen, but they would happen relative to a more uniform beginning, and would thus be less dramatic. In fact, average sentences might even rise, as judges become increasingly motivated to comport with the more reasonable Guidelines. Though this proposal would not solve the problem altogether, it would make manifestations of the problem less extreme, and would serve as a starting point for future reforms.

Currently, the loss calculation is based not on the actual loss but on the intended loss, which can dramatically overrepresent the amount of monetary loss and social harm caused by the crime. (91) Intended loss is a double-edged sword--on the one hand, it encompasses the full extent of potential damages that could have arisen from the scheme; on the other, it "includes intended pecuniary harm that would have been impossible or unlikely to occur." (92) The intended loss paradigm, which in many cases is substantially higher than the actual loss, (93) should be replaced by a sentencing factor more sensitive to the actual effect of the crime: actual loss. A calculation based on actual loss would better reflect not only socially perceived culpability, but also actual culpability. If a new system required judges to calculate sentences based on the actual loss caused by an individual's actions, it would be far more difficult for even the most well-informed member of a conspiracy to avoid prison time. (94) Moreover, if the loss calculation were calibrated such that it rested on real-world factors such as personal profit and actual loss, the new system could decrease losses. Structuring a crime so as to maximize the amount of money missing from the company upon discovery would be made less attractive by a loss calculation that incorporates actual, rather than intended, losses.

The precise effect that this change will have on average sentences is unclear. Because departures happen in approximately 36% of cases, (95) many of the sentences in the remaining 64% will decrease. However, deterrence as a whole will not decrease: it will instead be redistributed to those criminals against whom Congress originally intended to direct the WCCPA. Frauds that cause large actual losses--the Bernie Madoffs and the Enrons of the next decade-- will be the ones in which moral corruption and social harm will be quite clear. In these frauds, judges will feel little need to depart. These offenders will experience the full force of the WCCPA, more so than they do in today's scheme--their sentences will be high, and rightfully so. On the other hand, frauds that cause minimal actual loss are almost certainly the frauds in which departures are more common under the current sentencing scheme. These frauds will be sentenced lower, but again judges will feel minimal need to depart--their feelings of injustice are not triggered by a high-intended-loss-increased sentence. Sentences should thus begin to track the Guidelines, becoming far more consistent and predictable. Though sentences in the latter cases might drop slightly, the perception of fairness and the certainty of punishment will rise. (96)

In addition to increasing deterrence against white collar crimes both large and small, the actual loss standard would mitigate the unfair effects of the hypercriminalization that the WCCPA imposed upon mail, wire, and other types of fraud. Instead of being treated like the Ebberses of the world, Joe the check forger or low-level spammer would be treated more in accordance with the nature of his own crime. Because his actions did not affect the lives and livelihood of hundreds or thousands of people, and because the amount of money lost to his actions is minuscule in proportion to that lost by the major fraudsters, a minor criminal would face only the base penalty for bank and mail fraud, as well as any minimal enhancement for the relatively very minor nature of his actions. Because the base level of punishment would not be eliminated, future Joes are still deterred; because the hasty overreaction of Congress to the Enron losses is no longer being held against Joe the minor criminal, justice is being better served.

Importantly, such a change would not decrease society's ability to punish white collar crimes that are begun but fail to come to fruition. Attempt is criminalized in white collar crime as it is for other crimes. However, just as attempt in other crimes is generally punished less than the completed crime in order to reward would-be criminals for aborting their efforts, imposing an actual loss calculation on white collar attempt would ensure fairness in that area as well. Attempt should begin from a Guidelines level higher than zero and add loss figures to accommodate the actual harm caused by the attempt. Punishment under an actual loss scheme could not be avoided by failing to complete the crime--if anything, an actual loss scheme would be an inducement to abandon the activity before completion.

B. Increasing Financial Penalties

In conjunction with any of the above suggested changes, there is another aspect of punishment that may in fact be a stronger deterrent than any other factor: increased fines. The vast majority of white collar fraud cases arise out of an officer's desire to acquire more money than can be gotten legitimately in his or her position--in short, greed may be the biggest motivator behind white collar crime. Perhaps the best way to counter greed is the knowledge that, if caught, the offender will be required to disgorge all profits and be fined a substantial additional amount of money. More so than most other crimes, the financial calculation is strongly at the front of the minds of white collar criminals; theoretically, these individuals are sufficiently sophisticated to take into account the risk of steep financial loss, and to factor that risk into their decisions as to whether to break the law.

Hefty fines beyond reparations not only permit the corporation or individuals harmed to begin rebuilding after the discovery of the crime, but also provide a disincentive to commencing the criminal course of action in the first place. Of course there is the risk that a fine will be so heavy as to make the offender effectively judgment-proof; however, as a criminal fine cannot be discharged in bankruptcy, (97) individuals contemplating fraud will know they run the risk of becoming permanently impoverished. Many scholars have discussed the prospect of supplementing or replacing prison time with fines; (98) however, for the purposes of this Note it is sufficient to acknowledge the utility of punitive fines as a factor in white collar sentencing: even if the marginal disutility of additional prison years decreases, for almost all potential white collar offenders the marginal disutility of additional fines is bound to be high.

CONCLUSION

If the purpose of the WCCPA was to deter white collar crime, the statute's harsh penalties have not achieved their goal. Moreover, by introducing the potential for enormously disparate sentences for precisely the same crime, the WCCPA detracts from just punishment. This Note has proposed merely one way of reforming the sentencing process, in hopes that sentencing will become more consistent and predictable across judges and jurisdictions. The goal of this system would not be to make things easier for white collar criminal defendants. Instead, the goal would be to return potential prison sentences to their proper role as deterrent and punishing forces-- sentences that would be low and reasonable enough that judges would impose them, but high and harsh enough that they would both deter future crimes and serve society's sense of justice. Though it may be that no system will ever be perfect or completely remove disparities, it is essential to continue reforming in response to the realities presented by the system at hand. This Note is meant to serve as one step in the long ascent toward a fair, effective, and legitimate justice system.

NOTES DELETED

InfoMarks: Make Your Mark

What is an InfoMark?

It is a single-click return ticket to any page, any result, or any search from InfoTrac College Edition.

An InfoMark is a stable URL, linked to InfoTrac College Edition articles that you have selected. InfoMarks can be used like any other URL, but they're better because they're stable – they don't change. Using an InfoMark is like performing the search again whenever you follow the link, whether the result is a single article or a list of articles.

How Do InfoMarks Work?

If you can "copy and paste," you can use InfoMarks.

When you see the InfoMark icon on a result page, its URL can be copied and pasted into your electronic document – web page, word processing document, or email. Once InfoMarks are incorporated into a document, the results are persistent (the URLs will not change) and are dynamic.

Even though the saved search is used at different times by different users, an InfoMark always functions like a brand new search. Each time a saved search is executed, it accesses the latest updated information. That means subsequent InfoMark searches might yield additional or more up-to-date information than the original search with less time and effort.

Capabilities

InfoMarks are the perfect technology tool for creating:

- Virtual online readers
- Current awareness topic sites – links to periodical or newspaper sources
- Online/distance learning courses
- Bibliographies, reference lists
- Electronic journals and periodical directories
- Student assignments
- Hot topics

Advantages

- Select from over 15 million articles from more than 5,000 journals and periodicals
- Update article and search lists easily
- Articles are always full-text and include bibliographic information
- All articles can be viewed online, printed, or emailed
- Saves professors and students time
- Anyone with access to InfoTrac College Edition can use it
- No other online library database offers this functionality
- FREE!

How to Use InfoMarks

There are three ways to utilize InfoMarks – in HTML documents, Word documents, and Email.

HTML Document

1. Open a new document in your HTML editor (Netscape Composer or FrontPage Express).
2. Open a new browser window and conduct your search in InfoTrac College Edition.
3. Highlight the URL of the results page or article that you would like to InfoMark.
4. Right-click the URL and click Copy. Now switch back to your HTML document.
5. In your document, type in text that describes the InfoMarked item.
6. Highlight the text and click on Insert, then on Link in the upper bar menu.
7. Click in the link box, then press the "Ctrl" and "V" keys simultaneously and click OK. This will paste the URL in the box.
8. Save your document.

Word Document

1. Open a new Word document.
2. Open a new browser window and conduct your search in InfoTrac College Edition.
3. Check items you want to add to your Marked List.

4. Click on Mark List on the right menu bar.
5. Highlight the URL, right-click on it, and click Copy. Now switch back to your Word document.
6. In your document, type in text that describes the InfoMarked item.
7. Highlight the text. Go to the upper bar menu and click on Insert, then on Hyperlink.
8. Click in the hyperlink box, then press the "Ctrl" and "V" keys simultaneously and click OK. This will paste the URL in the box.
9. Save your document.

Email

1. Open a new email window.
2. Open a new browser window and conduct your search in InfoTrac College Edition.
3. Highlight the URL of the results page or article that you would like to InfoMark.
4. Right-click the URL and click Copy. Now switch back to your email window.
5. In the email window, press the "Ctrl" and "V" keys simultaneously. This will paste the URL into your email.
6. Send the email to the recipient. By clicking on the URL, he or she will be able to view the InfoMark.